Praise for Carlos Eire and *Waiting for Snow in Havana*

"Deeply moving . . . Eire's tone is so urgent and so vividly personal that his unsparing indictments of practically everyone concerned, including himself, seem all the more remarkable."

—*The New Yorker*

"This rich, engrossing memoir has the magic realism of Gabriel García-Márquez. . . . [A] magical memory tour."

—*People*

"*Waiting for Snow in Havana* is a lush and savory read, the cheapest trip to sunshine between two covers."

—*The Denver Post*

"A beautifully fashioned memoir. As imaginatively wrought as the finest piece of fiction powerful."

—*Publishers Weekly*, starred and boxed review

"Eire's recollection of his Cuban boyhood is to be savored. . . . The memories come in beautiful profusion, coalescing into a young life in a lyric memoir of the utterly vanished."

—*Kirkus Reviews*, starred review

"A passionate, wildly ambitious memoir that aims to document the social life and customs of his childhood while also, by the way, delivering a work of art. A tale of a child's life in the distinguished tradition of *Huckleberry Finn* [and] *To Kill a Mockingbird*."

— *Sun-Sentinel*

"In this open, honest, and at times angry memoir, Eire bares his soul completely and captivates the reader in the process."

—*Booklist*

"Eire's writing has the quality of an intense dream, almost as lush as the Cuban landscape he describes so passionately and wistfully."

—*The Star-Ledger* (Newark)

"Eire gently unfurls the rich tapestry of his tragic story, and the beauty of the struggle and exploration he portrays is unforgettable."

—*Hispanic Magazine*

Waiting for Snow in Havana

Confessions of a Cuban Boy

Carlos Eire

Free Press
New York London Toronto Sydney

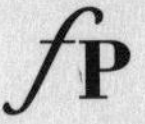

FREE PRESS
A Division of Simon & Schuster, Inc.
1230 Avenue of the Americas
New York, NY 10020

This is a work of nonfiction. However, the names of some people have been changed to protect their privacy.

First Free Press paperback edition 2004

FREE PRESS and colophon are trademarks of Simon & Schuster, Inc.

For information about special discounts for bulk purchases, please contact Simon & Schuster Special Sales:
1-800-456-6798 or business@simonandschuster.com

Book design by Ellen R. Sasahara

Manufactured in the United States of America

1 3 5 7 9 10 8 6 4 2

Library of Congress Cataloging-in-Publication Data

Eire, Carlos M. N.
Waiting for snow in Havana : confessions of a Cuban boy / Carlos Eire.
p. cm.
1. Eire, Carlos M. N.—Childhood and youth. 2. Cuban Americans—Biography. 3. Refugee children—United States—Biography. 4. Havana (Cuba)—Biography. 5. Chicago (Ill.)—Biography. 6. Eire, Carlos M. N.—Family. 7. Havana (Cuba)—Social life and customs—20th century. 8. Havana (Cuba)—Social conditions—20th century. 9. Cuba—History—Revolution, 1959—Personal narratives. 10. Operation Pedro Pan. I. Title.
E184.C97 E37 2003
972.91'23063'092—dc21
[B]
2002073875

ISBN 0-7432-1965-1
0-7432-4641-1 (Pbk)

For John-Carlos, Grace, and Bruno

I spit on fools who fail to include breasts in their metaphysics,
Star-gazers who have not enumerated them among the moons of the earth

—Charles Simic, "Breasts"

Preámbulo

This is not a work of fiction.
But the author would like it to be.
We improve when we become fiction,
each and every one of us,
and when the past becomes a novel our memories are sharpened.

Memory is the most potent truth.
Show me history untouched by memories
and you show me lies.
Show me lies not based on memories
and you show me the worst lies of all.

If all the characters in this book are fictional, none of them knows it yet.

All resemblances to actual persons
were preordained before the creation of the world.
It matters little that the names don't always match.

All the incidents and dialogue come straight from God's imagination.
As does the author himself.
And the reader.

Still, all of us are responsible for our own actions.
Not even Fidel is exempt from all this.
Nor Che, nor his chauffeurs, nor his mansion.
Nor the many Cubans who soiled their pants
before they were shot to death.
Nor the fourteen thousand children who flew away from their parents.
Nor the love and desperation that caused them to fly.

1

UNO

The world changed while I slept, and much to my surprise, no one had consulted me. That's how it would always be from that day forward. Of course, that's the way it had been all along. I just didn't know it until that morning. Surprise upon surprise: some good, some evil, most somewhere in between. And always without my consent.

I was barely eight years old, and I had spent hours dreaming of childish things, as children do. My father, who vividly remembered his prior incarnation as King Louis XVI of France, probably dreamt of costume balls, mobs, and guillotines. My mother, who had no memory of having been Marie Antoinette, couldn't have shared in his dreams. Maybe she dreamt of hibiscus blossoms and fine silk. Maybe she dreamt of angels, as she always encouraged me to do. *"Sueña con los angelitos,"* she would say: Dream of little angels. The fact that they were little meant they were too cute to be fallen angels.

Devils can never be cute.

The tropical sun knifed through the gaps in the wooden shutters, as always, extending in narrow shafts of light above my bed, revealing entire galaxies of swirling dust specks. I stared at the dust, as always, rapt. I don't remember getting out of bed. But I do remember walking into my parents' bedroom. Their shutters were open and the room was flooded with light. As always, my father was putting on his trousers over his shoes. He always put on his socks and shoes first, and then his trousers. For years I tried to duplicate that nearly magical feat, with little success. The cuffs of my pants would always get stuck on my shoes and no amount of tugging could free them. More than once I risked an eternity in hell and spit out swear words. I had no idea that if your pants are baggy enough, you can slide them over anything, even snowshoes. All I knew then was that I couldn't be like my father.

As he slid his baggy trousers over his brown wingtip shoes, effortlessly, Louis XVI broke the news to me: "Batista is gone. He flew out of Havana early this morning. It looks like the rebels have won."

"You lie," I said.

"No, I swear, it's true," he replied.

Marie Antoinette, my mother, assured me it was true as she applied lipstick, seated at her vanity table. It was a beautiful piece of mahogany furniture with three mirrors: one flat against the wall and two on either side of that, hinged so that their angles could be changed at will. I used to turn the side mirrors so they would face each other and create infinite regressions of one another. Sometimes I would peer in and plunge into infinity.

"You'd better stay indoors today," my mother said. "God knows what could happen. Don't even stick your head out the door." Maybe she, too, had dreamt of guillotines after all? Or maybe it was just sensible, motherly advice. Perhaps she knew that the heads of the elites don't usually fare well on the street when revolutions triumph, not even when the heads belong to children.

That day was the first of January 1959.

The night before, we had all gone to a wedding at a church in the heart of old Havana. On the way home, we had the streets to ourselves. Not another moving car in sight. Not a soul on the Malecón, the broad avenue along the waterfront. Not even a lone prostitute. Louis XVI and Marie Antoinette kept talking about the eerie emptiness of the city. Havana was much too quiet for a New Year's Eve.

I can't remember what my older brother, Tony, was doing that morning or for the rest of the day. Maybe he was wrapping lizards in thin copper wire and hooking them up to our Lionel train transformer. He liked to electrocute them. He liked it a lot. He was also fond of saying: "Shock therapy, ha! That should cure them of their lizard delusion." I don't want to remember what my adopted brother, Ernesto, was doing. Probably something more monstrous than electrocuting lizards.

My older brother and my adopted brother had both been Bourbon princes in a former life. My adopted brother had been the Dauphin, the heir to the French throne. My father had recognized him on the street one day, selling lottery tickets, and brought him to our house immediately. I was the outsider. I alone was not a former Bourbon. My father wouldn't tell me who I had been. "You're not ready to hear it," he would say. "But you were very special."

My father's sister, Lucía, who lived with us, spent that day being as invisible as she always was. She, too, had once been a Bourbon princess. But now, in this life, she was a spinster: a lady of leisure with plenty of time on her hands and no friends at all. She had been protected so thoroughly from the corrupt culture of Cuba and the advances of the young men who reeked of it as to have been left stranded, high and dry, on the lonely island that was our house. Our island within the island. Our safe haven from poor taste and all unseemly acts, such as dancing to drumbeats. She had lived her entire life as a grown woman in the company of her mother and her maiden aunt, who, like her, had remained a virgin without vows. When her mother and aunt died, she moved to a room at the rear of our house and hardly ever emerged. Whether she had any desires, I'll never know. She seemed not to have any. I don't remember her expressing any opinion that day on the ouster of Batista and the triumph of Fidel Castro and his rebels. But a few days later she did say that those men who came down from the mountains needed haircuts and a shave.

Our maid worked for us that day, as always. Her name was Inocencia, and her skin was a purple shade of black. She cooked, cleaned the house, and did the laundry. She was always there. She seemed to have no family of her own. She lived in a room that was attached to the rear of the house but had no door leading directly into it. To enter our house she had to exit her small room and walk a few steps across the patio and through the backdoor, which led to the kitchen. She had a small bathroom of her own too, which I sometimes used when I was playing outdoors.

Once, long before that day when the world changed, I opened the door to that bathroom and found her standing inside, naked. I still remember her shriek, and my shock. I stood there frozen, a child of four, staring at her mountainous African breasts. A few days later, at the market with my mother, I pointed to a shelf full of eggplants and shouted *"Tetas de negra!"* Black women's tits! Marie Antoinette placed her hand over my mouth and led me away quickly as the grocers laughed and made lewd remarks. I couldn't understand what I had done wrong. Those eggplants did look just like Inocencia's breasts, right down to the fact that both had aureolas and nipples. The only difference was that while Inocencia's were bluish black, those of the eggplants were green. Later in life I would search for evidence of God's presence. That resemblance was my first proof for the existence of God. And eggplants would forever remind me of our nakedness and shame.

A few months after that New Year's Day, Inocencia quit working for us. She was replaced by a thin, wiry woman named Caridad, or Charity, who was angry and a thief. My parents would eventually fire her for stealing. She loved Fidel, and she listened to the radio in the kitchen all day long. It was the only Cuban music I ever heard. My father, the former Louis XVI, would not allow anything but classical music to be played in the main part of the house. He remembered meeting some of the composers whose music he played, and he pined for those concerts at Versailles. Cuban music was restricted to the kitchen and the maid's room.

Caridad loved to taunt me when my parents weren't around. "Pretty soon you're going to lose all this." "Pretty soon you'll be sweeping my floor." "Pretty soon I'll be seeing you at your fancy beach club, and you'll be cleaning out the trash cans while I swim." With menacing smirks, she threatened that if I ever told my parents about her taunts, she would put a curse on me.

"I know all sorts of curses. Changó listens to me; I offer him the best cigars, and plenty of firewater. I'll hex you and your whole family. Changó and I will set a whole army of devils upon you."

My father had warned me about the evil powers of Changó and the African gods. He spoke to me of men struck dead in the prime of life, of housewives driven mad with love for their gardeners, of children horribly disfigured. So I kept quiet. But I think she put a curse on me anyway, and on my whole family, for not allowing her to steal and taunt until that day, "pretty soon," when she could take over the house. Her devils swooped down on all of us, with the same speed as the rebels that swept across the whole island on that day.

The lizards remained oblivious to the news that day, as always. Contrary to what my brother Tony liked to say as he administered shock treatments to them, the lizards were not deluded in the least. They knew exactly what they were and always would be. Nothing had changed for them. Nothing would ever change. The world already belonged to them whole, free of vice and virtue. They scurried up and down the walls of the patio, and along its brightly colored floor tiles. They lounged on tree branches, sunned themselves on rocks. They clung to the ceilings inside our house, waiting for bugs to eat. They never fell in love, or sinned, or suffered broken hearts. They knew nothing of betrayal or humiliation. They needed no revolutions. Dreaming of guillotines was unnecessary for them, and impossible. They feared neither death nor torture at the hands of children. They worried not about curses, or proof of God's existence, or nakedness. Their limbs looked an awful lot like our own, in the same way that eggplants resembled breasts. Lizards were ugly, to be sure—or so I thought back then. They made me question the goodness of creation.

I could never kiss a lizard, I thought. *Never.*

Perhaps I envied them. Their place on earth was more secure than ours. We would lose our place, lose our world. They are still basking in the sun. Same way. Day in, day out.

2

DOS

I shouldn't have been surprised that New Year's morning. There had been plenty of signs of trouble brewing, of changes to come. Even a sheltered child should have known something was about to snap. Later in life I would think back to that morning and try to link it to earlier events, just to make sense of what had gone wrong with all our lives.

Quite often, my wondering would come back to the day we almost died.

We were only a few blocks from my grandmother's house when the shooting started. It was near the botanical gardens of the Quinta de los Molinos. At first it sounded like a few firecrackers going off in the distance, *pop, pop, pop*. But within one minute, the pops were joined by *bang*s and *rat-tat-tats*, in a mounting crescendo. And the noise kept getting closer and closer. And louder.

My mother began to scream. "A shoot-out, a shoot-out! Oh my God, we're all going to get killed! Stop the car, Antonio, stop the car right here."

Antonio was my father's name in this life. Antonio Juan Francisco Nieto Cortadellas. This time around, my mother was called Maria Azucena Eiré González. Quite a comedown from Louis XVI and Marie Antoinette, but still quite high on the food chain. Marie Antoinette had been stricken by polio just before her first birthday in this lifetime, and her right leg was totally useless. Apparently being imprisoned in the Bastille and losing her head in 1793 had not been enough to settle her Karmic debts.

"If I stop the car now, we'll be killed for sure," said my father. "Stop shouting, you're frightening the kids."

It didn't seem to occur to him that the gunfire might be scary enough.

"Stop, stop, I beg you stop . . . we can get out of the car right here. I know the family that lives in that house right there," said Marie Antoinette, pointing a little ways down the street. In this neighborhood the buildings were all very close together, flush with the sidewalk. No front or side yards. Jumping out of the car and making a mad dash into a house was not too bad an idea.

"What if your friends aren't home?" Louis XVI asked. *Pop, pop, rat-tat-tat, bang!*

"They're not friends; I just know who they are," Marie Antoinette replied. "They're friends of friends of my sister." *Bang, pop, bang, rat-tat-tat, bang!* "And where else would they be on a Sunday evening?" *Pop, ka-pop, bang!* "My God, we're all going to die!" *Pop, bang, ka-blam!*

My brother Tony and I looked at each other in disbelief. This was just like a war movie! Finally, we were lucky enough to be involved in real gunplay. We had heard it in films, and often far in the distance, especially around bedtime, but never this close. It was so much louder! I thought of Audie Murphy in *To Hell and Back,* shooting dead all those evil Nazis and blowing up their tanks. My brother and I must have seen that movie at least a dozen times. Both of us wanted to be Audie Murphy, the most highly decorated American soldier in World War II. Since our father was a judge, we could go to any movie theater in Havana for free, and we went often.

"There are very good shows on television tonight," my brother chimed in. *Rat-tat-tat, bang, pop, pop, ka-blam!* "They're probably watching *Rin Tin Tin.*"

KA-BLAM! KA-BLAM! KA-BLAM!

"But grown-ups don't watch *Rin Tin Tin.* Grown-ups don't like shows about dogs," I said.

KA-BLAM! BOOM! BANG! RAT-TAT-TAT!

"Oh my God, Oh my God, Oh Mary Mother of God in Heaven. Oh Virgin of Charity! Stop the car! Stop the car! STOP!" Mom shouted even louder, over the sound of gunfire.

Maybe it was my overactive imagination, but I could have sworn I also heard a *Ka-ping*. A ricochet. The sound of a bullet bouncing off buildings, just like a war movie. Impressive. Then I heard a dull *thud*. Bullets penetrating buildings. Even more impressive.

Antonio Nieto Cortadellas swung the car over to the curb and stopped abruptly in front of the house my mother had pointed out. My brother and I were thrown forward against the front seat of the car. No one had seatbelts back in those days.

Maria Azucena Eiré González opened her door first.

Then it happened. Before she could swing out her good leg, a man bolted from the shadows. He grabbed my mother by both arms, crouching so low to the ground that his face was lower than hers.

"Save me! Hide me, please! They're after me! They're going to kill me!" The man's voice was shaky.

He started to push Mom back into the car.

"I beg you. For the love of God, hide me. Hide me, please, I beg you! *Por favor, se lo ruego!*"

I popped my head up above the front seat and got a good look at him. He had a round face and dark curly hair, and he was very sweaty. His shirt was open to mid-chest. He must have been in his thirties. I couldn't tell, though. All grown-ups looked the same age until they turned into old people.

The gunfire became ever louder. It made my hair stand on end, for the first time in my life. I heard more dull thuds and *ka-pings*, followed by sirens. Marie Antoinette gave a bloodcurdling shriek, just like the ones in horror films.

In the meantime, Tony had jumped out of the car, without having seen the man. As he rounded the car, the man grabbed him and held him tightly with one arm.

"For the sake of this boy, hide me!" he said through clenched teeth.

Louis XVI shouted: "Get away from us! You're going to get us killed! Can't you see my wife is crippled and that I'm trying to save my kids' lives? Go away! There's nothing we can do for you! Let go of my boy, now! Go! Run!"

The man looked straight at me. I had seen eyes like that before, on paintings and statues of Jesus Christ.

I had also seen them in my dreams. Very often, I used to dream that

Jesus would appear at the dining room window, carrying his cross while we were eating dinner. He would just stand there and stare at me, blood trickling down his face. And only I could see him. He didn't have to speak. I knew what he wanted and it frightened me to death. The rest of the family kept eating, oblivious. Then he would simply vanish.

And this man's eyes stared at me exactly the same way.

I ducked back down to avoid the man's gaze.

Then the man took a look at my mother's leg, released my brother, and ran away. As quickly as he had appeared, he disappeared. My brother would say forty-two years later, on the day that I wrote this, that he had never seen anyone run so fast.

We bolted out of the car, not even bothering to close its doors. Tony and I bent close to the ground, just like the soldiers in war movies. All those hours at the movie theater and in front of the television were finally paying off.

"Oh my God, oh my God, oh my God! *Ay, Dios mío!*" Marie Antoinette prayed, limping all the way to the door of the house.

KA-BLAM, BANG, BANG, RAT-TAT-TAT!

The noise was deafening. I heard the sound of bullets whizzing past us, too.

SWOOOOOOSH! KA-PIIING!

Marie Antoinette and Louis XVI started banging on the door loudly. King Louis used the door knocker, Queen Marie Antoinette pounded with her cane. The banging seemed to last an eternity, but finally a silver-haired woman opened the door a crack. Without saying a word, Marie Antoinette crashed through the door, and the rest of us followed in her wake.

"I guess she really does know these people," Tony said.

"Please, please, you've got to let us stay here until the shooting stops," said Marie Antoinette, as she limped past the living room. Without asking the woman's permission, she herded us to the first bedroom she could find and said: "Get under the bed, quickly."

Tony and I crawled under the bed and huddled together, shaking. I remember the bedspread was brown, and the marble floor was nice and cool. Our mother sat on the bed above us like a hen over her chicks, saying Our Fathers and Hail Marys under her breath. Our father and the lady who lived in the house came into the room too.

The grown-ups just sat, or stood, in silence. My mother's prayers had become inaudible. Outside, the sound of gunfire diminished gradually, moving farther and farther away. And then it stopped, as suddenly as it had started.

My parents thanked the silver-haired lady profusely and talked for a while in that boring way that grown-ups talk. Tony and I emerged from under the bed, and the lady gave us some candy.

And we went home.

That night I didn't fall asleep in the backseat, as I often did. We got home, our parents tucked us into bed, and sleep crept up on us slowly.

That night I didn't dream about Jesus and his cross.

The next day my parents read in the newspaper about the escaped prisoners who had been shot dead near the Quinta de los Molinos. Our desperate man was only one of several who had escaped from the prison at the El Príncipe fortress, a relic from colonial times.

"You know that man who asked us to save him last night? They shot him dead," said my father.

"The police killed him," added my mother.

Louis XVI wouldn't show us the newspaper, but somehow my brother and I managed to get our hands on it later. That's how we got to see the gory photo. He was sprawled on the ground, one arm horribly twisted the wrong way, bloodstains on his shirt, and a pool of blood under his body. A thin stream of blood trickled from his mouth. His eyes were open. But they didn't look the same as when he had looked straight at me. They looked empty.

Cuban newspapers were full of such pictures in the waning days of Batista's regime. Dead rebels. Dead escaped prisoners. Dead innocent bystanders. Blood everywhere. Flies, even.

We were live innocent bystanders. Not a drop of our blood had been shed. What good luck, and at how great a price for that man we turned away in his most desperate hour.

That's what the world was like before it changed. I should have seen it coming.

The year was 1958. Earlier that day, we had held a bon voyage party for my mother's sister, Lily, who was off with a tour group to the United States and Canada. We had gone down to the harbor to see her board the Havana-Miami ferry. It was a lot of fun to watch the cars drive into the huge ship. But it took a long time, and the fun wore off. I had brought only one comic book with me, and it was a bad one. Elastic Man. What a stupid superhero. All he could do was stretch. And he had a very stupid looking red suit without a cape.

As I lay on the cold marble floor under the silver-haired lady's bed, listening to murmured prayers and gunfire, I thought of Elastic Man. How would he have reacted to a shoot-out? By stretching himself completely flat against the ground? Or maybe by stretching himself so thin as to become nearly invisible? He certainly wouldn't have hidden under a bed, not even to avoid being ridiculed for his costume.

I was no superhero, for sure. Nor was anyone else in my family.

The seas were rough that day. So rough that my aunt was seasick all the way to Miami. After she returned to Havana, I was very impressed when she told us about the huge waves and the violent rocking of the ferry, and about how green her cabin mate's face had turned. I imagined my aunt Lily leaning her own green head out of a porthole, puking into the waves. One hundred and twenty miles of vomit. Very impressive. More impressive than her stories about New York City, Niagara Falls, and the Canadian Mounted Police.

Almost as impressive as the sound of bullets whizzing past my head, and the sight of Jesus at my dining room window, cross and all.

3

TRES

Havana at night. Some nightlife, I'm told. I never got to enjoy it, so I can't tell you about it.

Havana by day. Hot, yes, and radiant. The sunlight seemed at once dense and utterly clear. The shadows were so crisp, so cool. The clouds in the blue sky, each one a poem; some haiku, some epic. The sunsets: forget it, no competition. Nothing could compare to the sight of that glowing red disk being swallowed by the turquoise sea and the tangerine light bathing everything, making all of creation glow as if from within. Even the lizards. The waves, those turquoise waves, splashing against the wall of the Malecón, splashing, leaping over it to flood the road, lapping, lapping, lapping endlessly, eternally. Even in the worst of storms the waves were always a lover's caress, an untiring embrace, an endless shower of kisses.

Of course, I didn't think of it that way back then. Get lost. I was a boy. Images of hugs and kisses were unspeakably repulsive. Waves were fun, not sappy drivel. In the worst of storms my brother and I would ask our father, Louis XVI, to drive our car down the Malecón to be swallowed by the breakers. And King Louis was nice enough to comply.

"You know, kids, the saltwater will wreck the car," he would remind us.

But he would have as much fun as we did, perhaps more, driving through the surf. And he didn't really care that much about rust. We loved it, especially when a surging wall of water would nearly tip us over, and the windshield wipers couldn't race fast enough against the deluge. Sometimes we would pack as many of our friends as we could into the car, and my father would bravely take us all to be swallowed by the waves. Car surfing. Without seatbelts, of course. If Havana had been in the United States, the road would have been closed to traffic, and Dad would have been imprisoned for recklessly endangering the lives of children.

But Havana was not in the United States. That was the beauty of it, and the horror. So much freedom, so little freedom. Freedom to be reckless, but no genuine freedom from woe. Plenty of thrills, and an overabundance of risks, large and small. But so little margin for error, and so few safety nets. For the poor, opportunity knocked loudest in the lottery and the numbers racket. For anyone who wasn't poor, life could be beautiful, even if all was balanced on a razor's edge. As beautiful as a giant turquoise wave poised right over your head.

Havana was the capital of an island nation barely five decades into independence from the Spanish empire. My father's parents had grown up in a Spanish colony, with slaves in their households. Many of the men in his family had trained as army officers in Spain, and their chief purpose in life was to keep Cuba a colony. Many went to their graves denying the fact they were Cuban. My father's generation had been born in Spanish Cuba and had grown up along with the republic; his sister remembered hearing the blast that sank the battleship *Maine* in Havana Harbor. Fifty years is not that much time. How much can one expect of a nation as young as that, and especially of one so physically near to the richest, most powerful country on earth, and so dependent on it for its economic well-being?

Expect trouble.

But those waves, those turquoise waves, along with the sunlight, almost made up for the trouble. Almost. The divine, omniscient sunlight also shone on things warped and evil. Slums full of naked, parasite-infested children. Whorehouses. Bastards. Corpses. Bribes. Beggars. Bright green phlegm on the sidewalk. Bullies at school. And at night, the light was replaced by a menacing gloom, thick with bats, mosquitoes, prostitutes, and flying cockroaches. The turquoise waves turned inky black. Nothing frightened me more than the sight of that black water, except maybe for the sharks swimming silently beneath, and the malevolent magic of the *brujeros,* the voodoo sorcerers, who always did their dirty work at night.

Quite often, we awoke to find hexes on our front porch. All sorts of voodoo curses, none of which required written notes. Foul-smelling trinkets and coins. Rotting fruit wrapped in red ribbons. Bloody feathers. An occasional chicken head. Makeshift altars on which stuff had been burnt. These were all gifts left behind by the relatives of those men and women my father, the judge, sent to jail every weekday.

My father was a kind man, mild mannered and soft spoken. He had a very hard edge, but everything about him seemed soft and vulnerable, maybe because he was so fat. He was about five feet six or seven and weighed well over two hundred pounds. Thin, gray hair. He already looked liked an old man when he married my mother, at the age of thirty-seven. He collected fine porcelain and paintings, and all sorts of art. We owned a rare Palissy dish from the sixteenth century, one of the very first pieces of colored European porcelain. When my father lent it to the National Museum for an exhibit, it was assigned its own full-time guard. Years later, I would see an almost identical Palissy at the Walters Art Gallery in Baltimore. I wept like a baby right there, that sunny weekend morning in 1976, even though I was a grown man.

We had other valuable stuff, too. We had a Murillo painting of the boy Jesus hanging in the living room, along with a portrait of Empress Maria Theresa of Austria. Under their watchful gazes I watched television. American culture flooded our living room with a constant torrent of images, right under their noses: Felix the Cat, the Three Stooges, Woody Woodpecker, Laurel and Hardy, Mickey Mouse, Mighty Mouse, Betty Boop, Buck Rogers, the Lone Ranger, Roy Rogers, Hopalong Cassidy, Donald Duck, *Gunsmoke, Bat Masterson,* Fred Astaire, Pluto, Jimmy Cagney, Rin Tin Tin, Flash Gordon, Tarzan, *Sea Hunt,* Superman, *Perry Mason,* Zorro. But never ever *I Love Lucy*. Good thing, too. I think any American television show with a Cuban in it would have confused the hell out of us.

The child Jesus by Murillo, tending his sheep on a canvas blackened by centuries of candle smoke, always looked kind yet forlorn. He was obviously scanning the hills of Galilee for lost sheep. But that stern Maria Theresa. She scared me. In my dreams, she would often begin swearing at me like a sailor on shore leave, uttering the vilest language known to man.

When I told my father about these dreams and pleaded with him to banish the swearing Empress from our house, he had a very simple, historically accurate reply:

"Don't be silly. She was such a refined lady she could never swear like that."

Of course, I couldn't repeat the bad words to offer proof of Maria Theresa's expertise at swearing. If I had, he would have slapped me across the mouth. Foul language was not allowed in our household. Bad words—*malas palabras*—if uttered, were swiftly punished. Somehow, in my own numbering of the Ten Commandments, "Thou shalt not utter bad words" had come to rank first.

In my father's study, we had a silver reliquary containing bone fragments from seven different saints and two slivers from the True Cross. Imagine that: *the* True Cross! As if this were not enough, we also had a seventeenth-century painting of Jesus carrying his cross and bleeding profusely—the stuff of my dreams—and an Italian porcelain plate with the face of Jesus embossed in such a way that wherever you went, the eyes followed you. Blue eyes. My father loved to show that one off, and to taunt his visitors:

"I dare you: see if you can get away from His gaze."

Directly across the room from the staring Jesus hung a portrait of an English lady in her riding clothes, holding the reins of her steed. She only swore at me once. In a dream, of course, and in Spanish, just like Maria Theresa.

I only dream in Spanish now when I am visited by my father's ghost.

My father, Louis XVI, the Cuban judge, the art collector, the reckless wave rider, made the most beautiful dioramas out of seashells and coral. So inventive and so delicate. The shells became butterflies, the coral served as vegetation for the butterflies to alight upon. And no two pieces were alike. Louis XVI made the wooden glass-covered boxes by hand too, and they were crafted with the ultimate care, lined in velvet. Some of these hung on our walls, but most were given away as gifts. The shells and the coral came from a place that scooped up sand from the sea and sold it to construction firms. *La Arenera:* that's what we called it. The sand place. It was on the banks of the Almendares River, near a peanut oil factory that smothered the air with the scent of roasting peanuts.

I loved passing that spot on the way to my grandmother's house. "Here come the peanuts, here come the peanuts! Get ready to inhale!" I would cry out from the backseat. The aroma would rush into the car suddenly, as if we had hit a wall of peanuts, and linger inside for blocks and blocks, almost all the way to Grandma's house. "You know, that counts as your snack for the afternoon," Marie Antoinette would often say.

Every now and then we would make runs to *La Arenera* to sift for shells and coral. My father knew the owner. He seemed to know everyone. There were mountains of sand all over the place. White sand, gray sand, pink sand, brown sand, yellow sand. I mean mountains, literally, about five or six stories high. We could only sift at the bottom, though we itched to climb to the top of each and every mountain of sand. "Too dangerous, kids. Too dangerous," the owner would warn us as he handed us sifting trays. "I don't want you climbing on the sand, you hear?" Dad made sure we got the message. "You know," he would say as we were pulling up to *La Arenera,* "a lot of men have been lost in these sandpiles. Poor workers. They started to climb and sank into the sand. They disappeared, sucked in, drowned in the sand. Those sandpiles are full of dead men, you know. Once the sand sucks you in, that's it. No one can pull you out. Look at those sandpiles: they're just like the pyramids of Egypt. Tombs. Very large tombs."

It worked. We were rowdy kids, but we never took to climbing up the sand. As we sifted for treasures at the very bottom of the sandpiles, I thought of the skeletons that lay buried beneath the sand. *Maybe one day we'll be lucky enough to find bones,* I thought. But we never hit bones. Just beautiful objects, handcrafted by God Himself, about to be turned into art by my own father.

My father also made the niftiest kites out of brightly colored tissue paper. *Papel de China,* it was called. And balsa wood frames. My dad would slice the balsa wood with a special knife he saved in a special box, cut the paper into all sorts of shapes, arrange the colors in wild patterns, apply glue, tie some string, and, presto, a kite would appear. A tail made of thin strips of cloth, tied together in a chain of knots, was the finishing touch. Sometimes he would make a dozen or two at a time, give them to all our friends, pile us into the car, and take us to the seashore to fly them at the mouth of the Almendares River, not far from the sandplace.

I especially liked the fighting kites, which had double-edged razor blades embedded in their tails. We would hoist our kites high, far from one another, and then bring them closer and closer and try to cut each others' strings with the razor blades. Sometimes it worked, but most of the time the kites simply got tangled up and plummeted to the ground. But when a kite actually had its string cut, it was beautiful. It would sort of hang there in the air for an instant, confused by its freedom, and then fly off wherever the wind wanted to take it. Sometimes they landed on the roofs of houses. Sometimes they landed blocks away, or plunged into the turquoise sea. We would cheer and shout, unless of course the damaged kite happened to be our own. I hated to have mine cut, and the sad truth is that I never got to cut anyone else's. My father, Louis XVI, didn't seem to mind this wreckage of his handiwork at all. He seemed to enjoy it.

My father also sent people to jail every day, or fined them.

And sometimes these people would strike back the only way they could. They would curse us. Summon devils to rain misery upon us all.

Along with the devils came the presents too. Being a judge was not all that bad. Favors rendered, favors acknowledged. Once, a crate full of live chickens was brought to our door by a black man who simply said: "For Doctor Nieto. He'll understand." My brother and I set the chickens loose in the rear patio and shot at them with our water pistols. Still, we were kinder to the chickens than our maid Caridad; she wrung their necks and cooked them all. Another time a blue Cadillac pulled up to the house, and a uniformed chauffeur delivered a case of wine to the front door. The wine was immediately given away to a neighbor. Alcohol was not allowed in our household.

"Let someone else get drunk," said Louis XVI.

Along with the curses and presents, sometimes there were physical threats. When I was very little, my father took on the case of a notorious outlaw revolutionary known as *El Colorado,* or Red. Many other judges had turned down the chance to try this man in their courtrooms. It didn't matter much whether this was due to fear or bribery. What it meant was that my father stood all alone against this man and his supporters, and that our family became the target of intimidation. Notes were slipped into our mailbox. Phone calls from strangers came in the middle of the night. The messages were nearly as inventive as Dad's shell-and-coral dioramas, but in a perverse way.

"We know when your lovely wife takes the children to the park, along with your colored nannies. Her blue polka-dot dress is so pretty, and she fills it out so nicely, especially on top. Too bad one of her legs is so shriveled up. Maybe we should chop it off for her."

"Your little blond sons are gems. How do you think they'll enjoy our own very special playground? You know, there are plenty of dirty old men in Havana who would pay a fortune to spend time with them every night."

"Your dear old mother and aunt are so frail. Have you ever wondered how easily their necks might snap when we kidnap and rape them?"

"Quiz time, Your Honor: How would you like to watch your children tortured before you, and then to have your eyes plucked out and fed to them?" And so on.

God only knows how many bribes were offered along with these messages. At one point, some government minister showed up at our house, and a long cortège of cars filled the entire street. Dad and the Minister-of-Whatever went into his study and closed the door. I have always wondered whether Dad showed the minister his Jesus-with-the-moving-eyes during that visit. In the end, my dad, Louis XVI, prevailed. Or maybe Eye Jesus had something to do with it. Dad sent Red to prison and nothing happened. After a while, the police stationed around the clock outside our house simply vanished. Red was eventually killed in a shoot-out, after escaping from prison, but I didn't find out about it until I was thirty-eight years old. *El Colorado* lingered in our household after his demise, kept hostage in a perverse afterlife by my own parents. Other children's parents used the Bogey Man—*El Coco*—to frighten their children into behaving. My parents used *El Colorado,* who seemed as eternal and omnipresent as the Bogey Man.

"Stop doing that or *El Colorado* will kidnap you!" "Finish up that soup or *El Colorado* will shoot you!" "Look, there he is at the window!" "Look at that big gun he's holding! Oh, my God, he's about to pull the trigger!" "Go to bed now or we'll call *El Colorado* to come get you!"

I never saw a picture of *El Colorado*. But I imagined him being fat and red-faced, much like a sunburned American tourist I had once seen walking down the street. I can still see him in my mind's eye, clinging to the iron bars that covered my bedroom window, grinning fiendishly, his face glowing red, his Hawaiian shirt popping at the buttons. The God's honest truth is that he wasn't nearly as scary as Maria Theresa of Austria. Or Eye Jesus.

After *El Colorado*'s usefulness in behavior modification wore off, when I was slightly older, my father would occasionally take me with him to court in the summertime, when I was not in school. Sometimes he would take Tony too. Louis XVI began doing this when he was the judge of Regla, a poor district on the eastern side of Havana Harbor. Getting there was a lot of fun.

First we would take a bus all the way to the harbor. My father, the well-to-do art collector, former King of France, always rode the bus. Always. Even though we had a very nice car. This was one of his many quirks, like putting on his shoes before his trousers, or remembering his past lives and knowing about the past lives of others. The other judges made fun of him for this. "Hey, Nieto, did your chauffeur quit again?" "Nice bus, Nieto." "What's the matter, Nieto, too many girlfriends to feed and clothe?"

I don't remember him having any comebacks, especially for the jokes that had to do with sex, which in Cuba always outnumbered other kinds of jokes in a billion-to-one ratio, roughly. This was another quirk of his. He never spoke of sex and he loathed dirty jokes. This made him a rare bird among Cuban males. From first grade on, every boy's reputation as a genuine male was constantly tested through sexual humor and the free exchange of "bad" words. Anyone uncomfortable with that in first grade was taunted as a *mariquita,* or sissy. By third grade the insult was upgraded to *maricón,* or queer. And it couldn't ever get any worse than *maricón*. Even suffocation and entombment in a giant sandpile was better than that.

Anyway, back to the ride to Regla and my father's courthouse. Once off the bus, we would catch a small launch, jam-packed with people, and cross the harbor. At dockside, on either end, poor boys dove for coins thrown into the water. Most were my age, some even younger. The water was way past murky. Once the coins hit the water, they would quickly disappear from view. No turquoise here. This water was a deep, dark green, smudged with rainbow-hued oil slicks, and it smelled worse than it looked. My father's musings as we crossed the harbor made the boat ride scary.

"Just think of all the sharks swimming under us right now."

"You know, I once saw an old black woman fall off the side of the boat and drown, right here. And the guy who dove in after her was eaten by a shark. It was horrible."

"You know, one of these boats capsized once during a rainstorm, and everyone drowned. No, no, I take that back. Some drowned. The rest were eaten by sharks. It was horrible. What a tragedy."

"You know, some crazy man once drilled a hole into the hull of one of these water taxis and when it was about halfway to the other side it sank. It was horrible: those who didn't drown were eaten by the sharks."

Those poor boys diving for coins in water so dark that one couldn't see a shark coming seemed to me the bravest humans on earth. Or the most desperate. At the time I didn't know that desperation and bravery are usually one and the same thing. My dad would always give me a coin to throw in, usually a nickel. Sometimes it was a Cuban nickel, sometimes an American nickel. (Back then the currency was interchangeable, for the peso and the dollar were often nearly on a par with each other.) And the boys would scramble and fight one another to get to my nickel. The look of glee on the face of the boy who burst forth from the filthy water holding my nickel was priceless.

From the dock we would walk to the courthouse, a few blocks away. These were grimy streets, I thought, full of disgusting old buildings and poor people. The only color I remember seeing in that neighborhood was brown. The buildings were brown, the streets were brown, the people were brown. Even the statue of the Virgin Mary enshrined in the chapel of Our Lady of Regla was brown. The blazing sun remained far above, in its pure realm, unable to pass through the narrow streets. Not one tree in sight, at least on the way to the courtroom.

The courthouse seemed indistinguishable from the other buildings on that narrow street, probably because there was hardly enough room to step back and take a good look. The door seemed ancient and weathered. It was brown. The policeman guarding it was also usually brown. Once you made it past the door, you knew this was no ordinary building. It had jail cells, the only real ones I have ever seen. And there were people in the cells. Mostly brown people. We had to walk past them to get to Dad's chambers. They looked sad and angry and dirty, and they eyed me with malice, or so I thought. I was very glad to see policemen in that jailhouse corridor on the way to Dad's chambers. These were obviously bad people who had done something wrong. Who knew what they could do to me if my father hadn't locked them up? The jail cells reminded me of the lions' cages at the zoo, and the people inside looked about as happy as trapped beasts.

The most amazing discovery I made by visiting the courthouse was that my father was not just a goofy fat man who made kites and drove us through giant waves. He had power. Real power, the kind that makes other men grovel. Inside the courthouse, Dad was treated as if he really were the King of France, and my brother and I as if we were Bourbon princes. The court clerks would literally trip over one another fawning over him, and over us. Since I was always at the very bottom of the pecking order at school and at home, the attention and respect focused on me came as a shock.

The questions came at me fast and furiously from every man who worked for my father. Grown men with moustaches and slicked-back hair. "Can I get you a Coca-Cola? Or would you prefer Royal Crown? How about Pepsi-Cola? Orange Crush? Materva? Cawy? Maybe you'd like a milk shake? Should I turn up the speed on that fan over there? Is it too hot for you in here? Maybe you'd like some comic books?"

Once I had answered any of these questions in the affirmative, the man graced by my request would then snap his fingers and order some other man around. "Ñico, go across the street and get the judge's son a Coca-Cola." "Hey, Argimiro, run down to the newsstand and get the judge's son the latest Superman comic book." "Chucho, Chucho, Chucho! Snap to it! Go get this fine boy some Juicy Fruit gum!" A few minutes later, the request would be fulfilled. Being a child, I never thought about who paid for these items.

These very same men hovered around Dad's desk like worker ants, bringing papers and taking them away after he signed them. They asked if this or that had been done properly. And they always responded with a nod and a *"Sí, señor"* to each and every one of Louis XVI's orders. What a revelation that was each time I saw it. In the courtroom, the veil would lift momentarily to reveal a world of hierarchies, in which all five senses could detect power and discern its effect upon men. Lucky me, I was on top of the heap. And I thought it would be like that forever.

I knew this for sure when I got to sit next to Dad on his judge's bench. Yes, I could sit up there, next to His Honor. Those obsequious men would pull up a chair for me. There I would sit, elevated way above everyone else in the room, looking down on the guilty and innocent and on the victims. I told you Havana was not in the United States of America. My kite-making, wave-crashing father would hear testimony, question witnesses, uncover the truth, pound his gavel, and decide what was just, with his son sitting right next to him. In a world full of wrongs, it was his job to put things right: to absolve and to punish, to vindicate and to turn loss into gain.

It was amazing to watch him work. He dispatched his cases with great speed; even the most tangled arguments and disputes gave him no pause. I had heard of Solomon in school, and about the two women and the baby, and how Solomon had dispatched that case in the wink of an eye. Split the baby in two! Good God, my father was just like Solomon. He could spot the guilty ones in an instant by asking just one or two questions and render judgment in a flash. A fine for you: twenty pesos. Jail time for you: twenty days.

I sat up there transfixed. Everyone in the courtroom stared at me quizzically, as if asking "What the hell are you doing up there, boy?" One woman found guilty of something and fined fifty pesos looked at me pleadingly after my father pronounced her sentence. What did she think I could do?

I don't think the court sessions ever lasted more than two hours. After stepping down from the bench, Dad would sign some more papers and we would head back home. Back on the water taxi, back on the bus. Now that I think about it, my father's work day was about three or four hours long. No wonder he had time to do so many other things, such as typing out full descriptions of each and every one of his art objects on little cards, or building dioramas, or driving us to the seashore.

Once, after the world had changed and my father had been reassigned to a remote rural courthouse, we rode there on the train. It was the farthest I would ever get from Havana until I flew away for good. The train ride was very exciting, especially because the train was almost derailed. It took us about two hours to travel what must have been about thirty miles. Once he got to his courthouse, a small wooden building, Dad signed a few papers and back home we went. There were only two men working for him at that courthouse, and they were just as obsequious as the men at Regla. The only difference that the Revolution made was that there was nothing they could offer me. No sodas, no chewing gum, no comic books. Nothing. Not even a *guarapo,* a cold drink made from crushed sugarcane. Yet they still brought papers to my dad to sign, and took them away, and sought his approval.

Power is always power, and men are always men.

What a nice job being a judge. What a nice thing being the son of a judge. What a place, my Cuba. Lucky me.

Long before I rode the water taxi to Regla, many wise men and women had already discerned how best to approach such luck. One of these sages was Saint Jerome, the man who translated the Bible from Hebrew and Greek into Latin in the fifth century. Legend had it that Saint Jerome used to say, "Have mercy on me, Lord, I am a Dalmatian," while he beat his breast with a stone, struggling to suppress his own will and make his soul ready for God's abounding grace. What a wise man. He knew how deeply sin dwells in our skin. My own worst instincts still lead me to turquoise water, tangerine sunsets, and the judge's seat. I, too, find myself clutching jagged chunks of granite, beating my breast, seeking redemption. But I have to make a slight alteration in Jerome's prayer—a small change that makes a world of difference:

Miserere mei, Domine, Cubanus sum.

"Have mercy on me, Lord, I am a Cuban."

4

CUATRO

"Who discovered Cuba?"

Easy question. Nearly all of the boys raised their hands. Except those who thought it was too easy, and froze.

"Felipe . . . can you tell us?"

Felipe had not raised his hand.

"Christopher Columbus, in 1492."

"Very good," said our teacher, "but I didn't ask for the date. Good to know you weren't daydreaming. Now here is a tougher question: what was the first thing Columbus said when he set foot on Cuba?"

A couple of brownnosers thrust their hands into the air with more enthusiasm than anyone else. One of them even grabbed his upraised right arm with his left, as if to push it farther into the air. The teacher, as usual, called on someone who was sitting on his hands.

"Daniel, what did Columbus say?"

Daniel winced, and stuttered: "Uh . . . uh . . . uh . . . Thank God for land . . . at last?"

Laughs and snickers. A few more hands went up. The teacher shook his head and pounced on another seemingly distracted boy who hadn't raised his hand.

"Miguel, can you get it right?"

Looking the teacher straight in the eye, Miguel answered: "Columbus said, 'This is the most beautiful land ever seen by human eyes.'"

"Excellent. I'm glad to see not only that you were paying attention, Miguel, but that at least some of you have had a proper upbringing and were told about this at home, before we got to today's lesson. You know, what Columbus said is very, very important. It may be one of the most important things ever said about our island, and one of the most true."

"Yes, Cuba is a paradise," said Ramiro, unbidden. He was the one who had been holding his arm up higher than anyone else. "My dad told me that the Garden of Eden was here in Cuba, and that Adam and Eve were not only the first humans, but also the first Cubans, and that the entire human race is kind of Cuban. And he also said that this is the reason we don't have any poisonous reptiles at all."

"True, Ramiro, Cuba is a paradise, and it very well might have been the original Paradise, the Garden of Eden. How many of you have heard this before?"

A good number of hands went up.

"Yes, Cuba is a paradise. There is no other place on earth as lovely as Cuba, and that's why you should be so proud of your country. You're all very lucky to live in a paradise."

Lizards darted through my mind, and I stared through the window at the boy who was out on the playground, kneeling on the gravel under the bright blinding sun. I looked at the crucifix on the wall above the blackboard and the blood on the wounds. Few things scared me more than crucifixes, except for the Jesus who showed up in my dreams. And voodoo curses.

This is paradise? I strained to believe the teacher, and my own father too. Louis XVI had told me about Cuba being the Garden of Eden many times. I think he believed it, even though he couldn't remember ever having lived in Eden. It was one of the few things he didn't claim from memory. Could it really be?

Jesus H. Traitor-picking Christ. I didn't know it then, but that so-called Eden was far too close to the one in the Bible, and too close to what followed in that story, including the bit about Cain and Abel. I would have no foreigner to blame for the loss of my country, my home, and my family, or for all of the worst moments in my life. There would be no barbarian hordes I could point to, or invaders from beyond the sea. I would have only my own people to thank for my deepest scars, down to the most recent. But I would also owe a lot to them. Those fellow Cubans who would strip me clean, give me the Judas kiss, and crush me would also inch me towards paradise.

Loss and gain are Siamese twins, joined at the heart. So are death and life, hell and paradise. I struggled to deny this axiom as a child, and strain against it still on bad days.

Stupid of me to put up a fight. All along, I should have heeded what the Christian Brothers taught me. I didn't know it at the time, but those monks explained nearly everything to me. I owe them a lot, including my fear of chauffeurs.

Lucky me. I attended the finest primary school in Havana. El Colegio La Salle de Miramar. The Christian Brothers ran several schools in Cuba, but their outpost in the plush suburb of Miramar was the flagship, not just for their order, but for all private schools on the island. President Batista must have thought so, for he sent his children there. They were my schoolmates, as were the sons of many of Batista's ministers and generals. The sons of those who owned the sugar mills, tobacco factories, mines, department stores, and nearly everything else of value were my classmates, too, along with the sons of doctors, lawyers, and judges.

This was a Catholic school for boys, of course. It was run by stern monks, many of them from Spain and France, whose sole purpose in life was to make us aware of our base instincts and turn us into God-fearing Christians. Aside from a handful of Jewish children whose parents had come to Cuba from Europe fleeing Hitler and the Nazis, all of us were Roman Catholics. The Jewish kids would be excused from taking part in religion class, but they still had to sit at their desks while religion was taught. We all thought it was strange, but whenever we dealt with Bible stories from the Old Testament, they would chime in. And they knew all the answers. We couldn't figure out how they knew so much if they weren't taking religion class, but somehow they did. It was a mystery the good brothers never bothered to reveal to us.

You see, they didn't really explain everything. They only explained nearly everything.

The principal of this school, Brother Néstor María, was short and stout and spoke Spanish with a very thick French accent. You can imagine how much fun we good Christian boys had with that. French accents are just as funny in Spanish as in English. He would visit our classroom often and stand near the door with his hands behind his back, his huge belly testing the strength of the black buttons on his cassock. He boasted about the school to all the parents, and my mother still talks about it. "You know, that Brother Néstor María would always say that his school was attended by the *crème de la crème* of Cuban society."

The *crème de la crème*. Sure. We might have been at the top of the heap, but all of us were little thugs, putrid vessels of original sin. Not an hour went by without some kid being bullied or ridiculed. Not a day went by without a fistfight on the playground. Sometimes there would be two or three fights going on simultaneously during recess, each attracting a circle of spectators. The brothers would stand back and watch, intervening only at the first sight of blood. When more than one fight took place at the same time, the spectators would rush from circle to circle, trying to find out who was fighting. Some fights were better than others, depending on the reputation of the participants. What you wanted to see was a fight between two really tough guys. Watching a tough guy beat up on some *mariquita* was not much fun. The only kids who watched those fights were the *maricones*.

I wasn't counted among the *mariquitas* or *maricones,* but I was constantly tested. Abstaining from foul language placed me uncomfortably close to the line between *macho* and *mariquita,* and this invited all sorts of challenges to my budding masculinity. In the process, I came to be at the bottom of some pecking order I still don't understand. And I also took more punches than I care to remember.

I do remember winning one fight, though, and with merely one blow.

One fine day in second grade, out in the blazing sunlight, I was approached on the playground by the son of one of Batista's chief henchmen. Even at that age, I knew that his father was rumored to be in charge of all of the torturing in Cuba. No small task, on an island crawling with rebels. As often happens, the son tried to emulate the father. So this boy whose name I have forgotten was one of the worst bullies in my class.

Chief Torturer Junior approached me as I stood talking to another kid. He interrupted rudely, as bullies are supposed to do, and asked: "Why do you always stand with your hands on your hips, just like a girl?"

I looked down at my hands and, much to my horror, I saw that they were indeed resting on my hips. I had to think fast, especially since I had never heard that placing one's hands on one's hips was a telltale sign of femininity. But if this guy said so, it must be true. After all, the bullies were the lexicographers of *machismo*.

"I don't always do that," I replied as I removed my hands from my hips.

"Yes you do. I see you doing it all the time."

"No, I don't."

"Yes you do. Ask anyone. You always stand there just like a girl, with your hands on your hips."

Chief Torturer Junior turned to the kid who was with me. "Tell him. You saw it too. Doesn't he always stand like this?" And the bully struck a very feminine-looking pose, swaying his hips, placing one hand on his right hip and the other on his forehead.

"I . . . I . . . I don't know," said the other boy, afraid that he, too, was being challenged.

"I don't always stand around like a girl," I protested once more. "You're exaggerating."

"Are you calling me a liar?" huffed the bully.

"Uh . . . no, no."

"Yes you are, *maricón,* you're calling me a liar. You disgusting fairy."

He had done it. He had used the word. And we were only in second grade. This was getting very serious.

Chief Torturer *fils* pressed on. "You know, you make me sick. You stand like a girl, and you never say bad words. Here, prove you can say a bad word. Say *shit*. Say it. Say *mierda*."

"Uh . . . uh . . . I can't. That's a mortal sin. It's . . . it's against the first commandment."

"See. I told you. You can't even say *shit*. You know it's only girls who don't say bad words. Only girls and *maricones*."

"I can't say it. It has nothing to do with being a boy or a girl. I don't want to go to hell."

"So you're calling me a liar again, huh? Well, you can't do it! Say *shit*. Say *dick*. Go ahead, say *pinga*."

The next thing I knew my clenched fist was striking his head, right above his ear. It happened so fast he didn't have a chance to block the punch. He doubled over and stayed that way for what seemed like an eternity. Then he started to sob. I stood there holding my offending fist, which hurt a little, watching the bully sob. He sobbed and sobbed, and whined, and held his hand against his temple. I thought maybe I had ruptured his brain or something.

Then he spoke again between sobs: "You know, *sob,* you can kill someone by hitting them on the temple. *Sob.* That's a bad spot. *Sob, sob.* If you hit someone there, *sob,* the blow can go right to the brain and kill you."

I thought of saying, "Sure, you know this because your father kills so many people. I bet it's your father who taught you this. I bet he punches a lot of people in the temple. That's why you're such an expert." Instead of saying what I wanted to say, I simply stood there, breathing heavily. And I watched him weep.

The more he sobbed, the sorrier I felt for him. Waves of pity began to wash over me. But then waves of fear joined them. It dawned on me that I had hurt the meanest little bastard in class, whose father had the power to make people disappear. Now I'd done it. This meant death for me and my family.

Pity and fear twisted into a knot in my chest and forced me to say "I'm sorry."

The bell rang, recess ended, and we went back to class. Though I went home that afternoon and warned my parents about our impending doom, nothing bad ever happened. No police ever came in the middle of the night. No one whisked me away in a big black car during recess. The bully stopped taunting me. He didn't exactly become my friend, but at least he left me alone from that day forward.

I didn't realize it at the time, but I had stumbled onto one of the fundamental rules of the universe. Bullies are the ultimate sissies. *Mariquitas* at heart, all of them, maybe even *maricones*. Much later, when I ended up at a public high school in a rough neighborhood on the North Side of Chicago, where the tough guys carried knives and used them, memories of that weeping bully saved me from a lot of trouble.

Of course, the good Christian Brothers had told us repeatedly about the Sermon on the Mount, loving our neighbor, turning the other cheek, and the meek inheriting the earth. But it just didn't sink in. Original sin had us by the throat. We were all under the same curse, slaves to sin, blind as bats, and as happy as bats in a cave. We fought like God-damned savages, the whole lot of us. We hurled insults with abandon, laughed at the less fortunate, and looked down on nearly everyone else on our benighted island. We were, after all, number one. And everyone else was number two or lower. We knew it. Our parents knew it. The brothers knew it. Pride was our worst sin.

But all of us thought our worst sin was what the brothers called "dirty thoughts."

Ay Dios mío.

That's all I can say when I recall my formal introduction to sex in the classroom. I understand the good brothers wanted to warn us about storm clouds on the horizon, but in my case, at least, the warning and the storm clouds became one and the same.

In first grade, Brother Alejandro would come in and warn us not to have "dirty thoughts." At first, all of us sat there as silent as corpses, not daring to ask what in the world he was talking about. I thought of smelly laundry. But gradually his talks became more explicit. He told us about our shameful parts, and that most shameful of all male traits—erections—the gnawing, inevitable constant that led Saint Augustine to say, *"Ecce unde!"* (Behold the place!) If you want proof of original sin, said Augustine, just take a look at your penis. It has a life of its own. It can't really be controlled by reason. Behold the place. But don't behold it too much, and certainly don't hold it for too long after you're done peeing. And don't hold it at all any other time.

How Brother Alejandro came to be a sex education teacher for first graders I'll never know. Maybe because he was one of the few Cuban brothers at that school. He was the toughest of all the monks, the school disciplinarian. You didn't want to have him riding on your bus, if you rode the bus. And you certainly didn't want to get sent to Brother Alejandro if you misbehaved. He kept very strict discipline and was feared for his special bare-knuckle blows to the head. He also seemed to spend every single afternoon overseeing detention, making kids write phrases on the board hundreds of times. Some of the statements had a negative spin: "I shall never do X, Y, or Z again." Some were positive: "I shall always do X, Y, or Z." If he gave you more phrases to write than could fit on the blackboard, he would count up the lines, write down the number, ask you to erase the board, and keep going. If you complained, he would make you start counting all over again or ask you to return for more the next day. I learned all this from my brother Tony, who was sent to detention often. Sometimes Brother Alejandro would make the worst offenders kneel on gravel outside, in the hot tropical sun. These malfeasants knelt out there for what seemed an eternity. I could see them from my classroom, and I'd look at the clock on the wall. Every time one of those kids ended up out there on his knees, the second hand seemed to slow down. I was lucky, or perhaps even good. I never earned his wrath.

But I began to fear his visits to our first-grade classroom. There we were, six-year-olds sitting in a room decorated with Disney characters, listening to a monk talk about sex. I'm sure I wasn't alone in thinking that if we were being warned *not* to do something, it must have some pleasant side to it, like all of the other fun stuff you weren't supposed to do. One fine day, Brother Alejandro opened entirely new vistas of perversion and delight to all of us. "Don't ever look at your chauffeur's dirty magazines," he warned us.

One brave boy dared to ask the fundamental question on my mind: "Brother, what's a dirty magazine?"

"It's a magazine with pictures of naked women."

Naked women? Why would anyone want to look at pictures of naked women? *This must really be twisted,* I thought. All I could think of was old Inocencia and her eggplant breasts. Yuck. Why would chauffeurs keep dirty magazines within the easy reach of children? Maybe all chauffeurs were weird, like dwarves and cripples? Or maybe there was something I didn't know. Well, I didn't have to worry; we didn't have a chauffeur. My father rode the bus to work and drove his own car at other times.

Then it hit me. Although our family didn't have a chauffeur, my brother and I were driven to school by one every day. Each and every day we rode to school and back home in a chauffeur-driven, air-conditioned Cadillac, along with the son of the owner of one of the largest nickel mines in Cuba, who lived down the street from us. Four times a day we got into that car: to school, home for lunch, back to school, and then back home again. From that day forward I entered that yellow Cadillac with great trepidation. At any moment, I expected the chauffeur to whip out a dirty magazine and throw it to us in the backseat. This would be worse than a grenade, of course, since it could send you to hell for eternity. Instantly. All you had to do was see a naked woman and die the next moment, without a chance to repent. What if the magazine landed open right next to you, or on your face, and you actually got to see a picture of a naked woman just before the chauffeur, laughing insanely, crashed the car and killed everyone inside? Pretty soon I began to suspect that taxicab drivers also had these dirty magazines, since they, too, were called *choferes*. And I developed a fear of taxicabs as well.

I often wondered what kind of special treatment President Batista's children got at my school. Were they ever picked on by other boys? Were they subjected to the same sex talks? Did they ever have to write anything on the blackboard a hundred times? "I shall never forget my homework again," or maybe, "I shall ask my father not to torture anyone again." Did Brother Alejandro ever smack one of them on the back of the head?

I don't know. All I know is that the school was full of their bodyguards, outside and inside. Men who stood around all day, pacing back and forth, wearing suits or sport coats, even on the hottest afternoons. We knew they carried guns, and that they kept them concealed under their jackets. One day, on the way to recess, a boy in my class had the nerve to sneak up on one of the bodyguards and lift up his jacket, to see the gun. The bodyguard just smiled, and buttoned his jacket. I was lucky enough to see the gun in its holster and it looked huge.

I don't know about the other kids, but I thought that the bodyguards were there to protect the president's children from bullies. To protect them from me, maybe. And one afternoon in second grade I came face to face with the chance to be shot by a bodyguard. It happened suddenly. I was running down the hallway towards the grassy yard at the back of the school. Vendors of all sorts hung around back there all day, waiting for the kids to come out. Ice cream, candy, baseball cards, switchblades. These guys sold just about everything. Yes, switchblades. I told you Havana was not in the United States. If you had money, the brothers would let you buy any kind of snack that these men sold, or any size switchblade. One of these guys made the best popcorn I had ever tasted. He sold it in pastel-colored paper bags that would very quickly soak up the oil. They were a beautiful sight, those greasy bags. Anyway, I was running to buy something and—boom!—I ran into a first grader! Knocked him down. His popcorn went flying all over the place. I fell to the floor too, stunned by the collision.

When I saw whom I had knocked down, I froze. It was Batista's youngest son, the first grader. He looked a lot like his father. *Uh, oh,* I thought. *Now I did it.* The bodyguards will surely come and shoot me. Or maybe take me to jail, rip out my fingernails, and smack me on the temple. But before I had a chance to get really scared, Batista's son looked at me, and holding out his half-empty bag of popcorn, asked, "Would you like some?" He had the look of an angel on his face, the look of grace. I expected death or torture, or at least imprisonment, and instead I was offered the very same popcorn I had spilled.

The bodyguards never used their guns on me or on any bully, but they did need them after all. I found that out one sunny afternoon in second grade, when the school was suddenly surrounded by dozens of police cars. Brother Alejandro entered our classroom and handed a note to my teacher, who asked us to remain calm and wait for our parents to come pick us up. School was canceled for the rest of the day; we had to go home immediately. One by one, our parents showed up, looking troubled. One by one, we were plucked from our classrooms. My mother, Marie Antoinette, had the same look on her face that day as on the night of the shoot-out near the Quinta de los Molinos. As we were getting into the car, I noticed the switchblade salesman was not at his usual spot. There were no vendors, only police, some of them with their guns drawn.

"The presidential palace has been attacked," said my father, once we were safely in the car. "We need to get home fast. No one knows what will happen next." My mother was very quiet. A policeman waved our car on, and we passed through their barricade. It wasn't at all like that other time, when, at exactly the same spot, Louis XVI had picked us up by surprise and there was a puppy waiting for us in the backseat of the car.

The attack on Batista's palace failed. Although the rebels managed to make it all the way to the president's office and bedroom, Batista was not there. They had it wrong. I think he was at one of his *fincas* instead, one of his country estates. Dozens of men died that day, on both sides, providing the papers with a surplus of gory pictures. God knows what might have happened if the rebels had chosen to attack our school too. Batista's kids were there that day, one of them in the classroom right next to mine. If only those rebels had thought the way that *El Colorado*'s men had thought when they delivered all their twisted messages to my family. If only they had targeted the children instead of the father, the world might have changed even sooner than it did. Maybe one of the rebels killed that day would have survived, and Fidel Castro would have been eclipsed by him. Or maybe I would have died that day, and you wouldn't be reading this.

Idle speculation. Things happen the way they happen.

Planned they are from the get-go, eternal they are and eternal are we all. One and the same are we and those facts, forever. The way Brother

Alejandro's starched clerical collar moved as he spoke. The angle of the sunlight on the boys who knelt on the gravel. The shadows they cast. The taunts, the blow to the head, the tears, the dirty magazines, the bag of popcorn. Each grease spot on the bag of popcorn, and the trajectory of every popcorn kernel as it fell to the floor. The hand extended in goodwill. Each bewildering gift from on high. Every temptation, every glimpse of the plunging crevasse inside our souls. The Judas kiss. The basest humiliation. Everything. All of it seamlessly woven into the story of my fall, our fall, yours and mine, that deep and steep fall. That happy fall, that joyous fall during which we can always, in the wink of an eye, with grace, sprout wings and scrape the gates of Heaven.

5

CINCO

The pesticide Jeep rounded the corner, spraying death, and we jumped on our bicycles and chased it. It was usually Eugenio, Stinky, who could pedal the fastest, catch up to it, latch on to its rear bumper, and ride behind it for blocks. Eugenio would be lost in the cloud, invisible as the Jeep pulled away. Ten or twenty minutes later, he would return sweating and grinning, as happy as any kid could ever be, and give us a rundown on how far he had been pulled: "Ten blocks this time!" "Twenty blocks!" "Sixteen blocks!"

Few others could match this feat. Not even my brother, who could usually do nearly anything he wanted, such as swim out to the horizon by himself, along with the sharks and barracudas, and peer into the black abyss that opened up beneath him where the sea floor suddenly dropped hundreds of feet beneath the turquoise waves.

When the Jeep passed by, the world was transformed, and everything became invisible. You could barely see your hand in front of your face. The entire street was one giant cloud of pesticide. And it lingered forever. It must have been DDT, that awful poison banned in the United States. Mosquito control. Best way to curb malaria in a tropical paradise. What a beautiful sight, that red Jeep. What an exquisite color, that poison. Kind of blue.

I remember whirling like a dervish in the thick fog, inhaling with abandon, collapsing onto the street nearly delirious. I thought this was what heaven must be like: thick bluish clouds, and that wonderful smell. I have always inhaled with abandon. The world is so full of wonderful smells. Roasted peanuts. Olives. Popcorn. Bus exhaust. Turpentine. Kerosene. Talcum powder. Gasoline. New tires. Glue. Shoe polish. Bubblegum wrappers. Gunpowder. Thinly sliced potatoes and hot dogs frying in olive oil. When I matured, the strangest things began to emit pleasing fumes too. Freshly baked bread. Single-malt Scotch whiskey. Cigars. Roses. Bordeaux wines. New wallets. New cars. The back of a woman's knee after a hot bath. Other substances I dare not mention. Fumes are the fifth dimension, I'm convinced.

But nothing could beat that poison. So pungent, yet so sweet. We loved to fill our lungs with it, loved it so much.

Eugenio, our champion Jeep catcher, was the luckiest and the craziest of all of us. We were a close group of friends, five of us, all from the neighborhood. My brother and I, Manuel and Rafael Aguilera, also brothers, and Eugenio Godoy, who was unlucky enough to have sisters instead of brothers. When we first met him, my brother and Manuel dubbed him *El Apestoso,* or Stinky, because he smelled so bad. But then he started to use deodorant and we had to find another nickname for him. So we began to call him *El Alocado,* the Crazed One. We couldn't call him *El Loco,* the Crazy One, because we had to distinguish him from the homeless alcoholic who lived in the park, who already owned that spectacular name. Big difference between those two. Eugenio's father was a bank president, and his house and gardens took up half a city block. *El Loco* was an older man, scruffy and smelly, who often walked about the neighborhood muttering to himself. Sometimes he would shout, too, flailing his arms, shaking his head. We didn't know for sure where he lived, but we feared *El Loco.* He would show up unexpectedly, just like the DDT Jeep, only more often. And we didn't like that combination of frequency and unpredictability.

El Loco was crazy. We knew that and our parents knew it. They called him *El Loco* too. He was one of the very few people in my neighborhood—perhaps the only one—at the bottom of the heap. At least the maids and nannies got paid and slept indoors. *El Loco* had nothing but the filthy clothes he wore and a wide-brimmed peasant straw hat. He was a force of nature, wild and dangerous, capable of just about anything.

We, of course, were perfectly sane, and so were our parents. Unlike *El Loco,* who avoided the DDT Jeep like the plague, we had the good sense to discern the true, good, and the beautiful, and to chase down pesticide clouds. Our parents were enlightened enough to urge us on.

One of my father's brothers, Rafael, was the only adult who ever scolded us for calling this man *El Loco*. He had the odd nickname of Filo—which means "edge" or "sharpness"—and he was the only one in my father's family who touched alcohol. Maybe that had something to do with that peculiar burst of compassion on his part, for he was not exactly a compassionate man. Or maybe it was a premonition on his part, for Filo would one day be imprisoned and tortured, and lose his own mind. So it goes with revolutions. Anyway, Filo pricked our consciences just a little, but not enough to make us stop. We had no consciences, really. And *El Loco* was crazy, really.

Since we were all so sane, we thought it our right and privilege to taunt *El Loco* from a safe distance. "You're nuts!" "You're insane!" "Hey, what was it like at Mazorra?" (That was the name of Havana's largest insane asylum.) "Hey, how long before you go back?" Sometimes he would start shouting and chase us. Eugenio told us that *El Loco* had once pulled out a huge knife and chased him for two blocks.

We were fine specimens, the five of us. We also tormented a slightly retarded man who lived next door to Manuel and Rafael. Sometimes we would shout at him, and, since he moved slowly, challenge him to come chase us. "Mongo!" (Short for *mongoloid*). "Hey, how much is two plus two?" "Hey, what color was Napoleon's white horse?" "Hey, Mongo, why don't you show us how fast you can run!" And so on.

Back in the fifth century Saint Augustine bemoaned the fact that as a child he and his friends had stolen pears from a neighbor's tree just for the thrill of it. What an underachiever, that Augustine. When it came to committing mindless sins and manifesting unmistakable signs of total depravity, the five of us were gold medalists.

We rang doorbells and ran away. We called for taxicabs on the phone and sent them to the other end of the city. Using our deepest voices, we ordered groceries and hardware on the phone and had them delivered to our neighbors' houses. We uprooted plants from our neighbors' yards and from nearby parks. We picked fruit from neighbors' trees, not knowing that we were imitating a great saint. We took milk bottles from front porches and used them for target practice. We scattered thumbtacks and smashed bottles on the street and waited for cars to run over them. We blasted huge firecrackers—some of which were about the size of half a stick of dynamite—all over the neighborhood, wrecking shrubs, blackening porches, and scaring to death God knows how many old ladies. We crashed our toy cars into one another with the greatest force possible, smashed them with hammers, or blew them up with those huge firecrackers. We jammed wads of bubblegum into neighbors' front-door locks. We stole toy soldiers from Woolworth's. Sometimes we set those stolen plastic warriors on fire, just to watch them burn. We shot at streetlights at night with our water pistols, shattering the hot lightbulbs. When we didn't have water pistols on hand, we also threw rocks at the streetlights. We threw rocks at cats and dogs. We threw rocks at birds. We threw rocks at one another.

When we ran out of rocks and hard objects, we took to guns. We shot at birds with our BB guns and our pellet guns. Sometimes we even shot at people. Twice, the ever-feuding Aguilera brothers shot BBs at each other. I will never forget the sight of Rafa chasing his older brother Manuel on his bicycle, BB gun in hand, swearing, steering, and shooting at the same time. We laughed about that for weeks. Once my cohorts actually shot at passing buses with their BB guns from the roof of Eugenio's house. Somehow I missed that one. I think I was sick that day. But oh how I wished I could have been on that roof with my friends and brother. The four of them described in great detail how the passengers on the bus recoiled when the BBs hit near their windows. Eugenio even claimed he had shattered one window.

But why stop at buses and BB guns? Why not aim higher? At Eugenio's house there were a lot of real guns, with real ammunition. Rifles, pistols, shotguns. None of them were locked up, and his father never seemed to be around to stop us from using them. One day my four cohorts climbed to Eugenio's roof with a .22-caliber rifle and took turns shooting at passing aircraft. Yes, they tried to shoot down airplanes. I wasn't there, though.

Once again, I had missed out on great fun. What if they had actually succeeded? I tried to imagine the fireball and the explosion as the plane landed on someone's house.

We were capable of anything.

We also killed lizards whenever we saw them. In all sorts of horrible ways I can't yet reveal. All I will say now is that we sometimes tried to send them into outer space like the Russian dog Laika.

Poor lizards.

You see, it wasn't just my adopted brother Ernesto who was rotten. We were all rotten. The difference between him and us was that he did even nastier things and never got caught. Compared to him, the five of us were amateurs, and bad ones at that. We got caught every now and then and had to pay.

Like the day when the older boys ganged up on Rafa and me and put us through their version of Indian torture.

We had all recently seen a movie in which the ever-evil Hollywood Indians had buried some unfortunate ever-wholesome Cowboy up to his neck in the sand and smeared his face with something sweet. When the ants came out and ate his face we all squirmed and squinted, turning away from the screen and peeking through our fingers. But look we did. And the image took hold of us. This was one evil deed that cried out for imitation.

Rafa and Manuel's yard had several fire ant nests. One of them was huge. We knew they were *hormigas bravas* because we had all been stung now and then. We knew to stay away from them, and especially from that one big nest, which looked like a small volcano. Often, while playing in that yard, one of us would have a run-in with them and cry out in pain and run around like some demoniac. All of us learned to recognize the scream that came with their bite. It would take some time for the bite to swell, but the pain was there from the instant they bit you.

Those ants made the lizards look good.

But they weren't the only constant reminder of nature's treachery in that yard. The Aguilera yard was also blessed with a hot pepper bush. These weren't jalapeño peppers, with which just about every North American is familiar. No, they made jalapeños seem mild mannered. They were beautiful, tiny red peppers, and they could kill. They were truly exquisite to behold: such a bright shining red. Same color as a sports car, or the brightest red lipstick, and so smooth to the touch. They cried out, "Touch me, kiss me, eat me!" The ultimate deception. All of us had been tempted to sample them—cautiously, just on the tip of the tongue—and we rued having done it. One brush with their evil juice and you could brag about knowing what hell was like. They burned hotter than lava and made your flesh swell to the point of bursting.

I'm not exaggerating.

And one day, shortly after having seen the movie with the guy whose face got eaten by ants, the older boys decided to act out the fateful scene. Naturally, they used the two of us who were youngest and weakest to play the role of the hapless Cowboy. And they hit upon the very Cuban idea of combining the killer peppers and the fire ants.

The three of them—Manuel, Eugenio, and Tony—ganged up on Rafa and me, smeared our faces with the red peppers, threw us onto the fire ant nest, and held us there for a while. I had never thought it possible to hurt so much. And I didn't know which was worse, the sting of the ants or the burn from the peppers. But I still remember very clearly how I could feel my eyelids and lips swelling.

Rafa and I cried out, begging for mercy from our Indian torturers and for help from our moms. But our mothers were too used to our war games and our constant cries of distress and agony. ("Help, help, don't scalp me, no! Aaaaaaaay!" "Help, help, this grenade blew my legs off! AAAaaaaaay." "Oh no, my guts are spilling out. Ooooooh no!") No one came out of the house to rescue us, though we were shouting at the top of our lungs.

As soon as the Indians released us, Rafa and I ran into the house, wailing. Everything was blurry due to the hot pepper juice in our eyes and the swelling of our eyelids, but we found our way to our mothers in the kitchen, where they were chatting. I was crying my heart out, thinking that I was maimed for life, or on the threshold of dying. In between our sobs Rafa and I explained to our mothers what had happened, as they pelted us with questions and cries of alarm. Neither Rafa nor I had any idea how badly disfigured we were already, and how much that upset our moms. They rushed us into the bathroom, tossed us into the shower fully dressed, and soaked us thoroughly. I remember the two of them making more of a din than we two kids.

If you ever need to awaken quickly from a deep, deep sleep arrange to have two Cuban mothers shout at your bedside as if their children have been hurt. If you need to awaken from a coma, have them shout as if their older children have hurt the younger ones.

Rafa and I had our eyes soaked in something that made us cry even more and were slathered with ointment where the fire ants had left their marks. I don't know about Rafa, but I cried more on that day than I had ever cried before.

The older boys were rounded up for justice. They were unmasked before their fathers for the bullies they were, and they paid for what they did. I don't remember the punishment, but whatever it was, it must have been far too light for the crime they had committed. They never again did anything so cruel, but they joked about what they had done for years, and even bragged about it when we were in the company of other boys who hadn't been there. They probably bragged about the punishment, too.

After a while Rafa and I began to brag about it too, and even to laugh. It was the kind of story that always got the right kind of reaction from other boys.

With girls, it was different. The first time I told the story to a girl should have been the last. But I kept trying for years, thinking it would impress them.

Nowadays I play a game with my own three children. I ask them, suddenly and unexpectedly, at the oddest moments: "What is the Law?" They know the answer, and they pronounce the words as I have taught them, slowly and ponderously: "We shall not walk on all fours. We shall not drink blood." The answer is especially endearing when it issues from my youngest son's lips: "We sall not walk on all foahs. We sall not dwink bwood." They've never seen the movie this line is taken from, *Island of the Lost Souls,* with Charles Laughton playing the part of a deranged scientist, Dr. Moreau, who turns beasts into humans and has to keep them in line with a whip and the ever-central question, "What is the Law?" *Snap!* goes Dr. Moreau's whip. "What IS the Law?" *Snap! Snap! Snap!* "What IS the Law?" *Snap!* Moreau's creatures, barely erect, ask themselves and their creator, "Are we not men?" And they reply to Dr. Moreau's question in unison, slowly and ponderously, "We shall not walk on all fours. We shall not drink blood."

To this quiz on the Law I have added a third response of my own: "We shall not inhale poison."

My children think I'm joking when I launch into this pop quiz. But I'm deadly serious. I want them to know that there is a law, and that there is a beast inside each of them, always itching to ignore it and to break free. I want them to know, too, that there is a whip snapping over their heads, silent for now, gentle and silent. Someday, I tell them, they will hear the crack of the whip and realize they are wielding it themselves, standing erect, abstaining from blood, seeing poison for what it is, and avoiding it like the plague.

So, what is the Law? *Snap! Snap!* What IS the Law? *Snap!*

Your turn now. Go on. Answer.

6

SEIS

There He was again. How I wished He would stop this.

There He was, at the window, shouldering the weight of that huge, awful cross. He always showed up so unexpectedly. So swiftly. It's not as though He walked to the spot, or anything like that. He simply appeared. And He never made a sound.

How I hated it. How I feared it.

He just stood there, as always, blood trickling down His face, that nasty crown of thorns piercing His forehead. They were such huge thorns, and so sharp. His hair was long and messy, and bloody too.

He just stood there and stared at me.

My family kept eating dinner, as always, oblivious to the visitor. There they were, seated around the table, stuffing food in their mouths, making small talk, while Jesus parked Himself at our window, staring at me. "Pass the fried plantains, please." "Azucena, dish me out some more *malanga*." "Tony, eat your soup, it's getting cold. If you eat cold soup, you'll get indigestion." "Antonio, are you ready for dessert?"

How He stared. God, those eyes, those eyes, so full of pain. Brown eyes, not blue. So all-commanding, so all-consuming. Eyes that pierced right through to the very core of my soul, eyes that read my mind. Eyes that seemed to beg and command at the same time.

"Come, follow Me."

Go away, go away, go away, please. Vanish. Disappear, please. Stop torturing me. Why do you do this? I didn't have to speak. He knew what I was thinking before I thought it. And I knew He knew it.

He just stood there and stared at me.

I tried to speak to my family, but no words would come out of my mouth. It was useless to try. He let me know it was useless. He was there for me alone. And then He would vanish, as suddenly as He had appeared.

This happened so many times I lost count.

Funny thing, whenever Jesus appeared, I was sitting in my father's usual spot at the table, facing the window that looked out on the house with the breadfruit tree. When awake, I sat at the other end, facing the window that looked out on the house with the bitter-orange tree. Chachi's house.

Chachi was a girl my age. Her father was in the cigar business, and she was an only child. I don't know what her real name was; all I can remember is her nickname, Chachi. All of the adults in my house used to tease me constantly: "Chachi is so cute; she'll be your girlfriend someday." *Tu novia. Novia* means both "girlfriend" and "bride" in Spanish. It's that kind of language, especially when it comes to matters of the heart. *Te quiero* means both "I love you" and "I want you." They were merciless, relentless, my elders: "Wait and see: you'll grow up to marry Chachi." "You'll marry her someday." "What a cute couple you two will make."

How I hated her stupid lipstick. And what the hell was she doing wearing lipstick at the age of six anyway?

Knowing that your future is sealed is an awful thing when you're a child. I didn't know which was the worse window to face: the one where I could expect to see Jesus with His cross or the one where I knew I would see Chachi with her lipstick. Jesus let me know my future clearly: I was going to get one of those giant crosses and a crown of thorns. My family also predicted my future: I was going to marry Chachi and be smeared with her stupid lipstick for the rest of my life. Which was worse?

Both were frightening prospects. But there was a huge difference between these two beings, and their place in my life.

One was God, the other was not.

And there was another difference too: I saw Jesus only in dreams; I saw

Chachi in the flesh just about every single day. And I heard her voice all the time, drifting over the wall that separated our houses.

If my family had not soured my relationship with Chachi, we might have become good friends. I suspect her family also teased her about me constantly, in the same way. Cubans like to do things like that. I suspect that many Cuban mothers begin planning their children's weddings and arranging relationships for them before they even get married themselves. Anyway, whenever Chachi and I played outside at the same time, or even saw each other, we were like two positively charged magnets: a force field pushed us away from each other. I don't think we ever had a single conversation.

The closest we came was the time I got drunk at her aunt's wedding reception.

It was a nice party. Everyone was all dressed up, and Chachi was wearing more lipstick and makeup than usual. We must have been about eight years old. I was spending my time with Chachi's cousins Jorge and Julio, who were both younger than me. It was great to be the oldest one in a friendship rather than the youngest. And Jorge was very funny, and I liked him, despite the fact that Chachi was his cousin. Julio was too young to be funny, but I liked him too.

The party was being held two doors down from my house, at the home of Chachi's and Jorge's and Julio's grandmother. You see, Chachi's dad lived next door to his mother and father. This was not at all unusual. Jorge and Julio lived with their grandmother most of the time, and I never bothered to ask why. This, too, was common. Anyway, they were serving champagne at this big table and it looked good to Jorge and me. The thin-stemmed glasses were all set up, full to the brim, there for the taking. We didn't have to ask anyone to fill them. So we drank and drank and drank. It tasted so good, and those tiny bubbles were unlike those in any soda drink: they exploded in your mouth like a thousand microscopic firecrackers.

Chachi was there, weaving in and out of the crowd. I remember staring at her bright red lips and thinking that maybe they were not so scary after all. Even her black patent leather shoes no longer looked scary or incomprehensible.

Suddenly everything looked different at that wedding feast. I was so happy, so so happy. Jorge was happy too. We laughed and laughed at God knows what, not knowing we were drunk. And we got drunker and drunker. I remember asking myself: *Why does the world seem so much nicer all of a sudden? Why has Jorge held back on all these great jokes?* As I was puzzling over all of this, I said something Jorge must have found hilarious, for he laughed so hard that the champagne he was drinking came shooting out of his nostrils.

Two thin yellow streams, symmetrical and seemingly endless.

It was as if his nose had turned into a garden hose or he had become an elephant. I had seen elephants do this in Tarzan movies. The champagne streamed to the marble floor and made a yellow fizzy puddle at my feet. I laughed so loudly at the sight of this that my whole body shook and my eyes watered. Jorge stared at the puddle in disbelief, feeling the lingering droplets on his nose with his fingers, and his entire body convulsed, just like mine.

A large fat hand appeared from somewhere. This hand grabbed me by the shoulder. Then another hand appeared from somewhere else and grabbed Jorge the same way. My feet left the floor and all of a sudden I was horizontal. The last thing I remember was my father whisking me out of the wedding feast in his arms. Then I sank into a deep, dark, bottomless void. I don't remember being carried home, two doors down, or getting into bed, or undressing. But the next morning I woke up in my bed, wearing pajamas. I stared at the dust particles whirling in the shafts of sunlight, as I always did upon waking. Something was different that morning, though. I remember being disappointed by the fact that the world was no longer so nice and funny, and wondering why it couldn't always be that way.

Later that day, my parents explained inebriation to me. I didn't really understand what they said, all I could grasp is that I had gotten drunk at the wedding feast. *Emborrachado*. I did understand, clearly, that I had committed a sin, and that I should never, ever do it again. Dying drunk could land you in hell. What if you expelled so much champagne through your nose that you choked to death before you had a chance to confess the sin? And what if, on top of that, a chauffeur threw a dirty magazine and it landed, open, on your face, just before your heart stopped beating? Pretty scary. But not as scary as Chachi's lipstick. I resolved to stay away from alcohol for the time being, but I felt proud of having experienced something reserved for adults, and even prouder of having made Jorge's champagne shoot out through his nostrils.

Jorge and I talked about this for years, until I went away. We'd probably still be talking about it if it weren't for Fidel and his infernal Revolution.

Jesus, however, kept coming back again and again, all through my childhood, until I went away and became a man overnight at the age of eleven. He would show up unexpectedly. Right in the middle of other dreams, there I'd be at the table, facing the wrong window, in my father's seat, begging Jesus to go away. Every time I had one of those dreams, it shook me to the very core of my soul. He didn't so much read my mind as reveal to me what was there already. These dreams were the opposite pole from Chachi's aunt's joyous wedding feast: fear, terror, trembling.

I had no idea He was there to save me. Save me from what? Lipstick? Lizards? Bullies? Myself? The voodoo *brujeros* and their demons? I didn't know what to make of the cross, the crown of thorns, the blood, and the frightening message, "Come, follow Me." Why couldn't it have been Eye Jesus at the window, with his blue eyes? He was just a head on a plate. No cross, no crown of thorns, no blood, just a neat trick with His eyes. Now that I think about it, why couldn't it have been Jesus at the wedding feast of Cana, with His mother the Virgin Mary at His side, nudging Him, bossing Him around? Why couldn't He have come to turn my water into wine? Or into champagne?

It seems that Bloody Jesus had something to tell me no one else could.

My dad, Louis XVI, said you never passed the test in one lifetime. So much to learn, so many mistakes, so much to pay for. You had to keep coming back. You had to pay and pay, and learn ever so slowly, so painfully. A billion revolutions, a billion guillotines, a billion blades slicing off a billion of your heads would not suffice. Oceans of blood would not suffice.

Sometimes I think Jesus stopped by the window to tell me, as I sat in the place reserved for my dad, that this man who believed in reincarnation, this self-professed former King of France, was wrong. Dead wrong.

"Turn around. Follow Me, not him."

My mother, who never actually claimed to be Marie Antoinette until a drug reaction made her lose her mind for two days at the age of seventy-nine, didn't have much to offer in the way of lessons, especially in metaphysics and eschatology. She simply offered unconditional love. Sometimes I think Jesus stopped at my dining room window because He wanted to point her out to me.

"Behold your mother."

Or maybe He wanted to join us for dinner. I'm sure that fried plantains, *carne asada,* and *malanga* taste much better than plain broiled fish from the Sea of Galilee. *Sí, claro.* Yes, surely, Jesus was not just looking at me. He was staring at our food and smelling it.

Inhaling deeply.

Who knows what might have happened if God had become incarnate in a place with really tasty cuisine, such as Cuba? Questions like that have made me realize that Jesus was there in my dreams to say an infinite number of things. Messages too vast in number to be understood all at once, or even in a whole lifetime on earth. Vital messages such as:

"Behold your mother."

"Lipstick is wonderful."

"Lizards are beautiful."

"Demons are doomed to fail: I have defeated evil, and so shall you."

"Fear not death: You shall live forever, in a wondrous body, just like Mine."

"Drink champagne, and blow it out your nose."

When I think back to the Jesus of my dreams I always remember the curly-haired, desperate man we wouldn't rescue during the shoot-out, and I recall my father's challenge to all those brought face to face with his Eye Jesus plate: "I dare you: see if you can get away from His gaze."

Weird memories, even by Cuban standards. But useful, because the world is weirder than we can imagine, even in our dreams. Among the infinite messages conveyed by Jesus at my window in Havana, one stands above the rest in times of trial, those harsh, soul-crushing times none of us can escape. I didn't hear this back then, in my dreams, but I have heard it many times since, and hear it still.

"This pain, this cross, shall vanish as quickly as I did in your dreams; these stains on your soul shall be wiped clean, just like that lipstick smudge you once had on your cheek, that smudge you never saw, from the kiss you never felt, you drunken fool."

7

SIETE

Blackie the chimp was on the loose again. Running amok in Miramar, swinging from tree to tree, screaming loudly, scaring people.

This time he was dressed in olive green lederhosen. Yes, this fine African chimpanzee was dressed in Bavarian lederhosen, those stupid-looking embroidered leather overalls with short pants, running away from his prison in suburban Havana. Leaping from tree to tree, so far from his real home in the African rain forest, saddled with an English name in a Spanish-speaking country, seeking freedom.

His owner followed him closely on foot, along with a small retinue of servants, watching the chimp's every move, making sure he wouldn't get away for good. I saw Blackie in our ficus tree, out on the sidewalk, and his owner looking up anxiously at the branches, pleading with the chimp to come down, holding Blackie's Alpine hat in his hand. The hat was part of the outfit that must have fallen off, or been tossed away, by the runaway chimp. How vividly I still remember the colored feathers that poked out of the hat band. One red, one gold, one bright green. Blackie screamed loudly from his sanctuary, sounding just like Cheetah in Tarzan movies. Blackie also looked a lot like Cheetah but was a touch neurotic. Even a child could tell this chimp was not quite right in the head.

But you'd be neurotic too if you were as smart as a chimp and you lived in a little house, about ten feet by six feet, perched on a platform slightly larger than your dwelling, about eight feet off the ground, with a six-foot length of chain connecting your ankle to the platform floor. It looked a lot like Tarzan's tree house, come to think of it. The concrete supports that held up the platform had been carefully designed to resemble tree branches. They even had a rough barklike surface etched onto them, and truncated pruned limbs poking out helter-skelter. How I stared at those fake branch stumps when I played in that zoo garden. So much work to make something look natural. All for a chimp and its owner.

And you'd be even more neurotic than Blackie if you also had a bunch of snotty kids taunting you all the time, and throwing hard objects at you and your little house. Among all of those terrible things my friends and I used to do in the neighborhood, I glossed over our treatment of Blackie.

Poor Blackie, chained to his platform. How we loved to anger him. How we loved to yell at him and imitate his cries, or throw stuff at him. We always thought it was so funny when he yanked on his chain violently and threw around his brightly colored aluminum cup. How we loved it when he threw that blue cup at us, his only possession other than the chain. Hard to tell, then or now, whether the chain belonged to him, or he to the chain. The costumes were also his, I suppose. But he wore them only on special occasions.

Sometimes, if we made him really angry, he would defecate in his hand and throw turds at us. You can imagine how much a bunch of boys loved this, how we tried to shove one another in the path of those incoming missiles. Whoa, watch it! *"Oye, Cuidado!" "Prepárate!"* Get ready! We looked forward to the worst: would anyone get smeared with Blackie's stool? No one ever did, much to our collective chagrin.

Blackie belonged to one of our neighbors, the nickel mine magnate, the man with the Cadillac and the chauffeur who drove us to school. Gerardo Aulet, our neighbor, had turned his gardens into a zoo, just around the corner from us. A lion, a tiger, a panther, a chimp, some monkeys, other small mammals, and birds. All sorts of birds. Beautiful, exotic birds, held captive in cages large and small. Some of the cages were so large that later, after the world changed and poor people took over this zoo, some of them turned the cages into their dwellings.

Would that be a sign of progress or one of the saddest things on earth? You tell me. I still don't know.

All I know is that it happened to my birthplace and my people, and that my own memories are clouded by passion. As much as I have tried to escape, to obliterate what I was and ceased to be, I've been as successful at that as I've been at turning myself into a corn-fed, redheaded, freckled, Scotch-Irish farm boy from Indiana. Or Michael Jordan defying gravity. Or Captain James Tiberius Kirk commanding the starship *Enterprise* at warp speed, wooing every good-looking female that crossed his stellar path, human or alien. And speaking of fictional characters, Popeye might have been the wisest of all time, for he knew instinctively what it has taken me a lifetime to realize. "I am what I am," or as Popeye put it, "I yam what I yam."

I yam Cuban.

God-damned place where I was born, that God-damned place where everything I knew was destroyed. Wrecked in the name of fairness. In the name of progress. In the name of the oppressed, and of love for the gods Marx and Lenin.

Utterly wrecked.

I have pictures to prove it, from twenty years ago, when my mother went back to visit for one week, packing a Kodak Instamatic camera. Everything was already so thoroughly ruined then as to be barely recognizable. The entire neighborhood went to ruin, just like ancient Rome, only more quickly and without the help of German barbarians. The entire city. The entire country, from end to end. Rumor has it that our house collapsed about two years ago and Ernesto, the adopted one, had to move out. But we have no way of finding out. My mother, brother, and I haven't spoken with Ernesto in more than twenty years. On top of that, Havana might as well be on the other side of the moon, or on Pluto, or the planet Mongo, home of Ming the Merciless, or the outer fringe of the universe, where it's not houses, but time and space that collapse.

Anyway, I really don't give a damn about that house anymore. If it did indeed fall down under its own rotten weight, good riddance. If it didn't, the first thing I'll do when I return to Havana is rent a bulldozer and raze it to the ground all by myself. Or better yet, I'll stuff the house full of dynamite and blow it up. My final firecracker surprise for the old neighborhood, in remembrance of pranks past. I have a neighbor here in town who could teach me how to do it right and without casualties. He blows up things for a living, and his children play with mine. Such a nice guy. So expert with dynamite.

Would this make my current neighbors ordinary or extraordinary in comparison to those I had as a child?

Sorry, I digress. Back to my old neighborhood and Blackie's story: Aulet's son, also named Gerardo, was our friend. He was such a nice guy, Gerardito. If he hadn't suffered from severe asthma, he would have become a member of our gang, the sixth apostle of mischief. Such a funny guy, and always so frail, so sick, so pampered. We could play with him only at his own house, and in his own zoological garden.

Gerardito went to school with Tony and me and shared that perilous Cadillac ride with us every day. He never seemed scared of his chauffeur, though. They seemed to be buddies of sorts, if one could ever conceive of a rich white boy and a poor black man as buddies. They shared dirty jokes, even. And they both freely uttered bad words. But this made sense: bad words and the Aulet house went together.

On one of his rear terraces, Aulet had a mynah bird. A very special creature, this bird, a worthy competitor to the Empress Maria Theresa. He knew every swear word ever uttered in Cuba. And he screamed out these expletives so loudly you could hear him nearly a block away. *"Coño, coño, coño!" "Hijo de puta. Puta. Hijo de puta!" "Puta, puta!" "Carajo, carajo, qué mierda. Qué mierda! Mierda!" "Me cago en tu puta madre. Cago, me cago. Puta madre!" "Culo grande, culo grande y gordo. Culo, culo feo."*

I've taken great care to report only the mildest of his offending words. But I won't translate, for fear of landing in hell.

Aulet's mynah bird didn't have to worry about hell, though. Or about much else. He was well fed and sumptuously housed. And he obviously had a voice coach who put great effort into helping him master a highly specialized vocabulary. Back then, I used to suspect the chauffeur. But it could have been my friend Gerardito, or maybe his father. Or everyone in that household, for all I know. The amount of effort that went into creating this screwy masterpiece boggles the mind. The mynah bird, who had no name, knew only one clean phrase: *Gerardito, ven a comer.* Gerardito, come eat. It was spellbinding to hear "Gerardito, come eat" embedded in the midst of a long string of unconnected swear words and lewd phrases.

We played with our friend in his private animal garden quite often, and not without risk. Once, as my dad sat at one of the many benches in the garden, he suddenly felt a weight on his shoulders, what seemed to be two large hands pressing down on him. He turned around and he found his nose less than an inch from a lion's snout. The fact that he decided to say hello to my father might have had something to do with the fact that he was a portly man with lots of meat on his bones. Having faced the guillotine in a former life, my dad remained cool. Or maybe he was petrified. Fortunately, he sat perfectly still until the lion lifted his paws and sauntered off. Then, very cautiously and quietly, he rounded us up, one by one, and brought us into the Aulet house.

My dad, the hero.

Years later, but years ago, when my lovely wife was still my girlfriend, and when she was still in graduate school, she tried to argue in class one day that a tiger mentioned in one Latin American short story—a tiger in a house—didn't need to be interpreted metaphorically. The professor and the other students laughed her off. "Magical realism," they all said. But she knew so much more about what passes for Latin magical realism than they did, thanks to the stories I had told her. For one thing, she knew about the time Blackie took revenge on me.

We were playing hide-and-seek. I had found a very nice spot behind the tiger's cage. The tiger who would later die of indigestion and a failed enema administered with a garden hose. Hiding well was important to me, so important I braved the lizards in the thick foliage. So there I was, hiding successfully, minding my own business, listening for footfalls, as each of my friends were rustled from their hiding spots one by one. And looking out for lizards.

Then came the hug.

I felt someone's arms encircle my legs from behind, just above the knees. Thinking it was my best friend Rafael trying to startle me, even though it would have been immensely weird for him to hug me that way, I whispered: "Rafa, go away, stop it." Before I could turn around came the pain. Long, sharp teeth piercing through my jeans, sinking into my flesh. And the grip around my legs tightened as the teeth sank farther and farther into me. I'd been bitten by dogs and cats before, but this was a whole new kind of bite. And not just because it was my butt. Those teeth clamped down with resolve, as if they were seeking the seat of my soul.

I felt a primal terror, produced, probably, by one enzyme passed on to us by our forest-dwelling ancestors. The "you're-being-eaten" enzyme. Then the "you're-about-to-die" enzyme kicked in too, along with all those chemical compounds that encode and carry nature's most special gift to our brain, extreme pain.

It hurt. I hurt. Badly.

I knew it had to be Blackie, since lions and tigers can't hug you. These arms around my legs felt just like human arms, but I knew no human could bite like this. It's a good thing I didn't know at that time how awfully strong an adult male chimpanzee can be. I might have actually died from fright.

Fortunately, once he had dug his teeth into me as deeply as he could, Blackie released me. He was civilized, that chimp. He could have mauled me mercilessly, ripped my flesh from head to toe, punctured my aorta or my femoral artery, or inflicted God knows what other kind of damage. But he extended mercy to me. Grace, even. All he did was bite my rear end, the fleshiest, least crucial, silliest part of my body. Maybe it was the lederhosen and all the other costumes that had tamed him, taught him restraint? Maybe it was the cowboy outfit? The baseball uniform? The white linen suit? Maybe it was just Blackie the primate, my natural cousin, reaching down to his almost human soul, letting this boy go. Punctured, bloodied, but otherwise unharmed.

Blackie let out a shriek the instant his mouth let go of my butt. A victory howl that scared me almost as much as the bite itself. *I'm done for,* I thought. Then he shrieked and howled some more and jumped away, his knuckles pushing on the ground.

Then I let out a howl of my own, far from triumphant. I howled in pain.

"He bit me, he bit me! Whaaahh! Blackie bit me! Whaaahh!"

"Hey, you just gave away your hiding place," said Manuel from a few feet away, with compassion.

"I'm not joking. He bit me, he really did! *Ay,* this hurts! Waaahh!" And I cried like the little boy I was.

One by one my playmates came to my hiding place. And they all seemed to talk at the same time.

"I've got to see this!"

"What? You mean Blackie is loose?"

"Yaaaayy!"

"Hey, we'd better get in the house. We might be next!"

"You're lying. Let me see. I don't believe you."

From the upstairs terrace, the mynah bird chimed in: *"Coño. Carajo. Puta. Puta. Gerardito. Gerardito, ven a comer. Coño."*

My mother, who was inside the house talking to Gerardito's older sister, heard all the screaming and hurried out as fast as she could. Meanwhile my playmates gathered around me and saw I was telling the truth. Though I was wearing blue jeans, the bloodstain was easy enough to see. Then we all began to walk towards the house, keeping an eye out for Blackie. My brother tried to comfort me.

Before I knew it we were in the kitchen, safe from further chimp attacks. There, my mom calmed me down, wiped away my tears, and cleaned my wounds. To get to the bite itself, though, she first had to convince me to pull down my pants and my underwear. Since there were a lot of people milling about in that kitchen, who showed no desire to go away and refused to leave when asked, it took some convincing. Everyone wanted to see the bite on my rear end. And everyone saw it, I think.

The hydrogen peroxide and the iodine stung so much that I cried some more. The puncture wounds were deep, but no larger than the size of each of Blackie's teeth. He had only taken one bite, and it seems that my jeans protected me a little, especially since he had bitten right over one of the rear pockets. Thank God my father had received bolts and bolts of denim fabric from one of his many grateful acquaintances and that my mom had turned some of it into jeans for me. Ever since, blue jeans have made me feel safe.

I don't know who caught Blackie and chained him up again that day he bit me. Probably the gardener, or the guy who took care of handling the animals in Aulet's animal garden. But caught he was, and sent back to his little Tarzan-like hut. I went home with a sore butt and an increased appreciation of nature red in tooth and claw, our sweet world where every bough is dipped in blood and every bird's song conceals a dirge. I would like to think that on that day Blackie became aware of that law of the universe I had discovered on the school playground: bullies are the worst sissies in the world when the tables are turned on them.

I never, ever taunted Blackie again. Not even when it made me look bad in front of my friends.

As to the outcome of Blackie's lederhosen escape: of course, as always, he was captured and chained anew. But I don't know how this was accomplished. I only remember Blackie jumping from limb to limb, swinging furiously, making his way down our street on the green canopy provided by the trees. Aulet and his retinue followed close behind, yelling out his name. Aulet looked worried, and silly too, with that Alpine hat in his hand. Blackie looked regal in his lederhosen. He was King of Bavaria that day, and not one whit dumber or less majestic than Mad Ludwig II, builder of Neuschwanstein Castle, patron and friend of Richard Wagner. I rooted for him and urged him to run faster, to swing more furiously from branch to branch, to find freedom.

I wish I knew what happened to Blackie after I left the island on my own dash for freedom. He's always there, lurking in the back of my mind. Maybe he had something to do with the fact that a chimp puppet was the best man at my wedding, and that this puppet held a single blood-red rose during the ceremony. I have photos of that puppet, my best man, holding his red rose. I also have photos of him traveling in Europe with me and my bride, at all these places so far from Miramar. Outside the Jeu de Pomme museum, with the Eiffel Tower in the background. Crossing the English Channel, the white cliffs of Dover a faint haze on the horizon. Marveling at the Alhambra across a deep gorge, perched on the edge of a wall as white as the snow on the Sierra Nevada.

Gerardito ended up leaving by himself, just as I did. The rich boy, my friend, became a poor orphan the minute he set foot in the United States, just like me. I don't really know what he endured, for we never compared stories. Maybe he, too, searched vacant lots in ratty Miami neighborhoods at twilight, looking for discarded soda bottles that could be turned in for two cents apiece, hoping to come up with enough cash to buy a Twinkie or an ice-cream sandwich for dinner. His family followed a few years later, like so many others. His father, the nickel mine magnate, lost his fortune. He was forced to scrounge for lousy jobs in Florida, and to do without wild beasts in his garden, maybe even to mop floors and hear himself called "spic."

Where Aulet's bestiary ended up, I don't know. After a while you don't give a damn where anything went, not even your own stuff. Burn it, bomb it, send it down the vortex of a black hole. Let it all rot in hell. It was just stuff.

Dross. Sheer dross. Or so you think. Then a chimp puppet shows up at your wedding, years later, and you don't even realize why he's there, or why you are playing a joke on yourself. Then, when you finally get the joke, maybe you begin to reconsider the bulldozer and the dynamite.

Maybe.

Blackie was there in his Tarzan house that final morning I spent in Havana, there in the animal garden. He was there just a few hours before I left for the airport, a few hours before Louis XVI hugged me for the very last time in this life. I went to see Blackie on my roller skates that morning to say good-bye. It was the very last thing I did before leaving. He rattled his chain and made chimp faces at me, as always.

I swear, I think I also heard the mynah bird say, *"Culo, culo, culo feo!"*

All right, I'll translate, at the risk of eternal damnation. The bird said: "Ass, ass, ugly ass!"

8

OCHO

Cohetes. Without a doubt, one of the most beautiful words in the Spanish language.

Firecrackers, in English. A poor word, if you ask me. Impoverished. Lame.

Cohete is also the Spanish word for "rocket." *Cohetes* can take you to another world, to many other worlds. Flash Gordon and Dr. Zharkov flew around in *cohetes,* as did Buck Rogers. *Sputnik* had been launched with a *cohete,* and so had Laika. Poor Laika, the dog the Russians sent into orbit with a one-way ticket, propelled by a *cohete* to death by starvation.

Firecrackers? Not even close. When I first learned of the English word for *cohete,* all I could think of was flaming Saltines.

And I never did find any firecrackers in the United States as large as the *cohetes* I played with in Havana, not even illegal ones.

There we were in Chinatown, my dad, my brother, and I, buying firecrackers.

"I want some of these big ones!"

"How about one of those long strings? Two? Three? Ten? Please, *Papi? Por favor?*"

"We've got to have some of those round ones too!"

"Okay, Felipe, let's have ten boxes of these. And twenty of those."

Yes, Havana had a Chinatown, and a Chinese cemetery too. Lots of Chinese had somehow ended up in Havana, and some were named Felipe. You could buy any explosive you wanted on *Calle Zanja*—Ditch Street in English. *Zanja* sounds a lot like *Shanghai*. Is that why the Chinese ended up in that neighborhood? Or does it have anything to do with the fact that Chinese coolies dug a lot of ditches in Cuba?

Anyway, the Chinese had the best firecrackers in town, and we were amassing quite an arsenal.

How I stared at the merchandise in that store. Long, long strings of firecrackers in all sizes. From tiny ones as thin as rose stems, tied together in perfectly symmetrical rows of two, about the length of Pancho Villa's bullet belt, to huge ones as round as hot dogs, strung together in bundles the width of the average tomb. Small individual firecrackers as round as a pencil, two inches long. Medium-size explosives as round as a man's index finger. Large *petardos* about half the size of a dynamite stick. Jumbo *petardos* that could have passed for dynamite sticks, the only ones that King Louis wouldn't buy for us.

The most amazing thing was that this was not the only firecracker store in Chinatown. There was another one next door, and across the street, and next door to that, all over the street, and down some of the side streets, a nearly infinite supply of firecrackers.

We went to Felipe Wang's store because my dad knew him and always got a special deal. Favors. All those favors. The most gorgeous boomerangs in the world.

They were all red, those firecrackers. Blood red. Even the thin transparent wrapping paper around them. Chinese paper, the same stuff my dad used for kites, only slightly thinner. How I loved to handle that paper, to feel it with my fingers, to rub it, to inhale the scent of gunpowder, to hold it over my eyes and see the entire world turn blood red. All those dragons on the labels, they were so awesome, despite the fact that they were related to lizards. These were firecracker dragons, small gods of pure joy. And all those Chinese characters on the labels, too. Mystical words, secrets from another dimension. I was certain that somewhere in China there were these extremely wise men, a caste of priests who had discovered gunpowder, along with a whole other way of writing.

I saved the wrappers. I saved them in my sock drawer, and had to leave them all behind, along with Mom and Dad and almost the entire family, and all the stuff we owned. When I saw *Citizen Kane* for the first time, and got clobbered over the head by the great surprise of "Rosebud" at the end, my hair stood on end. If I were still a genuine Cuban, I might say that I fainted, or suffered a heart attack, or was felled by an *embolia*. But my powers of exaggeration have greatly diminished in exile. I have to admit that it was just a chill that went through my body. I knew what my Rosebud had been, and that was my chill of recognition. My love for those wrappers ran deep. I fear that when I die, my final words will be *"los papelitos rojos"*—the red wrappers—instead of something pious.

These treasures came from so far away, from the other side of the globe. My dad had told me that if I could dig a hole deep enough, right through the earth's core, I would end up in China. For a while I believed him, even though his geology didn't take into account purgatory and hell. The good Christian Brothers had told me about those two places, also under my feet. But I preferred to think my dad was right.

Chinatown was full of scary things too. Images of large dragons, in all shapes and sizes. Images of heathen deities, some looking like Christian demons. Statues of the Buddha. Very few statues of the Enlightened One totally at peace, though. Most of these Buddhas seemed lacking in insight, blind in the third eye. They reminded me of some of the Catholic images that also scared me: Saint Lazarus on his crutches, his legs being licked by dogs; Saint Barbara, holding a cup in one hand and a sword in the other. Images used by *brujeros* and by those who practiced *santería,* that quintessentially Cuban religion that masks African beliefs, symbols, and rituals with a thin veneer of Catholicism. I was especially scared by these very weird Buddha statues that I've never seen anywhere else since then, also available in all sizes: a very fat Buddha with tiny children crawling all over him, his pudgy arms held aloft, a goofy, almost sinister grin on his face. It looked as if the children were devouring him little by little. In some of the poorer neighborhoods, like Regla, or Marianao, or Old Havana, you could see these proudly displayed in front windows. My dad told me that people thought these statues brought good luck. They scared the bejeezus out of me.

Louis XVI liked the Enlightened Buddha, of course, because of his belief in reincarnation. That gave me the creeps too, the way he told me the story of Siddhartha so often. I was waiting for him to tell me that the story was wrong, that Siddhartha had not been the final incarnation of the Buddha, that he had been the Buddha too. He used to tell me about Christian saints, canonized by the Church, who came back. If heaven was not the final destination of the holiest men and women, why assume Nirvana was the Buddha's last stop? Fortunately, he never went that far.

Anyway, the firecrackers more than made up for everything unpleasant in Chinatown. We set off our little bombs all over the neighborhood. On the inner branches of flowering shrubs. On trees. On walls and fences. On neighbors' porches. On toys. On anthills. On lizards. Inside empty soda bottles. Inside storm drains. Some of these targets required lighting the firecracker in your hand and throwing it before it exploded. My brother and Manuel were experts at that. Daredevils, too. They took to playing a game that was a combination of Russian roulette and Chicken in which they would both light firecrackers in their hands at the same time and wait to see who would be the first to throw his. I did it a few times and always threw first.

Then there was the time when we tried to set up the first, last, and only Cuban space program. Inspired by Laika's flight into space, we decided to launch a living being into outer space. And what creature better than a lizard? So we captured a large green chameleon, taped it to the top of a large tin can, set our largest firecracker under it, and placed it on the sidewalk in the park at the end of my street. Having decided that one firecracker wasn't large enough to propel the can into outer space, we substituted several medium-size *petardos,* but then decided that there was no way that several fuses would burn in perfect sync and that what we really needed was a single huge explosive. So Eugenio came to the rescue. He ran home to get one of those huge *petardos* my dad wouldn't buy, the ones that resembled sticks of dynamite. His dad wasn't as much of a weenie as mine.

We couldn't hide our excitement from one another when Eugenio showed up on his bike, sweating and grinning, and pulled the giant *petardo* out of his pocket. We carefully arranged the explosive device under the can so that only the wick was sticking out. Calling it a mere "firecracker" would be an insult. It could have been a stick of dynamite, for all I know.

"I bet this can will go into outer space."

"Yeah, the thrust from the explosion should send that can past the clouds."

"What if the lizard actually goes into orbit?"

"That would be so great."

"How long do you think he'll last in space?"

Our reluctant astronaut squirmed under the white surgical tape we had used to bind him to his capsule. So green, so very green, that beautiful Cuban chameleon. The kind of green you see on tropical plants, and on new spring foliage in northern latitudes, but not on wildlife.

Since it was his explosive, Eugenio lit the fuse. Then we all backed up about six feet and waited for liftoff.

It was a long fuse. We stood there for what seemed an eternity, watching the sparks wend their way down the fuse towards the bottom of the can and the explosive under it.

BANG!

A blinding flash, a cloud of smoke. *Whoosh, whoosh, whoosh! Whoosh! Whoosh, whoosh!*

"What happened?"

"Hey, where's the can?"

"It blew up, stupid."

"What do you mean?"

"It blew up. Completely destroyed. Didn't you feel and hear those pieces flying by?"

"I saw it explode into a million pieces, I really did," said my brother Tony. "And one of those pieces of metal nicked my ear. Here, look: blood!" Sure enough, there was a little bit of blood trickling down the edge of Tony's left ear. We all inspected ourselves for damage. Everyone was intact. Except the lizard of course.

"Hey, do you think we might be able to find pieces of the lizard?" I asked.

"No, stupid, it's gone, all gone. Too soft to survive."

"Let's see if we can find pieces of the can," said Manuel.

"Yeah, maybe we'll find lizard guts on one of them," added Rafael.

We fanned out over a fifty-yard radius, leaving the charred epicenter behind. We did manage to find a few pieces of shrapnel, but none was very large. No trace of the lizard, or the tape. Our spaceship and astronaut had gone out of this world, yes, but not the way we expected.

We laughed and laughed like the idiots we were. Thinking back, I now realize it was a miracle that we weren't hurt by the flying shrapnel. Every mother's worst fear, metal embedded in her boy's eye. *Whoosh!* That's as close as we came to harm, an odd flurry of whispers following the explosion.

We were graced that day.

Fools. None of us did well in physics later. I thought then, and I still think now, that all so-called laws of physics are random acts, directly willed by God. The so-called laws could change any instant, as they did when that can blew up in our faces.

That's what could happen when we were unsupervised, which was most of the time. But every now and then my dad would want to join in the fun, and when he did we were more cautious. Often, when he joined us we would go to a park about two blocks from our house, on Fifth Avenue—*Quinta Avenida*—the nicest street in Miramar.

It was a grand old park that stretched across both sides of the avenue and it was full of ancient ficus trees that had trunks as big as houses. Ficus trees have these tendrils that grow from their branches, and when they reach the ground, they take root and swell, ever so slowly, and another trunk begins to form. Trunk upon trunk, ficus trees build themselves out. Sometimes a single tree is a forest of trunks, some bundled together, others standing at various distances from the center. They were so much fun to climb and to fill with firecrackers. So many nooks and crannies. So many lizards to blow up.

This park also had some sort of enormous marble gazebo, or band shell, held up by thick Corinthian columns. We loved to explode firecrackers in the *glorieta,* as we called the giant gazebo. The acoustics of the dome made it sound as if we'd set off an atomic bomb, or so we thought. It thundered and reverberated, and filled us with undiluted joy.

Then there was the smell of the gunpowder. The *petardos* gave off the most intoxicating fumes. But even the smallest firecrackers were worth smelling. We would all run over to the spot where our firecrackers had exploded and inhale deeply.

How I wished I could smell the gunpowder when real bombs went off at night. Imagine what a punch a bundle of dynamite can pack! More often than not, they were far off in the distance, but every now and then we got lucky and one would be close enough to rattle our window shutters.

Quite a few bombs went off in Havana those last few years of Batista's regime.

To this day, as I am drifting to sleep I often expect to hear a bomb or two going off in the distance. It was an almost comforting sound, a lullaby of sorts. And if it was a bomb followed by a shoot-out, then it was even more oddly soothing.

You knew, at least, that the world hadn't changed.

Sometimes you would learn later where the bomb had gone off, what damage had been done, or whether any people had died. The papers made sure to get photographs of those killed or maimed. Sometimes you never found out anything at all. When so many bombs are going off all the time, it's hard to keep track. Hard to care, too, unless one happens to go off next to you.

Nothing like that ever happened to us, however. Tough to say this, but I was kind of disappointed that I was never near one of these bombs, or that we didn't know anyone who had been blown up by one.

I loved explosions. I loved them in war movies. I loved them off in the distance as I went to sleep. I loved them even more close up when we set off firecrackers.

I loved the sound of the match head on the rough side of the matchbox, the flare: so suddenly there. I loved the sight and the phosphorus smell of the burning match as it approached the fuse on the firecracker, as it transferred that living flame to it. And I loved the sight and smell of the fuse as it came alive and was consumed, eaten by time and fire.

Such a perfect way of thinking about those fuses, and also life. You begin at one end, and as you make your way forward, point by infinitesimal point, you give off sparks. And what you leave behind is charred, consumed, transformed. But that glorious voyage towards the end: poets never grow weary of trying to describe it. The end, or *telos,* as Aristotle or Aquinas would tell you, is the very reason for existence, the purpose of anything that exists. Our *telos* as humans, yours and mine, is to abide with God for eternity. The sparks on our way there, large and small, call them love. The *telos* of a fuse on a firecracker is a nice explosion. The sparks on the way there, call them love too.

On a really good day, I will fight to the death with anyone who tries to tell me that those sparks are not also love, fight with my bare hands or the jawbone of an ass or a broken stump of a sword. Metaphors matter to me, especially perfect ones.

How I loved that instant when the fuse disappeared altogether, when its sparks were swallowed whole by the blood red firecracker. You knew what would happen next, but each and every time it was such a great surprise.

Absolute silence, for the briefest little pinpoint of time.

BANG!

Good ones shake you to the core, sweep over all your senses. Sight, sound, smell, taste, even touch. Yes, touch too: a good blast can be felt all over one's body.

A flash of light, one of those rare moments when raw energy makes itself visible, the very stuff of life, blinding the eyes to all else.

A roar, deafening, that suddenly cancels out all other sound.

Wave upon wave of particles of the exploding object filling the air, fumes that fill your nose and cancel out all other scents, even those of the sweetest flower.

Those same particles invading your tongue, vanquishing all other flavors, melding with your own spit.

And those shock waves, the air itself moving, our invisible ocean of gas ripped from top to bottom, just like the veil of the Temple in Jerusalem when Jesus died on the cross, the air pulsating with energy that seeps into your very skin, your pores, your nerves, and ultimately, your brain, making every other sensation vanish, making you say "Yes, I live." Sometimes the shock waves bombarding your skin force you to say "God."

Of course, firecrackers seem a lot less lyrical or cosmic when they blow up in your hand. At least while you're feeling the pain. I should know; it happened to me.

There we were at the park with my dad one day, the whole bunch of us, setting off firecrackers in the *glorieta*. This time, my mom was there too. She was sitting on a park bench under the shade of a giant ficus tree, watching her husband and her boys play with firecrackers.

On this day we had a few duds that wouldn't explode. *Duds*. Now, there's an English word so perfect that it almost makes up for the lameness of *firecracker*.

We'd watch that fuse disappear into the firecracker, and then nothing would happen. The firecracker would just sit there, right where we had put it, totally dead. Talk about frustration!

Yet even these insulting, faithless ones served a purpose. After waiting a minute or so, we would take the duds, slice them open, and light the gunpowder with a match. *Whoosh!* A flash rather than an explosion. Second best, but so nice. And such a great smell too.

It was probably my twentieth firecracker of the day. I lit it inside the *glorieta,* at the base of one of its columns. We watched the fuse burn, as always, with great eagerness. This one seemed to burn more quickly than most, but that might have been an optical illusion, or a trick my memory is playing on me. Dud. The fuse vanished, the last spark flew, and nothing. Zilch. I was mad. It was my third or fourth dud that day. I thought I had waited long enough, but as I reached for the firecracker my dad and my brother and my friends shouted at me in unison.

"No, not yet!"

"Wait! Wait!"

"Hey, no!"

"Don't, don't!"

Stupid dud. I was so angry, I ignored their warnings, grabbed the firecracker with my right hand, and made a fist over it, trying to crush it.

BANG!

It was so pretty. The blast turned my hand into light itself for an instant. It seemed totally aglow, ever so briefly. Bursts of light and showers of sparks shot out from the narrow gaps between my fingers. It looked just like the drawings in Superman comics when the Man of Steel crushed bombs with his bare hands. The thrill hovered ever so delicately and briefly.

Then the pain shoved the thrill aside, rudely, and conquered my brain. My hand was nothing but pain. It was burning, throbbing, seared by a pain beyond all thresholds. I kept my fist closed tightly, and held my right wrist with my left hand, as if trying to choke off the pain. I stood there, frozen, in shock.

A few images managed to embed themselves in my memory, snapshots of sorts.

My dad, brother, and friends rushing towards me.

My dad saying "I told you not to grab it."

Someone else saying "I told you to drop it."

My body refusing to sit down next to my mom at her park bench.

My body yielding to her voice.

My mom, sitting next to me, trying to open my fist.

My fist, refusing to open. My mouth letting out a strange sound, some kind of cry I didn't recognize as my own. It was more like a very loud whimper.

My fist letting go, opening, yielding to my mom's voice.

The sight of my hand. It was black and red, all over. Like some odd mixture of coal and raw meat. I remember feeling relieved that I couldn't see any bones. I remember being surprised by the fact that there was no firecracker left in that monstrous hand.

A long car ride to the hospital. Too long. I whimpered all the way there.

A shot in the arm at the emergency room.

A doctor opening my hand, with my mom and dad next to me. That same doctor swabbing my hand and fingers with giant Q-tips dipped in some fluid, for what seemed like an eternity.

My mom and dad telling me not to look.

My mom cradling my head in her hands, holding me tightly against her bosom.

More pain.

A nurse wrapping my hand in what seemed like miles of gauze.

Another shot, this one in my butt.

Calm, peace, relief, sleep. Fade to black.

Did this stop us from fooling around with explosives? Of course not. I gained a special respect for duds, but kept to my old ways, unfazed. Explosions are so hard to give up. Harder even when they seem as natural as sunlight and as common as heartbeats, and you live in a world out of joint—a world that seems to need a few bangs to set it right. If I had stayed in Cuba, the experience might have come in very handy later, for I would surely have tried to blow up much bigger things, just like my relative who ended up shot by a firing squad.

Wait. One more memory has just emerged from its hiding place. One final snapshot.

I'm in my first-grade classroom. It's nearly the end of the school year. I'm looking forward to summer vacation. Brother Pedro is at the blackboard, doing math. An essential prelude to physics. Those sorry-ass Disney characters are still there, all over the walls. Such hypocrites, always happy, except for Donald Duck, who actually showed his darker emotions, the only one who could explode. He was, and still is, the most decent of them all, and the only one I appreciated on the wall. Anyway, after glancing at Donald on the wall, I'm looking out the window at one of Brother Alejandro's malfeasants out on the playground, kneeling on the gravel under the blazing sun, reeling slightly. The sunlight is flooding into the classroom.

I'm peeling long strips of skin off the palm of my hand and marveling at the transformation. My hand is back. My old hand, not that other one the firecracker left behind, all charred and bloody. The skin I've pulled off my hand is so clean, so beautiful, so transparent. It feels a lot like the wrapper on firecracker packages, except that it's not red. I roll the white skin, knead it with my fingers, ball it up. Brother Pedro calls my name. "Carlos, pay attention!"

I drop my skin on the ground. I shed my skin.

Just like a lizard.

9

NUEVE

Parties, parties, birthday parties.

Fiesta! One of the very few Spanish words every American knows. Along with its narcoleptic cousin, *siesta*. Parties and naps, the only two things spics are good at.

Mel Blanc, voice of Speedy Gonzalez and a thousand other Hollywood cartoons, may you burn in hell forever. As one of your God-damned Hispanic Warner Brothers cartoon characters might have said: "*Sí, señor,* firrst I go to zee *fiesta* and zen I tayk-a *siesta,* beeforrre I go to anozzer *fiesta* a-gain. *Ole! Andale, ándale! Arriba, arriba!*"

I take it back, Mel. Sorry, I got carried away. Hell might be too harsh a punishment for your sins. You must have been clueless, truly. Maybe a better place for you would be heaven, where you might be surrounded by lazy, napping, partying spics who talk funny.

I couldn't make up my mind whether I loved or loathed those birthday parties back then, in sunny, breezy Havana. It has taken me such a long time to realize that few things in life are simple, that so many things are mixed. A bit of this alongside a bit of that. Good and evil dancing with each other so tightly, only one subatomic particle between them, while indifference looks on, as a chaperone, with her two lazy eyes, neither one of them capable of focusing. Here's a brand-new Spanish proverb for you, Mel Blanc: *la indeferencia es bizca.* Indifference is cross-eyed.

Anyway, they dance so fast, good and evil, these two polar opposites. So tightly and furiously. You can't dance with just one of these partners. If you cut into their dance, you end up with both, as a threesome. And if you fear cutting into the dance and taking a spin with good and evil, you end up dancing with the cross-eyed, ugly chaperone.

Even the deepest, most wondrous love can sometimes bring you to that dismal dance, and then every single tune is a tango. A bad tango composed by an angry, drunken Argentine just for you and your loved one. A tango that never ends.

But back to those Cuban parties: no dancing there. None at all. Furious whirling, yes, but no dancing of the literal kind. No Desi Arnaz orchestras banging on conga drums, their ridiculously puffy sleeves quivering to the beat. No rumba, no mambo, no cha-cha-cha. No tangos or string quartets. No waltzes. No Bartók, thank God. Cubans were much too smart back then to allow Bartók to be played anywhere on the island. I think there were laws against it and Bartók police who secretly spied on all the central and eastern Europeans in the country who might dare to pollute the atmosphere with music that not even Satan could dance to. Those who broke the anti-Bartók law were quickly rounded up and smacked on the temple, just above the ear.

The parties I went to just had games, costumes, and presents. No music, aside from the birthday song.

Oh, how the children of the fortunate ones celebrated their good fortune. How great, to be born to one of those families, and to have the children of similar families bring you presents and sing "Happy Birthday" in English as you blew out the candles on your excruciatingly well-decorated cake.

Well, I exaggerate a little. The lyrics were in English, but close to unrecognizable, at least the way we sang them. This is what I thought I was singing: *Japy berrssdéy tú yú, Japy berrssdéy tú yú.* It might as well have been *Abracadabra, hocus pocus,* or *meka-leka-hi, meka-hiney-ho.* It was a magical incantation in the language of the gods, the English tongue. In the language of the people who made movies and had invented every modern convenience.

Cargo cultists, all of us at those parties, and we didn't even know it. Just like South Sea islanders, mumbling their version of English phrases, expecting B-26 bombers to show up loaded with manufactured goods: knives, shoes, hats, screwdrivers, screws, jockstraps, cigarettes, and chewing gum. Phrases as "English" as ours, we fortunate boys and girls.

Pago-Pagoans we were, and we didn't know it. Tongans. Papuans. Bora-Borans. Nanumangans. Manihikians. Nukulaelaelans. Head-hunting cannibals, no better than grass-skirted, bone-in-nose savages, we were. And we thought we were Cubans. Urbane Cubans, mind you.

But there we were at party after party, singing *Japy berrssdéy tú yú* just before the painstakingly well-wrapped presents showed up. Mel Blanc would have loved to hear us. Good thing he never did.

Of course, we knew that we had brought the presents. And, of course, all of us were studying English at school and knew at a very basic level what we were singing. But it *was* a magical song. Sacramental, too. It was so much like the Latin used in church, which we both understood and didn't, and which brought about such major changes in the fabric of reality. *Hoc est corpus meum*. This is my body. *Hic est enim calix sanguinis mei*. This is indeed the cup of my blood. *Agnus Dei qui tollis peccata mundi, miserere nobis*. Lamb of God who takes away the sins of the world have mercy on us. *Per omnia saecula saeculorum*. For ever and ever, world without end. Or even the Greek that we mistook for Latin: *Kyrie eleison*. Lord have mercy.

Somewhere between South Sea savages and ancient Romans. Somewhere between London and Madrid. Somewhere between heaven and earth. But, oh, so close to heaven compared to so many other Cubans.

All the cakes had themes. American themes. Cowboys and Indians. Popeye. Hopalong Cassidy. You name it, if it was part of the American entertainment empire, we had it on a cake. *Keik*. Or more properly, in that relaxed, African Spanish of Cuba, *kei*. That's what we called them, *keikes*, or *keiis*, in the plural. Not *tortas* or *pasteles*, the proper Spanish names. Never, ever, ever did we call a cake a *bollo*, as in other Spanish-speaking countries. In Cuba *bollo* had somehow evolved into the swear word for a woman's private parts. Maybe this is why the English *cake* had taken over all the Spanish words? Or did *bollo* evolve into a bad word as a revenge for *keik*?

Anyway, those cakes were amazing. Some were mountains of multicolored meringue and icing. Others were dioramas worthy of display in a museum. Under the decorations there were surprises. Some of the meringue flowers and plastic figurines had jawbreakers attached to them, buried inside the cake. A treat within a treat. I didn't really like the jawbreakers, but I loved getting them. They made me feel lucky, even as I tossed them away into the shrubbery, passing on the treat to the lizards and fire ants.

And virtually every party involved costumes. Especially the parties for very young children. No special theme, just random costumes, like at carnival time. Clowns, cowboys, Indians, policemen, Cossacks, pirates, yachtsmen, baseball players, bullfighters, Dutchmen in wooden clogs, Bavarians in lederhosen, doctors in lab coats. But never ever monks, priests, or Cuban peasants. And never ever ever boys in their underwear diving for pennies and nickels at the Regla wharf.

Sometimes monkeys would show up in costumes, too, just like Blackie. I have pictures to prove it. There seemed to be a lot of pet monkeys in Havana, and affluent Cubans had a penchant for dressing them up, even though Cuba had no native primates. No monkeys or apes of any kind. No native humans either: all of the Arawaks, Tainos, and Caribs who lived there before the Spanish arrived had been wiped out by the end of the seventeenth century, their genes sent to oblivion.

None of the Indian costumes I ever saw at those parties were those of Cuban Indians, who tended to wear loincloths or nothing at all. No good Cuban mother would allow her child to go to a birthday party naked or almost naked. Someone might mistake your offspring for a boy from Regla, or think you were too lazy to make a costume—or even worse, too broke to pay someone to make it for you. They were all North American Plains Indians, those Cuban kids, most of them chiefs, too, with large feathered headdresses, war paint on the cheeks, fringed vests, beads, and moccasins. Some of them brought peace pipes along, or even said "How," the palms of their hands upraised in greeting. Well, really *Jao,* in Spanish.

When we weren't at parties we sometimes played cowboys and Indians. Never *conquistadores* and Indians. After all, we had no movies about our own history.

But that's what a colony is all about, isn't it?

I finally realized I had grown up in a colony years later, on a London bus, thanks to a Jamaican. So wise, that man, that Caribbean neighbor, reading his tabloid newspaper. I asked why the bus had stopped and its driver had disappeared, for no apparent reason. "Tea time," he said, in his blessed Jamaican accent. "The bus driver has to stop for tea," he said, turning the page, not even looking up. "And if you complain, *they* say *you're* not civilized." Then he laughed. A deep laugh that came from the very bottom of his soul, each "ha" so carefully enunciated, as perfectly spaced as beads on a rosary. "Ha, ha, ha, ha, ha, ha!" And he turned another page.

Sometime between first and second grade, there were no more costumes at birthday parties. Just games, cake, and presents. I was so glad when the changeover took place. I hated most of my costumes.

We played a lot of American games, of course. Pin the Tail on the Donkey. Bobbing for apples. Hopsack races. Tug-of-war. Blind Man's Bluff. We could have been in Ohio. But we also had *piñatas,* a small nod to our own culture. Cuban *piñatas* were just like the Mexican ones now sold in the United States, made of cardboard and brightly colored tissue paper, with room inside for candy and party favors. But there was one difference. Cuban *piñatas* were not destroyed by blows, much to our chagrin. Instead, they had long ribbons attached to panels at the bottom. Every kid at the party would grab a ribbon and at the count of three, or seven, or ten, all would tug, the bottom of the *piñata* would rip open, and goodies would rain down upon us.

The day I found out that Mexicans got to beat the crap out of their *piñatas* with sticks, I was so jealous. *That must be a far superior culture,* I thought.

Ripping open the *piñata* was one of the high points of every party. The instant those goodies hit the floor, all of us would lose control and jump on one another like American football players scrambling for a fumble. Or kids in Regla diving for pennies. Sheer pandemonium. Arms and legs flying all over the place. Pushing. Grabbing. Screaming. Punching. Kicking. No holds barred. Every now and then a kid would emerge from the huddle with a black eye or a bloodied lip.

I always made off with at least some candy. But never with one of those tokens for a really nifty party favor. My brother Tony always got those.

The mothers seemed to enjoy the melee. They shouted loudly and laughed their heads off.

These parties were full of mothers, you see. That was another very Cuban deal. Mothers stayed around for the party. None of this drop-off-the-kid-thank-God-see-you-two-hours-later American kind of stuff. No. These mothers stayed for the whole party, keeping an eye on things and talking to one another. How well I remember those phalanxes of moms, and my own mother among them.

When I was very young, I think the costumes used to scare me. So many familiar faces, so much else out of place. And I was dressed just as ridiculously as everyone else, perhaps even more so. I would orbit fairly close to Mom, and return to her repeatedly, as if she were some kind of safe haven.

Eventually I would leave her alone and go off on my own, to seek out what the party had to offer. Just as I would do on a much larger scale at the age of eleven, when she and my dad put me on a plane and sent me to Miami, with a suitcase containing two pairs of socks, two undershirts, two briefs, two shirts, two pairs of pants, one handkerchief, one sweater, and one jacket. No costumes allowed. No toys, mementos, money, or jewelry either. My brother Tony and I had to strip down to our briefs at the airport, just like the boys from Regla, so a government official could ensure that we weren't smuggling any of our property out of Cuba. Like my number two *Batman* comic book, or my firecracker wrappers, or family pictures.

The worst part was when they tugged on the elastic band of your underpants and peered down at your butt and your genitals to make sure you hadn't hidden anything there.

Wait, I take that back. I think it was even worse when they laughed at you.

I didn't think about parties that day I left, but it might have helped. I should have tried to recall the party to end all parties. Sugar Boy's party. The party that made it inevitable that I should end up in a small, stuffy room at José Martí Airport, a stranger peering down at my bare ass and laughing.

It was second grade. It must have been. Or maybe it was the first half of third grade. It couldn't have been any later than that, because the world changed over Christmas vacation in third grade. The exact date is inconsequential. What matters is that it happened, and I was there, and that I came away from it a changed boy.

I knew that some of the kids at my school were very wealthy. I knew this because even in my own neighborhood, our house was relatively small. Crammed with valuables, but still small. Eugenio's house was much larger, and so was Gerardito's. I knew this also because my parents told me that some of my classmates were fabulously wealthy. But I had no idea what wealth really was until I went to that party.

It was a birthday party for the son of the man who owned the largest sugar company in Cuba. This was sort of like owning the largest steel mills in Pittsburgh or Chicago around the same time. Or owning an American railroad in the late nineteenth century.

Sugar Boy was one of my classmates, and he invited the entire class to his birthday party.

No one else had ever done that. Birthday parties were rites of inclusion and exclusion. Always for a select number, never for all. But this family could do it. They could have invited the entire school, for that matter. Perhaps even every boy in the *Social Register,* some of whom were unfortunate enough to attend other schools.

I started off the day on the wrong foot.

"Oh my God, today's the day of the birthday party, and I forgot to buy a present."

This wasn't what I wanted to hear my mother saying.

"What do you mean? Are you saying that I won't have a present to bring to the party?"

"I mean I forgot about this party completely, and now we don't have enough time to go down to *Los Reyes Magos* to buy the kind of present we need. We only have one hour to get ready and another half hour to drive all the way out to the party."

Los Reyes Magos was the largest and finest toy store in Havana. And it was far from our house, eastward, in the heart of the city. The party was in the opposite direction, beyond the western suburbs of Havana.

That toy store was my favorite place in the whole world. A temple to be entered cautiously, with few expectations. Perhaps one might exit with a small token of its vast, wondrous treasure. Perhaps one might find some of the items displayed there under the Christmas tree, brought there by *Santicló,* or on January 6, by the Three Magi, who also brought presents, and after whom the store was named.

"Oh no, I can't go to the party without a present! I can't, I can't."

"Yes you can."

"How? Tell me, how can I go to this party without a present? You have to bring presents to a birthday party."

"Don't worry. I'm sure we can find something here at home you can bring."

This was worse than I had thought at first.

"No, no, no! I can't bring him one of my used toys. No!"

"Oh, yes, don't worry. We'll find something you've barely used, and no one will know it's not brand-new."

At this point I started praying for some kind of miracle.

"What? What do I have that isn't used? I play with all my toys."

How well I remember the exact spot where this desperate conversation took place. It was in the dining room, right by the window that faced Chachi's house and her bitter-orange tree, the window opposite to Visiting Jesus and the house with the breadfruit tree. It was the window under which my mom kept her sewing machine. Her favorite spot.

"Don't worry. Let's take a look in your room. We'll find something."

I refused and started crying. I might have thrown a fit of sorts too, throwing myself on the ground and pounding the marble floor with my feet and fists.

The next thing I knew I was in my room with Mom, pawing through my toys, looking for something that didn't look used. But everything looked well used. Destroyed, for the most part. It was hopeless. And didn't my mom know that all new toys came in specially designed boxes?

"What about a box, too? We can't bring a present in any old cardboard box. It has to be inside the original package."

"Oh, I hadn't thought of that," said Marie Antoinette. "But you just gave me a good idea," she added.

There would be no way out of this labyrinth of shame, I realized.

"What about one of your board games? They all stay in the original boxes, and they don't get that much wear and tear. Let's look through all of them."

So I climbed up on my bed and reached for the top of my wardrobe, where my board games were all neatly stacked up, dust-free. The maid dusted up there every day.

We inspected each game carefully. Monopoly? No way! Even a blind man could have told it wasn't new. Chess? Nice wooden pieces, but too banged up. Checkers? Not too badly scarred, but even my mom had to admit that you couldn't give the richest boy in Cuba a game of checkers for his birthday. Parcheesi? No good either. Banged up and way too low-class. Chinese Checkers? Even worse than plain old checkers and Parcheesi combined.

It was at the bottom of the pile that my mom found what she was looking for: a board game that hadn't been used very much. The corners on the box were slightly scuffed, and the instructions looked a little rumpled, but everything else looked almost new. I would like to emphasize the word *almost*. I knew then that the game looked used, beyond a shadow of a doubt, but she convinced me with that voice of hers that it was really all right. Everything would be fine. Everything she touched was always fine. And that voice of hers could convince me to do just about anything.

"Oy vey!" That's what the Jewish family that took me in four years later in Miami would have said. Or maybe *"Oy gevalt!"*

Louis XVI said nothing about the gift. He never got involved in birthday party details. So I went to Sugar Boy's party, tainted. When we finally got there, after driving way beyond any suburb I had ever seen, even Biltmore, we came to a huge gate flanked by tall royal palms. We drove through the gates and entered an earthly paradise.

Sugar Boy's estate had everything the world had to offer, and more. A colossal swimming pool. Tennis courts. A stable full of horses. An enormous garage full of luxury cars. A golf course. The house, if one dared insult it by using such a humble word, was no house, really. It was a palace. Not quite Versailles, Aranjuez, or Neuschwanstein, but definitely a palace worthy of the Loire Valley. A tropical Chambord. With palms and tropical foliage, of course.

The road that led to the palace from the gates was long and winding. The lawns were lush and green, and immaculately mowed. An emerald sea it was, with multihued accents everywhere. Crotons of all kinds. Giant philodendrons. Caladiums. Flowers. Palms in all shapes and sizes. Especially royal palms, so tall, so regal. So Cuban. Palms that pierce my heart and entrails to this very day.

Other cars streamed in with us, a caravan of guests bearing gifts.

And there he was, in the circular driveway that skirted the palatial garage, Sugar Boy, driving a miniature sports car. Not a homely go-cart, but a perfect miniature replica of a real Ferrari or Porsche or something like that. He was taking curves, honking his little horn, impressing the hell out of everybody. He didn't wave at me when I got out of the car. He didn't even acknowledge my presence.

All the other kids gathered around Sugar Boy and his car when he came to a stop, like ants around a sugar cube or some discarded jawbreaker.

"Look at that car! Look, *Mami*, look, *Papi*!"

"Yes, it's very nice," said Louis XVI, probably pining for those days at Versailles.

"Can I have one? Please? For Christmas? For my birthday?"

"Sorry, I think that's too expensive for us," answered the King of France.

I knew he would say that, but I had to ask anyway. Imagine having your very own car! I almost had the nerve to ask my dad to sell foul-mouthed Maria Theresa. But I bit my tongue. I knew better. He wouldn't exchange her to ransom me from *El Colorado* if he had to. Or from Fidel, as it turned out.

My mom seemed more impressed than my dad by this estate, probably because she had no memories of Versailles, the Louvre, and Chambord.

Tony was not with us. He hadn't been invited. He had stayed at home with my father's sister and Ernesto. But I didn't feel too sorry for him. He got to go to Batista's son's party every single year, and I didn't. One of the older Batista kids was his classmate.

After dropping off Marie Antoinette and his non-Bourbon son, Louis XVI departed. "See you at nine," he said, and home he went. I don't think he looked back once.

Unimpressed, he seemed. Nonchalant. Such a fine French word. It suited him.

So there we were, my mom and I, at Sugar Boy's party. I walked over to a small mountain of gifts and placed my stinking offering down at the bottom of the pile. How I hoped it would get crushed, that the pile would crumble on top of it. How I hoped he would never open it! That would be even better.

Then, as I turned to leave the gift pile, a woman handed me a huge box, beautifully wrapped.

"What's this?" I asked.

"These are your party favors," answered the well-dressed lady.

"But the party is just getting started."

"Yes, I know, but you'll need some of the favors during the party."

Talk about surprises. This one topped them all.

I went back to Marie Antoinette, who was already busy talking to other mothers, and sat as close to her as possible. And I unwrapped that beautiful box with the red ribbon around it. The wrapping paper was silver: two shades of silver, in alternating stripes that traversed the box diagonally. I can still see the paper. To this day, stripes remind me of wealth.

It was the Box of Infinite Humiliation, the Box of Infinite Remorse.

Inside I found a gun-and-holster set. A beautiful cap pistol and many, many rounds of ammunition. A leather belt, finely tooled in Western motifs, with a leather holster to match. Black. With silver trim. A sheriff's badge—metal, like the pistol, not plastic. Several other items, the memory of which exists only in the deepest, darkest, most secure dungeon of repressed thoughts.

I think I started to shake. If I had been able to do it, I would have said *"qué mierda."* I couldn't say that word then, due to my fear of hell, though I use it freely now, and often. This is what happens when you read too much Martin Luther.

"No, no, no!" That's what I said. "No, no, no, no, no." It turned into a mantra. A nearly endless string of no's stretching to infinity.

One of the moms sitting nearby chimed in: "Strap it on, go ahead, join in with the other boys."

All of a sudden I heard the *pops*. So many *pops,* coming from all directions. It was quite a shoot-out.

"Go on, *ándale,"* came the command from Marie Antoinette. So I joined in the shoot-out, until everyone's caps ran out.

Later that afternoon there was a scavenger hunt. I had never taken part in one before, so I had no clue how to proceed and I missed absolutely everything offered up in the hunt. It was immensely frustrating.

You see, the box of party favors was not enough for Sugar Boy's party. We had to roam all over the grounds of that wondrous estate looking for more toys, their location revealed only in cryptic messages. Great toys, mind you, not crap. It was largesse with an American twist: search for your treasure, wrinkle your brow, sweat for it.

I don't remember the cake and the presents. Those details are gone forever, buried in the vault of oblivion. I don't even remember what Sugar Boy looked like, or what expression he had on his face when he opened up my shameful present. Maybe he had the same expression for all of the presents, including mine. What could any of us have given him that he didn't already have ten times over?

The last thing I remember was the movie. As soon as darkness began to descend, we all gathered in an outdoor pavilion and were treated to a movie about King Arthur and the Knights of the Round Table. All I remember is knights in armor and horses in armor, fighting in the mud, and my rising, choking envy.

What I remember much better than that movie was the sunlight that afternoon. Every blade of grass seemed alive with light, every leaf on every tree. The light on the bush by the tennis court. The light on the silver wrapping paper. The light on a scavenger hunt toy found by some other boy. Everything ablaze, as if glowing from within.

Nothing seemed the same afterwards. I had seen what life was like at the summit. For just one long afternoon, I had been part of that charmed life, suffocated and enthralled all at once. Gift giver from hell redeemed by gifts given to him. I was tagged. Now I needed to be swept away when the world changed.

I'm sure the gaunt man with the pencil-thin moustache who peered down my underwear at the airport years later had never been to a party like that. I don't think anyone ever gave him a striped silver box full of treasures in exchange for a used board game. I don't think anyone who cried out *paredón*! had a similar experience either.

Gracias. Muchas gracias, Sugar Boy, for showering me with grace in exchange for my tawdry gift. A foretaste, I hope, of The Final Judgment, the ultimate party, when we show up bearing crappy gifts and, instead of being tossed out on our ear, to wail and gnash our teeth, are instead overwhelmed with superabundant largesse, with eternal gifts beyond our wildest dreams.

Thanks also for making me laugh years later when your family's name showed up in *The Starr Report,* which gave us all the sordid details of the affair between President Bill Clinton and Monica Lewinsky. Bubba Clinton was actually talking on the phone with someone in your family—no doubt trying to shake loose some change—while Monica played with his *pinga.* Was that your name etched in Monica's memory and in the White House phone log?

Still no more than colonial inferiors unworthy of respect, even when knighted by King Bubba. Sorry, Sir Sugar Boy. Guess we Cubans are still not civilized. Or is it ceeveelaaized? Ha, ha, ha, ha, ha, ha!

Gracias. Muchas gracias, oh sage, Jamaican man on the London bus. You're the closest I've ever come to those angels who walk the earth in human disguise.

Gracias. Muchas gracias, South Sea Islanders for being kindred spirits. *Japy berrsdéy tú yú,* Nanumangans. You too, Manihikians, and all you Nukulaelaelans. Time for presents!

Gracias. Muchas gracias, Mel Blanc, for giving me the chance to earn some points with God by forgiving your goofy ignorance, spicmeister. *Arriba, arriba, ándale, ándale.* Hope you enjoy sharing heaven with all of us spics, you colonialist doofus.

Gracias. Muchas gracias, compañero, whoever you were. Thank you, comrade, buddy, airport underwear checker, for tugging on my briefs, inspecting my butt and my family jewels, and thank you above all for laughing. Thank you, nameless brother, fellow Cuban, whoever you were. I turned into a Regla wharf boy, there at the airport, right in front of you, stripped bare, without a nickel or penny, on the way to a totally uncertain future and many years of Reglahood.

But you also set my feet on the path to enlightenment with the snap of that elastic band. You did, you bastard, you agent of heaven, brother of mine.

My party favor, I guess, for having attended Fidel's glorious, all-inclusive party.

Gracias, muchas gracias. I must have deserved it. I hope you spend eternity living in very close proximity to Mel Blanc, comrade.

Arriba, arriba! Fiesta time in heaven!

10

DIEZ

The master craftsman was at it again, creating other worlds in miniature. So many worlds to create. So much time.

Louis XVI cut into the cardboard box very carefully with a knife he reserved strictly for that purpose. He was cutting out a window or, more accurately, what would be a window. Right now it was just a rectangular hole in a brown cardboard box. The box would eventually be covered in plaster of Paris and turned into a house. A house in Bethlehem.

We had the whole town, and it grew every year. House by house he built it, house by house it grew, Bethlehem. We had the landscape too. Rocks. Hills. Ravines. Meadows. A few trees. Just a few, and scraggly ones at that. Even the palms looked beat. King Louis knew there weren't many trees in the area of Bethlehem around the time Jesus was born. He couldn't re-create a falsehood.

He had been there. He remembered all the details. No vault of oblivion for this man, my father.

"See this domed house over here? That was the first inn at which Mary and Joseph asked for a room. See that hill there? That's where the shepherds usually ate dinner around a fire. This house I'm making now was my house. See this window here, the one I'm slicing open? One of Herod's soldiers threw the corpses of my twin sons out of this window after he cut off their heads."

Jesus H. Dictator-fleeing Christ. Where did this man come up with so many details? And all these severed heads?

He seemed to remember everything. Or to have convinced himself that he did. He had a very fertile, nearly inexhaustible imagination, totally dedicated to inventing past lives and vanished worlds. And it wasn't enough to do this inside his once-severed head. No, he had to re-create some of these vanished worlds physically.

By the time I was seven years old, the town of Bethlehem and surrounding countryside took up most of our dining room. By the time I was nine, it had become too big to fit into any single room in our house, and King Louis had persuaded the Christian Brothers to display it in a large room at our school. He would set it up on sheets of plywood, which rested on sawhorses. Over the plywood he would lay out the landscape, some of it made from very stiff, painted fabric, some of it built out of chicken wire covered with plaster of Paris.

The town itself consisted of many buildings in all shapes, sizes, and colors. Many of them had domes for roofs. Inside each building was a lightbulb. Small ones, the kind that are usually strung on outdoor Christmas trees or used for night-lights. Some lights were red, others orange or yellow. He wanted to capture the glow of the hearths inside those houses, inns, and shops. To re-create it just as he remembered it, this time with the aid of electricity.

At night, light poured out of the windows, bathing the landscape in a soft, twilight glow and heightening the shadows on it.

All over the town and the countryside, naturally, there were people and livestock. Shepherds galore, out in the fields, and flocks of sheep. A few donkeys and cows. And camels, those inevitable camels. Wait, wait, I almost forgot the angels. There were angels too, suspended from the ceiling with clear, nearly invisible fishing line. Hand-painted ceramic figurines. And a dark blue, starry backdrop. Couldn't forget about that Star of Bethlehem, could he? He had, after all, seen it with his own eyes.

A nativity scene worthy of a cathedral. A very Spanish Christmas tradition, passed on to its colonies. Every church set up one of these tableaux, or so it seemed, but none that I saw could compete with ours. Many homes had them too, but they were all puny by comparison.

What a sight that miniature Bethlehem, especially in the dark. You could almost hear the people inside, gnawing on bones around their hearths, or licking their fingers, as ancients did. (My dad had enlightened me at an early age about the invention of the fork in the Middle Ages, and about how hard it was for people to get used to the concept, even among the nobility. "One of my brothers stabbed me in the forearm with a fork the first time we dined with them back in 1348, just before the Black Death wiped us all out.") All those people and animals milling about. The stable in which Jesus was born, so rustic, so incredibly detailed, off to the side of the town, somewhere near the shepherds and their flocks. Had my dad really seen moss hanging from the rafters of that stable?

He said he had.

My favorite characters were the Three Wise Men. The Magi. The Three Kings. *Los Reyes Magos.* Call them whatever you want. The Three Zoroastrians. The Three Astrologers. The Three Wisenheimers. Melchior, Gaspar, and Balthasar, bringing gifts on their camels. They were the only figures that moved across the landscape. On the first day in which Bethlehem went up in our dining room, the Magi would be placed way out on the edge, and with each passing day, we'd move them ever closer to the manger where Baby Jesus lay, His little chubby arms constantly outstretched, prefiguring the cross. Millimeter by millimeter. On the sixth of January, the Feast of Epiphany, these three very well-rested travelers and their camels would finally make it to the manger. Talk about slouching towards Bethlehem.

That same day we would also receive some presents, left for us by those same three Wise Men.

I liked the way we could move the Magi, but I hated thinking about their God-awful gifts. Gold, frankincense, and myrrh? What kid in his right mind would swoon over such useless grown-up crap, especially the myrrh? Even two thousand years ago, kids must have seen these gifts for what they were: useless stuff. What can a little baby do with spices, bullion, or coins? Jesus H. Diaper-changing Christ. What child is this?

A very unlucky child, I thought.

First these awful gifts, in a stinking stable, and then the cross at the end, in the prime of life. What kind of Father was God, to do this to His Son?

Perhaps none at all.

That's what I thought then. Any dad that puts his son through so much, making him cry out at the end, "Why have you abandoned me?" was no dad at all. Lucky me, I thought: my inventive, one-of-a-kind dad would never abandon me. No, he might even build a real town someday, just for me, and include in it a huge store filled with firecrackers. And he might just stand there laughing, beaming with pride as I blew up the whole town with my explosives. He'd do anything for me, except sell the portrait of Maria Theresa.

If you overlooked his unhealthy relationship with Maria Theresa and the other antiques in our house, my dad, Antonio, Louis XVI, was a great father. So much like the other gift giver at Christmastime, the *good* gift giver, *Santicló*. Merry Old Santa, swooping down from the pristine, ever-frozen North Pole, his sled brimming with really good presents that ended under our Christmas tree. Despite the fact that he labored mightily to keep alive a Spanish tradition at Christmastime, my father really resembled the imperialist American Santa Claus.

At Christmastime, you see, a silent battle raged in our house between Spanish and American customs. A battle between *Santicló* and *Los Reyes Magos,* between Bethlehem and the Christmas tree. And those Three Wisenheimers had no chance of winning the battle with Santa. Spain had no chance against the United States, just as in 1898. The past had no chance against the future.

Santa brought the best presents. And the Christmas tree: no contest. That tree was divine. I didn't know it at the time, confused as I was about the first commandment, but I was an idolater. I worshiped that tree, bowed down to it, praised it, loved it unconditionally, inhaled its sweet essence down into my cells, where it mingled with the sunlight.

Where these trees came from, I had no idea. Years later, when I moved to Illinois and saw balsams, spruces, and firs growing out of the ground, some of them three stories tall, I was thrilled beyond words. I might have even floated a few feet off the ground when no one was looking.

Now I take my children to a tree farm every December and we spend a very long time looking for the perfect tree, saw in hand. Even in the worst weather, even when my kids argue endlessly, I could remain there all day. Once, in freezing rain, mud and slush under our feet, one child running a fever, it took over one hour to find and cut down the tree God had grown for us.

When I die I would like to be buried at a Christmas tree farm.

The lights and houses of Bethlehem, so lovingly created by my dad, were no match for the lights on that tree, or for the ornaments. Exquisite ones, mostly hand-blown glass, finely spun into marvelous shapes and figures. I catalogued and memorized them all. But I think it would be better not to dwell on them. I might revert to my idolatrous ways if I get going on this topic.

My dad bore some responsibility for the Christmas tree, since he bought it, but it was my mother's Christmas symbol, not his. She, the daughter of Spanish immigrants, conceived on a transatlantic liner on the way to Cuba, wanted her children to be up-to-date. This meant being as American as possible. My dad favored the past, fought against the present, ignored the future. My mom looked towards the future.

I realize now that the battle between December 25 and January 6 was not just a skirmish between American cultural imperialism and Spanish tradition, but also a contest between Marie Antoinette and Louis XVI. And it was no contest, despite my father's best efforts.

Nature itself mocked my dad when it came to this battle for Christmas. My own dad, the former Louis XVI, looked and acted like Santa. He was as fat as Santa, and just as white-haired. So what if he didn't have a beard or a red suit? He looked as old as Santa, didn't he? If he didn't, then why did all of my classmates think he was my grandfather? So what if he had eyeglasses different from Santa's? He wore glasses, didn't he? Thick ones, too. He made toys, didn't he? He loved children, didn't he? Loved them so much he always brought strange ones to our house, like so many stray cats. He was generous. He never skimped on firecrackers. And he took us car surfing: a fine tropical substitute for sleigh rides.

"*Santicló* doesn't exist," said my brother to me one day. "All those presents come from Dad." Tony said this to me as we stood on the edge of our father's Bethlehem, in the glow of the lights that streamed from the windows he had cut out so carefully.

I didn't even bother to ask my brother about the Magi, because I didn't really care for them. They always brought inferior gifts.

Like all kids, I refused to believe the awful news at first, but the veil lifted quickly, and the clues all fell into place. In less than a minute, I came face to face with the truth. Santa and my dad were, in fact, one and the same person.

I had been lied to for years.

The veil lifted, and I beheld, virginally, the dreadful treasure unearthed by my ancestors. *Desengaño*. Disillusionment. The scorching, incandescent cornerstone of Spanish culture. You see, Spanish culture is built upon one warning: beware, all is illusion. Whatever you love, whatever you think you own, all of it is bound to disappoint, to prove false. Whether you know it or not, whether you like it or not, nothing you can embrace in this world will ever fill that yawning void in your soul. Nothing. No thing. No one. *Nada. Ninguna cosa. Nadie.*

Jesus H. Bungee-jumping Christ, save me! Find me the key to the vault of everlasting illusion! Take me to a place where the veil is never lifted, where the void can be ignored or seem full to the brim. Right there, looking down on Bethlehem, I prayed for release, for redemption. And it came from a very unlikely source, and much too fast.

Fidel came down from the mountains a few days later, swept down like an avenging angel burning with white-hot envy, frothing at the mouth. Beelzebub, Herod, and the Seven-Headed Beast of the Apocalypse rolled into one, a big fat smoldering cigar wedged between his seething lips, hell-bent on imposing his will on everyone. Hell-bent on ensuring there would be no king but he, no thoughts but his. He wrecked Bethlehem, leveled it, slaughtered all its children or drove them away. Burned all the Christmas trees in one fell swoop with a whirlwind of flame, a cyclone of hellfire, kindled by his cigar. Banished Christmas itself, made it illegal. Sowed salt on the landscape too, he did, enough brine to poison the entire island for more than the biblical forty years.

Two score and one, and still counting, as I write this. Man, oh man, God was surely pissed at us. So seldom does he exceed the number forty when venting his spleen or teaching a lesson.

I was one of the lucky ones. Fidel couldn't obliterate me as he did all the other children, slicing off their heads ever so slowly, and replacing them with fearful, slavish copies of his own. New heads held in place by two bolts, like Boris Karloff's in *Frankenstein,* one bolt forged from fear, the other from illusion. Even those Regla wharf boys lost their heads, they did, in exchange for a ration card and a ban on coin diving. And those that are still there, now grown men, with children and grandchildren of their own, are all walking around with rusty bolts on their necks.

Thanks to Louis XVI and Marie Antoinette, I was spared the head transplant. They battled over how best to save me, went to war with each other, pulled out weapons neither one knew they had. Like all real wars—as opposed to the ones staged in films—it wasn't very pretty or much fun to watch. Working with the skills she had honed so well in the battle over Christmas, my mom eventually prevailed. Louis XVI caved in to her, reluctantly. Caved in and collapsed, unable to resist her persuasive voice. On bad days I see my dad as an inflatable rubber Santa, the air all gone from inside, nothing but a red, wrinkly puddle on the ground. Or I see him as a plastic lawn ornament Santa, turned into shrapnel by a well-placed explosive. Dad-Santa, gone in an instant. Just like our lizard rocket.

Father, Father, why did you abandon me?

On good days, I cut my dad some slack. I think that maybe he convinced himself he was reliving what he had experienced in Bethlehem two thousand years ago, and, working with that knowledge, did the best he could. He listened to my mom and her very persuasive voice and chose to spare us the decapitation this time around. Louis XVI and Marie Antoinette hid me in the ruins and threw me out the window before Fidel's militiamen could get to me.

They threw me as far as they could, and so it was that I was driven into exile, along with my older brother. Threw me across the turquoise sea, all the way to our own Egypt, all the way to the United States, the vault of everlasting illusion.

11

ONCE

It was a huge wave. The biggest wave of the day. We had no surfboards, boogie boards, or rubber rafts, only our bodies. And we knew how to use them.

We could see this wave coming, bearing down on us and the beach. It was green. Light green, sort of jade, and foaming way higher than all the other waves in front of it. We fought with all our strength against those smaller waves, which weren't small at all, dug our feet into the fine white sand and let them pummel us.

"Wait for the big one!"

Four or five rows of these waves we wrestled against, knowing that the mother of all waves was not far behind. The closer it got, the bigger it grew. It was turning into a small mountain range.

We were all about fifty, maybe sixty yards from the edge of the beach, in about four feet of water. It was hard to keep your balance when the waves hit. We turned our backs to them and let them crash over our heads. We yelled at one another over the roar of the surf.

"Wait for that huge one!"

"Two more to go, and it's here."

"It's getting bigger!"

"Oh, no, it's getting scary."

"It's a monster, a monster!"

"Tidal wave!"

"Mount Everest!"

"Must have been caused by a whale fart!"

"No, no, it was one of Ernesto's farts!"

"Go to hell, Manuel, it was one of yours!"

"One more! One more to go!"

"Get ready, everybody, heeeere it is! *Aaaaaquí está!*"

"Whoa, whoa, whoa . . . ."

"Aaaaaaaaaayyyyyyyy . . . ."

It hit us like a freight train. Swallowed us whole, swept us away like straws in a tornado. We rolled in the green water, all of us, submerged, moving towards the shore at what seemed to be the speed of light and no speed at all.

I remember tumbling under the water, losing all sense of direction. I opened my eyes and saw nothing but green, and lots of bubbles in all sizes. The roar was deafening. Head over heels I spun, saltwater rushing up my nose. *Which way is the sky?* I asked myself. *Which way is the sand? How far left to go?*

I didn't have to wait very long for an answer. The wave crashed, and I was spit out onto the beach, head first, face down. Hard. With my mouth open.

And then, in less than a second or two, someone with a big butt landed right on my head and pushed it deep into the wet sand, burying it completely. Big Butt sat on me for a long time, or so it seemed. Just sat there on my head, his entire weight pinning my head under the sand. I suspected it must be Ernesto. None of us weighed that much. I had sand up my nostrils, sand in my ears, and sand down my throat. I think I screamed, or tried to. No sound would come out, though.

I thought I was going to die.

Then, mercifully, the weight lifted from my head, very slowly. I tried to raise my head out of the sand, but couldn't. I was stuck. Another huge wave crashed over my body, pinning me down. Just as I was beginning to pass out, someone grabbed my arms and pulled hard, freeing my head.

I blew sand out of my nose, coughed up sand, and gasped for air. I don't know how long it took me to catch a full, deep breath. All I know is that as I was busy trying to get air into my lungs, I also noticed I had sand in my eyes. And that hurt more than anything else.

Tony and my friends helped me crawl away from the pounding surf. The sand in my ears muffled the sound of children laughing at me, but I could make out what some of them were saying.

"That's the funniest thing I ever saw!"

"Did you see Ernesto sitting on his head?"

"They looked like some weird creature with two bodies and only one head."

"FrankenErnestostein . . . Moby Ernesto . . . Creature from the Fat Lagoon."

"Yeah, and did you catch the look on Carlos' face when we pulled his head out?"

"Never thought I'd get to see a zombie."

"How does that sand taste? Good? *Sabrosa*?"

"Here, let me slap your back."

Cough, spit, blow, wheeze. More of the same several times over. No words would come out of my mouth. Sand will do that to you. Having two hundred pounds or so land on your head doesn't help either. I wasn't just choking, I was stunned. And four boys pounding on your back with clenched fists don't help much either, especially four boys who think they've been given license to hit you as hard as possible.

Louis XVI and Marie Antoinette eventually showed up and rescued me from all the joking and the inept first aid. King Louis walked me over to one of the outdoor showers and helped me get the sand out of my head. I remember filling my mouth with water, gargling, and spitting out. I remember rinsing my ears, twisting my head sideways and pounding on my temples. Gently. I didn't want to kill myself. The club nurse helped me too, especially with the sand in my eyes.

What a great day that was, though. Great storm. Great waves. Great beach. Great parents who let us play in killer surf. Great beach club that let us in for free and allowed us to bring as many guests as we liked. Great management that had no lifeguards and allowed us to *tsunami*-surf with our bodies. Great coincidence, too, someone landing on my head. As soon as I got over the shock, I started laughing too, and joking. Especially about Ernesto's big butt.

Ernesto was not amused. But then again, he was seldom amused.

I'm not ready to speak about him yet, but I can say this much: he was not our friend. From the very start, from the day he first set foot in our house, none of us kids liked him. And we could tell he didn't like us very much either. It was one of those vicious circles in human relations that only keep getting worse. If some genius ever figures out how to tap the energy in vicious circles like that one, humankind will have a source of energy more abundant and powerful than cold fusion.

My mother tells me none of the adults liked him either. My father's mother was still alive that first day he came to visit. She had fifteen days left to live but didn't know it. And she pulled my mom aside and said, "Don't even allow this boy to use our bathroom." It's just about the last thing she ever said, that wise woman who seldom spoke, that gentle woman who ran her fingers through my hair.

The only one who seemed to like him was my dad.

Much of Ernesto is locked away in my vault of oblivion. But what's not in there scares me, and that's the reason for his shadowy, lurking presence in these pages up to now.

I have to admit, though, that having him land on my head and nearly suffocate me after we were both swept away by a killer wave is so perfect a metaphor for our relationship as to be my second proof for the existence of God.

Thomas Aquinas came up with five proofs for the existence of God, all of them based on causality. My proofs are based on similitude and the ways in which all things relate to one another, and to our limited yet eternal minds.

As long as I am on this topic, let me bring up my third proof for God's existence. Of course, it involves a head. Mine. And, of course, it's the kind of proof that no one who takes Immanuel Kant seriously would be eager to accept.

I have nothing but the utmost contempt for Kant, and so should you. He was foolish enough to trust entirely in one kind of reasoning alone, and verbose enough to convince many other smart people that he was right. Benighted fool, that lousy philosopher Kant, curse of the thinking class.

May you burn in hell forever, Immanuel, you obsessive-compulsive pedant, or find yourself in heaven, right next to Mel Blanc and the airport guy who laughed when he peered inside my underwear. And may you be eternally rid of the double set of garters that you wore on your precisely timed walks around Königsberg every afternoon, those jaunts that were a more accurate reckoning of the hour and minute than that of any clock in your gray Hanseatic town. You need not fear that your hose will slither down around your ankles in the afterlife, dear Immanuel, as you discuss the Categorical Imperative with Mel and Airport Guy. Or as you ponder the *ding-an-sich* and dissect *Vernunft* in a million useless ways with your two eternally doltish pupils. Socks and philosophy are even more useless in heaven than in the tropics.

I found that out early in life, along with my third proof for the existence of God, in a church. Let me get to the point with Prussian alacrity and precision.

It was years before the wave, years before Ernesto. I wasn't in school yet, not even preschool. We had gone to a baptism somewhere in the older section of Havana, in a very old church. There we were, sitting in a pew towards the rear of the nave, my parents, my brother, and I. It was a creepy church, just like all the others in that part of town. Pathologically Baroque. Dark and gloomy, with scary images everywhere. Gory crucifixes. The awful smell of incense and candles. The Mass that preceded the baptism had just started, and I was rolling around on the hard wooden pew, trying desperately to find some way of amusing myself while this guy dressed in a ridiculous robe mumbled words in a language that seemed oddly familiar but also very strange.

Dominus vobiscum. Dominoes vo-what? Why is he talking about dominoes, that game my grandfather loves to play with his white-haired friends?

Et cum spíritu tuo, came the mumbled response from the congregation. What was that? *Eco d'espíritu tuyo?* An echo of your spirit? Was he talking about ghosts' voices?

Louis XVI and Marie Antoinette had positioned themselves between me and Tony, as always. They never let us have fun in church. Always placing their index fingers up to their lips and saying "shush, be quiet," or simply hissing "shhhhhhhhhhh." Sometimes King Louis would smack us. I never had anything to do. Couldn't bring toys to church. Couldn't talk. Nothing at all, except to try to make sense of Latin and feel the burden of my own existence.

Ah, but suddenly I noticed this church was different. The pews didn't have solid backs. No, these were interesting pews. Their backs were carved in an intricate pattern. Row upon row of wooden slats in undulating shapes. Lots of rounded openings. What intriguing holes these were!

I tried to make sense out of the pattern, which looked a lot like that optical illusion you find in every basic psychology textbook, the picture that looks like the silhouette of a cup or an urn if you look at it one way, or the silhouette of two faces looking directly at each other, nose to nose. My very first paradox. This being a church, I guess the cup in the pattern must have been a chalice. But that's neither here nor there.

What matters is that I wanted to merge with the optical illusion, to live inside the paradox.

I got down on the hard wooden kneeler and ran my hands along the undulating shapes for a while. Then I stared at the rounded openings, puzzling over their affinity to the shape of my head. Round head. Round opening. Wow!

So I decided to put my head through one of these openings. I tested its breadth with the crown of my head. Amazing! The round hole was just wide enough to fit my head through by the smallest of margins. I had a bit of trouble inserting my head, but not much. A little twist of the neck here, another twist there, and bingo! Breakthrough! *Durchbruch,* as my dear friend the mystic Meister Eckhart would say. I had pierced right through the illusory plane, crossed from one dimension to another.

I stared in wonder from the other side of the pew at the pattern, looking sideways down the back of the pew at row upon row of cups-and-faces. It was the same from the other side! Incredible. And I had pierced right through, become one with the pattern, one with the paradox.

This was a great church. *We should come here more often,* I thought.

Oremus, I heard from my trans-dimensional vantage point. I remember mulling it over in my head, the head that was protruding out of the back of a pew like that of a malfeasant in stocks in some Puritan New England town back in 1689, maybe the very town in which I now live.

Oremus. There he goes again. Why is that guy with the funny robe always talking about oars? I thought he was saying *los remos*—"the oars." Oars made me think of the beach and the brightly painted rowboats they had at our club. I thought of cups-and-faces, pews, rowboats, and the beach. I thought of the turquoise sea, which called to me even at that early age.

Throughout this first rapture of mine, King Louis and Marie Antoinette remained absorbed in the Mass. Or maybe they were so relieved by my silence and lack of movement that they entered the fragile retreat of their own minds. Either way, they failed to take notice of me and my wonderful discovery.

Then came time for communion.

This meant that some people would have to get up and walk up to the communion rail to have that little white thing placed on their tongues. Then they would come back to their pews looking very, very serious. Not that many people went to communion back then, when all it took was one venial sin to make you unworthy of the body of Christ, but there were always enough holy people in any pew to make you move slightly as they made their way past you on the way up and the way back. More often than not it was women, with those dumb-looking veils on their heads, those folding fans in their hands, and those noisy high-heeled shoes on their feet. Why didn't men go up for communion? Why didn't they wear veils? Why did women wear such crazy shoes? Why did they snap their fans open so loudly, and fan themselves so furiously? Why did they shut those fans with an even louder noise? *Snap, whoosh, whoosh, whoosh, SNAP!* Why weren't men allowed to use fans?

More things to ponder from my trans-dimensional perch. More mind-bending questions to fuel my ecstasy from within the paradox.

Then came the rude awakening. A woman sitting in our pew had to go to communion. Which meant I had to move. But there was one problem, as I quickly discovered.

My head was stuck in the pew.

I tried and tried, but no amount of neck twisting or shifting into reverse could get my head out of that hole in the pew. Stuck in the paradox, I was. Somehow, either my head had swelled, or the opening in the pew had shrunk. My ears, especially, proved an insurmountable obstacle. So I did what any kid my age would have done. I yelled, at the top of my lungs: *"Mami, Papi, se me trabó la cabeza!"* Mom, Dad, my head is stuck!

The pall of silence that descended upon that church was thick indeed. It was as if I had made everyone stand perfectly still. As if I had made everyone hold their breath. As if everyone were suffocating.

Everyone except the man in the funny robe.

"Corpus Domini nostri Jesu Christi custodiat animam tuam in vitam aeter-

nam. Amen." I could hear the priest whispering at the communion rail, as he dispensed the body of Christ, Our Lord, to kneeling women, and a man or two.

"Mom, Dad, my head is stuck!" I yelled again. "My heeaaad is stuuuuck!"

"Corpus Domini nostri Jesu Christi . . ." (Whispered.)

Dad came over and started to pull on my shoulders. But every tug caused my ears to collide with the immovable wooden barrier of the hole's edge. And each attempt brought with it more pain.

"YAAAaaaaah! You're hurting me! You're hurting me! My ears! YAAAaaaaah!"

"Corpus Domini nostri Jesu Christi . . ." (Whispered.) Those dominoes again.

By now a small crowd had gathered around us.

"If this kid got his head in here, there must be some way to get it out," my father whispered through clenched teeth. These are the very first words of my father's that I remember with precision. So he tugged and tugged some more, and my ears felt as if they were being ripped right off my head.

My response was to yell even louder.

The crowd around us grew. People started whispering advice to my dad. "Turn his head this way." "No, no, don't turn his head at all." "Get some oil and rub it on his ears." "Put your hand on the top of his head and push hard."

"Corpus Domini nostri Jesu Christi . . ." (Whispered.)

My brother Tony came up with what seemed the best idea to me. "Dad, why don't you get one of your saws and cut the pew?"

I'm not sure, but I think I remember my dad muttering something under his breath that sounded an awful lot like, "Maybe what I should do is cut off his head."

You know about my dad and heads by now. I wouldn't put it past him to have said that.

In the meantime, as the crowd grew and my screaming became more frantic, my mother somehow worked her way to the other side of me. By that time, it seemed as if the Mass had stopped. Perhaps it had. I had the distinct impression that everyone in that church had their eyes fixed on me, including the guy in the funny robes, who was no longer whispering *"Corpus Domini nostri Jesu Christi . . ."*

"Here, Antonio, hold his head like this," said Marie Antoinette, placing her hands over my ears. "Hold his ears down as you pull, and gently twist his head. You do it. I can't really pull the right way from this angle."

Louis XVI did as his queen suggested, and in an instant, my head was freed from the paradox, effortlessly.

I rubbed my ears and sobbed for a while, and we all went home after the baptism. I may have looked exactly the same as I did before entering the church, but looks are deceiving. I had been transformed. I had come face to face with God.

So, you ask, what kind of proof is this for the existence of God? If I were a Zen master, I would give you no answer. Instead, I might whack you on the back of the head with a wooden plank, hoping the shock would bring you sudden enlightenment.

But I am far from a Zen master. No Cuban could ever gain the slightest toehold in the way of Zen, even after years and decades of reading up on the subject. Not even by living in a Buddhist monastery for a lifetime could any Cuban actually hear the sound of one hand clapping. We are not minimalists when it comes to paradox.

No, we like our paradoxes nice and complex. The more labyrinthine, the better. No single hands clapping, no. We don't like that. It's too reductionist, too minimalist, too close to a void. It speaks of absence and infinite loss and loneliness. We prefer to seek the coincidence of opposites, the infolding of the flame and the rose, the melding of face and chalice, head and pew, *Corpus Domini* and YAAAHHH!

And, besides, Cubans like to talk too much, and to explain everything in great detail. None of us could let anyone figure out a proof for God's existence on his own. Especially a proof that involves church pews.

As the eggplant and the breast speak of resemblances too numerous to be mere coincidence, as the perfect metaphor of near suffocation by an adopted brother sings sweetly of the relation between mind and the world around it, so does the head stuck in the pew announce our primal need to transcend linear logic, a craving as essential to our being as that for air, water, food, and love. So does the head in the pew reveal an intelligence beyond our own, but every bit as real as our own, an intelligence we seek.

Carajo, perdón. Damn it, forgive me, I've turned into a pedant from hell. Hoisted by my own *petardo*! How stupid to use linear logic in an attempt to blow up linear logic, just like that ever-cautious pedant Immanuel Kant and his bloodless, sallow brethren and disciples. I've tried to reason through a trinity of metaphors by reducing an infinity of meanings to a mere three. But to rely on reason alone is the surest road to heresy. And to hell, too. A more direct route than foul language.

Better to go for the infolding of Kyoto and Havana than to yearn for the singularity of Königsberg. Better to unthink, after all.

So go figure it out for yourself. Go ahead, after all.

Unthink.

Use your infinite imagination, and allow it to vanish on its own. Stick to the sense of sound alone, novice. I promise: no one will whack you on the back of the head with a wooden plank.

Imagine the sound of
boys thinking inside a giant wave . . .

Imagine the sound of
a boy screaming whose head is buried in the sand . . .

Imagine the sound of
a vicious circle . . .

Imagine the sound of
a philosopher's shadow moving over cobblestones . . .

Imagine the sound of
a head trapped in a paradox . . .

Imagine the sound of
a paradox trapped inside a head . . .

Imagine the sound of disillusionment and redemption
all at once . . .

And for Cubans only: imagine the sound of
memories that have nothing to do with Batista or Fidel.

12

DOCE

We pulled up to the house slowly, as always. Aunt Carmela's house was a house you had to approach slowly. It demanded respect.

It was so huge and so far back from the sunlit curb. A couple of mansions down, at the end of her street, there was nothing but blazing turquoise and the rhythmic breathing of the surf. But the house itself was enveloped in gloom, surrounded by a tall imposing wall and gargantuan, prehistoric-looking trees. An eclipse of the sun, contained in a parcel of land in Miramar.

When we passed through the driveway gate, I always slid off the backseat, dropped to the floor of the car, and closed my eyes.

"Do we have to come here again?" I whined.

"Oh, stop it, you know we have to visit her," came the predictable response from Louis XVI.

"Aunt Carmela is such a nice lady. And she always has some surprise for you." Marie Antoinette was always so much more soothing and persuasive.

"Come on, it's not that bad. She's not a scary lady at all." King Louis again.

"Remember, it was at Carmela's house that *Santicló* left our Monopoly game last Christmas." This was my brother speaking.

"I don't care. This house gives me the creeps."

"But it's a beautiful house," said our mother.

"Take me home, take me home. I want to go home."

"Stop it. Stop it right now . . . or . . . I'll make you spend the night with Aunt Carmela," threatened the King of France.

"Oh no. Pleeeaaaaase, no! No! You wouldn't do that to me, would you?"

"Try me."

"Stop it, Antonio—"

"Here we are," interrupted Tony. "Can't wait to see that butler again. And I can't wait to see what the surprise is today."

As always, I got out of the car, obedient but shaking with fear. We climbed the marble steps to the huge bronze double doors, and King Louis used the heavy knocker. *BLAM, BLAM, BLAM!* We could hear the echo inside.

One of the doors opened slowly. A tall, lanky man dressed in a dark suit appeared. He was thin and bald and had dark circles under his eyes, and he seemed to be hiding something. He looked down his long nose at us, and, as always, said, *"Buenos días, Doctor Nieto. Buenos días, Señora."*

Greetings for our parents, but not for us. But, as always, he stared at Tony and me with his dark droopy eyes. He knew we were there. He knew I was trying to hide behind my mom, peering up at him with one squinting eye.

"Come in. I'll go tell Doña Carmela that you are here. This way, please. Follow me."

This man didn't walk like other men. He kept himself straight and stiff as a railroad tie, yet somehow also as loose and fluid as the goop inside a Lava lamp.

The inside of the house was every bit as dark as the driveway and the large front yard. No lights on anywhere, and all the window shutters closed. Room upon room of furniture draped in white shrouds. This house was haunted by sofas, armchairs, and ottomans from bygone days. Each and every piece protected from the ravages of dust by an opaque white veil. Protected too from the insult of novelty, from the attempt to displace memories, from the affront of new human beings trying to supplant those who once sat on them, wrote on them, perhaps even kissed on them. Ghosts they were, really. Furniture that had once been alive. Springs creaking, chair legs scraping, tables receiving sweaty goblets that dripped on them. The occasional stain or gouge. Now they had no purpose to serve save that of filling the rooms, cloaked monuments to happier times, when the windows were open, the lights were on, and the future was not yet the past.

How I hated that journey from the front door to Aunt Carmela's study. Following that butler through room after dismal room, imagining what might be lurking under those white shrouds.

The study was different. The window shutters were open and light streamed in. Aunt Carmela had an enormous desk and beautiful glass paperweights and strange paintings on the walls. They were unlike any other pictures I had ever seen. Dalí, Gris, Miró, Picabia, Picasso, maybe?

"I don't know what she sees in this modern art," said Louis XVI.

She always came in so slowly, Aunt Carmela. She was nearly blind, and it seemed to take her forever to appear and to make her way to her desk, hobbling on her cane. On this day, as on all others, she was very cheerful. She had the nicest smile I ever saw on an old lady, and eyes that seemed far younger than the rest of her.

On this day, as on all others, we talked for a long time. And when we were done talking came the surprise.

"Here you go, boys, don't spend it all in one place," she said, handing us each a five-dollar bill.

Five dollars was a lot of money back in 1957, especially for children. Despite her advice, I blew it all on an entire box of Davy Crockett trading cards, which were all the rage at my school. One of those vendors outside the schoolyard sold them by the packet. But I came armed with five dollars one fine Monday and bought an entire box containing about thirty packets.

Desengaño. Packet after packet contained the same sets of cards. Out of two hundred or so cards, I think I only managed to get a sum total of half a dozen new ones. Five American bucks for cards I already owned, and all the other kids already had, too. I couldn't even trade them, so I threw most of them down a sewer outside the school.

I should have listened to Carmela. She was very wise. Perhaps the wisest of all of my relatives.

Tía Carmela was the only Nieto who seemed to have lived life to the fullest. Back when it wasn't the least bit fashionable, in the late nineteenth century, she had insisted on doing things her own way. She was a rebel and a liberal through and through.

I don't know the full story, but this is what I've been able to reconstruct.

Carmela was *Abuelo* Amado's first cousin. Her father was my great-grandfather's brother. She had been brought up in the strict, stultifying tradition of the Nieto family. This meant denying that you lived in Cuba. It also meant, if you were a woman, that you devoted your entire existence to your husband and children.

Not Carmela. She took up every cause she believed in, especially democracy, independence from Spain, and equal rights for women and the recently freed African slaves. She was vocal about it, ruffling every feather there was to ruffle. She loved socializing and parties, and fervently believed in having a good time while taking care of the needy.

Then, to top it off, she took up writing. She wrote fiction and newspaper columns in which she gave advice and championed her liberal causes. And if this were not odd enough, she married an American man. From Kansas, of all places. How he ended up in Havana, I don't really know, but they had three children: Daisy, Archibald, and Addison.

I'm sure those names went over very well with the Nieto family.

Then she did the unthinkable. She fell in love with another man, a Cuban. A hero of the War of Independence against Spain. A man who was married to another woman. She and the war hero allowed nature to take its course, and before long, trouble came their way. Carmela, you see, was no longer on very friendly terms with her American husband. So much so, in fact, that when she became pregnant, the man from Kansas knew with absolute certainty that she wasn't carrying his child.

He packed his bags, said good-bye to his children in English, and returned to Tornado Alley without ever looking back. He divorced Carmela and disowned his children. He never wrote a letter or ever inquired about Daisy, Archie, and Addison. Never answered their letters either. He abandoned them totally.

Years later, when Addison was in his twenties, he would seek out his father in the United States, but Kansas man refused to see him. He wouldn't even open the door for Addison. Through a closed door he told him to go away. "You're not my son," he told him. "Go find your Cuban father. Go back to stinking hot Cuba, where you belong."

Carmela and her war hero married eventually and had two children of their own, but their union came at a very high price. The entire Nieto family refused to have anything to do with Carmela after her scandalous divorce and remarriage. In the same way that Kansas man refused to acknowledge the existence of his children, the Nietos refused to admit that Carmela existed.

My father was the only relative who kept in touch with her through all of this, furtively. He dared not court the disfavor of the family openly. Decades passed and no one else in the family talked to the woman. When her war hero husband died, my dad was the only relative at the funeral.

While every Nieto was stone silent and invisible, Carmela continued to write, promote her causes, and enjoy life. She also became fabulously wealthy. How this happened, exactly, I don't know. But it did. Her house was ample proof. So was the hospital that she established in El Rincón, outside of Havana, to shelter lepers.

And no one said a word to her, until I came along.

I have no memory whatsoever of my role in breaking the ice. I only know what my mother has told me, which can always be trusted. According to her, I overheard some grown-ups talking about Aunt Carmela one day and asked why I'd never met her. When it was explained to me that she was an outcast, I couldn't understand how someone could be shunned for divorcing one man and marrying another. And I began to ask, with uncharacteristic persistence, that I be taken to meet Aunt Carmela. I became such a pest about it that Marie Antoinette finally convinced King Louis to break the ice. He called her and arranged for an open reconciliation. No more secret visits and phone calls. After a well-announced visit from us, the rest of the family also caved in, asked her forgiveness, and went back to loving the woman no one had really wanted to shun in the first place.

Blessed are the peacemakers, said Jesus. My blessing was to get to know that very nice woman and to visit the house from hell. The butler and the veiled furniture, you see, were the least of my problems. Beyond the study, at the end of the wide main hallway, there was a grand staircase. On the first landing of that staircase there was a giant fish tank, which I loved, flanked by two modern abstract sculptures that scared me to death. They were far scarier than Maria Theresa. They looked like something by Modigliani or Henry Moore, but they were black and odd looking, and reminded me of voodoo masks and costumes I had once seen at a museum at the University of Havana.

"Want to go see some little devils?" King Louis had said one day.

"*Diablitos?* Sure, let's go. Sounds great."

"Okay, I'll call this guy I know and he'll let us in. This is a special museum, you know. It's not always open."

So, as always, a bunch of kids piled into the car, and off we went, to the university. We might have done some car surfing on the way, who knows? It was a cool winter day, and cloudy. On days like that, the surf was usually whipped up by the northern winds that swept down all the way from the polar ice cap. It was a perfect day for car surfing, anyway, whether we did it or not.

What a rude surprise, those little devils at the university. We walked into the exhibit hall and I froze with panic. What I saw were life-size figures dressed in colorful grass costumes, most of them wearing pointy-headed masks. These African costumes displayed on life-size mannequins inside those glass cases terrified me as nothing else had ever done before. Maria Theresa and Eye Jesus and the Candlestick Lady (about whom I have not yet spoken) seemed like angels next to these devils.

"Get me out of here!" I screamed.

"What's the matter with you?"

"Get me out of here, now, please."

I felt as if I were in the presence of a malevolent force that wanted to annihilate me.

I would feel exactly the same terror, magnified ten thousand times, many years later when confronted with the Evil One himself in a dream. Don't think for a minute that just because it was a dream it was an illusion. The force behind those *diablitos* manifested itself to me, in a very real way, and let me know it was pissed at me. Pissed as hell, as only the Prince of Darkness can be. Yes, I did finally get to meet him face to face, the ill-tempered King of Assholes. He's very large, let me tell you. Huge. And he's a cranky bastard, the Father of Lies, and an ugly son of a bitch too.

Maybe someday I'll be able to tell that story. But not now.

I ran out of that exhibit as fast as I could, found my way to the car, and stood out there in the small parking lot at the rear of the university for a long while, waiting for everyone else to come out.

"You're such a coward," said my brother Tony when everyone finally emerged.

"Those devils were so nice," chimed in Rafael. "You should have stayed and taken a better look."

"You know," said Louis XVI, reassuringly, "out in the countryside some black people still wear those costumes. They dance around a fire at night and put curses on their enemies. And sometimes they're possessed by spirits and fly around."

Just what I wanted to hear. *Muchas gracias, Papa.* Of course, I didn't say that. I just said I wanted to go home.

The image of those *diablitos* dancing around bonfires out in the sugarcane fields would haunt me for years. Until the day I left Cuba, to be precise.

Anyway, the sculptures on the landing of Aunt Carmela's grand staircase gave off the same vibes to me. And so did the giant Saint Lazarus statue in a small shrine behind the kitchen. The leper hospital she had founded was named after Saint Lazarus, the patron saint of lepers, and that's why she had this giant statue in her house. There he was, life-size, just like the *diablito* mannequins, Saint Lazarus, hobbling on crutches, disfigured by leprosy, the sores on his legs being licked by dogs. Mean-looking mangy dogs.

Somehow, devotees of Saint Lazarus found out about the image at Carmela's house and came all the way to Miramar to venerate it. Most of them were ragged, humble people. Several times while I was visiting, I saw them knocking on the rear door, begging for admission to the shrine.

Lazarus had plenty of candles and votive offerings. Fruit. Coins. Trinkets. Cigars.

To African Cubans, Lazarus was someone other than Lazarus. He was an African deity in Catholic disguise. A powerful one. Hard to know how white Cubans got to like him, but they did. Need and despair know no race or class boundaries, I guess.

Years later, in Chicago, I knew a white Cuban family that kept a statue of Saint Lazarus in their living room and offered it glasses of rum and cigars. In Havana, they'd lived near the Plaza de Marianao. In Chicago their apartment building was right next to the El, the elevated train tracks, even closer than ours. Unlike the Lazarus at Carmela's house, which was large and frightening, this small exiled Lazarus was benign, almost comical. The cigar was always precariously perched on the edge of the wooden shelf on which Lazarus stood, and every time an elevated train rumbled by the cigar would do a little dance of indecision on the edge of the shelf.

Shall I stay at the feet of Lazarus, or shall I tumble to the floor?

This family took to thinking that Lazarus sometimes rejected their offerings. So whenever the cigar fell off the shelf, thanks to the El, they would go out and buy a more expensive one.

"Listen, little Lazarus, you have to grant me this favor I asked for. Look, I bought you a very good, expensive cigar," the lady of the house said one day while I was there.

Eventually, Lazarus made it all the way to Honduran cigars that cost twenty dollars each, which was a lot of money thirty years ago. Every now and then he'd get a smuggled Cuban cigar. Real Montecristos for the disguised African deity.

Greedy Lazarus. Avaricious little leper, exiled to a red brick apartment building on which the sun shone for only one hour a day in winter, on Winthrop Avenue, right next to a train line that never shut down, on the edge of a slum, two blocks from ice blue Lake Michigan and the high-rise towers of the well-to-do, just one block from our own basement apartment with the pipes running all along the ceiling.

All right, maybe I should be kinder to poor Lazarus. Maybe he wasn't greedy. After all, there he was, over two thousand miles from home. Maybe he felt imprisoned in that dark apartment. Maybe he didn't like the look of the little sliver of gray sky he could see from his perch in the living room. Maybe he was more than a little annoyed by that El train rumbling twenty-four hours a day, three hundred and sixty-five days a year—sixty-six in leap years. Maybe he would have liked Miami better. Maybe he longed for real Cuban cigars. *No El Productos, please. No Dutch Masters. No Tiparillos. If you offer me Tiparillos, I'll curse you.* Maybe he really wanted to help his fellow Cubans and felt empathy for them. Maybe it wasn't too much fun for him to watch the man of the house leave for work at midnight and return at ten in the morning, after his two teenage sons had already gone off to school. Maybe it was even less fun to put up with the six wailing children that the lady of the house cared for while their Cuban mothers went off to work at the Lava lamp factory on Lawrence Avenue.

Yeah, I take it back. Poor Saint Lazarus of North Winthrop Avenue. I need to cut him a lot of slack. Since all images are linked to their prototype in heaven—even images that mask African deities—that Lazarus in Chicago was constantly in tune with every other Lazarus in the world, and especially all the Lazaruses in Cuba, including the one in Carmela's very nice house, and the one at her leper hospital.

Imagine how he felt.

The Lazarus of Carmela's mansion was probably still there, on those very same days when I saw the cigar doing the El train dance on the shelf in Chicago. I don't know how long it stood there or whether it's still there.

Carmela died in my mother's arms in 1964, in her own bedroom, not far from her Lazarus, in her mansion, surrounded by her shrouded furniture and whatever memories were hidden beneath those veils. My dad was there too. I have no idea where Ernesto was and don't care to know. I don't know about the butler either. My brother and I were two thousand miles away, probably playing in the snow. We loved snow so much. It was such a novelty. Archie and Addison were there too. Daisy was in London, where she had lived for decades. Carmela's two children by her Cuban husband were in Miami. Archie and Addison remained in the mansion for some years after that, but death eventually came to claim them. And I don't know what happened to the house after they passed away, or what became of Addison's banana grove and his iguanas.

More about those two last items later.

I do know, however, where Saint Lazarus of the dancing cigar of Winthrop Avenue ended up. He's enjoying the sunshine in a nice neighborhood in Miami, somewhere around Southwest 135th Avenue. I can't be exact, but I know for certain that there isn't an elevated train anywhere near that house.

As to all the stuff that scared me, what can any of us say about the things that frightened us as a child? When do they stop being spooky, if ever? I can't say. I didn't get a chance to grow up with my scary things, so they remain scary, embedded as they are in childhood memories.

Occasionally, some things surface in dreams. Things I have every right to be scared of. But sometimes good things surface too. Things that heal.

Since I already had the nerve to tell you that the Evil One himself ambushed me in a dream, I should also tell you that my dad, Louis XVI, visited me regularly for a while. It's been about eight years since he's come around, but maybe that's because his soul is now at rest. His last visit was very sweet and very much in character.

In my dream, I'm asleep. All of a sudden, there he is. He shows up to tell me, while I'm sleeping, that he's finally at peace, that everything's all right. He embraces me and tells me that he understands and forgives me for every bad thought I've ever had and ever will have about him. He tells me that nothing should frighten me. Grace abounds, goodness prevails. He tells me pain is an illusion, ultimately, a little puff of smoke. He tells me that those spears that impale us and we actually see sticking out of our chests sometimes, those black iron harpoons that pierce our hearts and stay there till we die, and take years and years of practice to ignore, are really gifts of the Holy Spirit, one and the same with tongues of flame. Even those launched by love gone wrong, love unreturned, love thwarted, love unfulfilled, love thrown away.

In my dream I catch on to the fact that I'm asleep and missing out on my father's visit. He's here. At last, he's here, with me. I haven't seen him for so long, since that day at the airport. I've missed him so and cursed him so. And he's here, embracing me, finally, preaching redemption and healing, not reincarnation. But I'm asleep. Why can't I wake up? This is as good as it can ever get.

So as I struggle to awaken in my dream, I plead with Louis XVI, "No, no, not in a dream. Don't do this in a dream. Don't do this to me. Show up while I'm awake."

"Ven cuando yo esté despierto," I plead, in Spanish.

"Estás despierto, hijo. Más despierto que nunca," he says, and then he vanishes.

"You're awake, son. More awake than ever."

And I was, damn it.

13

TRECE

Thirteen is a volatile number. Schizoid, highly charged, unstable, unpredictable.

If thirteen were a human being instead of a number, and it lived next door to you, what would you do? Could you live with the anxiety of not knowing how this neighbor might behave? Generous to a fault, this neighbor, capable of lending you lawn mowers with a full tank of gas, or murderous to the core, capable of skewering you with a fireplace poker and of sacrificing your children to Satan on your own kitchen table, slowly, with your dullest butter knife? Better to skirt thirteen, when possible, or to remove yourself from its presence.

If I can't avoid thirteen though, what then? Should I invoke the goddess Fortuna? Why not talk about luck? But not my own luck. No. That's like knocking on that unpredictable neighbor's door with an empty cup in my hand.

Better at this point, when speaking of luck and the lottery of existence, to reach back into the past. Better to deal with people and events that influenced me, but for which I bear no responsibility. And, after I make the briefest of appearances, exit quickly. Better to offer fragmentary sketches of luck, and odds, and improbable coincidences. Fragments of family history that mirror too much. Fragments of mirrors that hint at a carefully crafted plot.

Some of these fragments, I believe, have Fidel's face on them, mirrored endlessly.

Out of a very long list, I have chosen thirteen items. Thirteen, of course, to placate the ever-smoldering goddess. Do I have any choice, divine Fortuna?

1. One of my great-grandparents—the father of my father's mother—won the top prize in the Spanish lottery three times. *El Premio Gordo*. The Fat Prize, literally. Lucky man, I think. Family tradition has it that someone tried to hack him to pieces with a machete for the money.

2. One of my great-great-grandmothers was chased out of Mexico in 1820, during the Mexican Revolution, and she and her family fled to Cuba on a boat. This boat apparently drifted aimlessly in the turquoise sea for a while, and they were all forced to drink their own urine. They lost everything they owned, too, which was a lot. According to my dad, whose facts can't really be trusted, she and her family, the Butrón-Múgicas, owned practically the entire city of Guanajuato. On some days, my dad said it was the whole state of Guanajuato. Unlucky woman. She won *El Premio Flaco,* the Thin Prize.

I had to hear this story endlessly as a child, along with that of Louis XVI and the guillotine. I'll spare you the details of what they ate on the boat, along with their urine cocktails.

3. After arriving in Cuba, Great-great-Grandma Múgica, now bereft of her fortune and much skinnier, married a Spanish army officer named Nieto who had fought against the Mexicans for ten long years, only to lose the war. As a reward for his efforts, futile though they were, and possibly for his wounds, Captain Tomás Nieto was given some land in Cuba. So he gave up whatever waited for him back in Spain, married the thin woman who used to own Guanajuato, and the two of them raised a whole new batch of army officers, who were trained to ensure that Spain wouldn't lose Cuba too.

Spain lost Cuba anyway. And Guanajuato remained in the hands of others.

But I had another ancestor who had already beaten the Múgicas to the finish line in the lose-everything sweepstakes by three centuries.

4. There's a very good chance that the original Nieto, Alvaro, the first for whom there are written records, was a Jew. Or at least the son of a Jew, forcibly converted into a Christian. Alvaro Nieto packed his bags and fled from Albuquerque, in hot, dry Extremadura, Spain, to seek a new life and a new identity in cool, green Galicia. Many converted Jews had to do this back in 1500, to escape prosecution for practicing Jewish rituals in their homes. Many of them fled to other places, and pretended not to be Jews, or the children of Jews. Many of them had all of their property confiscated by the Inquisition, or lost it, before fleeing.

Why do I suspect that Alvaro Nieto was a Jew, or the son of a Jew? Funny thing. We never ate pork at our house. Never ate clams, or lobster, or crabs. And it had been that way for generations. Cubans love pork and all that other stuff we never ate. It was unnatural for Cubans to observe Jewish dietary laws, especially without knowing why.

But that's not all. Another ancestor also lost everything for the sake of his faith.

5. On my mother's side of the family, one of my great-great-great-great-grandparents was chased out of Ireland in 1649 by Oliver Cromwell and his English Puritan army. Ultra-great-Grandad Francis Eire and his Irish family fled to Spain, leaving everything they owned behind, so they could remain Catholic. And family tradition has it they owned a whole lot. Unlucky, I guess. But his son was lucky. He fell in love with a woman in Galicia whose family owned a lot of property and married her. Luck of the Irish?

Much of her property remained in my family's hands until my grandfather came along and fell in love with the wrong girl. Not wrong for him, mind you, only for his parents.

6. My mother's father and mother left Spain in 1920 because their parents didn't want them to get married. They eloped. Got on a ship, and crossed the ocean to Cuba. My grandfather left behind everything he owned and everything he hoped to inherit—which was a lot—just so he could marry the girl of his dreams. Lucky, lucky man, at least when it came to love. So lucky, he lived with that girl, Josefa, for fifty-eight years, and they had three lovely children. Yes, of course, it was a lot that he gave up back in Galicia. I know this because I went there and saw it for myself. Everyone kept pointing out to me what would have belonged to my grandfather.

"Sabéis, esto debería ser vuestro." You know, this ought to belong to you, they said. Orchards. Vineyards. Meadows. Houses. Stuff. Now, it all belongs to other relatives. One of them showed me a trunk full of fine china and silverware, tucked away in an attic, and said, "I shouldn't let you see this: it was supposed to go to your grandfather."

This same grandfather started to make his way in Cuba, but his house burned to the ground and his oldest daughter came down with polio. There was no insurance to cover either tragedy. He started all over again, and when the banks failed in 1929, he lost all his money once more. So he started over again, working as a truck driver. One day, shortly before I was born, he bought a lottery ticket, and it turned out to be the winning number. *El Premio Gordo*. The Fat Prize. But that very same night, right after he learned he was a wealthy man, his house burned down again. And inside the house was the winning ticket, which was devoured by the flames. No ticket, no prize. Those were the rules of the Cuban lottery. He lost his house, his belongings, and the Fat Prize all in one night. So he started over again, driving his truck day after day, and saved enough money to buy a very nice house for his retirement years. And along came Fidel and Che Guevara, and one fine day Che seized all the money in the banks. And my grandfather lost all his savings in one day. Again. Lucky or not? I can't tell. He always seemed so happy. And he had nothing against lizards.

7. His name was Amador. In English this means "lover."

8. My other grandfather, my father's father, was named Amado. "Loved one," in English. What are the odds of having grandfathers named Lover and Loved One? A trillion to one? Probably much higher than that. Somewhere just short of infinity, I guess.

9. Amado, my father's father, met his wife, Lola, my grandmother, while watching Lola's house burn down. There she was, standing outside the house with her family, watching everything go up in smoke, and along came Amado, a previously unseen young neighbor, and they got to talking, and the next thing you know, they're getting married. Lucky pair.

By the way, the house they were watching burn down was the house owned by Lola's father, the man who had won the lottery Fat Prize in Spain three times, the man who was nearly murdered for money.

Amado chose not to follow a military career, like all of his male ancestors. He went to medical school for a while but dropped out because he didn't like the idea of having to find his own cadaver to dissect. (Back then, each medical student had to find their own cadaver, which meant that many of them stole corpses from cemeteries.) He finally ended up in the real estate business. He and Lola had four children, the youngest of whom was my dad.

Lola's sister, Uma, lived with them their entire married life. She was a musician and a very well-respected piano teacher. She never married. Family tradition has it that Uma had fallen in love with Amado the night of the fire, and had always remained in love with him. But he had fallen for her sister, and married her instead. Unlucky Uma. Was living under the same roof with her sister and the man she loved the seventh circle of hell, or could it have been just what she wanted, and a foretaste of heaven? Uma thought Amado was the funniest man in the world. Or at least in Havana. This is what she told my mother over and over again. No one was funnier than Amado, or nicer.

10. Amado is the only grandparent I never got to meet. Too bad. He died young, at the age of fifty-six. Killed by an envelope. Unlucky Amado. While licking an envelope, he nicked his tongue with its sharp edge. A small paper cut on the tongue. It was a tiny, ridiculous wound, but there were no antibiotics in 1927. His wound became infected and he died. Unlucky. Definitely. No doubt about it.

I never lick envelopes. And I yell at my children every time I see them do it, just like my father did to me. "Do you know my grandfather died from licking an envelope?"

They think I'm making it up.

Lola was widowed in her mid-fifties. She and Uma, and her unmarried daughter, Lucía, and my father, Antonio, moved to Miramar a few years after that. To a house on the very edge of civilization.

11. Then my dad met my mom. He met her through a psychic he used to visit regularly, a woman who claimed to have intimate connections with the spirit world. My mom and her family were not at all interested in psychic mediums or the spirit world, but they had a neighbor who knew someone who knew the medium, and somehow, in the weird way these things sometimes happen, my mom and dad were introduced to each other through her.

Louis XVI recognized Marie Antoinette the minute he laid eyes on her, and he began to court her furiously. She was not too interested at first. But slowly the persuasive woman was persuaded. Louis XVI wouldn't take no for an answer. This is what can happen when a man thinks he has met the woman who has been his soul mate for thousands and thousands of lifetimes.

He did outrageous things, such as stand outside her house with flowers in his hand for hours and hours. In the hot sun. In pouring rain. He used whatever intermediaries and advocates he could find. He sent letters. Presents. And he stood outside her door until she caved in. They started seeing each other, with chaperones of course, as was the Cuban custom, and before long, my mom fell in love with King Louis, in spite of the fact that she thought that all of this reincarnation stuff was utter nonsense. Non–Marie Antoinette she was to herself, Marie Antoinette to him. Non–Louis XVI he was to her, Louis XVI to himself. Dad was also twelve years older than Mom and not exactly the best-looking man in Havana. Whereas, if you had stood my mom next to Rita Hayworth in 1944, you would have been forced to say that Rita just didn't measure up. Although my mom did have one bad leg and Rita didn't. Still, in spite of every glaring difference between them, in spite of my mom's leg, and all the odds stacked against this pairing, my parents got married.

King Louis brought Marie Antoinette to live in that house in Miramar. Brought her there to share the house with his mother, his aunt, and his sister. The neighbors took bets on how long the marriage would last. No one bet on more than one year. And no one won.

12. Sometime in the 1930s, a Jewish refugee fleeing from the Nazis landed in Havana. He had been wise enough to see what was looming on the horizon and had managed to escape with his whole family and several valuable works of art. Strapped for cash in a strange tropical land, this refugee sold off the art piece by piece. Much to his dismay, most of the items sold for a fraction of their real value. Havana during the Depression was not a good place in which to market works of art. Unlucky refugee.

One day, while scouring antique shops in Havana, trying to find more objects with which to fill up that house into which he would bring my mother, Louis XVI found a portrait he immediately recognized. A thrilling find. It was none other than Empress Maria Theresa of Austria. The painting was a bargain. A steal, practically. The shop owner had bought it from another dealer, who had bought it from the Jewish refugee for a pittance and was selling it for not much more than he himself had paid for it. About one hundred pesos. Nobody wanted that portrait. Such a dour-looking woman. Maybe she cussed out all potential buyers, telepathically, scaring them away.

Louis XVI purchased the portrait gleefully and hung it in a place of honor. The portrait of his mother-in law.

Empress Maria Theresa of Austria, you see, was Marie Antoinette's mother.

Lucky Dad. Unlucky me.

Coño. Qué mierda.

What were the odds of a portrait of Empress Maria Theresa of Austria ending up in the hands of a man who claimed to have been her son-in-law in a former life? What were the odds that this strange man and the portrait would have crossed paths in Havana, of all places?

Only God could calculate those odds. Perhaps. Maybe not even He.

13. Finally, let me tell you more about *Abuela* Lola, from the luck angle. Houses that burn down, fortunes that are lost, tyrants and revolutions that force you into exile, these are all part of my family's luck. And so is the lizard-loathing gene. It was my luck to end up with it. She gave me that special gift.

How I wish Lola could tell you about this herself. I may have inherited the loathing from her, but have never fully fathomed it. I know for certain she understood it intimately.

Speak, Grandma. Please. *Llegó la hora.* The time has come. You, who loved speaking with the dead, speak now. You who were so superstitious, to you I offer the thirteenth place in chapter thirteen.

(..)

Oh hell, all I get is silence. History of my relations with the spirit world. But I can guess at some of the things she might have said, for she had a great fear of reptiles. Fear and disgust. And I am a keeper of the fear.

Some things on this earth are truly scary and loathsome. Pond scum. Slime. Eggs. Ooze. Dragons. Salamanders. Newts. Alligators. Iguanas. Lizards. Toads. Frogs. Big-eyed frogs. Croaking frogs. Fly-catching frogs. Pissing frogs. Copulating frogs.

When God got angry at the Egyptians, He sent them a plague of frogs. Disgusting frogs. Frogs without number. Slimy, lusting frogs. And the Egyptians died by the thousands. Died like ugly frogs because of frogs.

And could we forget the snakes, we keepers of the fear? Forget the serpent?

If they can't poison you, then they crush you. If not in the light of day, then in the dark of night. If not in the tall grass, then in the baby's crib. They can sneak into your bed, under your pillow, and kill you while you're dreaming, or making love.

If not by poison, or brute force, then by merely being there, and sharing this world with us, they bring us to the grave. Death itself carries them in his pocket, and loves to brandish them by the handful. The mere sight of their beady eyes and vile, camouflage skin slays as swiftly as any guillotine, even more swiftly sometimes.

Vipers. Boas. Adders. Rattlers. Mambas. Cobras. Pythons.

Snakes writhing over one another. Serpents, copulating, hissing with delight. Writhing over all of creation. Slithering. Since the beginning. Living, writhing guts. Intestines with heads. Sexed intestines. Nothing but ingesting, digesting, expelling, hissing, and mating.

Male and female He made them. First two. Then thousands. Millions. Billions. Trillions. Be fruitful and multiply. Hiss, writhe. Mingle your cold, cold blood. Cold as the absence of light. Cold as the heart of a fallen angel. Colder than the loins of Adam and Eve before It came along.

There was a snake in the garden. A serpent. It talked to the woman with its forked tongue, or maybe not. Spoke without speaking, maybe. Didn't have to speak at all, maybe. Just showed up and manifested its scaly rainbow skin, which said: "Look at me, woman. I have entrapped all the colors of the rainbow, and you have not. I know things that man over there will never know. Stupid man. What does he know? You know more than he does, but what do you know, really?"

And the rest was nothing but trouble, so the Bible says.

God-damned serpent.

Abuela Lola was among the lucky few. It flowed through her veins, this memory, and she passed it on to me. This is why she stroked my hair all day long, silently, while she lived. While her blood was still hot, before her blood, that final day, became as cold as theirs. Wordless. No words at all can I recall. Not one.

Only a simple, wordless message that said: flee; kill or be killed.

Why speak? We both knew. Loathsome breathing rainbows, all of them. The enemy. Crush their heads. Annihilate them. Erase with abandon the awful mistake. Redemption shall never extend to them. Redemption is their extinction. God the Father Himself hates them. Jesus hates them. Cursed for eternity, they are.

The reason *Abuela* Lola held me up to the front-door window pane, inside our living room, to watch for my brother's return from school, rather than out on our ever balmy tropical front porch, was that she never set foot outdoors.

Never.

And the reason she never stepped outside was her fear and hatred of reptiles.

When she and her sister and daughter and son first moved to that house in Miramar, after the tragic death of her husband, it was on the very edge of Havana. Too close to undeveloped land, full of lizards, iguanas, and frogs. Her son, my father, the onetime Louis XVI, had to kill many an iguana. Crushed their heads with a wooden plank.

Eventually the iguanas learned to live elsewhere, as the neighborhood grew, and he and other dutiful sons in other homes crushed their heads with abandon. By the time I came into that house, the iguanas were gone. I never saw one anywhere in that neighborhood. They merely existed in my father's tales of chivalry, of King Louis the dragon slayer, crusher of iguana heads.

The lizards were far too numerous to disperse. But you know this already. They were always there, and shall remain until the earth melts like wax.

There were frogs in the neighborhood back then, too, back in the beginning, before the City of Man paved its way over their garden. Frogs of all kinds and sizes, I hear. They had gone to the same place as the iguanas by the time I arrived. The only frog I ever saw in that neighborhood was a small one, squashed as flat as a pancake on the street. A foolish frog, no doubt, who tried to return to the garden.

But in the beginning, long before I arrived, the frogs had not yet learned to stay away. And one sunny day, as Lola sat on the porch, a giant loathsome frog jumped on her lap. She was so horrified, so shaken to the core by this surprise encounter with the enemy, that she retreated indoors for the rest of her life. Vowed never, ever to step outdoors again, and she never did.

From the day she made the vow until the day she died, the earth circled the sun about twenty times. For two decades, Lola was a self-made prisoner in her own house. I doubt she viewed herself as a prisoner, though. It was the world full of loathsome reptiles that was a prison. Her house was a sanctuary, a fortress. She was a recluse, a nun. A holy woman, keeping alive the impulse to crush the loathsome heads of reptiles, passing it on to some of her progeny.

My father's mother, my grandmother. Never fully at home in this world. Convinced that reptiles were evil, that, somehow, they were not included among those creatures mentioned in the Bible, in Genesis, about whom God felt good at the dawn of creation.

I don't know how she felt about envelopes, but I guess she had a fear of them too. Everyone in my family feared envelopes.

What we didn't fear enough was loss. Exile and loss. So much lost, so much regained, only to be lost all over again.

Always starting all over again. Ignoring the neighbor who is lusting after our stuff. Forgetting the taste of our own urine. Buying lottery tickets. Licking envelopes absentmindedly. Marrying the wrong women. Fumbling miserably with the right women. Tossing away our inheritances for the sake of love or faith. Hating those lizards, crushing their heads. Blowing them up with firecrackers.

Hoisted on our own *petardos,* over and over and over.

Lucky as hell, all of us.

14

CATORCE

"Bless me Father, for I have sinned . . ."

I was practicing my first confession before my family, who sat in stunned silence. They didn't want to hear it, but they seemed to me the most appropriate audience. After all, they were the people with whom I screwed up most often. I was seated at the dining room table, with my back to the Jesus window, the same table under which my brother Tony had once, years before, smoked a cigarette stolen from our grandfather Amador and gotten so sick that Dr. Portilla was summoned for a house call.

"Come quickly," I remember my mom saying on the phone. "I think one of my boys is dying."

It had all started so suddenly. There we were, watching a Popeye cartoon on television, and my brother started to make groaning noises behind me, from the couch.

"Ooooooh. Ooouuuarrghhh. Ouououooh."

I turned around to look, from my rocking chair, and was shocked by what I saw. Tony's face was actually greeen. As green as a dead, rotting chameleon, I swear. And he was holding his stomach.

Maria Theresa saw the whole thing. If you can find the portrait, just ask her. I'm sure she'd give you a very colorful account.

Our next-door neighbor, Chachi's father, figured out what had happened before Dr. Portilla showed up, black bag in hand. Only someone in the cigar business could have made that instant diagnosis.

My mom had summoned Oscar. Just for company, in an hour of need, because my dad was not at home and there was no man in the house. In Cuba, you see, neighbors always came to your aid. Oscar, *"Quinientos Pesos,"* did his duty and took his turn at hand-holding. Well, not literally. Cubans don't like that. If you ask Cubans to actually hold hands, especially Cuban men, you might get punched in the face, or worse.

How I hate being forced to hold hands with people other than my wife and kids at Mass during the Our Father, Sunday after Sunday. It's not intended as a penitential rite, but it's one of the harshest punishments ever imposed on me by the Church. Stupid American custom. I'm sure if I checked into it, I'd find out it was started by a heretic.

"I think this kid smoked some tobacco," *Quinientos Pesos* said. "Search the house for a cigarette or cigar butt. I bet you'll find one. Look for a place where he could hide to smoke it. This shade of green comes only from tobacco, I'll bet five hundred pesos on it."

We called Chachi's father *Quinientos Pesos* because everything he boasted about seemed to be worth exactly that much—five hundred pesos. His air conditioner had cost *quinientos pesos,* his television, his sofa, his dog, and on and on. Everything, even the most expensive items, such as his Cadillac, had cost exactly five hundred pesos. This was more than some Cubans brought home in a year.

He loved to boast. He built himself a wondrous house right on the seashore, miles west of Havana, way past Sugar Boy's mansion. The only problem was that construction began about the same time that Fidel rode into Havana on a Sherman tank. By the time this house was finished—and how splendid it was, how modern; it looked like a spaceship, or something from a science-fiction film—he and his family got to live in it for only a year or so. Then they left it behind, and all of its furnishings, and fled to Tampa.

Leaving something like that for the sake of principle must be tough. Especially if you're over the age of forty and you've spent all of your life boasting. Even tougher if all you have to look forward to is a crappy apartment and a menial job in another country where almost everyone thinks that all you're good for is mopping floors and cleaning out urinals. Not easy, the transformation into a spic. Not at all like a chameleon changing his color.

How well I remember that day in sixth grade, at Everglades Elementary School in Miami, when some freckle-faced kid named Curtis told me to keep my "stinkin' mitts" off his lunch tray.

"What are mitts?" I asked, in my still-accented English.

"Dumb shit spic, yer all so stinkin' dumb, why don't y'all go back to yer stinkin' country," was his reply. One of those "stinkin's" was really another English word that begins with "f." I had never heard it before.

It was our maid, Inocencia, who found the cigarette butt under the dining room table. The table had a very long wine red velvet tablecloth, which reached all the way to the marble floor. Tony had hidden under there to puff on his stolen cigarette, and the smoke had all been trapped under the table. Keep in mind these were Cuban cigarettes. Unfiltered. They made Camels and Lucky Strikes seem like kids' toys.

Tony stole cigarettes from *Abuelo* Amador and smoked them in secret at the age of eight. I didn't ever do that—though I took a few puffs from Tony's cigarettes now and then—but I was a sinner too, and had amassed all sorts of blotches on my soul. Now, in second grade, it was time to come clean. I had to confess my sins to a priest, I had to lay out my whole sordid seven-year-old past.

"These are my sins, Father . . ." I began my mock confession.

No one dared play the role of the priest, but they all listened to my sins, wide-eyed, as I read them off one by one. They remained as silent as stones, there, at that table, within sight of the Jesus window, under the eighteenth-century French tapestry that depicted a hunting scene. It was the *Bois de something-or-other,* my dad said, with authority. After all, he had been there, in that very same forest, chasing the prey, hadn't he?

"See those hounds? I loved my hounds. They were so sweet, so smart. But the revolutionaries slaughtered them all and ate them. You know what else they did? They broke into the chapel of Saint Denis, the birthplace of Gothic architecture, that jewel built by Abbot Suger in the twelfth century, and they desecrated the tombs of all the French kings. They ripped the heart out of the corpse of my grandfather, Louis XIV, and ate it. They ate his heart. His dead, dead heart."

What a neat little list of sins I had. But I don't think pride was anywhere on that list, not even in disguise. Just the opposite, in fact: I was so, so proud of the list.

A list. Things you check off as you read the items, one by one. Groceries, things to do, wishes, blots on your soul.

Taco sauce, milk, sponges, orange juice, razor blades, cat litter.

Fix the faucet, mow the lawn, rake the leaves, adjust the brakes on the bicycle, clean out the gutters, renew the passport, fire all the secretaries.

New cars with ten-year warranties, a toolshed, a rooftop apartment in Paris overlooking the Île de la Cité, bathrooms that never need cleaning, a way to undo the past, an end to death.

Lies, bad words, bad thoughts, disobedience, theft.

I knew theft was just about the worst sin on the list after bad words, and I might have actually felt sorry for it. I say "might" because I'm not sure I felt any genuine remorse. I loved to steal. Busy little kleptomaniac I had been. Toys, mostly. What was this deal where the store made you pay for the stuff on the shelves? If they had the toys out in the open, where anyone could grab them, why make you hand over this stuff called money? Especially when they had so many other copies of the same thing you were putting in your pocket. In a bin full of army men or cowboys or cars, what difference does one less make?

"Hey, where did you get that?" The question always seemed to surprise me. How did my mom know I didn't have this toy already? But every single time she caught me. And every time I was shocked by her omniscience.

"Uh . . . what do you mean?"

"Where did that toy come from?"

"Uh . . . I've had it for a long time. You just don't remember it."

"Are you sure?"

"Yes, of course."

After the first question-and-answer session, Marie Antoinette would usually walk away. Then she would return a minute or two later.

"I don't think I ever saw that toy before. Are you stealing again?"

"No. I told you, I've had this soldier for a long time."

Then came the stare. That piercing stare that went straight to the core of the soul. The same gaze you see on some Byzantine icons of Christ. That gaze that says "I know what you've done, and you're a big liar."

What could I do when pierced by those all-knowing eyes? Confess, of course.

"Well . . . *sí,* I took this from the soldier bin at Woolworth's yesterday."

"I thought so. How did you do it? I was watching you carefully."

"I waited until you started talking to that lady with the blue hair. By the way, why do so many old ladies have blue hair? How does it get that way?"

"Don't change the subject. It's hair dye. You know stealing is wrong, don't you? It's a mortal sin."

"Yes, I do. I'm sorry." Sheepish look on my face, with no genuine inner contrition. I knew I'd do it again as soon as I had the chance.

"Next time you do this, you're in for a big surprise."

I'd heard that one before, and the surprise never came. I knew she was bluffing.

But the surprise finally came one day. It was at the Plaza de Marianao, that awful, stinking hellhole with all the butcher shops where they slaughtered animals right in front of your eyes and the air itself seemed soaked in blood. I always found myself breathing through my mouth so I wouldn't have to smell the blood. I also walked around with my fingers in my ears to block out the sounds emitted by animals as they are turned into food.

So different the meat at the Plaza, so unlike the silent, odorless hunks of flesh wrapped in plastic at the Stop & Shop or the Piggly Wiggly. Freshly slaughtered animals, cut up or whole, hanging from hooks, dripping hot blood.

My mom really liked one butcher shop at the Plaza, and we went there too often.

There was a toy stand at the Plaza, tucked away in a corner on the upper level that actually received some sunlight and didn't smell too bad. The toys were awful, like the rest of the place, but they were toys. And they cried out to me:

"We're yours for the taking. Take us. We know you don't like us, but please take us home with you. We'll feel so much better in your sweet-smelling house. Do us a favor, please, take us away from here. Save us. It's not just the smell, you know, but also the screams of the pigs and chickens that drive us insane within this dusty bin. Look at the dust, too. No one ever brings kids here to buy us. We linger here, unloved, unwanted, surrounded by death, suffocating in the stench of blood and freshly cut flesh. Take us, please. Put us in your pocket."

Who could resist such a heartrending plea?

I glanced around for watchful eyes, found none, plunged my hand into a bin without looking down, and put some Cossacks in my pocket. Yes, Cossacks. Dad had told me what they were called, but I still had no idea what they were, really.

Anyway, I walked out of there with Cossacks in my pocket. But how many had I freed? I had to know. So the great Cossack liberator made the mistake of attempting a body count in the backseat of the car as we were driving away from the Plaza. I pulled up the booty to the edge of my pocket and peered down. One, two, three. Great! I didn't even care that these were really ugly toy soldiers. I could always make use of them, maybe by setting them on fire or blowing them up with firecrackers.

"What are you doing?" came the question from the front seat. Marie Antoinette was looking straight at me.

"Uh . . . nothing . . . just looking at my pocket, that's all." I've always been a very unimaginative liar.

"What's that red thing sticking out of your pocket?"

It was there all right. The tall skinny Cossack was sticking halfway out of my pocket, and his red jacket was hard to miss. I didn't even try to lie.

"It's a Cossack . . . I took it." I hardly ever said that I "stole" anything. I merely "took" things.

"This is it." She pointed her index finger straight at me without raising her voice. She never raised her voice.

"Antonio, turn the car around, we're going back to the Plaza."

"What for?"

"Carlos stole some toys again, and we're going to make him give them back to the store from which he took them."

"Okay, good idea." The judge agreed, and turned the car around immediately.

"You're in big trouble now," observed my brother.

"No, no, please. Don't make me do this. I promise, I won't ever do it again. I promise. No, no . . . Can't you or *Papa* take them back for me? I promise, I won't take toys again."

"It's time you learned this lesson," said Louis XVI.

Once back at the Plaza de Marianao, I was sent back in to return the stolen Cossacks. I had very clear instructions: I was supposed to confess to the woman minding the store and hand the Cossacks back, one by one. But I was sent in all on my own, and entrusted with this painful, impossible task. Neither of my parents went with me to ensure that the penance would be performed. You can guess what I did. As soon as I was back in the toy store, I simply reversed my tactics: I looked around for witnesses, and, finding none, pulled the Cossacks out of my pocket and dumped them back in their dusty bin, all the while breathing through my mouth.

How that place stunk. Good God, how it reeked of death.

And how I ran.

I got back into our brown Chrysler, panting.

"Did you hand back the toys?"

"Did you do as we asked?"

"*Sí,*" was my simple reply. No elaboration on this falsehood.

"Good. We're so proud of you," said Mom.

"I guess you'll never steal again after this," added Dad.

Not bad, for a bad liar.

A few months later, perhaps even just a few weeks, I found myself at a very small *quincalla,* a store that sold odds and ends, and the toy soldiers called out to me again from their dusty bin. It was a store named Saxony. Once again I couldn't resist the pleas of the poor, neglected toy soldiers. These weren't Cossacks. They were American army men. Nice and green. I had all of them already: bazooka guy, radio-telephone guy, crawling-with-rifle guy, standing-up-shooting guy, kneeling-shooting guy, grenade guy, bayonet guy, binoculars guy, pistol guy, flamethrower guy, mortar guy, minesweeper guy, pointing guy. But it didn't matter that I had others like them. They called out to me.

"Take us home. We're yours. We belong to you. Free us. We will fight for you."

Using my well-honed skills, I pocketed a few green army men. Freed them from imprisonment in a store named after the land of Martin Luther. Freed them from captivity in the land of arch-heretics, without knowing it.

This time I was much more careful. I knew better than to inspect my pockets in the car. But I got caught at home, damn it, as I was playing war on the marble floor.

"Hey, where did you get those soldiers?" Marie Antoinette, as always.

"What do you mean? I've had these for a while."

"But I thought you only had two grenade guys. I see you have four now."

"Uh . . . no. I've had four all along."

"No, I don't think so. I put them away all the time, and I know you only have two. Where did the other two come from?"

"Uh . . . oh, now I remember: Jorge lent them to me."

"Are you sure? I haven't seen Jorge around for a few days. When did he give them to you?"

"He gave them to me last Saturday."

"But we spent the day at Grandma and Grandpa's house last Saturday."

Then came the stare. That all-knowing gaze. Laser beams aimed straight at the conscience.

"Tell me the truth, come on."

What could I do but confess?

This time around the penance imposed on me was the same as at the Plaza de Marianao, but with a wicked twist. This time, when I went back to the store, both of my parents followed me into the store.

"My son has something he wants to tell you," King Louis informed the clerk behind the sales counter at Saxony. Louis XVI put his hand on my shoulder. I remember the way his hand seemed to have no weight at all and an awful lot of weight at the same time. Light as a feather. And as heavy as my conscience, which finally, at that very instant, seemed to have sprung to life.

Everything that happened in the store after my dad put his hand on my shoulder is now in my vault of oblivion. No details left. This means, of course, it was a reverse peak experience, a Mariana Trench of the soul. I only know that I did what I was supposed to do because my parents praised me for it and wagged their fingers at me some more.

"I bet this cures him," Marie Antoinette said to King Louis as he started the car.

"How bad was it?" asked my brother, who had wisely refused to go into the store.

Silence from me. I couldn't talk for a long time. Maybe even the rest of the day.

I felt genuine remorse for the first time in my life. Or at least I felt embarrassed. Ashamed. Humiliated. Exposed as a thief. Is that the same as remorse? I still don't know.

But I do know that from that day forward I never stole anything. Not even when I was slowly starving in Miami, at that foster home for juvenile delinquents where Tony and I were fed only once a day, at five in the afternoon.

How wonderful those Twinkies and Moon Pies looked on the store shelves. How they sang out to me.

"Take us! Unwrap us! Touch us! Squeeze us! Taste us! Eat us! We belong inside of you. Hear that rumbling in your gut? Listen to that. That's no rumbling, it's a roar. Listen more closely. Hear that nearly imperceptible sound? Those are your bones. They're gasping, bending, growing crooked. And, by the way, when is the last time you went to a doctor, or had a dessert?"

Tempted as I was by the song of the Twinkies, I resisted their siren call. Stealing was wrong, but not just because it was a sin. Stealing was an affront to the mother and father who had driven me back to Saxony and stood with me as I confessed my sin. Stealing was a betrayal of those memories that mattered most to me.

Stealing seemed so wrong that I couldn't bring myself to go along with some of the thugs who lived with me and wanted me to help them steal stuff. Couldn't do it, even when they threatened me with harm. One of them, Miguel, got it into his head to steal an outboard motor from a boat moored at the Miami River, not far from our foster home. We used to go there often to watch fishermen catch nothing or, every now and then, fight off water moccasins with their rods. The place was crawling with all sorts of snakes.

Miguel wanted me and Tony to help him steal this outboard motor and carry it all seven blocks to our foster home, and he threatened to hurt us if we refused. What he wanted to do with that motor, I'll never know. We had as much chance of gaining access to a boat as we did of having an air conditioner installed in our room, or of winning the Spanish lottery. Tony and I refused to join Miguel, but he ended up finding someone to help him and somehow managed to lift it up onto the flat roof of our orphanage.

Social workers called it a "foster home," but it was really an orphanage. Twelve children living in a rundown, three-bedroom house infested with roaches, mice, and scorpions, under the care of two adults who didn't really care for us. Four or five kids to a room. Two in the glassed-in porch. One in the living room. No air-conditioning, no fans. In Miami, mind you. One tiny bathroom for all of us. One meal a day, and plenty of menial labor. Physical and mental abuse from adults and housemates alike.

Anyway, Miguel got his outboard motor. And one evening, as I was in the backyard throwing out the trash, Miguel snuck up behind me and hit me as hard as he could above the knees with a huge, crudely made club, larger than a baseball bat. I think he was aiming for the knees.

"I broke your legs! I broke your legs! Ha, that'll teach you!"

I thought he had broken my legs for real, it hurt so much. He laughed loudly and swung the club over his head as he did some kind of dance all around me, chanting.

Well, he didn't really break my legs. I managed to get up off the ground about ten minutes later. But I did get the largest bruises I'd ever seen, and I had trouble sitting down for a while.

Miguel ended up getting caught by the police a few days after he whacked me. They came to our house, found the outboard motor on the roof, and took him off to jail. His partner had ratted on him.

Very odd, how my conscience gained the upper hand and prevailed. I still resent that victory, deep down. And that, my friend, is a very big problem. After all, a huge chunk of the message delivered unto Moses by God Himself had to do with keeping your stinkin' mitts off things that belonged to others. Check out Exodus 20:15–17: "Do not steal."

"Do not desire another man's house; do not desire his wife, his slaves, his cattle, his donkeys, or anything else that he owns."

Good God in heaven. Even desire is forbidden. Is this harsh or what? Especially the part about donkeys? You can't crave what belongs to others, ever. If you do, your soul is stained. And if it's stained, you're in big trouble.

That's how the Christian Brothers explained it to us. In order to get to heaven, your soul needs to be pure. Think of it as pure whiteness, that's what they told us. Blazing, blinding white, that's how God wants your soul to be. Just one large stain is enough to land you in hell for eternity. One stolen toy, that's all it takes. One covetous glance at a pair of nice new shoes, or the person wearing them, or whatever belongs to someone else. That's all it takes to be plunged into a sulfurous burning pit, where you will be horribly tortured by hideous demons for eternity.

But there's a remedy, we were told. Your soul can be made pristine, scrubbed white, as pure white as a consecrated host. You can make that happen by receiving the sacrament of Penance, by going to confession, and exposing each of your stains to a priest.

And confess I did, after rehearsing in front of my family. Since I was a male I had to face the priest directly in the confessional box. Only girls and women got to hide behind a wicker screen. At the time I didn't know that the screen was there to protect the priest from temptation. I thought women were getting another unfair break.

I read my list of sins to the priest, at San Antonio de Miramar, that cool, air-conditioned Art Deco church surrounded by beautiful homes, bathed in light straight from the highest heaven.

Theft was high on my list. Bad words were nowhere on the list, of course. They frightened me so much, they were never a temptation back then. Bad thoughts? You bet. Nearly everything was a bad thought if you dwelt on it long enough. Lots of malice towards others, especially. Wishing lizards harm, and making your wishes come true. No naked women, though, no dirty magazines. Nothing to do with that troublesome *ecce unde* down yonder, not yet, not really. But I confessed that sin anyway, just in case I hadn't understood Brother Alejandro correctly. Maybe I had. After all, you had to touch it every time you peed. Disobedience? Of course. All the time. Lying? Every single day. My whole life was one big, stupid lie. A transparent lie, too, especially to my mother.

"For all of these sins and any others I have overlooked I am heartily sorry."

"Una confesión muy buena, hijo." That was a very good confession, my boy. Go in peace, your sins are forgiven.

Much to my surprise, I did feel relieved as I stepped away from that confessional. I felt as if some weight had been lifted off my shoulders, maybe the weight of a father's hand.

I also felt proud. So proud of myself for making such a good confession and being spotless inside. If they'd been able to assign grades for this exercise, I was sure the Christian Brothers would have given me the highest possible mark, *Sobresaliente,* Outstanding.

I didn't tell any lies that day or the next, and I didn't kill any lizards either. I managed to resist temptation at many turns, and to make it to my First Communion two days later with a fairly white soul and a perfectly tailored, perfectly bleached white suit, white gloves, and white shoes. The white suit looked oddly out of place at the beach later, at the reception that was held at the Havana Yacht Club. Odd, but as white as my soul.

Or so I thought, standing on the pier of the Yacht Club, sweating profusely in the blazing sunshine, feeling the sharp edge of the starched collar against my neck, looking down at my white shoes rather than at the sea, eating a ham salad sandwich, a perfect triangle of white bread, all white on the outside and pink inside, every trace of the brown crust carefully excised.

One stain had been missed, though. Forgiven, of course, under the rubric of "any other sins I have overlooked." It was the stain of pride.

I remember thinking how nice it was to be at the Havana Yacht Club, how well it suited me, my classmates, and our families. I knew at that age that I was lucky and thought God owed me that luck simply because I richly deserved it. Deserved it more than others.

I would have Fidel to thank for pointing out this pride to me, and "stinkin' mitts" Curtis too, who made me realize for the first time in my life that I was a Cuban.

Thanks, guys. *Muchas gracias.* You gave me what I truly deserved.

And thanks also to the heresiarch who came up with the idea of having everyone in church hold hands during the Our Father. You have no idea how you wound my pride and remind me that I am Cuban. Every Sunday you put me in touch with the abysmal root of all my problems.

I can see that monstrous root now in a way I never could at the age of seven. My first stab at confession was like a leap off a cliff, blindfolded. I rehearsed with my family in the same way Evel Knievel did before any of his motorcycle stunts, with the likelihood of a crash landing in mind, but no real acceptance of the chasm about to be spanned, or the pull of gravity.

"That was an excellent confession," said Marie Antoinette as I finished my rehearsal at the dinner table. Everyone else remained silent.

"Did I leave anything out?"

"No, you didn't. If you confess like that later this week, you'll have covered everything. And you don't have to say you're a thief. You're not anymore."

"Are you sure?" I looked at Marie Antoinette, and then at the others. Everyone but my mother looked away or pretended not to be at the table. Tony hid his face in his armpit.

My mother looked me straight in the eye and said, "Yes, I'm sure."

Total silence. Everyone got up and left the dining room. Tony zipped out of his chair at the speed of light. I remained glued to my seat for a while.

Fast-forward forty-three years. I am confessing to a priest, face to face, cataloguing my soul's dark stains in a sunlit room. The worst ones get the most attention, and this time around they happen to be as dark as they come. Jesus H. Crucified Christ, the gloom inside me is formidable. I recognize these blots for what they are: states of mind and deeds that I am attached to, or even love, but which cause pain to others and diminish me in the process. I am brought face to face with my desire for what's wrong and my dogged avoidance of what's right. Can I really repent for things I don't feel totally sorry about?

I say I'm sorry for not being truly sorry.

The priest looks me in the eye the same way my mother did forty-three years before and says: "Go in peace, your sins are forgiven."

All I can say—all I am supposed to say—is what I say every time: "Thank you, Father."

What I should add, but don't, is: *"Hasta luego, Padre."* See you again soon, Father.

15

QUINCE

Most families give you the keys to the car when you turn sixteen and tell you to go and have fun. In our family, all you get is the key to the family pantheon at the cemetery, and then you're told how to take care of the dead."

This is what my cousin Fernando said to me one day, when I was about seven or eight years old.

"Prepare yourself for the speech that comes with the key," he added. But I didn't need to prepare. I'd already heard all the key phrases many times, even though I was far from sixteen.

"Here you go, Son, when we're dead and buried make sure we get flowers on the right feast days. Here's the list of feasts, take it, and always keep it near the pantheon keys. Also make sure the place is kept clean. Make sure enough masses are said, as required by our last will and testament. Here's the will, keep it with the keys too. And make sure that our bones are moved to the ossuary after a few years to make room for the newcomers . . . like you. And after we're dead, don't you dare do any of the things we've forbidden you to do, like dancing, or wearing loud clothes, or going out with the wrong kind of girls, or—especially—swimming right after a meal.

Remember, you must always stay out of the water for three hours after you've eaten. If you disobey this rule, you will suffer an *embolia* and join us in the pantheon prematurely. Here's the list of forbidden activities. Keep that in your pocket at all times."

Still, Fernando was a good teacher. Better than any I had in school. He had good, practical information about our family.

"Learn this and learn it early, so it doesn't come as a shock later: our family is interested in three things only: ancestors, death, and good taste. But there's a family paradox too. Though we are obsessed with death, we avoid many things that could bring it on, such as wearing shirts without undershirts or taking a shower with the windows open."

Fernando was a very sensible guy. He flew jet airplanes for the Cuban Air Force, and he drove a purple 1947 Plymouth from which he had intentionally removed the muffler. Within a year of revealing the secret of the pantheon keys to me he would also be smuggling weapons and planting bombs all over Havana.

He was the only sensible guy in our family.

How I loved it when he came to visit our house. I never did see enough of him, though, since he was always busy learning to fly jet planes, detonating bombs, or, later, getting sent to prison on a thirty-year sentence.

Fernando was one of my first cousins, the younger son of my father's brother Filo, and he was about eighteen years older than me. He was a grown-up, as I saw it, but he wasn't like any other grown-ups I knew. No one else, for instance, had taken the muffler off his car. No one else would pick me up and throw me in the air, so high that sometimes I almost hit the ceiling. He always caught me too. I never feared being dropped.

The nicest part of being with Fernando was that he always seemed to be having such a good time. No one else in my family seemed to enjoy themselves so much. Not even his brother Rafael or his sister Maria Luisa, who were also lots of fun to be with. They actually had a sense of humor, those three. But Fernando won the prize, hands down.

Vroooooooom, vroooooooom, vrooooooom. You could always tell when he was coming. His car was louder than the pesticide Jeep. And when he left our house, my brother and I would go out to the curb to wave him off so that we could stand as close as possible to that wonderful noise. I also liked to inhale the unfiltered exhaust.

How often I've toyed with the idea of removing my muffler. It would make the car sound and smell so much better. But I now live in the United States, where it's against the law to drive around without mufflers on cars.

Coño. Qué mierda.

I shouldn't dwell too much on Fernando's car, though, for it ruined his life and brought him within an inch of dying. I'm not talking about a crash or a wreck, not at all. More about this later.

Back to death and the dead, one of my family's favorite subjects.

The dead lived with us. They watched us constantly, always criticizing or spewing out rules. At least that's how I felt. My mom wasn't responsible for this. It was my dad and his entire family. Always talking about our family history, always trying to contact the dead, always speaking for the dead.

Before I was born, I'm told, seances were held regularly at my house. Grandma Lola, Aunt Uma, my dad, his sister, and others would sit around the dining room table and try to contact the dead. The same table at which I ate all my meals, the table of my dreams, too, from which I would see Jesus standing at the window. My cousin Rafael told me about this when I was forty-one years old.

How much fun it might have been to see this happen. Imagine hearing the voices of the dead coming through your grandmother or some other living relative. My cousins Rafael and Fernando had a lot of fun, or so they tell me. They used to live in the house, you see. Their father was a diplomat, and while he served in faraway places like Seville, Washington, and Mexico City, they were left in the care of *Abuela* Lola, *Tía* Uma, and my dad. Louis XVI had been a surrogate father to them during much of their childhood. And they loved him.

Fernando and Rafael would always be chased out of the house when the seances took place, but they didn't let that stop them from enjoying themselves. Often, they would eavesdrop just outside the dining room window. They could hear everything clearly through the closed shutters.

Once, they brought a friend along to listen, however, and all hell broke loose. It started as all seances did, with an invocation of the spirits of the dead.

"Oh, spirits, speak to us from beyond the grave . . ."

"Oh, spirits of the dear departed, come join us anew . . ."

"Wait a minute, guys, I've got a great idea," whispered my cousins' friend.

"What?" whispered back Rafael and Fernando.

"Wait and see." Whispered, of course.

"Oh, dear spirits, please, harken unto us . . ."

"Dear souls, we approach you, we implore you, speak . . ."

Silence. Dead silence.

My cousins' friend rose and pulled himself up the dining room window's iron grate—pulled himself up in such a way that he was literally standing along the full length of the window. No one inside could see him, of course, since the shutters were closed. Then, as the silence was at its deepest, this kid let out a very, very loud burp. According to Rafael it was a long, monster burp.

"BRRROOOOOUUUUGHAAAAAAOOOOOOOUUURRRRPPP!"

Panic inside. Chairs moving quickly. Gasps. A scream, probably from my father's sister, the woman without desires.

The dead had spoken in a foreign language.

"Oh, my God, what was that?"

"Ay, qué susto!" Oh, what a scare!

My cousins and their friend ran away from that window as fast as they could. According to Rafael, no one inside that dining room ever found out who had burped. He's still convinced that some of them might have actually taken it for a genuine burp from beyond the grave.

But it wasn't just talking with the dead that was routine in my family. My dad claimed he saw the dead, too. Said he saw them all the time, and heard their voices.

One dark moonless night, walking back home from the Roxy theater with my dad and brother and friends after a stupid Mexican cowboy movie, we passed a house with a large yard and a barking dog, and Louis XVI said to us, "Listen, that dog can feel the presence of ghosts. Dogs see them all the time. And they understand what the dead say, too. They see things and hear things most humans can't see or hear."

"Can you see ghosts?" Manuel asked my dad.

"All the time," responded Louis XVI. "There are several here in this yard, right now, and they're trying to tell us about their tragic deaths."

Dead silence, for a while, until King Louis started to tell us about the buried pirate's treasure that some Chinese ditchdigger had found not far from the Roxy Theater years and years ago. That got the conversation moving again.

Ghost stories were as much a part of my childhood as toys, pranks, firecrackers, and rock fights. Ghost stories told by someone who believed in them and often narrated them as first-person accounts. They must have really scared me, for almost all of them are locked away in my vault of oblivion. All I'm left with is some vague memory of a house where the walls dripped blood, which my dad claimed to have seen with his own eyes.

No wonder when it came time for me to face the dangerous world of romance, years later, I was so ill equipped and messed up so horribly. Boys should learn more than ghost stories from their dads. They shouldn't be taken on too many trips to the cemetery either.

But we went to the cemetery all the time. *El Cementerio de Colón*. Columbus Cemetery. Since Columbus is buried in Seville, Spain, the name was purely honorific. What a place! A true city of the dead, with real streets and marble pantheons that looked like houses. It looked as if it had always been there and would always be there. When we passed under the huge front gates I always felt that we were entering eternity itself.

On most days it was fairly empty of live people, and extremely quiet. Eternity has no noise. Except on certain holidays. On Mother's Day and Father's Day, the place was mobbed, and very noisy. Cubans talk loudly, even in cemeteries. Put together dozens and dozens of families talking loudly on any street of a densely packed cemetery and what you have is a mildly delirious sort of din. We always had to line up in the car just to get in, and then we'd have to fight traffic inside the cemetery itself. Family upon family, all delivering flowers, cleaning the marble grave sites, greeting the dead, grooming their future burial places.

Most of the families we knew had a pantheon—some enclosed, some not—in which preceding generations were buried, and in which succeeding generations would be buried. A few years after each burial, the tombs would be opened and the remains of the dead removed from the burial crypt. Out with the old, in with the new. In most cases, the tropical climate worked wonders with decomposition. A few years, and all you had were clean bones. Most pantheons had smaller niches called ossuaries, where the bones taken from the graves would be collected. Then the crypt would be ready for the next dead relative.

Every now and then, a family would be surprised by a relative who hadn't decomposed. Louis XVI knew about all these problem cases, of course, and told us about them in great detail.

This recycling arrangement meant that every time you went to visit the dead, you were visiting your own future grave. Our father, of course, loved pointing this out to me and Tony.

"You know, this is where I'll be buried. And you'll be buried here, too. And so will your children and grandchildren. That is, unless you build a bigger and better pantheon and move us all. You know, I'd love for us to have a better pantheon. Maybe someday you boys will build us one. Maybe one like Aunt Carmela's?"

Aunt Carmela had a pantheon that resembled its original namesake in Rome. We went there once, and it was cavernous. The marble walls were a golden yellowish hue and very shiny, as though polished with a vengeance. I stared at the wall in front of me for an eternity, or so it seemed, spooked by the sight of Carmela's name etched deeply into the marble above a huge sarcophagus.

"Why is Carmela's name on there if she's not dead yet?" I asked Louis XVI.

"Because it's good to be prepared."

"But death is always so far off," I said, foolishly.

Louis XVI laughed. "Who told you that?"

"Mama."

"Well, don't listen to her. Death is always just around the corner, always ready to surprise you."

Good God Almighty, what a thunderbolt that was. To this day, whenever I see marble, I think of death. Maybe this is why some overdecorated Italian restaurants unnerve me.

And whenever I think of the beach I also think of death. Sudden death. *Embolias* and *calambres.* Strokes and cramps. Somehow I put together my dad's warning in the cemetery with another warning I constantly received at the beach, and the result was an odd association as lasting and peculiar as the one between chauffeurs and dirty magazines.

"You can't go in the water yet. Not for another hour."

This was my mother speaking. She irritated me to no end, and I played the role of a logician, right there, in that fine white sand, with the turquoise sea as a backdrop. And those clouds, those never-finished, ever-changing poems; and the blazing sunshine, that transfiguring, everlasting kiss; and those waves, those endless caresses—all of them bore witness to the dialogue between a son and his mother. Ask them if you can track them down and find them. Not even Fidel could make that beach vanish. And I've long been convinced that every word ever uttered anywhere is somehow preserved at that spot.

"Do I have to wait that long? Why? Maybe you shouldn't have given me lunch, then?"

"You know that if you go into the water before your food is fully digested, you'll suffer an *embolia* and drown."

"What's an *embolia*?"

"It's bad. It can kill you."

"But what is it? What does it do to you?"

"It's something that happens in your brain. It paralyzes you, and if you're in the water, you'll sink to the bottom immediately and drown."

"How does it happen? What does food have to do with it?"

"Your body just can't handle digestion and swimming at the same time. It's some sort of overload. Too much for your body to bear."

"Then why are there so many people in the water? I saw some of them eating a little while ago. Look, they're all fine."

"They're all in grave danger, risking too much. If they don't get an *embolia,* then they may get a *calambre*."

"What's a *calambre*?"

"It's when your muscles get all cramped up and you can't move them. They're also very painful. If you get a *calambre* in the water, you'll drown."

"Even in shallow water?"

"Yes, you might fall down so quickly no one will notice, and you'll be unable to get your head out of the water. Especially if you get an *embolia* on top of the *calambre.*"

I didn't find any of this scary, just irritating as hell.

Mom continued: "I've known of many people who have gone into the water too soon after eating and drowned, or nearly drowned. Most of them got *embolias*."

"Who? Anyone I know?"

"My uncle Emilio, who had just arrived from Spain. He didn't know about the three hours, since they never went to the beach in Galicia. They found him all twisted up in the water. *Todo jorobado*. All twisted up, but he was lucky enough to survive drowning. But one of my childhood friends drowned from an *embolia*. And a lot of other people you don't know."

"But why don't we ever see anyone drowning at this beach?"

Silence. I continued pursuing my line of logic: "I see people eating and swimming, and I never see anyone getting *emboliado.*"

She set me straight: "You don't get *emboliado,* you suffer an *embolia*. And the answer is still *no,* you can't go in for another hour. Your body is still digesting its food. If you go in now, you could die."

"So why did you give me lunch, then? If I have to wait three hours before swimming every time I eat at the beach, it's not worth coming. If I have to wait another hour, it will almost be time to go home when I finally get in the water. Why did you give me lunch? Why?"

"Because if you don't eat, you'll be too weak to swim. And you could drown."

I gave up and went back to digging my trench in the sand.

Maybe if I dig deep enough, I thought, *I could get to China*. I thought that in China, maybe, they jumped into the water right after eating or even ate *in* the water. *Anyone who made firecrackers,* I thought, *had to be smart enough not to have such stupid rules.*

So I dug furiously, dug and dug, until I hit water. "Carlos, be careful. If you hit water in that hole you're digging, don't put your feet into it. You could get an *embolia* that way, too."

No way to win. None.

Embolias and *calambres* at the beach were just the tip of the iceberg. The world was an infinitely dangerous place for my family, full of risks at every turn. *Pulmonía* was always a possibility. Pneumonia. And it was always fatal.

Here are some of the ways in which my family thought you could catch pneumonia and die: standing in front of an open window with wet hair. Going outdoors without a shirt on, except at the beach. Going outdoors in the daytime wearing just a T-shirt, except at the beach. Wearing a shirt without an undershirt. Wearing shorts between November and February. Going outdoors without a jacket between November and February, no matter what the temperature. Taking a shower with water that wasn't warm enough, no matter what time of the year, even on the hottest days. Wearing shoes without socks.

Catching a chill, under any circumstances, was a death sentence. And you could catch a chill in a million and one ways. Being out in the rain for too long, even with an umbrella. Running too quickly from an air-conditioned room into the tropical heat, or vice-versa. Eating ice cream between November and February. Standing in front of an open refrigerator too long. Scraping frost from the freezer and eating it.

God forbid you should ever bathe or take a shower while running a fever. Sudden death would surely follow after that first contact with the water.

These were not superstitions, mind you, but quasi-scientific *theories,* based on centuries of cumulative experience and thousands of reports of *pulmonía* felling someone you never knew directly.

Then there was traffic. Tales of people who had been run over by cars were a constant source of conversation, especially for my father. *Arrollado.* Run over. *Sí, pobre tipo.* Yes, poor guy. *Arrollado.* He didn't see the car coming. *Wham!* Gone. *Pobre mujer.* Poor woman. She didn't look both ways before crossing the street and a bus hit her. Knocked her to the ground, ran over her with its wheels, and then dragged her for a block. And she was pregnant too.

"Ay, Dios mío." Oh, my God. Always a woman's voice for this phrase. Only women were supposed to say this. Don't ask why.

My dad had to deal with a lot of these accidents in court, so I'll cut him some slack. In his world, at least half the people were *arrollados.* The other half were the drivers who ran them over. And I'm sure he had to linger over all the gory details. It was his job.

But for us, *arrollados* were only in stories. Except for the afternoon I actually got to see a guy get hit by a car, while out with my dad.

Well, I really didn't see it happen. I only heard it—a loud noise off to my left as we were crossing a wide boulevard in Vedado, one of the older suburbs of Havana. It was, I must admit, a most disgusting-sounding thud. It sounded like twenty watermelons dropping onto the ground at once. After the thud came the squealing of brakes.

Then I remember hearing a woman scream near us, *"Ay, Dios mío!"* And people running, and more screaming and shouting. And my dad saying, *"Mira eso!"* Look at that. And my dad turning my head with his hands.

A very fat man lay sprawled on the street about a hundred yards away. He was wearing a white shirt and green pants. The man lay motionless on the street, flat on his back, about ten yards behind a car with a smashed-up hood and a broken windshield. His limbs looked awfully funny—twisted like a rag doll's. And he didn't have any shoes on. Some people knelt around him. Soon a circle of people enveloped him and he disappeared from view.

"Look at that. He must have gone sailing over the roof of the car," said the judge.

"What do you mean, *Papa*?"

"I mean that when he got hit, the impact sent him flying over the car, and that's why he's lying there so far behind it. I bet he's dead. No one can survive an impact like that. Look, the car even knocked off his shoes. Whenever that happens, forget it, you're dead."

"How come I don't see any blood?"

"Internal injuries. Bad sign."

"Can we go take a look close up?"

"No, no. Better not . . . ah . . . here are the police. Good. They'll handle it. Let's get going. I'm glad this isn't my district, and I won't have to hear the case. I have more of these than I can stomach."

And that was it. I had seen proof of the danger of traffic. Cars did hit people. It wasn't at all like *embolias, calambres,* and *pulmonía.*

But I was still annoyed by the restrictions placed on my bike riding. Strict boundaries. Can't cross Seventh Avenue. Can't cross this street, can't cross that street. Not by yourself. Never. *Te puede arrollar un carro.* A car could run you over.

I knew it could never happen to me, but I obeyed all the same.

My brother Tony never listened to these rules. I think he rode his bike all over Havana, and my parents never knew. He did this with Manuel and Eugenio. But I didn't, and neither did Rafael, or Jorge, or Julio. We were younger and dumber.

Now, years later, I pray every night that my children will be even dumber than I was.

And then there were always bad people who wanted to snatch you away and hurt you terribly. *Mala gente.* Not just *El Colorado* and his cronies, but legions of bad people whose sole purpose in life was to inflict pain on others. There were specialists among the *mala gente* who targeted children. This we heard from very early on. I guess my dad was all too familiar with this kind of danger too, and had trouble handling those cases.

Like every kid on earth who is warned about *mala gente,* I didn't pay much attention to this. I learned not to accept candy from strangers or to climb into cars with people I didn't know, but I didn't learn to be as cagey as a fox. Which is what you need to learn about when dealing with bad people. They're usually much too clever, especially when they are hell-bent on damaging the lives of others.

How I wish I had listened more carefully to that item on the list of dangers. Right in front of my very own house, one day, after the world changed, not long before I left Cuba, one of those bad people would try to harm me. And if it hadn't been for our neighborhood wino, *El Loco,* who rescued me, God knows what might have happened. But that story will have to wait. Not now; I'm not ready. Just let me say that the guy looked perfectly normal, and that a knife was involved.

For now all I can do is focus on one sweet irony. My family had lots of rules for avoiding peril, and death lurked everywhere for us. Yet we played with firecrackers and went car surfing under killer waves. We also swam in shark-infested waters all the time. Fernando, who understood the rules so well, ended up becoming a jet pilot, and later, a bomber and gunrunner. How could this be?

My family's logic, like Kantian logic, can only take you so far. Maybe if you think about death all the time and are always trying to communicate with the dead, you'll eventually find all sorts of odd ways to flirt with danger, even with death itself.

So, though we sat on the beach for three hours after lunch, waiting for our food to be fully digested, we got to throw rocks at one another. And my dad watched us do it. Sometimes he even helped us find good rocks.

Those were splendid rock fights we had. I can't count how many times we did it, because we did it practically all the time. Usually at vacant lots, or on the street, or down at La Puntilla, on the seashore, where we also flew kites. The best rocks were there. They were all pointy and sharp edged. Killer rocks.

Once, for three or four incredible months, when the gas company dug trenches for a new pipeline in our neighborhood, we not only had an endless supply of the most beautiful chunks of quartz to heave at one another, we actually had trenches, too. And we stocked up on those quartz chunks for future fights. Rocks are recyclable, you know. Even when bloodstained.

What we usually did was break up into two teams and throw rocks at one another. Was there a point to this? Any rules? Any end to the game? No to all three. Stupid questions. This was sheer, pointless anarchy.

We all had scars to boast about. Especially the ones that had required stitches. Eugenio's blond head was full of scars. Manuel had a very nice scar on his head, which always gleamed through his shortly cropped black hair. Tony had one too, though smaller. I had a nice scar above my left eyebrow back then. When my thin blond eyebrows turned into the Black Forest later in life, the scar was swallowed up, and I've lost track of it. Maybe it's still there. I was very proud of it. Especially because it was a scar caused by an almond, rather than a rock.

Yes, an almond. Almonds can do a lot of damage. Forget the almonds we all buy at the store, which have all been removed from their hard, pointy shells. I'm talking about almonds fresh off the tree. The fresh almonds we had at the play yard at my school, La Salle de Miramar, and which we loved to throw at one another.

All this under the approving gaze of the Christian Brothers, of course.

One day we were having a monster almond fight, which was fairly common. We were divided into two camps, facing each other about twenty yards apart, throwing almonds at one another as hard as we could. I was enjoying myself as thoroughly as I always did when throwing hard objects at other children. Then, *WHAM*! I didn't see it coming, but I felt it hit for sure, right above my eye, that almond. A bright, bright flash of light and then utter blackness.

The next thing I know, I'm in the arms of one of the Christian Brothers. It might have been Brother Pedro, since I was in first grade. He was swabbing my forehead with a handkerchief, and it had red stains on it. My forehead hurt a lot. And so did my whole head. And I felt very dizzy.

The almond fight was over, and a circle of kids hovered over me.

"Hey, that's a nice hole."

"Yeah, look, it's so perfectly round."

"A hole? I have a hole in my head?"

"Yes," said the brother softly, "but don't worry, it's not that big."

I felt for it with my fingers, and found it. It seemed big enough to me. And deep.

"I think you'd better go home early today, Nieto. Have your mom take care of you, maybe take you to a doctor. You might need stitches."

Well, as it turned out, I didn't get any stitches. But I did get to go home early and I spent the rest of the day in bed with a very bad headache.

Mothers of the world, imagine what might have happened if the almond had hit me directly in the eye, a fraction of an inch lower? That point was sharp. Very sharp. *Ay, Dios mío.*

Yes, I was lucky most of the time, and so were all of us, come to think of it. We all took direct hits to the head and face, and no one lost an eye or a tooth. I did get hit in the eye by a rock once. Jorge threw it at me. I think what saved me was the fact that Jorge was only about seven years old at the time and couldn't pack much of a punch. I had a very nice black eye for a while, but no eye damage.

I also took direct hits to the ears, twice, and to the mouth, three times. I lost count of how many rocks bounced off the back and top of my head. How about the forehead? Just a few hits, but none as tremendous as that almond.

But Ernesto was not so lucky. No.

Ernesto didn't know what to do in a rock fight. He was so inexperienced. But every now and then, there he'd be, and he'd try to join in. Like that one day at La Puntilla, when my dad brought him along with the rest of us. On that fateful day we had a monster fight. Maybe Ernesto's presence brought out extra hostility in our rock throwing that day.

As always, we picked up rocks so fast we hardly had time to look at them. Some were on the large side. We scurried over those sharp-edged rocks like crabs looking for their lunch in the tidal pools, picking up whatever we could find and throwing it. Then we started to throw more furiously than usual. A few hits here and there. The requisite *"Ay!,"* the occasional, forbidden *"Coño!"* The laughter. You should have been there. We laughed every time someone got hit. We laughed when we missed. We laughed and laughed. If Adam and Eve hadn't screwed up so badly, and their children had been able to play in the Garden of Eden, they would have laughed just like we did that day, when we threw rocks at one another on the edge of the turquoise sea.

But we were in a different garden. And we were picking up larger and larger rocks to throw. Fist-size rocks at first. Then larger and larger and larger. We couldn't throw these big ones as far or as hard, but it was fun to watch them fly, and to hear them thud when they hit the ground. These big rocks were easy to duck, at least when they came at you one at a time.

But it was raining big rocks. And it was getting harder and harder to throw and duck at the same time. Experience was the key to survival.

My dad watched this all with a bemused look on his face. Not a word from the King of France. Maybe he had watched peasants doing this for amusement on Sundays and feast days. He seemed totally unworried.

Eugenio, *el Alocado*. Crazed Eugenio. You should have known better, nutty Eugenio. You picked up a jagged rock way too large, about the size of an American football, and you heaved it with both hands. We all saw it fly through the air, twisting and turning as it valiantly tried to defy gravity. All of us saw it except Ernesto, who had bent down to pick up a rock of his own. The rock began its descent just as Ernesto was raising his head. And it became painfully clear to all of us that Ernesto's face was in the path of the rock, and that it was moving too fast for him to avoid it.

I know it happened quickly, but it seemed to take forever, that meeting between Ernesto's face and Eugenio's rock.

Few noises in the world compare to that of a large rock breaking someone's nose. I won't even try to describe it; really bad things are better left to the imagination. Imagine the sound of a nose being totally flattened all at once. Imagine, too, the sound made by the consciences of seven boys who don't know if they feel all that sorry to see another boy's nose crushed.

Ernesto passed out. He was knocked out cold, just as I had been by the almond. But this was no almond. This was a small boulder. And it put out Ernesto's lights with fifty times the force of my stupid little almond. King Louis rushed over immediately, moving faster than I had ever seen him move before, and cradled Ernesto's head in his arms.

Ernesto was bleeding as none of us had ever seen anyone bleed, not even in a movie. Blood was streaming out of what had been his nose like two small rivers. Not at all like the champagne that had spurted out of Jorge's nose for a few seconds at that wedding where he and I got drunk. Not at all like the tiny rivulets that dribbled down Kirk Douglas' face in *The Vikings* when his eye was mauled by a hawk's talons. These were two swiftly flowing rivers pouring forth from Ernesto's nose, two strong red gods. And they had no intention of drying up, or going away anytime soon. But my dad managed to tame them, to slow down the bleeding with his handkerchief.

I've often wondered if cousin Fernando's nose bled like that when he was tortured by Fidel's men. Did his nose bleed more or less when he was beaten? About the same? Did anyone laugh while the blood flowed? I've also wondered: did Fernando's gums bleed as much when he pulled out his teeth with his own fingers, one by one, in his dark, dark cell, during those twenty-three years in prison?

Ernesto was out for a long time. King Louis tried to revive him, gently, but Ernesto just lay there, as limp as the *arrollado* I had seen get hit by a car. We all stood there speechless, examining Ernesto's face and my dad's. Antonio Nieto, my father, looked so pained, so worried, so angry. I was too green and too thickheaded then to know that love and worry are two faces of the same coin, and that if you flip that coin fast enough, you can also see anger. I just thought he was angry at us.

When Ernesto finally came to, my dad helped him into the car and rushed him home so he could clean up before going to the hospital. Only a Nieto would do something like that. God forbid you show up at the emergency room with a broken nose, and possibly a concussion, bleeding profusely, with bloodstains on your shirt. Clean shirts were a must. And you had to have that undershirt, too. A clean one.

It took a very long time for Ernesto's nose to heal, and it never looked right again, even after surgery. The doctors managed to give him a nose again, but it was all twisted, and he was left with the queerest whistling sound as he breathed. You could always tell when he was near because of that whistle. It was an angry whistle, I swear it was. Every breath Ernesto took from that day forward was filled with resentment, and each of those whistles, each and every breath, was a word of sorts. An angry word, each breath, forming sentences, and paragraphs, and pages, and books. Volumes and volumes of God knows what kind of bitter invective against us, Judge Nieto's sons, and towards all of our friends.

We who weren't Ernesto went on living our lives as always, under the blazing sunlight by day, under our white mosquito tents by night. We woke up almost every single morning to the sunlight streaming in, revealing dust in the air, swirling silently. If we had listened carefully enough, I'm sure we could have heard the dust and also the sunlight falling on each speck of dust. I know we could have, if we'd only tried. I know this as I know other things that are hard to prove.

Some mornings we woke up to find a lone mosquito trapped in the tent. The buzzing was loud enough to be mistaken for an alarm clock, or a car without a muffler, especially when the mosquito landed on your ear. And sometimes they did just that. Those mosquitoes didn't know when to quit. Trapped inside the tent all night, a whole human body all to themselves. They would gorge themselves so much they could hardly fly.

Too happy for their own damn good, those bugs. Too noisy too. Buzzing so happily, so deliriously. So loudly. *Vroooooooooommmm.*

Maybe as loudly as the dust and the sunlight. Maybe as loudly as twenty watermelons hitting the ground all at once.

Those of us who weren't Ernesto, I repeat, went on living our lives as always, breathing through both nostrils, silently, waking up sometimes to find a lone fat mosquito in our tent. I don't know about the others in their beds, but I always made sure that the big fat mosquitoes who had spent an entire night drinking my hot red blood paid for their last supper. I squashed them all, flattened them like Ernesto's nose. They popped between my fingertips, and I loved to hear that sound.

And my own blood would go spurting out of their tiny little squished bodies, flying out in tiny droplets that stained my fingers and the mosquito tent in the same pattern as hibiscus blossoms. And I heard that, too.

I had no fears. Not then. Not yet. Pantheons, *embolias, arrollados,* bad people, rocks in the eye. Death. Heard about them all, and didn't really hear at all. All of them for others, not for me. What did I know, really? What did any of us know? We couldn't hear the dust specks. Couldn't hear the sound of our own end approaching, second by second.

Vroooooooooooooooooooommm!

"Hey, Carlitos, jump in! Let's go plant some bombs! Jump in, quick!"

Vrooooooooooooooooooommm!

How I wish you'd asked me, Fernando. How much, how deeply I wish you had.

16

DIECISEIS

They appear suddenly, out of nowhere, when I least expect it. They float into view, and linger there longer than all the others, without changing shape, or changing so slowly as to fool me into thinking they can't change at all.

They claim a lot of the sky, always making sure that there is plenty of blue between them and all the others. In all directions. And they're never upside down. Sideways, sometimes. But upside down, never.

They come in all sizes. Perspective is their favorite language for kidding around. Some of them are foreshortened. Some are elongated. Some are compact. Some are almost abstract. Some are cubist. The cubist ones are my favorites because they know they are puns.

What to make of these clouds I see so often? These clouds in the shape of Cuba?

In the past thirty-eight years I've seen eight thousand nine hundred and seventeen clouds in the shape of the island of Cuba. I know this because I keep count, and the number is always etched accurately in my brain and in my heart. When I die, feel free to saw open my skull and paw through my brain. I bet you'll find a spot that looks like a cloud in the shape of Cuba.

Feel free to open my chest, too. I bet you'll also find a scar on my heart that looks like a Cuba cloud.

You accuse me of making this up, or worse, of being insane?

Okay, yes, I'll admit it: I'm making up the exact number. I don't really keep count. Who could? I do see them all the time, though. As to being nuts, well, maybe I am—but not in the way you think.

I saw one of those Cuba clouds this afternoon, on my way home from work, hovering over the highway. If you'd been in the car with me, I could have pointed it out to you. And you would have been forced to say, "My God, you're right."

The first time I saw one of these clouds was in the Pedro Pan refugee camp for kids who had come to the States without their parents, in Homestead, Florida. There we were, sitting outside the dining hall, another newly minted orphan and I, our backs against a chain-link fence, and this other kid says to me, "You know, the clouds in Cuba were so much prettier."

"Naah, you're just homesick," was my reply.

"No, I mean it, take a look. These clouds just don't compare."

I looked up and inspected that Florida sky full of puffy clouds. I tried to find a difference between the sky I was looking at and the sky I had seen all of my life until ten days before that one, but I couldn't detect any difference at all.

"I don't really see what you mean," I told my fellow orphan.

"You're just blind, that's all. This sky is very different. It just doesn't compare to the sky in Cuba."

I started thinking how this guy was already well on his way to becoming a very bad poet, and then, out of the corner of my eye, I saw it. A long cloud in the shape of Cuba, and it even included the Isle of Pines, that smaller island to the south of Cuba where my cousin Fernando was imprisoned.

I had never seen a cloud like that before. It came as a great shock to me then, and it still amazes me every time I see one. It's too grand a practical joke on the part of God, or nature, if you prefer.

They pursue me, these clouds. I've seen them everywhere. In Bluffton, Ohio, over a whole town without fences. In Reykjavik, Iceland, of all places, not far from the Arctic Circle. In Mexico, as I neared the summit of the Pyramid of the Sun. In Minneapolis, at sunset, through subzero air. In

Wolfenbüttel, Germany, right above a pet store named *Vogel Paradies*. In Tarzana, California, over a freeway as wide as the Mississippi River. In Watseka, Illinois, suspended above one of the sorriest looking parks on earth. In Rome, while strolling through the Forum, just as a snake emerged from the ruins. I've even seen one in Kalamazoo, poised directly over a conference of scholars, unnoticed by a thousand and one medievalists.

Do they see me?

Under these clouds I pursue the life given to me. Under them I pine not for what I lost but for what I've never had and perhaps shall never have. What is always out of reach. These Cuba clouds are not so much reminders of my past as omens for the future. But what future? What could they possibly, silently, forecast?

Spun from dreams, they seem, in spite of themselves, in spite of their appearance and presence. Yet I won't be too surprised the day a bolt of lightning surges from one of them, cleaves me in two, and reduces me to mere cinders and vapor. I should expect it. Maybe even indoors, in the unlikeliest place, I'll be struck while my back is turned, when my guard is down. Maybe while I'm sitting in someone's wood-paneled office. Maybe in the presence of superiors, one of them will annihilate me. Those clouds are capable of the worst treachery, I'm sure.

Perhaps they are pesticide clouds. Exquisite breathtaking poison.

Time ran out on me this afternoon. Ran out with a vengeance. Shortchanged, I shuffle off. Arriving at my home, I leave a Cuba cloud outside, allowing it to disappear on its own terms. If I can't see where they come from, I feel I shouldn't keep track of them or try to see where they end up. Besides, I don't know which one of them might kill me someday.

My youngest son emerges from behind a wall, as always, runs towards me at full speed and plows into me, head first. His hard little skull slams into my gut like a cannonball. I wince, as always, let out an honest *ummph,* and thank him for being such a brave charging bull, as he wraps his pure little arms around me.

"Good bull hug, Bruno. Great. One of the best, ever."

My daughter Grace smirks and rolls her eyes. I wink at her. My oldest son, John-Carlos, smiles. I pray for that moment never to run out, as all the others have, as this afternoon ran out. I ask that the bull hug and the smirk and the smile never evaporate or turn into clouds, too.

But I know better.

Next time I emerge from this house in the woods, bound for some other point A, or point B, or C, or N, or Q, or Z, any finite point, another cloud might or might not be there. I never know when exactly, or where, but I know there will be one, for sure, when I least expect it, when my guard is down.

"There it is again," I'll say when it appears out of nowhere, the crocodile-shaped island, my once and future lizard. So sublime, so ethereal, so far from reach, so clever and unfathomable, so supercharged with the power to enchant and annihilate me at the same time.

Such an odd, silent clue. Such rare evidence, so absurd, this, my fourth proof for the existence of God.

17

DIECISIETE

"Here, have some more, you'll grow up to be just like me."

Nilda, my nanny, God bless her, was just trying to get me to eat some more rice and black beans. She meant, of course, that I'd grow up to be big and strong, with a back as straight as a royal palm, and a heart that could cheat death a thousand times over.

But that's not what I heard. No.

What I heard Nilda say from my high chair was that if I ate some more rice and beans, my skin would turn black, just like hers. The color of black beans. *Negro.* I would turn into an African.

I knew even then that there was something awful about being black in Cuba. African Cubans weren't too lucky, from what I could see. They seemed to do all the hard work, and to have inferior bathrooms, like the one at the rear of our house, where I saw Inocencia's breasts.

As to the possibility of turning a different color, it seemed very real to me. Didn't some lizards change color all the time? Those green, green chameleons could turn brown in an instant, as you looked at them and they looked right back at you. I'd seen it often enough at that early age. The lizards were everywhere, always flaunting their metamorphic prowess. If lizards changed color so easily, why not humans?

For a very, very long time after that experience with Nilda, I wouldn't eat any food that was black or brown. Nothing dark. Not even chocolate.

I remember my mother, especially, trying to reason with me.

"Please, Carlitos, how about trying this nice Nestlé, this chocolate bar?"

"You know, it won't turn you black. It won't."

"Believe me. Trust me. Why won't you believe me? Go ahead, try these raisins."

But the thought of turning into a black boy, an African boy, scared me even more than Candlestick Lady.

In one of his many display cases, Louis XVI had a porcelain candlestick from the eighteenth century with the figure of a woman on it. She was wearing something green, and she was crouching. The hole for the candle was actually behind the woman's back. I think she was a fairy of some kind. Candlestick Lady was the first woman in my dreams, and the first dream bully. She was there long before Maria Theresa, even before Window Jesus, the Jesus of my dreams. In my dreams, she used to come out of the display case and chase me all over the house. And I knew she meant me harm. How, I don't know. I just knew she was up to no good at all.

Fortunately, she never caught me. I always woke up just as she was about to touch me with her evil little hands.

Sometime after I started dreaming of Candlestick Lady, she was joined by an even scarier character, Torso Lady. What a tag team. Candlestick Lady and Torso Lady, chasing me all over that scary house, my house, in my dreams.

Torso Lady was unique. She was just a torso, with tiny little stumps where her arms, legs, and head would have been. She was about the same size as Candlestick Lady, maybe about five inches high at the most. Six, tops. She ran pretty fast for a tiny headless midget without legs. I think she ran faster than Candlestick Lady, as a matter of fact, because she was always in front, and always about to catch up with me.

Where she came from, I don't know. Maybe I had seen too many mutilated carcasses at the meat market. Maybe I drew upon pictures of ancient Greek or Roman sculptures that lacked heads and limbs.

I know it wasn't the Venus de Milo. I know because the very first time I came face to face with her at the Louvre in Paris, at the age of twenty-nine, I broke down and wept. She was so beautiful I couldn't stand it. Even without arms. Her stumps made her seem all the more gorgeous because they made her seem so vulnerable, so much less of a statue, so much more like a living, breathing woman. It was this, I think, that took her straight the core of my soul and ignited it.

What a fool. I've always been such an idiot in this department. Maybe this is why I hate Immanuel Kant so much. Hate and envy are always close to each other. Maybe I envy a guy who can love his garters and his narrow reasoning so much. A guy like that could never fall for a beautiful woman, or even an ugly one. And certainly never for an ancient statue of a woman without arms.

Anyway, back to Torso Lady: she bore no resemblance to Venus de Milo, and this is how I know that the statue at the Louvre was not the inspiration for my infernal dream stalker. Torso Lady was squat and chubby. As far from heavenly as possible, and she ran so awfully fast. Venus de Milo would never run like that, and if she did it wouldn't look as if she were hurrying at all. That's how it is with beautiful women. Nothing they do seems to be a strain for them, even when they outrun you, or pin you to the mat, or outwit you, or tell you to drop dead.

One day I got up the courage to petition Louis XVI.

"*Papa,* please, could you get rid of Candlestick Lady? Could you sell her? She scares me so much. She chases me almost every night in my dreams. She's so mean."

"Don't be silly. It's just a *candelabro*."

"Please?"

"No. *De ninguna manera*. No way. You're just being silly."

"Could you at least hide her so I won't have to see her?"

"No. She's very rare and valuable. She's one of my prize items."

"Please?"

The answer was always no.

I learned at a very early age what mattered most to King Louis: those objects in the house. They consumed him. Eventually, he would choose to stay with them rather than join us in the States. I know it's infinitely more complex than that, but anyone looking from the outside, or a child looking from the inside, would have to say that the man preferred his art collection to his very own children. So, in a way, Candlestick Lady and her cohorts did end up chasing me out of the house.

Sorry, *Papa,* but that's how I've seen it for a long time. But you've already forgiven me for this in a dream, so you can't hold it against me. And you chose to forgive me in the same dimension as that in which your objects cursed me and pursued me, wishing me harm.

Someone, stop me, please, before I try to turn this into a fifth proof for the existence of God.

No one would be better suited to stop me than the Chinese hot dog man. No metaphysics involved in his trade. His hot dogs and french fries transcended all others on earth without philosophizing. The taste was heavenly, true enough, and I think that hot dog man knew the spiritual secrets behind his cooking, but he was always tight-lipped about it. I don't think he knew much Spanish, as a matter of fact. Only enough to take orders from his customers and repeat the order in a thick accent. I tried talking to him many times, that sage, but he remained silent.

"Hot dogs. Fried potatoes. Very good." That was the sum of his philosophy.

Those hot dogs and fries were out of this world. I've spent the rest of my life searching for something to equal them. They were tiny little fries. Shoestring fries. He cooked them on the spot for you, in an oil-filled wok. He had them all cut up already, and he would take a handful or two and throw them into the hot oil. They would hiss and sputter and make the nicest little bubbles as they cooked. And the smell. Inhaling fifty thousand dollars worth of cocaine would never get you as high as you could get beside his wok, at the corner of Ayestarán and Bruzón, right around the corner from my grandparents' house.

My grandmother was annoyed that my brother and I preferred the Chinese guy's hot dogs to her Spanish cuisine, but she grudgingly put up with it. Hard to beat the Chinaman, after all. He was as wise and expert as those priests who made firecrackers back in China.

We went to my grandparents' house every single Sunday, without exception. It was great to spend Sunday at another house so far from our own, in such a different neighborhood. The buildings there were all so close together. No front or side yards at all. And most buildings were occupied by two families, one on the bottom floor and another on the top. The street-level apartments had porches, the second-story ones had balconies.

My brother and I loved the balcony. It was such a good spot from which to launch paper airplanes, or from which to spit.

How we loved the spitting. Gathering up enough saliva in your mouth to launch a great big liquid bomb was a challenge in and of itself. But we would do it, time and time again.

"Big one!"

"Bigger than yours! Look at that splat on the sidewalk!"

Sometimes we'd try to get as close as possible to the pedestrians underneath without actually hitting them. Sometimes we failed, and the huge drops of spit would land on them. Then it was time to hide in my grandfather's room or on the staircase, and pretend nothing had happened.

One time my brother threw lighted matches over the balcony, and one landed on a man and burned his shirt. The man knocked on the door, furious, and came up and made quite a scene. My brother, master of lies, denied he'd done anything. The man kept pointing to the burn hole on his shirt and demanding that we buy him a new one. The more he ranted and raved, the calmer Tony's lies became and the more hurt he acted. Finally, my grandfather gave the guy five pesos, and he went away, cursing. But on the way home, Tony pulled the matches out of his pocket and showed them to me.

There was also a lizard's tail in his pocket. He loved to pull them off. Sometimes he caught lizards just so he could rid them of their tails, and watch the tails wag, all on their own, apart from the lizard. They had a life of their own, and it was amazing to see them move. On most lizards, I think, the tail grew back. But on some, it didn't. We had one lizard in the backyard we always recognized because of its stump of a tail. It looked almost human, with its tiny stub at the rear.

I loved going to my grandmother and grandfather's house. The sunlight on their porch was so bright, and they got the Sunday newspaper. We never got the Sunday paper at home, so theirs was the only place where I could enter the worlds of *The Katzenjammer Kids, Alley Oop, Prince Valiant, Terry and the Pirates,* and other American comic strips, all translated into Spanish, with titles that didn't always resemble the English originals. *Alley Oop* was *Trucutú*. Good thing, too, for Cubans would have pronounced that as *Ah-yey-Óh* and turned the caveman into a disguised African deity, like Saint Lazarus and Saint Barbara.

Before the world changed I didn't spend much time talking to my grandparents, or to my mother's sister and brother. That would come later. I was way too young to care about talking to grown-ups, before Fidel came along. And by the time I began to talk to them, it was time to leave.

But I always felt so calm around them. Their presence was so soothing. *Abuelo* was a mountain of sorts, with snow-white hair, so solid, so silent, so unmovable, so sure of himself. *Abuela* was so sweet and so solid. Years later, when I made the trip to her ancestral home, I would come to understand how much she resembled the stone houses of Galicia, with their walls about two feet thick.

And I loved the way they spoke Spanish. Both of them had very thick accents and lisped their *c*'s and *z*'s with utter abandon. Sometimes they made fun of the way we mangled the language of their homeland.

"Listen to these little Cubans: they speak Castilian so poorly. How cute they are."

My grandparents always called Spanish "Castellano" because their native tongue was Gallego, the dialect spoken in Galicia. Some Gallegos take their own language very seriously. When I finally got to meet my grandfather's only surviving brother in Galicia, who looked just like Alec Guinness, he refused to speak Castilian Spanish.

My mother's sister Lily was so affectionate and sweet that my brother and I could only respond by being mean to her. How we loved rifling through her jewelry box, which looked to us like a pirate's treasure chest. Tony and I would take pieces of her jewelry and hide them all over the house. For the remainder of the week, Aunt Lily would have to spend time looking for her jewelry as she dressed for work each morning. Sometimes she would phone our house and ask if we could please tell her where we had hidden her necklace, or her pin, or her earrings.

And she never seemed to get angry about this, or yell at us. On the contrary, every Sunday she greeted us with the biggest hugs and told us how much she loved us, her very own Katzenjammer Kids. And every Sunday we would find better places in which to hide her jewelry.

She is the closest I think I have ever come to unconditional love.

My mother's brother Mario was even more of a mountain than our grandfather. He was about six feet three inches tall, a tightly wound bundle of energy, self-confidence, and good humor. He always called me Cabo, which means "corporal" in army ranks. And he loved to smack me and

Tony on the head with his knuckles while he told us jokes. Forty years later, he is still one of the funniest people I know, and one of the most optimistic.

I've forgotten when and why Uncle Mario began to call me Cabo, but I shall never forget the nameless hot dog man from China, *El Chino de los perros.* Those fries, I tell you, were a work of genius. The onions too. I don't know how he managed to dice onions into such small chunks. Any smaller, and they would have been microscopic. And the smell of the stuff frying in oil was nice enough to make me ignore the exhaust from the buses that passed by just a few feet away.

I often wonder how he ended up in Havana and what he thought about as he silently prepared food for Cubans. I wonder how it felt to be the lone man from China there, at the corner of Ayestarán and Bruzón. After all, we can adapt quickly to the strangest circumstances, sometimes better than animals, but we can't change the color of our skin, or the way our tongue handles unfamiliar sounds.

We can't regrow anything either. Once we lose some appendage, all we are left with are stumps. Like the stump on Louis XVI's neck after his run-in with the guillotine in 1793. Or the stumps on the ever lovely Venus de Milo.

I often wonder where *El Chino* might be now. He was only about fifteen years older than me, which means that there's a good chance he's still alive somewhere. I'm curious about him, personally, but would also like to know if he's still making those killer hot dogs and fries.

Back to Nilda and the black beans and rice, then, as long as I've circled back to the subject of food. Nilda was very kind to me, and always attentive. But she hardly ever spoke to me. As she took me for seemingly endless strolls through the park or watched me play, she said nothing. Except, of course, for her invitation to become an African.

She might have spent more time with me during the day than my own mother, or my grandmother. I had Nilda, and my brother had Hilda. We each had our own nanny, and we had them for a long while.

Rearing three children of my own has made me wonder about my parents and the lives they led. Especially because my wife, Jane, and I have done it without relatives, nannies, or baby-sitters of any kind. My parents had one nanny for each child, a maid to do all the housework, one grandmother, one great-aunt, and one aunt in the house.

No wonder my dad could type labels for each of his objects, make kites, referee rock fights, and take us car surfing. No wonder my mom could make us costumes for parties and spend so much of her day designing and making clothes. There wasn't even a lawn to mow. Plenty of tiles and plenty of *canteros,* or planting beds, full of foliage and flowers, but no lawn. How I've envied them sometimes, my parents, especially after three hours of mowing. All that time they had on their hands.

Whatever work needed to be done in the house was done by African women. And whatever hard work needed to be done in the world, that is, my world, always fell to African Cubans, men and women alike. All the Regla boys who dove for coins were brown or black. And Regla itself was full of brown people. I couldn't help but notice that the neighborhoods and houses of dark-skinned Cubans tended to be downright nasty.

I noticed the absence of dark-skinned Cubans as much as their presence. There were no black or brown kids in any of the schools I attended. Not even light-skinned mulattoes. Not one kid with African features, except, perhaps, for President Batista's kids, who were rumored to have black ancestors. There were no blacks allowed at the beach clubs. No blacks ever attended the same movie theaters we did. No blacks ever went into the same churches that we attended. They just stood outside begging.

Of course, there were no Chinese people at any of these places either.

So when Nilda asked me to join her in being discriminated against, my immediate reaction was to panic. It wasn't exactly a hunger strike. It was more like a boycott—out of fear, not for the sake of some principle. The worst part of it was not being able to eat chocolate. Those Nestlé bars and all the ice cream that suddenly became poison. It was too much to bear. I don't know how many times my mother and others tried to tell me that it was impossible for dark foods to turn you into an African. My entire family repeatedly tried to show me that nothing could happen by eating chocolate or black beans, or by drinking coffee right in front of me and saying: "See? Nothing can happen. You won't turn black."

I simply didn't believe them. I thought it was some kind of curse placed directly on me, and me alone. I was the only white person who would be turned black by dark foods.

I stayed that way for months and months. Maybe even longer than a year.

Then one day, suddenly, I decided to brave it. When the ice-cream wagon came around, I decided to ask for a chocolate-covered ice-cream bar. It was a beautiful horse-drawn wagon, the same one that came past our house almost every day. The driver, of course, was a black man. My mom was there, as always, money in hand, ready to pay the ice-cream man.

"You're ordering chocolate?"

"Sí."

Silence.

I unwrapped the ice-cream bar and hesitated. It was so brown. As brown as the ice-cream man. As brown as Nilda. As brown as the woman with no legs who begged outside several churches in Miramar. You couldn't avoid her. Even if we went to a different church, she always seemed to be there, wherever we went. It was almost as if she were following us, Sunday after Sunday. She had no legs, only stumps. And she used to pull her skirt up so we could see her stubby, mutilated legs, which were horribly scarred at their rounded ends, above where her knees would have been.

I closed my eyes and took a bite from the chocolate-covered ice-cream bar, thinking this might be my last moment on earth as a white boy. I savored the ice cream in my mouth, allowing the chocolate crust to slide off the vanilla ice-cream core and melt on my tongue. Such a wonderful, familiar taste, just as good as I remembered it to be. I had trouble opening my eyes after that first bite. But when I finally opened them, I immediately glanced at my hand.

I was white. White, as I'd always been. Whew!

The ice-cream man caught me looking at my hand and grinning, and gave me one of the strangest looks I ever saw as a child. Then he tugged on the reins, made a clucking sound at the horse, and rolled away to sell more ice cream to white kids.

They'd been right after all, those who told me that dark food couldn't turn you into an African. What they didn't know was that it would take only one brief plane ride to turn me from a white boy into a spic. And I'm reminded of it every time I have to fill out a form that lists "Hispanic" as a race, distinct from "white" or "Caucasian."

It wasn't any food that stripped me of my whiteness. No. Just one forty-five-minute plane ride over the turquoise sea. Well, let me correct myself. Since I flew out of Cuba a few minutes after sunset, the water wasn't turquoise at all. It was starting to turn dark blue, and the farther north we flew, the darker the water became.

By the time we had reached the lights of Key West, the sea was black. Pitch black.

And behind me, in the inky darkness, my tail was flapping like mad in Fidel's pocket.

18

DIECIOCHO

She bought us comic books every Wednesday, the woman without desires, my father's sister. Tony and I would wait eagerly for her to get off the bus and walk home from the corner.

"Did you get me a *Batman* this week?"

"How about me, did you get me a *Donald Duck* with Scrooge in it?"

I was the *Batman* fan. Tony liked Scrooge McDuck because he had a vault full of money and a diving board from which to jump into it. That was always his aim, my dear brother, to be as rich as Scrooge McDuck and to be able to dive into a vault full of money.

He never made it. He told me today, again, during one of his daily phone calls, that he loved me and that he had no money at all. He also tells me he's close to death all the time, and I believe him. He can barely walk twelve feet without feeling short of breath. He has no teeth, no job, and no hope. Maybe this is why he won't stop eating hot fudge sundaes, even when dangerously close to a diabetic coma.

He's a mere shadow now, a specter trapped inside a failing body. But back then, in Havana, he was a spirited boy with braces on his teeth and dreams of becoming a multimillionaire.

My ambition was to fight evil in a great costume like Batman. Of course, I would have liked having awesome preternatural powers like Superman, but fighting evildoers on a purely human scale, like Batman, seemed more heroic to me. After all, I knew I'd never develop X-ray vision or the power of flight, but I hoped that someday I'd be able to jump from rooftop to rooftop.

I still have no idea what my father's sister, Lucía, dreamed of doing, or whether she ached for anything at all. She was such a shadow of a woman. Very nice, and loving, in her own cool distant way, but not quite there most of the time. Her room was at the rear of the house, right next to the dining room. She kept the doors closed most of the time and hardly ever emerged.

She read a lot. Sometimes she would watch television with us. But aside from that, I don't think she did much else. She never attended the university. Never worked either, not until she was already fifty-nine years old and her mother died. Then, freed from her mother's supervision, she took a part-time job at one of the finest jewelry stores in Havana, selling expensive stuff to rich ladies.

It was a great store to visit, full of display cases that were lit from within. The smaller counters were full of all sorts of jewelry. The larger display cases, which stretched a long way to the back of the store, were full of bulky silver objects: teapots, pitchers, platters, candelabras, picture frames. I think most of Brother Néstor María's favorite crème de la crème mothers and grandmothers shopped at that store. I know President Batista's wife did. She was one of their best customers.

The store, Petriccione's, was next door to a restaurant called El Carmelo, and next to the restaurant was a newsstand that sold comic books. Every Wednesday, when the comics came in, our aunt bought us each a new one.

Sometimes, on those rare occasions when King Louis and Marie Antoinette went out together, Aunt Lucía would be left in charge of us. Tony and I hated those nights because she made us go to bed at seven. Her own bedtime was around eight o'clock.

Tony and I would resist, but we always caved in after some mischief, such as jumping back and forth between our beds. Once, on one of those nights when she was in charge, we jumped on the beds so wildly that Tony broke one of them. *My* bed, of course.

After a couple of years we figured out that if we were quiet enough to fool her into thinking that we'd gone to sleep, she'd go to sleep herself and we'd be able to stay up until our parents came home, listening to the radio in our room, playing games, or breaking each other's furniture. Once she went in there and shut the door, that was it for the night. Even if all hell broke loose.

Years later, with Ernesto in the house, this would prove to be a very bad thing.

But while we were little and Ernesto wasn't there, it was harmless enough. We always hated the way she said *pyjamas* (peeyahmas) instead of *pajamas* (pahyahmas), but once we learned to take advantage of her lax supervision, we didn't mind her baby-sitting at all.

Years later, when I was a college student, she would end up living with my mother and me in our basement apartment in Chicago. I discovered that she had once played the piano very well and that she was fluent in English. She knew a lot about history and art and music, but she seldom shared her knowledge with any of us or tried to put it to use. She was an immensely proud woman who seemed to know a lot about who were the "right people" and which were the "good families." But she was proudest of all about her self-confinement and self-restraint, a demeanor that she expected from all of us.

She scolded me in Chicago for listening to the wrong music, dancing, drinking beer, keeping my hair long, and growing a beard. As always, what she said had little effect on me.

I couldn't understand her. Even then, knowing her better, I couldn't detect any kind of burning desire in her. She read a lot and watched television. She was more of a shadow than a woman, and it seemed she had always been like that.

My mother tells me that Lucía never had any friends and that she never even had suitors when she was young. Her whole life before the Revolution was spent at home with her family. No parties, no chaperoned dates. No lovers. No dancing, none at all. No nights out on the town. No days at the beach. In Havana, of all places!

Which goes to show you that just about anything is possible.

But is it really possible to have a life without desire? I still refuse to believe it. Not even Meister Eckhart, wrapped invisibly in the cold fog in fourteenth-century Cologne, achieved a life without desire. Forget selflessness. Forget *gelassenheit:* forget forgetting the world and what the "I" lacks.

We all hunger for so much that we imagine even the dead still need us. So we frequent cemeteries and place flowers on graves.

Saint John of the Cross, who fervently desired not to desire anything but God, also failed. Poor Saint John, fellow spic, at least he was honest. He admitted his failure. He knew that the shortest distance between two beings is always a labyrinth, and that its very design is desire. He also knew that his passion for God was not different in kind from any other love and that desire itself was the ultimate proof for the existence of God. Who on earth could fail to recognize his plea, save those with hearts of granite?

> *Show yourself to me,*
> *and let your gaze and your beauty kill me;*
> *for the wound*
> *of love, it can't be healed*
> *save by your being here.*

Forget the five proofs offered by Saint Thomas Aquinas, forget the ontological proof of Saint Anselm of Canterbury, forget Blaise Pascal's wager, forget the four contemptible proofs I have offered here. Saint John made them all superfluous. Desire proves itself most eloquently and painfully. Desire is God, and God is desire.

In the dark of night, the frogs piercing the gloom with their ceaseless croaking, my loved ones asleep, both far and near, my own wound festering, I refuse to believe that Lucía had no desires.

I simply refuse.

And so does Saint John in heaven. It doesn't take a mystic or a poet to know this. Any moron listening to the radio should know, instinctively. Desire oozes from every piece of music. Twenty years ago, the Cuban writer Guillermo Cabrera Infante sat in my sky blue Volkswagen Karmann Ghia, about ten inches away from me, and told me:

"Las canciones populares han reemplazado la poesía en este siglo." Popular songs have taken the place of poetry in this century. He was dead serious.

I agree. And this is why I play my stereo as loudly as possible.

My aunt must have had unrevealed desires, at least a labyrinth or two into which she tumbled. In that world, before the Revolution, the world of Lucía Nieto and many other Cuban souls, male and female, the world of those who could afford to be stiffly proper and hold their emotions in check, much could be hidden.

I got a glimpse of Lucía's desires after the world changed. Two glimpses, actually. First, I saw her strike up a friendship with her cousin Addison after he returned from the States for good. They became very good friends and often went out together. I asked my mom once if he and Lucía would ever get married. "What a silly question," she said, laughing.

I didn't think it was silly. But of course, at that time I didn't know there was something odd about Addison sharing his home with a sixteen-year-old boy who was a circus acrobat.

I wonder whether my aunt ever suspected Addison of being gay. Did it matter? She seemed to enjoy Addison's company, and at the very least she desired his being there, as Saint John might have said.

He was the only friend she ever had.

I got another glimpse years and years later, when she was close to death, living in a nursing home in Uptown, one of the worst neighborhoods in Chicago. She was about ninety years old, so frail that she was unable even to watch television or eat solid food. So I began to bring her milk shakes from McDonald's. Vanilla shakes, in paper cups, with a plastic straw.

She lived for those shakes. She told me she did. But she didn't have to tell me. Her guard was down, obliterated by age and by exile. There she was, living in a place she hated, surrounded by strangers and all sorts of the "wrong people," betrayed by her own aging body, so far from home, so far from sunshine.

Her eyes lit up like klieg lights at a Hollywood premiere whenever I walked in with that shake in my hand.

She had lost so much. A whole lifetime lost. Property lost, too. I didn't know it when I was a kid, but Lucía owned our house in Havana. Not King Louis, as anyone would have assumed. We all lived in *her* house. And she lived in the rear of her own house, nearly invisible. The house had belonged to her mother and she had inherited it.

"Go get your own house and stop turning mine into a museum," Lucía could easily have said to my father. But she never did.

She was supposed to die in that house, her own house, in her own room, as her mother and aunt had died, nursed and ushered into the after-life by her family rather than by orderlies in a noisy, busy, over-lit Chicago nursing home that reeked of disinfectants.

Instead, she left the house behind, and her one friend, her cousin Addison, at the age of seventy-six, because she couldn't stand what Cuba had become. She left her brother King Louis and Ernesto in charge of the house that now belonged to all the people of Cuba. She knew life would be tough in the States, but she never could have imagined how tough it would really be.

"Ay, Carlitos, gracias por el batido." Thanks for the shake.

"De nada, tía." You're welcome, aunt.

She grabs my hand and squeezes it, feebly.

Flashback.

I'm running on the sidewalk that is shaded by the breadfruit tree, running to greet my aunt, who has just stepped off the bus. It's a Wednesday, and the weather is perfect, as always. The edge of the shadows on the cement are razor sharp. The cigar-shaped, blood red hibiscus blossoms are opening wider with each passing second. As I run by them, they sigh with relief. I'm too busy now to rip them from the bushes and dissect them, or to tie them up so I can see whether the force that opens them is strong enough to pop the string, so I can find out how strong their desire really is. Tony is right behind me. A tail-less lizard is hiding nearby, hiding so well we don't see it, the very same tail-less lizard that Lucía will mention immediately upon getting off an airplane in Chicago years later, on a cold, cold, gray day, the tail-less lizard who, as she put it, asked her to tell Tony and me not to hurry back to Havana, please. Aunt Lucía is wearing one of her dark old-lady dresses with polka dots. Her gray hair glistens in the sun like one of the silver teapots at her jewelry store. She walks slowly, as always. Tony and I reach her as she steps over the curb, at the corner. She's walked about twenty feet from where the bus dropped her off. My brother and I have run about half a city block in the same amount of time. We ask for the comic books, and she pulls them out of her large purse. She gives each of us our Wednesday present, slowly. Our hands don't touch at all. There's a hint of a smile on Lucía's face, but I'm too busy to notice. I take what is rightfully mine, what I desire and deserve each and every Wednesday, and purely out of habit, the habit she expects me to have, I say the proper words.

"Ay, tía, gracias por el Batman."

"De nada, Carlitos."

19

DIECINUEVE

The shoe slid like a hockey puck across the marble floor, hit my big toe, bounced off, crashed through the glass on the display case, and landed right inside an eighteenth-century cup, heel first. Cup and saucer wobbled a bit in protest but ended up accepting the presence of the shoe.

Goal!

But that wasn't what we were trying to do at all. Tony and I had taken off our shoes inside the house, which was strictly forbidden except at bedtime, and he was trying to slide his shoe down the long hallway from the living room all the way to our bedroom. My toe just happened to be in the way. It was a one-in-a-billion shot.

The instant that shoe bounced off my toe and headed towards the display case, we both knew we were in big trouble.

The shoe stuck out of the cup at an angle and looked uncomfortable. The cup looked disgusted. The glass shards on the floor and inside the display case looked devastated. My big toe was bright red and it throbbed like Yoruba drums during a spirit-possession dance. Just then, as I was about to start crying, Louis XVI emerged from his study.

"What was that? I heard glass breaking."

Silence, for an instant.

"Oh my God, my Louis XV cup! Oh—My display case! . . . Aaaaarghh!"

That awful guttural sound made my skin crawl. But the sound of the belt sliding off his baggy trousers was more awful still. It was a very familiar sound. All too familiar.

Swwissshhhhhhhhhhhh!

Without even asking who was responsible for filling the cup with a shoe, Louis XVI swung his leather belt over his head and brought it down on my shoulder.

Swishh, whack!

Up again, *swishh,* down again: *swishh, thwack!*

Right across my back, just as I was trying to get up.

Up again, *swishh,* down again, *whack!*

The back of my neck this time.

I was screaming and crying at the same time: "But . . . it wasn't my fault . . . *Ay!* . . . I didn't do it . . . *Ay! Ay!* . . . *No hice nada* . . . I didn't do anything . . . really . . . I didn't."

Swish, thwack!

Across my butt this time. By now I was standing up, though doubled over in pain.

And Tony was nowhere in sight. He had fled the scene of the crime instantly, leaving me all alone to face the wrath of the Great Collector.

I tried running away from my dad while trying to explain what had happened, but it was no use. The Judge had weighed the evidence with his customary speed and pronounced me guilty on the spot. Then he had instantly turned into an executioner. Twenty lashes with a wide leather belt! Scourge away, show no mercy! There's nothing like swift justice, administered by a real judge, believe me. The welts stayed with me for a while, but not anywhere as long as the memory of my brother's betrayal or my father's wrath.

You didn't want to mess with his collection. No way.

Our house was not a place in which we frolicked. Everywhere you turned, there was something fragile and valuable. Lucky for us we lived in the tropics and could play outside all the time. Even when it rained, we could play on the porch. Or in our room, where there was nothing to break, except our beds.

I got whacked for the bed Tony broke, too. He was the great evader, the master escape artist, the king of blame shifting.

Tony must not have been as skilled in evading punishment at school, though, for I do remember him having to stay late for after-hours detention, and sometimes even for Saturday detention. He wasn't among the worst, though. Not once did he have to kneel in the gravel out in the hot sun.

Ernesto *was* among the worst, but he never got punished for anything around the house. No, instead he ended up with all the goods. Justice might be most intensely blind in a judge's own home.

Hey, but that collection was something else. Something sacred, at least for my dad. It was what he cared about the most, what had sunk deepest into the core of his soul. If I'd been a Calvinist minister instead of a Catholic and his son, I would have accused him of idolatry and blasted his ears with censure: "Inflamed with love for graven images and baubles of all sorts, a supplicant at their empty, bogus feet. Idolater! High Priest of false gods! Inflaming yourself with idols at every antique store!"

And if I'd been a *santero,* I'd have said something like: *"Reparte los dioses, compay!"* Share the gods, buddy! Don't keep them all to yourself! Dot the landscape with shrines!

Eye Jesus should have had his own church in Havana. God knows what the voodoo and *santería* crowd would have dreamed up for him to do. Maybe they'd have turned him into *Jesús de los Buenos Ojos:* Good-eyed Jesus, protector supreme against the evil eye. Or maybe X-ray Jesus, *Jesús de los Rayos X,* supreme advocate of those who wished to see right through women's clothing. Or *Jesús de la Pelota,* Ball Jesus, supreme guide of all baseball players who must always keep their eye on the ball. Or *Jesús de la Lotería,* Lottery Jesus, great visualizer and prophet of winning lottery numbers.

I can hear the prayers, even now, in far-off Connecticut: *"Oye, Jesusito lindo, mírame con esos ojitos azules tan chulos, persígueme con tu vista, y dime que número va a salir en la lotería mañana."* Listen, pretty little Jesus, look at me with those cool little blue eyes, pursue me with your gaze, and tell me which number will win the lottery tomorrow.

Every one of those objects in our house could have had its own church or temple, and altars full of votive offerings. Eye Jesus could have collected eyeglasses by the thousands, and lottery tickets, and baseballs. Perhaps even dresses and underwear taken from those women who had been scoped out and successfully wooed by men with X-ray vision.

Imagine also the Shrine of Maria Theresa, patroness of everyone with a foul mouth, where all the prayers would end with *coño* instead of "amen," and where all the votive offerings would involve dirty magazines—and chauffeurs, of course.

Or the Basilica of Candlestick Lady, patroness of lithe, shapely legs, healer of varicose veins, avatar of sexual encounters, advocate for pursuers of fugitives, and guardian against power outages.

Or *El Sagrado Templo de la Taza del Zapato,* the Sacred Temple of the Shoe Cup, which would have been bizarre enough to attract an infinite, inexhaustible number of devotions, most of them probably having something to do with gambling, love potions, and foot fetishes. Sex and money would surely be the most popular dimensions of devotion to this cup and to any other sacred object in Cuba.

Of course, since these objects belonged to my father, we could have pocketed a good percentage of the donations made at these shrines. This income would have allowed Louis XVI to travel and buy even more objects. What a happy cycle of buying and setting up shrines my dad could have enjoyed! How fabulously rich we could have become!

But no, my dad kept the objects all to himself, guarding them like Cerberus, the dog at the gates of the Underworld.

God forbid that one of our friends should damage his stuff! More than once, some friend broke something or came perilously close. More than once, friends were expelled from our house and barred from re-entering it for a long time. Once one of our friends came dangerously close to being banished forever.

Of course, it was Eugenio, *El Alocado.* One day, as he ran into the living room, Eugenio knocked over a small enameled picture frame. It crashed to the floor, the enamel on one corner of the frame disintegrating on impact with a sound like a very small, very weak firecracker.

"What happened?" My dad bolted out of his study and into the living room. "Oh, my God, no, no, not the frame! No! Nooooooo!"

Not a word from any of us. Eugenio tried to slink away.

"Who did this? Who?"

"Eugenio did it," Tony was quick to point out.

"Get out! Get out of this house right now, and never, ever come back. You hear me? Never, ever. You're never setting foot in this house again. Out! Out! Now!"

I had never seen King Louis yell so loudly and so angrily at one of our friends. Eugenio made himself as small as possible and, without saying a word, walked out the front door. Then my dad called Eugenio's parents and told them that he never wanted to see their son again.

Coño, qué mierda!

Somehow, eventually, Eugenio managed to have his sentence revoked. But whenever he played with us after that, *El Alocado* always hesitated before entering our house.

Any day could turn into Judgment Day at our house. A thousand and one booby traps surrounded you, all set to trigger the worst possible reaction from our judge, father, and executioner.

It was a lot like life itself, at least as my teachers would have it. Life was a labyrinth freighted with booby traps of all sorts. Temptations to commit sin. Temptations to choose evil instead of good. Temptations by the billions and trillions and numbers beyond naming. Temptations that could ruin your life in the here and now. Temptations that could lead to woe at Judgment Day and, afterwards, for eternity.

At the end of every life, we were told, a Judge awaits. God the Father, God the Judge. Or was it Christ? I don't know about the other kids, but I was a bit confused. Who judged you, and how many times? There was a judgment when you died and one at the end of the world, the Final Judgment. Or were they one and the same? And if they weren't the same, was it the Father who judged you first, right after death, and the Son later, at the end of time? I couldn't sort those out. All I knew was that judges who were fathers could be tough as hell.

Hell. Ah, *el infierno*! Fire, endless fire.. Torments beyond any that Batista's police could dream up. Demons. Ugly, mean ones. Much worse than the *diablitos* at the university museum. Everlasting suffering beyond anyone's imagination. An infinite number of firecrackers blowing up on every part of your body constantly, forever and ever. An infinite number of apelike demons biting your ass and every part of your body, forever and ever. An infinite number of fat demons sitting on your head and burying it in red-hot sand forever and ever. An infinite number of pointy almonds striking every part of your body, forever and ever. An infinite number of friends lying to you, breaking promises, betraying you forever and ever.

Repetition was key to the representations of hell our teachers unveiled to us. Without repetition, the eternal dimension would have seemed flat and less frightful. Hell, they emphasized, lasts forever.

And what did forever mean?

"Ah, Carlos, good question. Infinity is beyond comprehension. The best we can do is employ images to convey a sense of infinity. You want to know what 'forever' means in terms of hell and the suffering that awaits us there? Well, answer this question first: if all of the oceans on earth were to be filled with sand, and a bird were to remove one tiny grain of sand every million years, how long would it take for all of the sand to be removed?"

We gave all sorts of answers, but all of them were wrong.

"All right, you want to know the right answer? The right answer is this: ridding the earth of all that sand, grain by grain, in one-million-year increments would take only a fraction of the time one would spend in hell. The whole process would be only an infinitesimally insignificant fraction of the eternity that is hell. So small a fraction as not to count at all. Almost the same as zero. Eternity has no end."

And one sin could take you there. Just one.

My third-grade teacher was the master of hell and damnation. Rumor had it that he had tried to become a Christian Brother but hadn't made it. The rumor was probably true, because this man really knew his eschatology.

He was short. Probably between five feet three and five feet four. And he looked a little bit like the Mexican actor Cantinflas, except without the silly moustache. His hands were in proportion to his slight frame but had very long, thin fingers. They reminded me of the tines on the pitchforks that devils supposedly carried around in hell—those pitchforks with which they loved to skewer you forever and ever.

Imagine my surprise when, many years later, I stumbled across the work of Caesarius of Heisterbach, a thirteenth-century Cistercian monk who collected stories such as the ones that our third-grade teacher told us. What a revelation to discover that I'd been reared in the Middle Ages. What a thrill to discover that it was Caesarius who had been speaking to us third graders in Havana, within sight of the turquoise sea, at the very same time that tourists flocked to our island seeking all sorts of pleasures, most of which were unavailable or illegal back in their homelands. Brother Caesarius had spoken to us from beyond the grave even as Fidel Castro was waging guerilla warfare against Batista's forces in the eastern end of Cuba.

I remember most of the stories *el profesor* told us in third grade, along with the beads of sweat that appeared on his face while he told them. I have to share two of these with you.

Here's the first one. A little boy once fell in with the wrong group of friends. He had been a very good boy up to that point in his brief life, but these bad boys started to twist his soul towards the devil. One day, these evil friends encouraged him to take God's name in vain, and he did it. That night, he went to bed as usual, but in the middle of the night a huge, terrible, smelly black dog came into his room and took him away. The next morning his parents found his bed charred beyond recognition and no trace at all of their boy. The devil himself had come to drag him down to hell.

Of course, the specific words uttered by the boy were never revealed. This made it more suspenseful, and brought you almost to the brink of coming up with your own execrably vain name taking.

Now for the second one. A little boy once fell in with the wrong group of friends. He had been a very good boy up to that point in his brief life, but these bad boys started to twist his soul towards the devil. One day, these evil friends encouraged him to blaspheme, and curse the Virgin Mary, and he did it. That night, he went to bed as usual, but in the middle of the night a violent thunderstorm erupted, and a bolt of lightning came right through the window and struck him as he slept. The next morning his parents found his bed charred beyond recognition and no trace at all of their boy. The devil himself had turned into a lightning bolt and dragged him down to hell.

I warned you about the repetition.

How about one more? One that involves beads of sweat.

One night a monk is praying in his cell. This monk has not exactly been living up to his vows. (Once again, no specific mention of what was being done, or not done, by this monk.) Well, there he is praying away but not feeling too sorry for his sins, and *whooosh!* one of his fellow monks, now dead, shows up, enveloped in flames. The heat and the stench are unbearable. The live monk asks the dead monk: "What are you doing here?" The dead monk says he's been sent up from purgatory to warn his fallen brother to stop sinning, repent, and go to confession, lest he too end up in the flames. The live monk asks: "Are you in hell, then, brother?" The dead monk replies: "No, brother, I'm in purgatory." The live monk makes the mistake of saying: "Well, then it can't really be all that bad for you, brother. After all, it's only purgatory." Wrong thing to say. "Hold out your hand, brother," says the dead monk. The wayward monk puts out his hand obediently, though he is frightened out of his wits. The dead one wipes a single drop of sweat from his brow. And then he lets this tiny, lone drop of sweat fall upon the open palm of his live brother. Ouch! Ouch! Ouch! That drop of sweat sears a hole the size of a host in the monk's hand and then hits the cold stone floor, fizzing and hissing. Then, as expected, comes the lesson from the dead monk on a five-minute furlough from purgatory: "If that's what a single drop of sweat from purgatory can do, imagine what it will be like for you to endure these flames for thousands and thousands of years. Then imagine how much worse hell will be! Amend your life, brother, and pray for me, so I may be released from this torment."

Snuck in hell, didn't I? Just like my third-grade teacher used to do.

Second grade had been a different kind of hell. I've told you about this already: that's when we learned to distinguish between venial and mortal sins. What I haven't told you is that it was in second grade that we learned about hell on earth, too.

Hell on earth was our classroom.

Practically every inch of space on our walls was taken up by dead animals that had paid a visit to the taxidermist. And the taxidermist was none other than our teacher. Most of the animals were native to the island, but there were a couple of common dogs and cats too. I remember bats, iguanas, several kinds of rodents, birds, turtles, fish, and, in the left front corner of the classroom, a large *majá,* or Cuban boa, curled around a suitably sized tree limb. You can imagine how much I liked that boa.

We never heard a word about these animals. Not a single lesson on Cuban wildlife. I think the teacher just wanted to intimidate us. Cross him one time too many, and the next item on the wall might be your carcass.

And it was so easy to make this guy mad. Very irritable, this man with the big black moustache and the thick glasses. Any time something happened that he didn't like he would punish the whole class. For instance, if he heard a noise he didn't like but hadn't seen who'd made it, he'd ask us all to turn in the offender.

"Who did that? Who whistled? Tell me now, or no one gets to go to recess today."

Most of the time we squealed willingly on one another. Then *el profesor Taxidermista* would design some punishment for the guilty boy and let us off the hook. One of his favorite penalties was to make the malfeasant stand in the corner of the classroom for the remainder of the day, next to the boa. If the offense was committed just before lunch or late in the afternoon, this wasn't too bad. But if the punishment was inflicted when the whole morning or the whole afternoon yawned before you, the consequences could be dreadful. You see, so long as this reprobate stood in the corner, he wasn't allowed to go to the bathroom at all. Not even during recess.

I don't know how many times I watched my classmates holding their crotches, dancing in pain by the boa, and pleading with *el profesor* to let them go pee. But the more they squirmed or pleaded, the angrier he became, and the more he threatened to extend the torture to the next day, and the day after that, and even for a whole week. Naturally, no seven- or eight-year-old boy will persist in the face of such threats.

I don't know how many of my classmates I saw pee in their pants, up there by the boa. I lost count. *El profesor Taxidermista* would then ask one of us to fetch the janitor. The janitor would show up with a bag of sawdust, a push broom, and a large dustpan. After heaping some fragrant sawdust on the yellow puddle, he'd allow it to sit there for a minute or two, and then sweep it all up and take it away. Then he'd come back with a mop and wipe down the floor under the boa. Meanwhile, the boy with wet pants was not allowed to move for the remainder of the morning or afternoon.

They stood up there, all these boys with wet pants, their shame on display. We were too young and untamed to feel sorry for them, or at least to let others know that we did. We laughed, sometimes, and made fun of them afterwards.

Coño, qué mierda.

But it didn't always work that way.

Sometimes none of us knew the identity of the offender. Then there was hell to pay. No recess, or even worse. Like the time someone left an offensive drawing on *el profesor Taxidermista*'s desk during lunchtime, while he was out of the room.

"Who left this on my desk? Who drew this? Tell me now, or no one gets recess for the next three days. And no one gets to go to the bathroom either."

Silence. None of us knew who had drawn whatever had offended *el profesor* so very much. We didn't know what had been drawn, either, since he wouldn't show us.

"One more chance, boys. Tell me immediately, or it's three days without moving from your desks all day, except to go home for lunch."

We all looked at one another, hoping the guilty party would confess. Having the burden on your conscience of seeing all of your classmates punished for what you alone had done was often enough to make the offender buckle. It was an old Nazi trick. We knew it from American war movies. Sometimes, in these films, the Nazis would wipe out a whole town full of people as punishment for the wrongdoing of one individual. Maybe *el profesor* had seen the same films?

But this wayward artist must have had no conscience at all. Or maybe too much fear. Whatever his reasons, the little bastard sealed his lips and allowed us all to be sentenced to hell. For three whole days.

I was one of the first to pay the price. I paid it that very first afternoon. I'd had a lot of lemonade to drink with lunch. Really good lemonade, made with freshly squeezed lemons and tons of sugar that you could see at the bottom of the pitcher, a thick, cloudy sediment even after you stirred it. Someone had brought us a whole basket of lemons that morning.

Afternoon recess came and went and there we were, still in our seats. My bladder had been sending me signals since before the time that would have been our recess. Very soon after our non-recess, the signals began to intensify. Then they turned to pain. Enough pain to make me raise my hand and beg for a chance to go to the bathroom.

"No. No one gets to go anywhere. No exceptions. Maybe *you* can tell me who drew this awful picture?" He held it up backwards, so none of us could see it.

"But . . . but . . . I don't know who drew it. Could I please step out for a minute? Please? I really need to go. It's hurting a lot."

"No. And if you keep asking I'll extend the penalty for two more days for the rest of the class."

Dirty looks from everyone.

By that time, the pain had become so unbearable that I lost control completely. And what a sweet feeling it was to let go. I think that might have been my first genuine ecstasy, emptying my bladder, right there at my desk, feeling the warm pee trickle down my legs. *Gelassenheit*. That's what it was. I let go, completely, utterly.

But the ecstasy faded fast. I looked down at my feet and noticed, much to my surprise, that a puddle was forming at my feet. The yellow puddle kept growing and spreading to my left and right, across the narrow aisles that separated my desk from those of my immediate neighbors.

I tried to pretend nothing had happened.

The guy to my left, however, noticed soon enough.

"Eeeww, Carlos wet himself. Look at the puddle: it's huge!"

Everyone craned their necks to look at my feet. And I panicked.

"It's not me," I said. "It's Pepe, there, in front of me. It's his puddle. Remember, he has trouble holding it. He wet his pants in the corner of the room a couple of weeks ago."

Pepe, of course, stood up and showed everyone his pants were bone dry. And he asked me to do the same, while he gave me a dirty look. I gave up pretending then. Those seated around me could see my wet pants.

Meanwhile, *el profesor Taxidermista* sat back and watched my humiliation with detachment. When everyone was done laughing at me, he asked Pepe to fetch the janitor. After the sawdust had been spread and swept and the floor had been mopped, I sat there all afternoon with wet pants and a red face, looking out the window and trying to pretend I wasn't there.

The classroom had a beautiful view of the Gulf of Mexico and the cloud-dappled tropical sky above it. So did my third-grade classroom. Such beauty, such peace in sea and sky.

Not always, though. One rare stormy day in third grade, a kid said he had spotted a tornado over the water and we all rushed to the windows. Much to our disappointment, no one saw anything that resembled a twister or a water spout. The kid swore up and down that he had seen it, but I didn't believe him. Neither did most of the class.

False prophet.

But maybe he had seen something else. Maybe, I thought, he had seen Jesus returning to earth, on his way to judge everyone and destroy the world.

El fin del mundo. The end of the world. The words sent shivers up and down my spine, and still do. I'd seen illustrations of it in my religion book, even though we skipped over that lesson, and also in a popular magazine at my grandmother's house. Long-haired, bearded Jesus seated on a throne up in the clouds, surrounded by armies of angels. Chaos and utter ruin on earth. People frightened out of their wits. The earth opening up, mountains crumbling, the seas full of giant tidal waves. The dead rising from their graves, all bare-ass naked. Very scary stuff. Especially the part about being naked in front of God and everybody.

The article I had seen in that magazine, *Bohemia,* was entitled "Will the World End in the Year 2000?" And it contained all sorts of information that had been neglected by my teacher, *el profesor Infierno*. There were umpteen quotations, taken straight from the Bible, that proved without a doubt that the end was very near indeed. I subtracted 1958 from 2000 and came up with forty-two. Forty-two years!

If I'd been a girl I might have said, *"Ay, Dios mío."*

Instead, I sank into a silent panic. I thought about that article for months, all through third grade. And I kept all the fear and worry tightly bottled up. As I saw it, the world was scheduled to end in my lifetime. I would be old, yes, a gray and wizened fifty-year-old geezer, bent over, perhaps confined to a wheelchair, but I'd live to see it.

I began to wonder whether the prophecies were off by a few years. What if the experts had miscalculated by a decade or two? How about three decades? Four? Maybe the end could take place at any moment?

Then one Sunday, in church, the priest read aloud the passage from the Bible in which Jesus says that the end of the world will take place when people least expect it. Yikes! They'd left that one out of the *Bohemia* article! Maybe the world was about to end in a few days!

I began to scan the blue sky for signs of the end. I tried to peer into the clouds, hoping I might spot Jesus approaching astride one of them before everyone else did. I wanted time to run to the first priest I could find and confess all my sins before the lines at the confessional became too long. I went to bed in a panic many a night in third grade, fearing the end was near. It would be so hard to beat the others to the confessional in the middle of the night.

But it was the daytime sky I focused on the most, the sky outside my classroom. I saw the most beautiful clouds in all shapes and sizes, and in all shades of white and gray. (No Cuba clouds back then, no.) Hundreds of them, thousands, tens of thousands maybe. I didn't count them. I looked for Jesus, that's all I did. Soon my grades began to plummet, and my eyes to fail. I couldn't read the blackboard or the subtitles on films at the movie theater. Everything looked fuzzy, as if it were turning into a cloud.

It was at the Miramar Theater, as we watched Cantinflas and David

Niven in *Around the World in 80 Days,* that my mother noticed me straining to read the subtitles.

"Here, try my glasses, Carlitos. Tell me if you can see better with them on."

It was a miracle! I could see again. The fuzziness was gone!

She was nice enough to suggest that I keep her glasses on for the rest of the movie. She was also wise enough to point out that no one would be able to see me wearing women's glasses in a darkened theater. They were pale green harlequin frames, with curving tail fins at the ends.

A few days later we went to the optometrist and I became a four-eyes. I picked out big square eyeglass frames made out of real tortoise shell. Cuban tortoises, I bet, probably the same species as one of those on my classroom wall. The same kind of frames Fidel wore back then. I'd seen his photo in *Bohemia*. Come to think of it, I'd seen a picture of Fidel holding a rifle in the very same issue that had the article about the end of the world. I thought his beard was cool. And also his eyeglasses.

I knew Fidel was somewhere in the mountains, fighting against Batista. Anyone who was against Batista must be good, I thought. Batista tortured people and ran a corrupt government. I'd heard about the corruption from my dad, who was no great fan of any politician. He preferred a monarchy, of course, and for him all politicians were bad simply because they weren't kings. He gave us no details on the corruption, but I believed him. As to the torture, I'd heard about it since first grade, from many sources, but more recently, I'd heard about it from my uncle Mario. His wife's brother had been arrested and tortured by Batista's police. He didn't go into details, but he said his brother-in-law had been subjected to awful cruelty.

That was all I needed to know. Anyone who treated human beings like lizards couldn't be a good president. He had to go. And the sooner, the better, so we Cubans could at least enjoy a brief spell of decent government before the world ended.

Equipped with my Fidel glasses, I scanned the clouds even more feverishly than before for signs of the end. Such great details I had missed! I could see every leaf on every tree, every billow on every cloud. Now, for sure, I'd be able to spot Jesus riding those clouds, descending into Havana over the turquoise sea, ready to pronounce sentence on us all. I knew that God the Father figured in there somehow, but I wasn't sure exactly how. It was Jesus who worried me because he was the one pictured in the illustrations I'd seen. He worried me because all judges worried me, as did fathers. I knew what they were like up close. All too well.

Swwissshhhhhhhhhhhhh! Whack! Swishh, Thwack! Swishh, Whack!

Of course, instead of inspecting the clouds, I should have been scanning the hills and mountains of eastern Cuba. Doomsday really did arrive that year, when I was in the third grade. And the judge sported a beard all right, just as in Catholic iconography. But the rest was all wrong. He also dressed in olive-green fatigues, sported cool-looking tortoiseshell eyewear, smoked large Cuban cigars, and rode a Sherman tank.

Surprise!

The entire world shall be judged on one spot, at Doomsday, the Bible says. But it shall not be Jerusalem. It shall not be the Plain of Megiddo, when the Battle of Armageddon is over and done, and the whole world is awash in blood. No. If you read the Bible carefully, with the right inspiration, and your third eye open, you'll see it for yourself. Most of the world is in for a big surprise.

Prepárate! Get ready.

Swwissshhhhhhhhhhhhh!

Any day can turn into Judgment Day, anywhere, when you least expect it. Don't look for it up in the clouds. Look way down deep, and all around, at all the hells you've helped create in and around yourself.

Expect more than one Doomsday, and one judge, and one end of the world. Expect the unexpected. Expect unjust verdicts and crushing punishments, along with just ones and others that are way too merciful. Expect some sentences to be both fair and unfair at the same time. Expect mercies that are punishingly beautiful and beautifully punishing. And at the very end, the end of all ends, so goes the rumor, all things shall be well.

And who knows? Maybe what we mistook for the most unfair verdict of all will turn out to have been the most merciful.

20

VEINTE

The light outside was a faint, dim blue, and we were unwrapping our presents. We had been waiting for this moment all year long. Christmas morning, 1958.

We always got up before dawn on Christmas. It was my brother who couldn't wait and always woke me up so early. Some years he barely slept at all, I think. We'd get to the tree in a hurry and paw through the presents like starving kids looking for edible scraps at the garbage dump. Some presents were too big to wrap. Once, years before, we'd woken up to find a Lionel train set under the tree. Another year, it had been Ivanhoe's castle, full of knights in armor. And one memorable year it was Fort Apache, complete with U.S. cavalry, a tribe of Indians, and all the characters from our favorite television show, *Rin Tin Tin*.

That morning it was bicycles. A brand new bike for my brother and one that looked strangely familiar for me.

"How do you like your new bikes, boys?"

Our noise had woken up Mom and Dad, and they'd come out to the living room.

"I love it!" My brother was very happy.

"Is this Tony's old bike?" I was confused.

Although it was green, with hand-painted yellow stripes, a new seat, spiffy new whitewall tires, and multicolored plastic streamers coming out of the yellow handlebar grips, I could have sworn it was Tony's old red bike.

"Why would you ask that?" Louis XVI seemed surprised by my question. "Look, it's green, not red, and it's totally different." My father, like his father before him, and his grandfather, had been educated by Jesuits. He was an expert at the art of casuistry.

"Yeah, I see the color, and the streamers, and the seat, and the light on the handlebars, but it looks a lot like Tony's bike."

"Look, that's Tony's bike right there." Marie Antoinette pointed to the shiny twenty-six-inch blue bike with the streamlined light on the front fender. My mother hadn't been educated by Jesuits but instinctively thought like one.

"Yeah, that's Tony's *new* bike. Where's the old one? This one looks a lot like it."

I ran down the hallway to the side door where we kept our bikes stored. No one tried to stop me. One look was all I needed. My old bike was still there, as beaten up as ever, but Tony's was gone. I shouted at my parents from the side door, down the long hallway where the shoe had once hit my toe, "Hey, Tony's bike isn't here! Where is it?"

Silence.

I felt an odd mixture of enlightenment, anger, and disappointment that my ancestors had recognized as disillusionment, or *desengaño.*

"Hey, you gave me an old bike for Christmas. You gave me Tony's bike—all you did is get it painted and put some new stuff on it."

"It looks brand-new," said Marie Antoinette.

"But it's not. It's not. It's Tony's bike and it's no good. It's not fair."

"Come look at your other presents. You have so many of them," Marie Antoinette said, using the most powerful weapon in any mother's arsenal: distraction.

"Oh, look at this giant box," she continued. "I wonder what could be inside?"

She triumphed. After two or three more transparently diversionary suggestions, I gave up complaining about the bike.

The big box contained an Erector set. What a marvel, those things. You had to put everything together using real tools. Screwdrivers. Wrenches. Pliers. Some genius in New Haven, Connecticut, had come up with the basic idea, and his company kept manufacturing and marketing endless variations of it. Little steel rods with holes in them. Screws and bolts. There were even little electric motors, gears, and winches on the better sets, like the one we got that Christmas. Thick instruction booklets—junior blueprints—guided you through the assembly process and suggested all the different machines and structures you could make. Eugenio's set had a real steam engine.

It made you feel like a man, an Erector set.

We were taking out the first few pieces when we suddenly heard loud, persistent knocking on our door. There, peering through that same glass pane through which my *Abuela* Lola and I used to look out onto our street, stood a nervous-looking man.

Marie Antoinette looked up, alarmed. "Oh, my God! What's that man doing here at this hour?"

Louis XVI peered right back through the glass, and spoke to the man without opening the door.

"What do you want?"

"Could you please let me use your telephone?" The man's voice was muffled.

"Why do you need a phone at this early hour?" Marie Antoinette called from the couch.

"My car broke down about a block away from here, and I need to call home."

King Louis and Marie Antoinette exchanged puzzled looks. The stranger outside kept looking back over his shoulder, and he seemed to be growing more agitated.

"I'm sorry," said King Louis, "but there's a taxi stand about a block from here that's open around the clock. Why don't you go there? You can call from their phone, or take a cab home."

The man looked over his shoulder, then back at my dad.

"I can't do that. Please let me in to use your phone. It's an emergency."

"Sorry, but we don't really know you and this is an odd time for you to be out knocking on a stranger's door."

"But . . . but . . . your house was the only one on this block with lights on."

"It's still an odd time for you to be knocking on our door. It's Christmas, you know? As you can see—" Louis XVI pointed to us, sitting cross-legged under the Christmas tree, clutching tools from the Erector set, our eyes fixed on the door.

"Please, please, *señor,* I beg you, let me in, I really need to use the phone."

He was starting to look a lot like the man who had accosted us during the shoot-out by the Quinta de los Molinos.

"Sorry, go to the taxi stand. It's down this street, to your left, and down another block, also to the left—"

"But, you've got to let me in, *señor.* Okay, I'll tell you the truth: I've got to call the police. I saw some men digging up the street about a block away and they were very suspicious looking. So, please, let me in before it's too late and they blow up the neighborhood."

Marie Antoinette stood up and joined King Louis at the door.

"Some men are digging up the street on Christmas morning? That doesn't make any sense—"

"*Sí, señora,* they're there, right now, and I think they're planting a bomb." He looked over his shoulder about three times as he said this.

"Nonsense," said King Louis. "The only one who's suspicious looking around here is you. Sorry, we can't let you in at all. Go to the taxi stand."

The man looked down the street once more and, in a flash, leapt away from the door and over the fence that separated our house from the neighbor's yard with the breadfruit tree.

I had never seen anyone jump so fast or so high. I was amazed. That guy was just like Batman.

Louis XVI passed sentence quickly, as usual: "I tell you, that guy's up to no good at all. I bet you anything he's running away from the police. Good thing we didn't let him in. How dumb does he think I am?"

Probably as dumb as you think I am, hoping I wouldn't recognize Tony's bike with new paint on it. The thought crossed my mind, but I didn't dare to say it out loud.

Marie Antoinette was pleased with the judge's quick thinking. "Yes, you did the right thing. That man looked crazed. God knows what he's up to. Probably one of those revolutionaries, or something. *Ay, Dios mío. Qué susto!* Oh, my God, what a scare! God knows what he would have done if we'd let him into our house."

"But what if someone is really planting a bomb down the street?" I hoped it was true. A bomb, on our own street! Finally!

"No way," said King Louis. "First of all, you don't need to tear up the street to plant a bomb. Also, no one would be dumb enough to dig up a street at dawn, on Christmas morning, in this neighborhood where there are so many children. Half the neighbors are up, just like us! Someone would see it happening and call the police immediately from their own home. Also, why would anyone want to blow up this neighborhood? The rebels blow up people, police stations, power lines, and government buildings, not neighborhoods like ours."

So logical, the judge. What a spoilsport. I wanted a bomb on our street! Some Christmas this was turning out to be! First I found out from Tony that there was really no *Santicló*, then I got a used bike, and now I had to hear that there was no chance of a bomb on our street. It was a Christmas of total *desengaño.*

The night before had been so much nicer.

That Christmas Eve, like all others, we had gone to my grandparents' house to celebrate *Nochebuena.* The Good Night. Pronounced as a single word by Cubans: Goodnight. And every single year it *was* a good night.

We gathered early, around two in the afternoon. My grandparents, my uncle Mario and his wife, my aunt Lily, and the five of us from Miramar, including Aunt Lucía. We were six at home now that Ernesto had moved in with us, but he'd gone to celebrate Christmas with his own poor family. I think my dad had given him enough money so that his parents could buy a decent *Nochebuena* dinner and some presents for their six children.

There wasn't much of a welfare system in Cuba in 1958. If someone like my dad hadn't helped Ernesto's family, they might have had no Christmas at all. President Batista's wife used to collect toys for poor children whose mothers would line up outside the presidential palace in Havana to pick them up. I saw the line one day. It stretched for blocks. And almost everyone in line was dark-skinned.

My uncle's wife, Hilda, didn't look very happy that Christmas Eve. Her brother had just been released from jail and he was in bad shape. He's the one who had been badly tortured by Batista's police. My uncle Mario, as usual, joked around the whole time.

Everyone in Cuba who could afford it would eat roast pork on Christmas

Eve. *Lechón asado.* The whole pig, preferably, with something in its mouth. I'd heard one slaughtered once, down the street from us. One of our neighbors had the gumption to pull this off in his backyard, much to the chagrin of the entire neighborhood. The sounds made by that pig as it was ineptly slaughtered still ring in my ears, along with the neighbors' complaints.

I wonder if the pig felt as anxious as the man who knocked at our door that Christmas morning. I wonder what might have happened if that pig had been able to leap over tall backyard fences.

Anyway, my grandmother didn't go for the *lechón asado*. She made a nice, neat pork roast, or some *carne asada,* or *ropa vieja,* or *picadillo,* or *arroz con pollo,* along with all kinds of Cuban dishes, including *yuca, malanga,* avocado salad, and fried plantains. She might have skipped the whole pig, but no longer cooked like a Gallega, thank God. She did make *caldo gallego,* a wonderful soup, and *tortilla española,* an omelette with potatoes, onions, and sausage, but that was it for Spanish dishes.

Thank God for that. I'm glad she didn't ever cook calf heads and rabbits whole, or serve fish with their dead eyes looking right at you, or boil up *paella* crawling with crustaceans and mollusks and slimy invertebrates, or plop an entire octopus complete with suction cups in front of you and say, *"Buen provecho."*

Spanish cuisine is not for the squeamish.

I'm still surprised that the Spanish didn't adopt lizards as their favorite food after they stumbled upon the New World. Lizards cooked and served whole. Steamed, probably, with as few spices as possible, with maybe a little parsley garnish, and an almond or an olive in their mouth, served on a bed of eels or slugs or, better yet, snakes. Or, why not all three? *Paella Infernal:* so many beady little eyes to stare into, so many little heads to bite off, so many little bones to pull out of your mouth as you chew.

That Christmas Eve we had a wonderful time. We ate a lot of good Cuban food. Slave cuisine, most of it developed by the Africans who had come to Cuba against their will and had ended up cooking for the Spaniards who owned and sold them like cattle.

We talked and talked. Stories of long ago. Stories from the recent past. I loved hearing my grandparents tell stories about their childhood in Spain. I especially loved hearing about snow and ice on Christmas Eve. I'd ask them hundreds of questions: What does snow look like? What does it feel like when you touch it? Does snow smell like the frost in our freezer? What does it feel like to wear coats and hats all the time? Did you ever make a snowman? Did you ever have snowball fights?

I thought our Christmases in Cuba were inferior because we didn't have snow. Christmas was all about snow, and here we were, eating Christmas Eve dinner in our shirtsleeves, with palm trees waving in the wind outside. We Cubans were getting cheated out of the real Christmas.

Coño, qué mierda.

Little did I know that years later I would nearly freeze to death in Galicia, in one of those stone houses where my grandparents grew up. Or that I would almost burn to death in the same house when my electric blanket caught on fire.

Little did I know that I would one day end up in Minnesota, where winter is eight months long and the lakes freeze so solidly that you can build houses and drive big, heavy trucks on them, and the heating bills sometimes add up to more than your paycheck.

My favorite story that night was the one my grandfather told about finding a wolf who had frozen to death. "There he was, the beast, totally stiff, hard as a rock. I tried to bend his legs, but they were like steel. So I picked him up and threw him, and he sounded just like a rock when he hit the ground. And one of his ears broke off. Just snapped right off, cracked as easily as a mirror, it did." I tried to imagine air cold enough to freeze a wolf solid, but couldn't.

After dinner there were wonderful desserts, and nuts, and *turrón,* or nougat. There are many different kinds of *turrón,* from very soft to tooth-cracking hard, and I liked them all. I especially liked the thin waferlike covering on the hardest *turrones* because it was made out of the same stuff as the host we got for communion at church. Imagine, covering a piece of sweet candy with a huge host! A host that didn't require you to be pure and holy in order to eat it.

Tony and I loved tearing the hostlike wafers off the *turrones* and eating them with utter abandon, usually after we'd hidden some of our aunt Lily's jewelry or spit on some pedestrians from the balcony.

I also loved cracking walnuts and filberts—pure, good food from the land of snow and *Santicló,* and all good TV shows and movies. I loved playing with the nutcrackers too—those simple metal ones, not the wooden Russian ones. I'd beg to crush those nutshells for everyone in the house. It amazed me that two pieces of metal enabled me to do something I couldn't with my bare hands.

That Christmas Eve my grandfather showed me how to take two walnuts in the palm of my hand and crack them both by pressing one against the other. How I wish I could have learned a few more things like that from him. He knew so much more, like how to throw a frozen wolf, or how to build a house from scratch. He was an amazing man, and so quiet. How I envied his reserve. My mother tells me he could get weepy, but I never saw that side of him. All I saw was the stoic, stone-hard Amador.

He sat on the balcony after dinner. Sat in a rocking chair, with his beret on and a bottle of wine next to him. He drank and rocked and remained silent, looking up at the stars, thinking perhaps of frozen wolves and everything that had slipped through his fingers, and all the relatives he never, ever saw again. He must have missed them terribly.

Still, he was tough. And he wasn't the least bit scared of lizards. Once, when we were sitting side by side on a park bench near his house, a huge chameleon dropped out of a tree and landed on his shoulder with a loud thud. I jumped out of my seat, looked over at him, and instantly panicked. That lizard was huge—one of the largest I had ever seen. And he was looking straight at me, examining me with his beady eyes, threatening to jump on me. My grandfather turned his head ever so slowly. It was as if he were moving in slow motion, as lizards sometimes do. He showed no surprise, no concern, nothing at all. Just like a lizard.

He looked the chameleon straight in the eyes. They rolled away from me and over to meet his light brown eyes. He stared the reptile down for an instant and then, with a quick swipe of the hand, he knocked it off his shoulder. It flew through the air and landed on the ground with exactly the same kind of thud as when it had landed on his shoulder. Then it scampered off with its long green tail wagging, as if nothing had happened at all.

My grandfather didn't say a word. He just sat there on the bench next to me, as quiet as ever. I sat there quietly too, dumbfounded. Forget Batman, Superman, Aquaman, or any other superhero. I had just witnessed a heroic act of the highest magnitude.

My grandmother was every bit as reserved as her husband, and probably every bit as heroic. I just didn't get to see her in action. That Christmas Eve, she spent most of the time in the kitchen or talking to her two daughters. As always, I didn't pay attention to what any of them said.

I was too busy cracking nuts.

How still the night air was that Christmas Eve. No wind. Just the soft murmuring of other families on their porches and balconies. Families like ours, enjoying one another's company—or, maybe, not enjoying it very much.

My uncle Mario and his wife left right after dinner. They had to go spend time with her family, who lived two blocks away. She looked kind of glum, maybe because of her recently tortured brother.

My dad and his sister Lucía just sat there most of the night, counting the minutes until it was time to leave. They seemed so stiff and uncomfortable.

We didn't know it then, but it would be the last time my entire family would spend *Nochebuena* together at my grandparents' house. That's what God had decided, as my grandmother would have said. In her world, God decided everything, down to the smallest little detail. Every time she spoke about any event in the future, even minutes away, she would preface or conclude her remarks with *"Si Dios quiere."* If God wills it.

As all of us sat on that balcony after dinner, unable to discern God's will, Fidel was very close to winning his war against Batista. In eight days, it would all be over—his guerilla war and our future as a family.

My grandmother would discern very soon after he assumed power that Fidel was up to no good at all. She had a way to tell.

"You know, that Fidel can talk for hours on end and promise all kinds of things for the future, but he has never ever said *'si Dios quiere,'* not even once. He's up to no good. He doesn't know what he's talking about, and he is a fool. He may also be an atheist, and that can only mean trouble."

That beautiful silent night God willed that we drive home the long way, down the Malecón, the boulevard that ran along the seashore, the road where we always went car surfing. My brother and I were wired up, abuzz with anticipation. But we didn't need to talk about it. Really good things don't need words. No. The best thing about really good things is that you can just sit there with someone else and not say a word. And you both know.

That, my friend, is the sweetest of all feelings in the universe.

God willed that certain families decorate their houses with garlands of

Christmas lights, house after house, and God willed that I should love those lights beyond measure. God willed it, too, that some families place their Christmas trees by their front windows, so that I could see them as we drove by.

God willed that my father take a special detour so we could see the street decorations on La Rampa, a wide, busy boulevard. God willed it that those decorations should be splendid that year. Better than ever.

God willed it that the sky should be clear and the stars very bright over Havana that night. And God willed it that each and every star in that swath of sky should be reflected in my Fidel glasses as I stuck my head out of the window with an upturned face. God willed that the smell of the saltwater should embrace me, that the soft murmur of the waves should caress me, tenderly, and that the warm tropical air should kiss my hair and make it whirl about in absolute rapture.

God willed that my mother and father sit quietly in the front seat, saying nothing to each other. He also willed that my aunt Lucía fall asleep on the way home.

God willed that we arrive at a darkened house and that I run to the Christmas tree and plug in its lights. God willed that I ignore the Nativity scene my dad had worked so hard to create.

God willed that Ernesto be home with his own family that night, and He also willed that it should be the very last time that would happen. God willed that Ernesto be adopted by my father, against all of our wishes. God willed that Ernesto inherit Eye Jesus, Maria Theresa's portrait, and everything else in that house.

God willed that I get my brother's old bike as a Christmas present the next morning, and that an anxious man should knock on our door to remind us that there was trouble brewing on the streets of Havana.

God willed that Fidel and his army be close to victory that night, and that the rebels would take over Cuba a few days later, destroying our world.

God didn't ask my permission for any of these things. Should He have asked?

God willed that I should have no clue whatsoever about the way in which He runs His universe, or any say in how He chooses to redeem us, or not.

God willed it, even, that I should still be asking Him impertinent questions and that I should still be doubting the wisdom of his plans, brooding over the logic of the Virgin's womb and the Word.

God wills it all. And it's our job, our very purpose in existing, to submit graciously, like the lizards who fall off trees onto the shoulders of white-haired grandfathers and are swiftly brushed off.

Just like lizards, I'm afraid.

21

VEINTIUNO

The air was a huge, all-enveloping knife. Even through the thickest layers of wool, the wind coming off Lake Michigan, two blocks away, would plunge the blade deep into you. It was about minus ten degrees Fahrenheit. Cold enough to freeze your spit in two minutes or so. I knew from empirical observation. I had just timed it, right there on the elevated train platform, after I'd coughed up a huge jade green wad of phlegm.

I'd come a long way from Havana. A very long way.

I was standing at the Bryn Mawr El station in Chicago, waiting for an A or B train to take me all the way past the Loop, to the Harrison subway stop, where I'd get off and walk the four blocks to my night job at the Conrad Hilton Hotel.

Long underwear, two sweaters, gloves, ear muffs, wool socks, fleece-lined shoes, and a long, hooded woolen coat weren't enough to keep me from getting stabbed. My face took the brunt of the assault. My nose was gone. Couldn't feel the damn thing, though I could taste the snot that dripped from it onto my lips.

The elevated train platform lurked over Bryn Mawr Avenue and all its lousy shops at second-story level. Most of the platform straddled the street, but the rest of it looked out upon the gritty, rear façades of buildings that stood tightly pressed against each other. I was facing the brown bricks of the Bryn Mawr Theater, which screened second-run films at a price that was just right for refugees.

ALL SEATS FIFTY CENTS read the permanent sign on the marquee, right under the movable letters that spelled out GOLDFINGER. SEAN CONNERY AS JAMES BOND 007. The Bryn Mawr Theater was a poor substitute for the Miramar Theater, but it was good enough. Especially on those rare days off from work.

Goldfinger was one of my favorite movies. Right up there with *The Vikings.* Oddjob's killer hat was every bit as cool as Kirk Douglas' flying axes. And Sean Connery was cooler and smarter than Kirk Douglas. He didn't burn for any single woman. No. He burned for all good-looking women, and he knew how to get them to burn for him, at least for a few hours. Which was all he wanted to see of them, anyway. Detachment, shaken not stirred.

The elevated train turned into a subway just a little bit south of the Armitage station. The tracks plunged rapidly and deeply into a dark tunnel, and the dank smell and the noise of the steel wheels grinding on the steel tracks in that deep gloom made you feel as if you'd plunged into the Underworld.

That's what I felt, anyway, on the way to my dishwashing job at the Conrad Hilton, in January 1966. I counted every lightbulb on the way as I prayed for the perverts to stay away from me, especially at two a.m.

Two thousand, four hundred and thirteen lightbulbs.

What a long, long way from Havana I had come. It was a dream to me by then, sunny Miramar, where there wasn't a single brown brick to be seen and no face-searing wind. It was not one whit different from all the fantasies my brain spun as I slept on a sofabed in the living room of our basement apartment on the North Side of Chicago.

My brother and I had lived as orphans in the States for more than three and a half years in camps and foster homes, and, most recently, with our uncle Amado in a small town in central Illinois. I was very happy in Amado's house, happier than I'd been most of my life. But our mother had finally managed to get out of Cuba, after three desperate years of trying, and she'd been sent to live in Chicago by Mr. Sandoval of the Cuban Refugee Center in Miami.

"Well, let's see: you don't speak a word of English, you're physically handicapped, and you've never had to work a day of your life. Your husband is in Cuba and you have two teenage boys you haven't seen in over three years. I think Chicago is the place for you. *Sí*, Chicago. There are lots of factories up there. Just about everyone we've sent up there has landed a job in a factory. Do you know anyone there?"

"No, not really . . . except for the cousin of one of my friends. But I don't know her very well. Not very well at all. And she's only been there for a month or so."

"That's great! At least you know her. That's better than most of the cases we handle. Chicago it is, then!"

That's how we ended up in Chicago, thanks to *Señor* Sandoval's quick thinking. Excuse me, I think he had become "Mr." Sandoval, just like any other Cuban refugee.

My mother still thinks of Sandoval as a nice man.

Marie Antoinette met us at Union Station early in November 1965. Tony and I had taken the train upstate from Bloomington, carrying all of our belongings in two beat-up suitcases purchased in a hurry at the Salvation Army thrift shop. My luggage had decals on it for Saint Moritz, Monte Carlo, and Rock City, Tennessee. We'd been torn from Amado's house and all of our good friends with less than a week's notice. I'd barely had a chance to say good-bye to anyone.

We rode through the November darkness past a hundred and twenty miles of flat, bare, harvested fields of corn and soybeans. As the train began to roll past the steel mills and oil refineries on the South Side of Chicago, it seemed we had passed through the gates of hell. We saw acres and acres of smokestacks shooting out flames, huge twisting labyrinths of pipes, mazes of twisting stairs, giant spheres, and colossal storage tanks. But it was the flames that made me reel. Big, noisy flames. Balls of flame. Jets. Plumes. Flares. Soft, dancing flames that swayed in the wind and made the chimneys look like giant candles at Satan's dinner table. Fountains of fire. Satan's Versailles. We could hear them through the closed windows of our train.

Whoooosh! Fffrrrrrrrggshhhh! Sssswrrrroossshhh!

Marie Antoinette was shocked by our appearance. We'd grown so much. She couldn't believe that I was taller than my older brother. Later, she would say that the sight of me nearly made her faint.

She looked about the same, except that her hair, which had been brown when we last saw her, was totally gray.

We ended up living for two months with the cousin of my mom's friend, the one she didn't know all that well. Two whole months, the three of us sleeping on one sofa bed in someone else's living room. Four adults and two teenagers in a two-bedroom apartment. Two families that didn't know each other very well. One family with no income at all.

That's Cuban refugee hospitality for you.

Marie Antoinette didn't know how to look for work. She'd never done it. She did the best she could, under the circumstances, applying only at those places where other Cubans had found jobs.

No place wanted to hire her.

So we went to the public aid office to ask for help. But Mr. Fajardo, the Puerto Rican social worker who saw us at the welfare department, wasn't very helpful.

Marie Antoinette didn't know that you weren't supposed to dress nicely when you applied for welfare. She wore a fine suede coat that a wealthy friend had given her in Mexico, where she had spent the first six months after leaving Cuba, waiting for an American visa. It was a beautiful light green suede coat.

"You've got two grown sons, lady. Both of these guys could find jobs in an instant. Nope, we can't offer you anything, *señora*. This country is all about work. Work, work, work. Look at me, I came here with nothing but the shirt on my back. I had nothing when I came here. Nothing at all, and I've worked my way up to this job. I didn't have a nice leather coat like yours."

"Yes," said Marie Antoinette softly, "that's admirable. But you have to understand, that shirt on your back was probably the only one you owned in Puerto Rico. We had a lot in Cuba, and we lost it all. We lost absolutely everything we owned. And this is a suede coat, not leather, and it was a gift from a friend."

That was it. Mr. Fajardo stiffened and he started talking very, very fast.

"How old are you?" he asked my brother.

"I'll be eighteen in two weeks."

"Great. Wonderful. You can get a full-time job during the day and go to high school at night. Lakeview High has a night school up on the North Side."

"And how old are you?" he asked me.

"I'll be fifteen in two weeks."

"You guys don't look like twins. Do you have the same birthday?"

"Their birthdays are only two days apart," said Marie Antoinette.

"Well, your case is a little more complicated," said Mr. Fajardo to me. "Only fifteen, huh? That means you can't go to night school. You have to be sixteen to do that. That means you have to go to high school during the day. And you also have to be sixteen in order to work in this state. Huh, that's a tough one. Well, here's what you can do: go to high school during the day and get a full-time job at night. Lie about your age. Tell everyone you're seventeen. You're tall. You can fool everyone. Lie about your age and work at night. And as soon as you turn sixteen, drop out of day school, and switch your schedule around."

Silence from the three of us.

"Yeah, you boys can take good care of your crippled mother here. Work, work, work, that's what this country is all about. I think I can get you a welfare check for one month, while you boys look for work. After that, it's up to you two to earn the money. I doubt your mom will ever find a job."

Lucky thing Tony found a job a month later, in a print shop on Lake Street. A good union job that paid slightly more than minimum wage, with lots of overtime. And he would get to learn a trade, on top of it all.

He went to night school at Lakeview High, for a year or so. Then he dropped out. Never finished high school.

But Tony has always been such a good con man, he managed to get into the night program in the business school at Northwestern University three years later. He didn't finish that either, but at least he got in. Without a high school diploma.

I had a harder time finding a job. Not easy when you're in school all day, in a strange city, and you don't have a clue as to how to look for work. Even harder when you're lousy at lying.

Tony couldn't help me: he was always too busy working overtime, or resting. Our mother tried to earn some spare change by doing a bit of sewing, but the two customers she found through the Cuban network would pay her with yards of old fabric rather than cash.

Lucky thing we ran into another Cuban, *Señor* Mancilla, at the Woolworth's on Bryn Mawr Avenue around Christmas, as we were picking out a Nativity set. We had to have one. Had to, even if it was from the *"Tén-cén,"* or ten-cent store. Mancilla recognized us as Cubans by our accents, came over, introduced himself, and within two minutes, solved my unemployment problem.

"Hey, I can get you a job tomorrow. A good job. Washing dishes."

Señor Mancilla had once been a small-scale Sugar Boy in one of the eastern provinces of Cuba, where his father owned a sugar plantation and a mill. Now he ran one of the freight elevators at the Hilton Hotel on the night shift. And he knew all the Puerto Ricans who ran the dishwashing department.

That's how I ended up at the Conrad Hilton Hotel, working as a dishwasher. I told them I was eighteen.

But, Jesus H. Wonder-working Christ, what was this cough I had?

I couldn't stop coughing. Neither could my brother. Cough, cough, cough. That's all we did, all day, all night, since shortly after Christmas. Coughing so intense, so deep, it nearly turned you inside out. Sludge denser than rubber in our throats and lungs. This wasn't any garden-variety green phlegm, the kind we'd seen on the sidewalks and curbs of Havana, but a vicious, lung-clogging gunk that could seal shut your windpipe and leave you gasping for air.

A couple of times Tony and I came close to death, or so we thought. Tony actually turned blue one time, right there under the ceiling pipes. I smacked him on the back as hard as I could, harder than I'd ever hit him, harder than I'd ever wanted to hit him. Our mother was screaming at the top of her lungs, "Do something, Carlos, please, do something, he's choking to death! *Ay, Dios mío!*"

I pummeled him mercilessly and mercifully at the same time, in a panic. I knew just what he felt like, gasping for air. I'd been there myself, a couple of times already. Once, on the way to the elevated station, all alone on a quiet side street, and once at the Conrad Hilton, in the employee's restroom on the fourteenth floor. Both of these times, I nearly passed out from lack of oxygen, but somehow managed to expel what was clogging my windpipe by pounding on my chest as hard as I could.

I hammered Tony's back with my fists as if I were a prizefighter.

At last Tony coughed. Out came the industrial-strength phlegm, and in went the life-giving air. His face gradually turned from blue back to a sort of normal color. Then Marie Antoinette made a panicky phone call to a man who lived down the street, the only Cuban we knew who owned a car. She asked him to drive us to Edgewater Hospital, about seven blocks away.

Señor Pujol told my mom that he couldn't do it. "Too risky," he said. "If your son dies in my car while I'm driving him to the hospital, then you could sue me. That's what people do in this country. No, sorry, *lo siento mucho,* but I can't risk having your son die in my car and then having you sue me afterwards. Sorry. Call someone else."

And no one thought to call for an ambulance or a cab. Too expensive. So we didn't go to the hospital. Marie Antoinette thought it was way too cold to wait for a bus out on the street.

But it didn't occur to her that Tony waited for the El train and two buses each and every day, and that he'd be doing it the next morning, when it was even colder. He didn't miss a single day of work. He couldn't. Without his paycheck, we were sunk. I was earning $1.25 per hour. My take-home pay for a forty-hour work week, after taxes, was a whopping $35. My brother earned twice as much, or more with overtime. So we couldn't take time off, even though the coughing wouldn't stop. Never.

Both of us had whooping cough, but we didn't know it.

Whenever our schedules gave us a chance, we would go to a man known as Dr. Piedra, who always seemed to be playing poker with his friends in the backroom of his office. He did nothing except give us some shots and say, "You'll be fine, it's just a bad cold."

I still don't know what he injected into us. We asked, and he said *"medicina."* If we'd been back in Cuba, our mother would have pierced through his lame smokescreen in an instant. But she seemed to have lost her bearings so completely, she let this go. Just as she had let everything else go.

We'd cough all the way to Dr. Piedra's office, and all the way home, in the subzero cold. We'd cough all day and all night, and our coworkers would say, "Hey, kid, you need to see a doctor." Both of us would say the same thing, "I just went to the doctor, and he gave me a shot and said I'd be fine." Some of the wiser ones among our coworkers would say, "You should find a different doctor." But poker-playing Dr. Piedra was the only doctor we knew, through our limited network of fellow refugee Cubans. God forbid we should dream of consulting an English-speaking physician. Marie Antoinette still harbored illusions about taking care of us, and she insisted that we see a doctor she could talk to. Tony and I just went with the flow.

One lady at the Hilton gave me the name of her doctor, but his office was in the wrong part of town. Somewhere on the Northwest Side of Chicago, where the Polish people lived. I didn't have time to ride the bus all the way out there after school and then make it to work on time. And it would have taken almost all of one of our precious days off to get there and back.

I finally got the correct diagnosis much too late, when the coughing had nearly stopped. It came from the guy who sat behind me in homeroom that freshman year of high school, who returned to school one day after being gone for nearly a month and diagnosed me on the spot.

"You worthless piece of scum, you know what you gave me? Whooping cough. I thought I was going to die. All that coughing of yours made me catch it. You gave it to me. And now I've missed a whole month of school. Damn spic."

I didn't miss a single day of school. And I didn't miss a single day of work either.

My schedule was so simple, so predictable. Every day from Wednesday through Sunday I would work at the Hilton from four in the afternoon until two in the morning. Monday and Tuesday were days off. Every day from Monday through Friday I'd go to school, from eight in the morning until three-fifteen in the afternoon. A mad dash to the elevated station, six blocks from my high school, would get me to the train just on time. And the train always got me to work on time. Always. Chicago elevated trains stopped for nothing or no one. Not even four feet of snow.

I had no time for homework, except for Mondays, Tuesdays, and one period of study hall every day. Tests or assignments due on any day of the week after Tuesday were a challenge, but manageable.

Fortunately, a guidance counselor at Nicholas Senn High School had assigned me to very easy classes for all the wrong reasons.

"Oh, you did well on these placement tests. What a surprise! Amazing, for a Latin!"

"How well did I do?"

"Uh . . . uh . . . you got perfect scores on all the tests. Amazing! So unusual, for anybody. And your grades at that other school downstate were pretty good, too."

"Yeah, straight A's aren't too bad," I boasted.

"Well . . . I think you should go into regular classes. Honors classes would be too much for you. After all, English is not your native language."

"I know English better than Spanish by now. I've forgotten a lot of Spanish."

"Well, still, I think the best thing would be for you to take regular courses, just like all the other Latin kids."

End of story. I wasn't about to argue with an adult, even though he seemed awfully dense.

The classes I attended that freshman year were full of troubled kids and led by teachers who should have been doing something else with their lives. I spent more time trying to survive than learning.

One guy in art class became my worst enemy within a week. He wore a leather jacket and steel-toed boots, and reeked of cigarette smoke. He punched me in class, tore up my homework, tried to extort money from me, and challenged me to fights daily. I think I must have been the weirdest kid he'd ever met.

"Sorry," I'd say. "I can't fight you. I'm a Christian, and I'm supposed to turn the other cheek. You can insult me all you want, and tear up my homework every day, as you did today, but I'm supposed to forgive you, love you, and pray for you."

It was just weird enough to work. You should have seen the look in his eyes every time I said this. After a while he stopped bothering me.

I learned early on never, ever to set foot in a restroom at Senn High School. This was where all the greasers, gang members, and troublemakers hung out, and where most of the stabbings took place. I'd wait until gym class and use the urinals in the locker room. Those were fairly safe because nearly everyone else was following the same tactic. Safety in numbers.

But not always. One day, one of the most violent guys in the school ran into me as he rounded a corner in the locker room. He smacked me on the jaw several times, hard, and barked: "Stay out of my way," and added a long string of four-letter words to that sentence. Every single day, every year of high school, this guy had at least a dozen hickeys on his neck, each in a different stage of development. Some were bright purple. Others were kind of yellow, with a touch of green. His neck was one giant hickey museum. I'm sure he could have made the *Guinness Book of World Records*.

He was killed by the enemy in Vietnam a year or two later.

I didn't know who was worse: my teachers or my fellow students. My English teacher, who was fresh out of college, rambled nervously most of the time. The rest of the time, she'd have us diagram sentences, or she'd scream at the top of her lungs for us to quiet down. The guy who sat behind me in English class loved to punch me in the back and call me names, but she never yelled at him. I tried the same trick on him as on the guy in art class, but it didn't work. He kept right on punching and taunting me all the way into June.

My history teacher also rambled and yelled a lot. He loved to address us as "Mr." or "Miss" even as he insulted us.

"Miss Theodoropoulos, you miserable wretch, the Maginot Line was not imaginary."

"Mr. Hashimoto, you miserable wretch, the bubonic plague did not cause people to grow boobs on their necks!"

My science teacher and math teacher both shared the same talent for making the simplest things seem complicated. I would walk into the classroom thinking I knew something and walk out confused. Then I'd have to straighten myself out in study hall later. My art teacher did little more than read at his desk. Rumor had it that he nestled *Playboy* magazines inside those large books of his.

Chicago. I hated everything about the place. Even the name was an awful joke. In Spanish "*cago*" means "I defecate." I had made fun of the name when I was still in Havana. *Me cago en Chicago.* Now I lived there.

I should have known that all of those flame-throwing smokestacks I'd seen from the train were omens of woe.

Attending Senn High School was a delight compared to working at the Conrad Hilton, the largest hotel in the world. I despised the tens of thousands of dishes, glasses, forks, spoons, knives, cups, creamers, pitchers—all needing to be cleaned, sorted, and put away. Over and over and over, without end. It was just like the repetition my third-grade teacher, *el profesor Infierno,* had used to scare us into holiness.

If you've ever attended a convention or a large banquet, try to imagine what happens when the dirty dishes leave your table. Picture tens of thousands of items, all dirty and smelly, needing immediate attention. Those busboys just kept bringing them in through swinging doors. Tray upon tray of stuff for us to sort out, scrape, bring over to the giant dishwashing machines, pull off the conveyor belt, sort, stack, put away. Every night the same thing. Over and over and over.

The worst part was the smell. It's not that the food started to rot instantly, it's just that the odd combination of smells was a real witches' brew. Fumes from hell, worse than those at any butcher shop.

The only "good" job was that of pulling the clean dishes off the conveyor belt. But that was reserved for the foreman's favorites. He tried me out once, but I broke so many dishes that he never dared to pick me again.

My coworkers, all of whom were Puerto Rican, had taken to calling me "Cubita," little Cuba. They all knew I had lied about my age, even the foreman. They put up with me, and ribbed me in a good-humored way, because they understood how much I needed the job.

I was a terrible dishwasher. Probably the worst dishwasher who ever worked at that hotel. I must have cost Mr. Conrad Hilton more in broken dinnerware than he paid me. It got to the point that any time something broke, my colleagues would shout, *"Tiene que ser Cubita!"* Must be Cubita! Or they'd simply start shouting, in unison, at the sound of breaking glass, "Cubita! Cubita! Cubita!"

On weekend nights I got to ride the subway and El home with my patron at the Hilton, *Señor* Mancilla, the elevator man, and it wasn't so bad. But on weeknights I was on my own. That was the worst part of the job—walking the four blocks to the Harrison Street subway station at two or three in the morning, past all the topless bars, flophouses, and missions, waiting for the train on that platform, usually with a few other weird-looking men, or all by myself, and riding the train home.

After a while, I got to know some of the winos on the way to the subway, and they got to know me. Those guys couldn't hurt anyone but themselves, but at the time I didn't know it. We learned to keep our distance, but every now and then we'd scare one another.

Looking through the large front windows of the topless bars was a sin, so I tried not to. But Mancilla got me into the habit of doing it. And some habits are hard to break. Especially habits that are a sin, when you're fifteen years old.

I couldn't figure out how those tassels stayed on the women's nipples. I'd never seen any glue that strong. They spun those tassels around like airplane propellers, and they never came off. Amazing.

Beneath the sidewalk, in the subway, this bad habit of mine made little difference to God. I must have had a squadron of guardian angels looking over me, as I rode that train home through some of the worst neighborhoods in Chicago, night after night.

Only once did a pervert show up. I knew I was in trouble when he got on at the Monroe Street station and made a beeline for the seat next to me, even though the entire car was empty. *Please, God, please, make him go away.* I started praying.

Baneful little man. Degenerate. Miscreant. Lost soul enslaved by demons. He sat next to me and started squeezing my knee.

I froze. I didn't know what to do. I just sat there, mute, praying up a storm inside, ignoring the man and his squeezing. Just sat there, and looked out the window while he clutched my knee.

What if he had a knife, like the pervert who'd accosted me back in Havana four or five years earlier? A sharp, shiny knife, this time without lizards reflected in the blade?

He squeezed my knee for what seemed an eternity. About five station stops. That's all he did, that miserable wretch. He fondled a fifteen-year-old boy's knee on the subway for about ten minutes at two in the morning, way down under the earth, and then he got up when we reached the Fullerton station, the first one above ground, and, as the doors opened with a *whrackettetat,* he looked back at me before exiting and said "good night," dolefully.

I looked him in the eye. I fired heat-seeking missiles into his depraved soul. I don't know if they hit their target, but I tried. I felt rage and shame all jumbled together. James Bond wouldn't have sat there and taken such crap. No way. Neither would Batman.

But I didn't have a license to kill, or weapons designed by Q, or a superhero's costume or a cape, so my fear got the worst of me. All I had was long underwear and a pair of corduroy pants. And my prayers took me far away from him and that subway car, so far that I couldn't even hear the screeching, rumbling, and squealing of the subway, down under the streets of Chicago. I was elsewhere, in another body.

Gone back to Miramar. To the beach, at the Club Náutico. I saw clouds, beautiful white clouds, hovering over the turquoise sea. I heard the waves, and in the distance, from the club bandshell, a live orchestra playing a soft and sweet cha-cha-cha, the kind King Louis despised. I smelt the saltwater, even tasted it, and felt the sting in my eyes. I felt the sun on my skin and the warm breeze. I felt the wind whip through my hair, just as it had that *Nochebuena* when we made our way home past the seawall of the Malecón.

When I got home to our apartment building on the southeast corner of Winthrop and Hollywood, Marie Antoinette was peering out the basement window, her head level with the sidewalk, waiting for me, as always. She had struggled mightily for three years to get to us, given up everything, including her husband, mother, father, brother, sister, and homeland, only to find herself spending all day and all night in an empty apartment. She cooked for us and cleaned the house and did our laundry, which was a welcome change from what we'd grown used to, but aside from showering us with love, that was all she could do.

My brother and I became her guardians. We supported her. We found our apartment. We bought our furniture. We found the used TV, the radio, the dishes. We spoke for her. We read newspapers for her and interpreted movies and television programs. We took her places on buses and trains. She could never give us advice on anything that mattered, or so we thought. And we barely spent any time in her presence.

Her love for us was boundless, even when we were blind to it.

That night I hugged her when I walked in the door, as always, took a shower, scrubbed my knee raw with a washcloth, and went to sleep on my sofa bed in the living room, under the pipes, below street level, no more than twelve feet away from the rushing traffic on one of the busiest streets in Chicago, a stone's throw from the rumbling elevated train.

Three hours later, Marie Antoinette would be up making breakfast for Tony, as always. And two hours after that, I'd be back at school again, as always.

I never told my mother about the pervert. It would have broken her heart. She still doesn't know, and, unless this is translated into Spanish sometime soon, she will never know in this life.

Thank you, Fidel. Thank you very much. *Muchas gracias, compañero.*

Whooooosh! Fffrrrrrrggshhhh! Sssswrrrroooosshhh!

"Fullerton. Next stop, Fullerton."

Whrackettetat . . . "Good night."

22

VEINTIDOS

The bullets were wonderful. Bullets in all sizes, from harmless-looking .22-caliber midgets to huge, armor-piercing monsters. The ones we liked best were those with pointy tips. They looked more lethal than the rounded ones.

Any time we saw a bearded guy in fatigues, we'd say, *"Tienes balas?"* Got any bullets?

There were plenty of bearded guys in fatigues roaming the streets those first few weeks after Batista fled and Fidel took over. Most of them were on the young side and, in our neighborhood, they were usually the grown children of affluent parents, or friends of theirs. Hard to believe, but there were well-to-do idealists in those early days of the Revolution who genuinely thought that Cuba could become a much better place. Idealists who set themselves up, and everyone else, for the ultimate *desengaño.* Some of them came back to our neighborhood after triumphing up in the mountains of Oriente province and sweeping through the island in a matter of days in January 1959.

Those bearded guys didn't stick around much past 1959, if that long. They either shaved and put on regular clothes, or they went back underground, to fight against a gathering dictatorship known as the Revolution. Or they fled elsewhere, usually to Florida. Some of them would return with the Bay of Pigs invasion. A few became the new ruling elite, taking over abandoned houses even bigger and better than those of their parents.

Those who simply shaved and sat down to dinner with Mom and Dad each day, and danced the night away in nightclubs, smelling of Old Spice and Brylcreem, those heroes, they didn't necessarily "sell out" as American hippies might have said around 1968. No, they'd fought the good fight and now got down to the business of living in a halfway normal country.

Isn't that why most young men fight revolutions, so they can dance the night away, fall in love with the girl of their dreams, and feel great about it?

I fell in love with three blondes that year. Marilyn Monroe, Kim Novak, and Eva Marie Saint. Eva Marie was a distant third, Kim a mind-blowing second, and Marilyn was so close to God that it was hard not to confuse the two.

Forget that bitch Tinker Bell, and even Doris Day, who had also struck some very deep chord in my soul. Forget Brigitte Bardot, too, that French tart. Couldn't feel the pull, not the same way.

I loved those three blondes. They were much too old for me, I knew that—real love, real sex had little to do with it. I didn't know anything about sex, except that there were dirty magazines and that chauffeurs loved them. These women just tugged on my soul as if it were a wide lapel, and pulled me close to their heavenly faces, and I could almost smell them.

Poor Jimmy Stewart in *Vertigo,* I knew just how he felt about Kim Novak, and I didn't even have to practice looking as lost as he did. It just came naturally whenever I thought of Kim.

What was that fire within, that burning? Why did I dream about them? It was such a relief to dream of women other than Maria Theresa, Torso Lady, and Candlestick Lady. And such a great gift to undergo that meltdown of the soul, to bask in their presence, to feel fully redeemed. Sorry, God the Father; sorry, Jesus and the Holy Spirit; sorry Brother Pedro, and all the other brothers, and *profesor Infierno,* and all my other teachers at La Salle, and every priest to whom I have ever confessed my sins. Bless me fathers, bless me brothers, for I have sinned: this was the only redemption I could genuinely understand. That attraction, that meltdown, that total invasion of the self by the presence of a beautiful woman.

Blondes and bullets in Havana. My world in 1959.

Hey, but those bullets. Once, Eugenio talked one of the bearded guys into giving us the bullet belt that he had strapped across his chest.

"Okay, kids, they're yours. I don't need them anymore." He undid the belt and tossed it at us.

We collected them as if they were gems. We each had our own stash, though we often traded or, on rare occasions, shared our loot. And we did very dumb things with them. We loved to pull a bullet out of its shell with a pair of pliers, spill the gunpowder on the ground, and set a match to it, as close to our faces as possible. *Whoooooosh!* We also threw the bullets down on the ground as hard as we could to see if they would go off. Or we pounded them with rocks and hammers.

We also threw them at one another, wondering whether we could actually toss them hard enough to tear through flesh, just like a gun. I had visions of my bullets sticking to people like darts.

Lucky for us, none of them ever exploded, or stuck into anyone, or poked out an eye. Much to our disappointment, of course. Not one bang. No wounds. Not even when Eugenio took a very large bullet and put it in a vice, and then struck it on the bottom with a hammer and a Phillips screwdriver, really hard. He thought that was as close as we could come to approximating the action of a real gun.

Good theory, but it didn't pay off. We wanted some bangs, and also some blood. Not too much, just some. Well, what we really wanted were real guns. But not even the craziest revolutionary would give a rifle or a pistol to a nine- or ten-year-old boy. We knew because we tried repeatedly and failed miserably.

It was a good start to a revolution. All these guys with beards and long hair, and all these kids playing with bullets. Kids who saw far too many war movies, and too many Westerns, and too many films with blondes in them.

I was lucky enough that year to see three Marilyn Monroe films. First *Some Like It Hot,* then *The Seven Year Itch,* and finally *Gentlemen Prefer Blondes.* Something about that woman was unearthly. I've been trying to figure it out since 1959, and am no closer to understanding it now than I was then.

My lovely wife, fortunately, gives me no grief about Marilyn. Once, when we were living in Madrid, she asked a guy at a newsstand for a poster he had of Marilyn—an advertisement for Winston cigarettes—and the guy gave her a funny look, the kind only Spanish newsstand guys can give you. "My husband is in love with her," she said, with an obviously American accent. The guy gave her look number two, a more intense version of the first funny look. "It's all right," my wife said, "she's dead." And the newsstand guy smiled from ear to ear, threw up his hands, nodded, took down the poster, and gave it to her, saying, *"Muy bien, entonthess."* Very good, then.

At least this is what she tells me.

Kim Novak had more or less the same effect on me, but there was something too gloomy and menacing about the character she played in *Vertigo.* I felt the pull, no doubt about it, but there could be no comparing her to Marilyn. No way. Apples and oranges.

Years later, I ended up befriending a guy in high school whose father had dated Kim Novak, when she still lived in Chicago. "Did you know Kim Novak could have been my mother?" he once said to me. "Well, if she had been, then you wouldn't be you, would you, and it would be some other guy sitting in your chair, wouldn't it, if he were sitting here at all?" I said, applying as much logic as possible to raw emotion.

I guard my memories fiercely, especially when it comes to these blondes. Sometimes I think these memories are as religious as Fidel's men were in 1959.

Many of the bearded guys wore rosaries around their necks when they came down from the mountains. Some wore several of them, and religious medals, too, which they proudly kept in view, rather than tucking them away under their shirts. It seemed for a few days that these young men who had come from the mountains were saints. Selfless holy men, who prayed as much as they fought, modern equivalents of the Knights Templar, or Knights of the Order of Santiago. Good Catholics, all of them, devoted to the Virgin Mary and the Sermon on the Mount.

Come to think of it, many of them looked like Jesus, with their long hair and beards. One of Fidel's right-hand men, Camilo Cienfuegos, looked so much like Jesus I wouldn't have been able to tell the two apart if it hadn't been for the big hat that Camilo always wore. He looked just like Eye Jesus, especially. Maybe this is why Fidel made him disappear early on in the Revolution.

Fidel too looked a little like Jesus. Those first few weeks of 1959, a poster appeared, plastered everywhere, which showed Fidel in a pious-looking pose, gazing off into the distance, or heaven, or both, with a nimbus and a hint of a halo surrounding his head. There were even cardboard fans with this image on them. These fans were a necessity for many Cubans. Without air-conditioning or electric fans in the tropics, you'd better be ready to fan yourself a lot. And a cheap, mass-produced cardboard fan with a thin, flat wooden handle works just fine, sometimes better than one made from expensive silk and mother-of-pearl. All the poor people in Cuba had these fans. Too many to count. Fans for the fans of Fidel.

At that same time, some genius came up with the idea of teaming up that image of Fidel, the haloed one, with a catchy slogan. The resulting poster caught on like wildfire. It depicted Saint Fidel hovering over the words: "Fidel, this house is yours." Cubans framed and hung these posters in their homes by the hundreds of thousands.

Fidel, I think, took the invitation a little too seriously. Within two years, every house was his indeed, literally, legally. No more private property.

Yes, I know, everything became the property of all Cubans, to be equally shared, according to need. Yes, I know, Fidel didn't expropriate anything all by himself, or for his own gain, not even a pencil sharpener, or a discarded shaving from a pencil stub. I also know that Fidel wasn't as interested in anyone's house, literally, as he was in their souls. He wanted to rule over every household, totally, and forever. He wanted to own all Cubans, not just their homes.

And he succeeded.

How different it was in Hollywood. Take Jimmy Stewart in *Vertigo* and *Anatomy of a Murder* or Cary Grant in *North by Northwest*. These guys wouldn't put up with any such crap. They didn't need to fawn over any revolutionary, or worship him, or cave in to his bullying.

I wanted to be Jimmy Stewart, not just because he got to be close to Kim Novak and Grace Kelly, but because he was so totally himself, always, regardless of the character. He reminded me of my grandfather. I'm sure Jimmy would have brushed lizards off his shoulder with the same aplomb as *Abuelo* Amador. I also wanted to be Cary Grant. He was so much in control in *North by Northwest*, no matter how absurd the world around him became. You can be sure that Cary and Jimmy would never have offered up their houses to Fidel, or to any other revolutionary simply because they were Americans. I knew Americans had no need for any such thing as charismatic leaders.

After all, everything was perfect in the United States. Americans were perfect, despite the ridiculous clothes they wore when they came to Cuba as tourists. They made all the great movies, didn't they? And they made the best cars, too, and Coke and Pepsi, and all the good comic books, like *Batman* and *Superman*. And they had snow at Christmas. And they had beaten the Germans, and the Japanese, and the Indians, and anyone who was an "enemy" in any really good movie. And they had women like Marilyn Monroe, Kim Novak, and Eva Marie Saint.

By 1959, at the age of eight, I knew I wanted to marry an American woman, preferably one who looked like either Marilyn Monroe or Kim Novak. Meanwhile, nearly everyone around me was worshiping a man with a black beard whose name was not Jesus.

We went to see Fidel make his triumphal entry into Havana on Epiphany, the day of the Three Kings, the feast that celebrates when the Messiah became known to the world beyond Bethlehem. Louis XVI wouldn't go, of course, but the rest of us did. We went with Inocencia, our maid. And we stood outside the grocery store where we did all our shopping, the store owned by Fernando Chan. Fernando was a very nice Chinese man who always gave us free olives and raisins when we went to his store. We loved shopping day because boxes full of stuff would be delivered to our house by Fernando, and we could make forts out of the boxes and the merchandise. Towers made from cans of condensed milk. Turrets made from cereal boxes.

That's what I thought about as I stood waiting for Fidel to pass by, those towers of condensed milk. Fernando was there with his children, who were about the same age as us. He was as excited as everyone else in that crowd, and so were his kids. Everyone was smiling and joking and feeling genuinely happy.

Fernando Chan and his family would end up in the United States, too, like so many in the crowd that January day. In less than two years, his store would be taken away from him by the state. About the same time, all of his savings would be declared nonexistent, too, just like everyone else's. It would be Che Guevara's idea, to wipe out all the bank accounts and level the playing field. His ultimate plan was to do away with money altogether, but that proved impossible.

Too bad for Che that Fidel set him up for a tragic death in Bolivia. He had such a nice Mercedes-Benz and such a nice mansion, just three blocks from my house. It was so huge an estate, it took up an entire city block. He should have remained in Cuba and danced the night away, smelling of

Old Spice and Brylcreem, instead of inciting revolutions south of the equator.

I got impatient waiting for Fidel to show up that day. Too much waiting and not much to look at, except all the people lining the parade route. The whole street was full of Cubans, two or three deep, as far as the eye could see. It was a wide avenue that led to the military camp of Columbia, west of Miramar.

Finally, Jeeps, trucks, and tanks began to show up, each and every one of them made in the United States. I'd never seen a tank up close before. They were sublime. Better than in the movies. Those cannons on the tanks looked lethal. And the noise they made was so beautiful. A deep, deep rumble that made the earth shake under your feet. You knew they meant business. And, best of all, the tank tracks left deep scars on the asphalt. You could see where they'd rolled, exactly. And you knew those dents on the street would be there for a very long time. Forever, perhaps.

How I wished cars had tracks just like those on tanks. Why not? Tank tracks and no mufflers. Perfect. You'd think that Americans would have thought of that already.

All of these vehicles were full of bearded, long-haired men, as well as a few women. Most of them carried weapons, and every now and then one of them would shoot into the air. And we waved at them, and they waved back at us. And everyone shouted, loudly. Cuban flags everywhere, on the vehicles, in the hands of the rebels, in the hands of those in the crowd. Fidel's flag—the red-and-black July 26 flag—flew from many of the tanks and trucks, but it was outnumbered by Cuban flags.

"Viva Cuba Libre! Viva Fidel!"

How great it was. How I wished that one of the bullets fired into the air would fall into my outstretched hand, which I held out like a farmer at the sight of a dark cloud during a drought.

Forget the Macy's Thanksgiving Day parade in New York, or the Parade of Roses in Pasadena, or the Bastille Day Parade in Paris. Forget them all. Phony, childish displays of crass commercialism and mindless patriotic drivel. Fidel's triumphal parade was the best in the history of the human race.

But where was Fidel? When would his tank show up?

Zip . . . Whoa . . . Oops! *Coño, qué mierda.*

He came by so quickly, I missed him completely. I was there, and he rolled by on his Sherman tank about fifteen feet from where I was standing, but I didn't lay eyes on him. I saw his tank receding into the distance, over the heads of all the adults, but I didn't see the man himself. Not then.

I'd get to see him in person a couple of years later, from far away, at the Plaza of the Revolution, but by then I despised the man.

But that Epiphany I did get to see him on television. It was Fidel's first major speech to the whole nation. He stood where he'd stand hundreds of times later, perhaps thousands, at the base of the towering monument to the Cuban poet and patriot José Martí, at what came to be known as the Plaza of the Revolution, a vast, open space that could hold tens of thousands of people. Batista had built it, but Fidel turned it into the navel of his universe, the place from which he would fill Cuba with empty words that far outnumber all the black holes in the universe.

Tens of thousands of Cubans gathered around that monument to hear Fidel. The cheering and chanting were unbelievable, even on a small black-and-white television. It was sheer elation, overflowing, filling the land, ripping through the air like lightning. Even an eight-year-old could feel something special was happening. I don't remember the speech at all. What I remember is that one moment when hundreds of doves were released.

The doves flew in all directions, like hundreds of Holy Spirits descending on new apostles. One of the doves, a nice white one, landed on Fidel's shoulder. As he held the microphone with one hand and gestured with the other, the great revolutionary kept talking, filling the plaza with his words, the white dove on his left shoulder.

"Look at that dove," Marie Antoinette said. "This must be a sign from heaven."

Louis XVI, who was watching all this with a look of detachment and no small measure of suspicion, perhaps even déjà vu, said to his wife: "You'd better take a closer look."

"What do you mean?"

"Look at his shoulder, look at what the dove did."

"Ay, Dios mío!"

"What? What? What did the dove do?" I asked.

"The dove took a crap," said Tony.

"Now, there's a sign from heaven!" said Louis XVI.

This might have been a sign from heaven, indeed, that many Cubans missed. But in January 1959, Fidel seemed nice enough. I didn't even think much of all the people who were rounded up and shot to death on television. That's just what happens when you topple a dictator, I thought. Big deal. At least I've got some bullets as souvenirs.

"Preparen! Apunten! Fuego!" Ready! Aim! Fire!

Those three words burned their way into everyone's brain quickly, along with the chant, *"Paredón! Paredón! Paredón!"* Up against the wall! Up against the wall! Up against the wall!

There must have been a lot of very thick walls in Cuba, because they never seemed to run out of *paredones* against which to line up people and shoot them dead. Lots of pock-marked, bloodstained walls in Cuba in early 1959. The blood came off easily enough, but the bullet holes were harder to expunge. The bodies were entombed easily enough, or incinerated, or whatever, but the memories were harder to bury on both sides—memories of the crimes committed by Batista and his people, and memories of all the killing that took place under Fidel, in the name of justice.

But back then, in those early days, nothing important changed for me or for anyone around me. Batista's kids weren't in school after Christmas break, and neither were a few other kids whose fathers were close to the former president, the loser Batista. My least favorite bully was gone, the one I'd hit on the head. The parking meters were gone too, every one of them smashed by the people. But that was it.

So I went about the business of being an eight-year-old Cuban boy. I rode my "new" bike past old boundaries, and I scuffed it up as much as possible, just to get back at my parents for trying to fool me with that paint job at Christmas. I played with my friends and my bullets, set off firecrackers, taunted Blackie the chimp, and climbed trees. I went to the beach often and to church every Sunday. I saw new movies nearly every week and allowed Hollywood to claim one more piece of my soul with every visit to the theater. After seeing the film *The Vikings* that year, I began to pine for fjords, and flying axes, and all things Norse. I even got a plastic model of a Viking ship, and so did Rafael, and both of us stared at them for hours after we assembled them. I also kept scanning the clouds for Jesus. Every now and then, I still dreamt of Jesus at my window, but I also dreamt of beautiful blonde women.

I was clueless, but, then again, so was nearly everyone else on that island.

Except Louis XVI, who did nothing, absolutely nothing with the wonderful knowledge he had about things to come. "This guy's up to no good. No good at all," he said when Fidel came down from the mountains. He prophesied our doom but failed to rescue us when there was still time.

We sneered at King Louis and his prophecies. The future seemed bright, even though the present was awash in blood. I did my share for the Revolution by pursuing lizards so I could wipe them off the island, perhaps even the face of the earth. They were so hideous, so base, the absolute opposite of Marilyn and Kim. And there were so many of them, these stinking reptiles.

If I'd had a chance, I would have rounded up all the lizards, each and every one of them, lined them up against a wall, and shot them all dead, one by one. I needed a lot more bullets, and a gun, but I'd have done it, for sure, if I'd had the chance. Preferably with Marilyn at my right and Kim at my left, helping me to finish up more quickly.

What do you think of these lizards, girls? *Qué dicen, muchachas?*

Paredón! Paredón! Paredón!

Okay, *muy bien,* my blondes. All together, now:

Preparen! Apunten! Fuego!

23

VEINTITRES

Kirk Douglas stood tall above Tony Curtis, sword in hand. He had just broken Tony's sword, left him with a little stump of a weapon in his hand, slumped on the ground, his back against the wall. There they were, these two American Jews, playing Vikings in a Hollywood film, standing at the very top of a medieval tower somewhere in England, on the edge of the deep blue North Sea, their hair waving in the wind like wheat on the Russian steppes.

Vikings. Jewish Vikings. Sons of Jewish migrants from Russia playing Vikings.

And there I was, a Cuban boy in the Miramar Theater, the grandson of migrants from Spain, the descendant of Jews, possibly, watching this drama unfold in air-conditioned comfort while the tropical sun blazed outside. My brother Tony sat next to me on one side, my friend Rafael on the other. Manuel was there, and so was my father. I would like to think Ernesto wasn't there, but he probably was. A very nice theater full of Cubans watching this American film about tenth-century Vikings, shot on location in Norway and England, at a Saturday afternoon matinee in a suburb of Havana. All the others had paid to get in. We had gotten in for free.

Kirk Douglas looked surprised. Very surprised. He hadn't expected Tony's sword to break. The suspense was almost too much to bear. How long before Kirk ran Tony through with his nice, long, intact Viking sword? Go on, Kirk, what are you waiting for? Tony Curtis was already missing one hand. How could he possibly win? A stump of a sword in one hand, and a stump instead of a hand, wrapped in leather, at the end of his other arm.

Kirk stood there, hesitating. His blind eye, mauled by a hawk's talons at the start of the film, looked downright fiendish. It was Tony's hawk that had blinded Kirk. Tony had also stolen Janet Leigh from Kirk. Wondrous Janet, so beautiful, so desirable, had been won over by Tony. Janet loved Tony. They had even kissed already, in a sun-drenched, flowery meadow somewhere on the coast of England, on the edge of the deep blue northern sea. And Kirk wanted Janet so badly. Kirk was a bleedin' volcano, to borrow a phrase from Mick Jagger. Burned as hot as the core of the sun, Kirk did. You could see it in his one good eye, and even in the bad eye, all white and cloudy, which also radiated desire in its own warped way. This was the moment for revenge. The one chance to gain possession of heavenly Janet. Think of her eyes, Kirk. Those blue eyes, as blue as the northern sea, God damn it. Yours, all yours, for the taking. Go on, Kirk, stab him. Run him through. What are you waiting for?

A one-eyed Jewish Viking versus a one-handed Jewish half-Viking. No contest. How long could the suspense last?

Stupid Kirk. He waited too long. As he hesitated, Tony stabbed him in the gut with his little stump of a sword. Whoa! What a surprise! A guy stabbed with a broken fragment of a sword. Pure genius! For the first time ever, I grasped the power of inventiveness.

Kirk just stood there for a long time, looking totally surprised. His one good eye spoke for him: "What the hell just happened? This cretin just killed me with a little stump of a sword."

Then Kirk keeled over and died.

The saddest thing of all was that Kirk and Tony didn't know they were half brothers. We in the audience knew that this was fratricide, that he and Tony were both sons of Ragnar. Sons of Ernest Borgnine. Yes, Ernest Borgnine was a Viking too. Ernest had raped some English lady at the very start of the film. She had gotten pregnant, and given birth to Tony Curtis, who had been sent to a monastery somewhere in the British Isles. Then the monastery had been raided by Vikings, and, as fate would have it, Tony ended up in Norway as a slave of his father, Ernest, and half brother, Kirk. And then Tony's hawk had blinded Kirk, and started a whole lot of trouble.

What a great scene, that attack by the hawk. Kirk struggling against the hawk, the talons digging into his eye socket, the blood streaming down his face. And Kirk didn't even cry. Vikings don't weep or register pain, I learned that day. I thought them capable of plucking out their own eyeballs without wincing.

God, how I wanted to be a Viking. How I wanted to sail on a Viking ship, hold a Viking shield, wield a Viking sword, and cry out "Odin!" as I died a heroic death. Maybe someday I, too, would get to leap into a wolf pit, just as Ernest Borgnine had done, sword in hand, invoking the name of the chief god of Valhalla. Then I could have a Viking funeral, just like Kirk Douglas, my corpse set out to sea on an empty ship, flaming arrows shot from shore, ship and corpse set ablaze on the bright blue northern sea at sunset. A pale Nordic sunset, mind you, not a bright tangerine Cuban sunset.

Nordic fantasies in Havana, in 1959, as the Revolution enjoyed its first few triumphal months. Not much had changed yet, except for all the men who had been executed by firing squads. All those men, so many of them. It seemed there were thousands, and rivers of blood.

Paredón! Paredón! shouted the mobs. Hard to translate. A *paredón* is a large wall, any wall against which you can line up your enemies and shoot them dead while they can't defend themselves. Get rid of them. Quickly, and with industrial efficiency.

So many Cubans were killed this way, shot dead without a real trial. I saw it all on my black-and-white television, under the watchful gaze of Maria Theresa and the Good Shepherd boy Jesus. The so-called trials. The rhythmic chanting by the mobs that never seemed to disperse. *"Paredón! Paredón! Paredón!"* The executions. Amazing, how quickly a human body can crumple and fall when hit by bullets. Amazing how long a man can writhe on the ground before the *coup de grâce* is administered to the head. Blow of grace, so-called, a holdover from the days of the Vikings, when cudgels and maces were used instead of firearms. Thank you very much, sir, for putting me out of my misery. Thank you for filling me up with lead, missing my heart, and then blowing my brains out. I must have deserved it. *Muchas gracias.*

This was no war movie. This was real life.

But it was on television. And that gave it an air of make-believe, put it all at a safe distance. The men wielding the rifles were as threatening to me as the torpid guards of Ming the Merciless on *Flash Gordon*. And my attention that year was really focused on *The Vikings,* which I must have seen about ten times. That film was so much better than all this shooting on television. It was in color, and it showed you men fighting and dying up close. There was one scene where a guy was crushed to death by a battering ram, and another where a guy got shot through the head by an arrow. And *The Vikings* had axes, lots of them. Axes flying through the air. Kirk Douglas was so good with those axes. He could even cut off a buxom wench's blonde braids from across the room and do no harm to her head, neck, or body. All this while dead drunk on mead, or whatever it was that Vikings drank.

Years later, in Chicago, I would meet two girls roughly my age who had seen their own father dragged from their house weeping and screaming, "Please don't kill me, please don't!" He had soiled his pants on the way to the *paredón,* and begged for his life until the split second when the bullets ripped into him. These girls had seen it, lived through it. His crime had been working for the Batista regime. He hadn't killed or tortured anyone, they said. I think he had been mayor of their town. When they told me the story everything I had seen on television years earlier, under the care of Maria Theresa, seemed so different.

I didn't know it at the time because my parents shielded me from it, but I had a relative who ended up at the *paredón* too. And he had been as brave as Ernest Borgnine at the wolf pit, maybe even braver. Instead of invoking the father of all the gods, Odin, he had grabbed his crotch with his right hand, though his arms were bound around his chest, and shouted, "Shoot here first, *maricones!* Shoot this!"

That would be the Cuban way, so different from the Viking way.

Cojones. Balls. Not Odin, father of the gods, King of Valhalla. Balls. My balls, *maricones*. Go to hell, you fags, I'm going to die like a man.

Too bad I didn't find out until I was forty-one years old. Knowing this earlier might have changed my life.

My father, the former Louis XVI, watched all this with a sense of déjà vu, perhaps even with ennui. Here we go again. Mobs, chants, trials, death sentences based on mere suspicion. Executions for all to see. Ho-hum. Interesting, how they use rifles now, and how television makes it possible for so many more to witness the killing. That square in Paris now known as the *Place de Concorde* never did hold enough people. So few, so relatively few were able to see me lose my head. Ho-hum, I think I'll go find some more stuff for my art collection.

The judge, my father, watched at home on his television and did nothing. I don't mean to say that he should have tried to stop the killing, as a judge, as a representative of the law. Only a suicidal maniac would have placed himself between the firing squads and their victims. This wave of executions was a giant *tsunami,* stirred up in an ocean of hate and pain. There was no stopping it. Everyone knew that. No, what I mean is that he should have thought of fleeing the instant the first bullet tore through the flesh of an *esbirro,* as Batista's supporters were known. It still makes me wince. He did nothing but buy more stuff.

He, of all people.

What was going through his head? The head he had supposedly once lost to the guillotine? Why didn't he pack up his whole damn art collection, find the first ship out of Cuba, and take us to the United States? Or to Spain, where we had family? Or even better, to Norway, where the Vikings lived, and there were no lizards at all? All I remember him saying on the day Fidel Castro rode into Havana astride a Sherman tank, was, "This is no good. Expect trouble. This guy's no good. *Este tipo es malo.*"

A few months later, there we were, sitting in the Miramar Theater, watching *The Vikings* for free, as our world began to crumble. Hadn't he learned enough from that sorry experience in 1789?

We would keep going to the movies until the day we left. And he kept buying stuff even after we left, until the day he died. Kept adding to his collection until there was no longer any room left in the house for more stuff.

At least the stuff was there to keep him company. And Ernesto. He was there with him as he died. And he remained there as custodian of the collection and occupant of the house. You can't really "own" anything in Cuba, you see. The state owns everything—excuse me—the *people* own everything. So you occupy houses and take care of the stuff in them, even though it's never yours. There is no "yours" or "mine" in a Marxist-Leninist paradise. We hear rumors Ernesto has sold it all, piece by piece, despite the fact that he doesn't legally own any of it.

Funny, how I ended up with a half brother of sorts, just like Tony Curtis and Kirk Douglas in *The Vikings.* The difference in my case being that I never had even a little stump of a sword to wield against him. Good thing, too, I think. Fratricide has a strong gravitational pull, let me tell you. That's why a fragment of a sword will sometimes suffice.

My father didn't have a Viking funeral after his heart burst. He was buried quickly at the family pantheon, and by the time I learned of his death, his corpse was already ten feet under ground in our marble vault, two thousand miles away from me, and his immortal soul was on its way to a new body somewhere else, perhaps already in some woman's womb. Maybe in Norway, somewhere near a fjord.

How I wish I could let go of the images I have of the death I never witnessed and the funeral I never got to attend, let go of what doesn't belong in the core of my soul, let go of all the passions that rule me. Letting go is a worthy goal, perhaps the worthiest of all.

Saintly Johannes Eckhart, Meister Eckhart, who was nearly declared a heretic in the fourteenth century for all the wrong reasons, had it all figured out. The only reason we suffer, he said, is that we are attached to stuff and to people. What you have to do is to stop loving. No attachment, no pain. So simple. So thoroughly German. *Gelassenheit*. What a concept. The Meister came up with it. It's what we should all aim for, he taught. The state of letting go. Letting-go-ness. You even have to let go of God, he warned. "I pray God may rid me of God," he said.

Maybe a German can let go, in the thick autumn fog of Cologne, in the dead of a dim northern winter, when the sun barely shines for six hours a day, if it shines at all. But can a Cuban ever let go? Sorry, Meister Eckhart, it must be that sunlight. I love you, dear Meister, love you dearly, but that damn sunlight stays with you forever. It's burned into your cells. God is light, is he not, *liebe* Meister? What do you do if your very self is already suffused with the essence of God? If your memories themselves are rays of light from heaven? How can you let go?

Poor Saint John of the Cross, the Spanish Carmelite monk. Born Juan de Yepes, descended from Jews, transformed into Juan de la Cruz when he took the cowl. He enjoyed less sunshine than Cubans, but more than Germans. He tried to be German, like you, dear Meister. He tried so hard to be like you that his Spanish Carmelite brethren had to lock him up and physically abuse him on a daily basis back in the sixteenth century. He read what your Dutch and German disciples wrote. And look what happened to him. He wrote the greatest love poems of all time. And what did he say in these poems?

Love hurts. It never stops hurting. God is love, God is pain. Pain and joy are one and the same. Life is longing. Pure longing. Nothing but unrequited love.

Blame it on the sun, and the sunlight. It makes as much sense as anything. With all that light, Cubans have a hard time letting go. Even if they only lived in the place for one day before being whisked away, the sunlight is forever trapped in their blood. We love much too deeply. I see this trait in my half-Cuban children, full-blown at times, and they haven't even been to Miami yet.

Time to think Nordic once again. Which is what I tried to do as a child, mindful of the effect that sunlight was having on me.

I would look at maps of the world and long for northern latitudes. I actually used to think that the farther north you went on the globe, the purer things became. I remember stretching out on the cold, white marble floor of my house, the closest I could get to ice, and staring at maps for hours and hours, wondering what it would be like anywhere north of Cuba, and especially above latitude forty-five degrees North. Or even better, fifty degrees North, no, eighty degrees North. How I wanted to live in Norway, Sweden, Finland, Iceland, Greenland, Alaska, Siberia, Yukon, Baffin Island. The North Pole. All that white ice, all that snow and cold air. So pure, so good. Snow was grace itself, falling from heaven; it didn't simply hide evil, but vanquished it. And I longed for it, fervently, there in Havana.

The very thought of darkness for twenty-three hours a day also seemed so inviting. Wasn't the Miramar Theater always dark and cold? How nice it was, so different from the blinding sunlight outside and the heat that came with it.

Plus, didn't Santa Claus live at the North Pole? He must know what he is doing. He is, after all, the nicest guy on earth. Wouldn't the nicest guy live in the nicest place?

I had it all figured out, and *The Vikings* helped me put it all into place in air-conditioned darkness. Northern was better. Definitely. Greater tolerance for pain, greater valor, and no lizards on top of it. Axes. Big axes flying through the air. Arrows and battering rams. Swords. Sword stumps, even. No firing squads, no cowardly shooting at men in soiled pants who were tied up and couldn't defend themselves. If you had a score to settle, you fought hand-to-hand and you gave your opponent a chance. You didn't just round up those who didn't like you and shoot them dead by the thousands.

And you could still love up North. Burn like a bleedin' volcano, you could, like one-eyed Kirk. But you could also achieve *gelassenheit,* if you so wished.

That's what happened to one-eyed Kirk at the end of the movie, you know. Just as he gained the upper hand against his own half brother, just as he was about to win the object of his affections, he decided to let go. He stood there, dumbstruck and scared at the prospect of winning, of being attached. He thought of Janet Leigh's blue eyes, thought of the deep blue northern sea, and he let go. I bet he prayed to Odin: "Help me let go, Odin, grant me *gelassenheit.* Rid me of desire, rid me of passion."

How I envy Kirk. Odin heard him, in Valhalla, and Kirk was saved from himself. Rescued from burning passion. No such luck for me.

I yam what I yam. *Soy Cubano. Cubanus sum.*

And even in New England I wait for snow.

24

VEINTICUATRO

The fireflies were out that night. *Cocuyos.* They came out of the shrubs, and the trees, and the lawns, and they blinked with abandon, flashing green when you least expected it. They zigged and zagged, hovered and rose and descended, and made your heart skip a beat. Kids all over the island chased them down and trapped them in jars with metal lids that had holes punched into them with a hammer and a nail.

Never mind the new world in the making. On hot tropical nights like that there were too many parties to count. Rum, limes, beer, loud music that unmasked veiled mysteries, and far too many cigarettes. Shouting, sweating, dancing, whispering, and far too many hands, hips, and lips on forbidden places.

And prayers, too. Always. Some blasphemous, some devout.

We walked down Fifth Avenue with large candles in our hands, our lights shining like giant fireflies in the night. Hundreds of human fireflies: insects challenging the gloom of night on the feast of Saint Anne, which also happened to be the sacred anniversary of the Revolution. Well-to-do insects, for the most part, out for a transcendent stroll on a hot night in late July, just a hair or two south of the Tropic of Cancer.

It was a grand procession, on the grandest of avenues. We had filed out of the Church of Jesús de Miramar, that temple to wealth and privilege, and made a circle up one side of the elegant boulevard for a few blocks and back down the other side to the church. *Quinta Avenida* had such a beautiful park right in the middle, all along its median strip. It stretched for miles.

What a church that was, so full of murals depicting the passion of Jesus of Nazareth. Huge, colorful murals, most of them densely packed with crowds and people. The oddest thing was that many of those who had paid for the murals had been included in these crowd scenes. Louis XVI loved pointing out to me people that he knew, and, even more, fingering people who were there in church, a few pews away.

"Look, there's Saint Peter, and there's Saint John. Look, there's Mary Magdalen. Look, there's Joseph of Arimathea, and Veronica. Look, there's Longinus, the Roman centurion."

And, sure enough, there they were. They looked a little older, all of them, but the artist was so good, he had captured their likenesses perfectly, almost as well as in a photograph.

What a great deal. Your face preserved on a church wall, for all to see, until Doomsday, portraying a character from the Bible. Imagine that.

"Hey, why aren't any of us up there?"

"It costs too much money." A simple and honest reply from the former King of France. He preferred to spend his money collecting art: better to own a painting than to be in a painting.

"Is Judas here today?"

"No. Think about it. Would anyone pay to be Judas?"

"What about that guy with the funny hat?"

"The High Priest Caiphas? No, he's as bad as Judas."

"What about Pilate?"

"Yes, he's here today. Look, over there, in the third pew."

And there was Pilate. Wow.

I still see that man's face every time Pilate's name comes up in the Creed, or the gospel readings during Holy Week. It's the only face Pilate will ever have, or could ever have.

"He's a judge, you know. We went to law school together. He's just like me, except he's a magistrate and earns a lot more."

"But wasn't Pilate a bad guy, like Judas? Didn't he condemn Jesus to death?"

"No, he wasn't bad, really. He was just doing his job . . . and he washed his hands . . . and he repented later and became a Christian before he died. I think he might even be a saint. It's not easy to be a judge, you know. It's a great honor to be Pilate in these murals. I wish I could have afforded it."

Pilate, like all the other males in that church, had to take the heat like a man. Out came the white handkerchief now and then to wipe the brow and dab the upper lip and chin and neck. But no fanning. Real *machos* knew how to take the heat without removing their jackets.

Women got to cool themselves off and, sometimes, their little children. Mary Magdalen really knew how to whip out that fan. She was the best of them all, the one who set the rhythm for all the other women, and determined the appropriate number of fannings between the opening and closing of those instruments of femininity.

The delicate, lacy veils the women had to wear over their heads would dance a little, fluttering in the self-made breeze.

Oremus.

"Hey, *mami,* could you fan me a little? It's so hot in here."

Swishhh, snap, fan, fan, fan, fan, fan, fan, fan, swishh, SNAP!

"Is that it? Keep going, please . . . It's so hot in here."

"Shhh, pay attention to the Mass. Offer the heat up as a sacrifice. It's a good penance."

Agnus Dei, qui tollis peccata mundi, miserere nobis.

How I hated that word *sacrificio*. How I hate it still.

It's the same with "patience." What a hateful word. It may earn you salvation to be self-sacrificing and patient, but there's no denying the fact that it's a pain in the here and now to put up with unpleasant things. Like the heat in church. Or like waiting for your mother to buy fabric in one of those infinitely boring stores on *Calle Muralla,* owned by Jewish immigrants from Eastern Europe who prefer to call themselves Poles, rather than Jews.

Rumor had it that the artist who painted the passion murals had used a young *Polaco* from *Calle Muralla* as his model for Jesus. But it was just a rumor, fueled by the fact that no one at that church came close to looking like the Jesus in the murals. My dad didn't know for sure. But he did know he had seen a few Jewish guys who looked just like Jesus.

Of course, he remembered what Jesus looked like from one of his previous lives.

Anyway, I couldn't decide what I hated more, a hot church or a fabric store. Both required patience and self-sacrifice. Could there be anything more boring than Mass or a store full of nothing but bolts of cloth?

"Are you done yet? When will Mass end? How much longer?"

"Be patient."

"And why can't you fan me some more?"

"Offer it up as a sacrifice."

The legless black woman who was always outside, sitting on the steps that led to the parking lot, certainly had a lot of patience. She just sat there Sunday after Sunday, her stumps on display, her little drooling boy stretched across her lap, her hand outstretched for alms. Oh, I think I forgot to tell you about the drooling boy before, when I mentioned this woman.

Yes, she had a little boy about my age who could do nothing but drool and stare into space with empty eyes. He was so thin he looked more like a skeleton than a living, breathing boy.

I don't know how she managed to get herself to church every Sunday, along with her boy, without legs and without a car. But there she was, every Sunday, on the church steps, following us, it seemed. If not at Jesús de Miramar, then at Santa Rita, near that park where the firecracker blew up in my hand, or at San Antonio, where I took my first communion.

And she smelled so bad, this beggar who sat in the bright sun every Sunday morning. It was a stench like no other. Very different from the awful smell of butcher shops, but definitely in the same league. She made me close my eyes and hold my breath as I walked out of church every Sunday morning. But sometimes she caught my eye. And that was such an awful thing, when she stared right at me and held her hand out close to my face. I had no tolerance for her pain, or her neediness, or her drooling boy.

"Why is this woman here all the time? Why does she have to beg for money?"

"Because she doesn't have any money," said Marie Antoinette.

"Why not?"

"Because she is poor and crippled."

"And why is her son like that? What's wrong with him?"

"Some people are born like that."

"Why?"

Both of my parents spoke at the same time. "Because they led a very bad life in their prior incarnation," King Louis replied. "Because God has a special role for them to play in this world. It's His will," said Marie Antoinette.

I didn't like either answer. And I didn't like to see that woman and that boy at the end of a long, boring ritual.

Fortunately, the woman wasn't there on the night of our Saint Anne's procession. And come to think of it, she vanished completely around that same time. Suddenly, one Sunday, she wasn't there anymore. I rejoiced, of course, and put her out of my mind. I thought that my mind was better suited for other things. Finer things.

As I walked in that procession up the street and back, I wasn't thinking about the legless beggar, or her boy, or Saint Anne, the mother of the Virgin Mary and grandmother of Jesus. I wasn't thinking about Jesus, or even the candle I held. I was thinking of that new television show, *Bat Masterson*, and the way Gene Barry wielded his gold-handled walking stick.

Whack! There goes the bad guy's gun, flying out of his vile hand. Justice served, the weak and helpless protected from thugs, once again, in the American Wild West. I pretended that my candle was a walking stick just like Bat Masterson's. Not at all like my mother's cane, no. That was just a cane, and its only purpose was to help my mother walk. Bat Masterson didn't need a cane. He was a hero, and way too cool. No cape, just a walking stick.

Elsewhere in Havana there were different celebrations, some honoring the seventh anniversary of Fidel's uprising against Batista, others marking the uniqueness of the passage of time in more personal ways. The new wig. The new baby. The wedding feast. The funeral. The new job. The new hubcaps for the Ford. The big favor granted by Saint Barbara. That first kiss. The visit from Grandma. The return of Grandma to her home in Santiago, after a two-month visit. That one hundred and thirty-fifth visit to the brothel. That lucky number for the *bolita*—the numbers racket, where every cipher had a name—the *mariposa,* the *jicotea,* the *mala mujer,* the *novia China*. The number, your number, your luck, your party. You name it. I'm sure there were at least a hundred thousand ways in which that night was special in a city of nearly one million people.

Good Catholics that we were, our party was a candlelight procession in honor of Jesus of Nazareth's grandmother. And we marked the occasion, and marked our territory, sanctified it by turning into fireflies.

Fireflies must seem so frivolous to ants and bees. What do they accomplish, glowing in the dark as they do, on summer nights? Where is their devotion to the community as a whole, their team spirit, their selfless dedication to the greater good?

Yet there we were, glowing, mating, reproducing, just like fireflies. And praying, too, unlike insects. Such pointless, criminal behavior. Praying for things to remain as they had always been, praying, in thanksgiving, for the privileges we enjoyed, and asking for more on top of that. Thanking God, beseeching Him through His human grandmother to smile upon us, to save us from lizards, and foul-mouthed empresses, and drooling boys, and bullies. Praying for love and health and a stay from executions. Praying fervently and absentmindedly, praying with Bat Masterson in mind.

The big man, Fidel, had big plans to turn us all into ants and bees. That night would be the last time we were allowed to be fireflies out on Fifth Avenue in Miramar, or anywhere in Cuba. No more public processions. No need for opium in a permanent Revolution. Who needs religion when you've got Agrarian Reform?

I didn't know what Agrarian Reform was, exactly. All I knew was that some landowners were being forced to give up some of their property, and I had to draw posters proclaiming the wonders of this. Yes, even the good Christian Brothers got into the act for a while, before Fidel kicked their cheek-turning butts out of the country. We all had to draw posters praising Agrarian Reform in fourth grade, in a Catholic school run by the Christian Brothers.

La Salle del Vedado.

No, I didn't make a mistake. In September 1959 our parents sent us to a different school, one that wasn't so obviously tainted with the aroma of Batista. This La Salle was run by the same order of monks, but it was in an older suburb and it was attended mostly by middle-class boys. And some other transfers from Miramar, like us, who were pretending not to be part of the elite.

The elite, you see, had a habit of getting into trouble by the end of 1959.

Take Louis XVI, for example. King Louis drove a big, black 1956 Buick Special, with three nifty streamlined, chrome-plated holes along both sides of the hood and spectacular chrome fenders, front and rear. It was a beautiful car, with budding tail fins and a panoramic windshield, as Louis liked to call it: a single windshield, rather than the divided, two-panel windshields that cars used to have before the era of tail fins. It was a great car, but it wasn't exactly a luxury item, like a Cadillac. In fact, it was three years old and was missing one of its hubcaps. But that car, which wasn't even worth a second look to an American dentist or accountant, earned my father a lot of trouble.

Any time he drove that car outside of Miramar or El Vedado, he ran the risk of being pelted with stones. Once, while stopped at a red light in a poor neighborhood, a group of angry men and women began to rock the car back and forth, shouting insults at him. This made him so nervous that he traded it for a two-tone, vanilla-white-and-sky-blue 1951 Plymouth without a panoramic windshield. It had a cool hood ornament, which must have been a streamlined version of the *Mayflower*, but it didn't have those three holes on either side of the hood. And it had a lot less room inside, especially on the floor of the backseat, where I liked to hide when we drove up Aunt Carmela's driveway.

Our school also made him so nervous that he transferred us to La Salle del Vedado.

And what an awful school that was. My fourth-grade teacher actually made me long for *profesor Taxidermista* and *profesor Infierno.* This teacher, who was tall and lanky, and had a nose like an eagle's beak, made it clear he didn't like any of us. He had rules for everything and graded very harshly and unfairly. God was in the details for him, entirely. Miss one tiny detail and your grade would plummet. Use the wrong kind of ink and your assignment wouldn't be accepted at all. Look out the window for a second and you'd receive extra homework, graded extra harshly.

But it wasn't the teacher who bothered me the most. It was my classmates. I had no friends at all, just enemies, the only genuine ones I've ever had. They wished me harm every day of school and did all they could to make me miserable.

Maybe it was the chauffeur-driven Cadillac that started the trouble. You see, Gerardito Aulet had also transferred, but his father wouldn't go as far as mine when it came to changing his automotive skin. We rode Gerardito's Cadillac in the morning, and it picked us up in the afternoon. Cadillacs were still fairly safe as long as they stayed in Miramar and Vedado. At noontime we would ride the school bus home and back for lunch.

The other boys always gave us such funny looks when we pulled up in the Cadillac.

Anyway, these kids tormented me in the classroom and the schoolyard, and excluded me from any games they played. The guy who sat behind me during the first four months or so was the worst. Unrelenting, this pit bull of a bully. A hundred times worse than the worst bully I had ever encountered.

Asking King Louis to have a talk with the teacher was probably the worst mistake I made that year. He came to class with me one day and stood at the teacher's desk, talking to him for about ten minutes. After they were done talking and my dad left, the teacher asked the guy behind me to switch desks with another kid a couple of rows away.

From that day forward, things worsened. All that I had accomplished was to confirm my status as a weenie. And the insults were now directed not only at me but at my fat, bald, and very old weenie of a father.

No wonder there are only four days I remember clearly from fourth grade.

Day one was my first day in that strange classroom, in that old building, surrounded by boys I'd never seen before, listening to the teacher tell us what kind of notebook we had to get, which color and brand of ink (*only* Pelikan), and which kind of pen we had to use (*only* Esterbrook), how we had to write our capital letters, and so on. A thousand and one rules, each of which would be strictly enforced. I missed my view of the sea and the clouds so much.

Day two was the fateful day my father showed up and failed to make things better for me.

Day three was the day when we were forced to draw posters for the Agrarian Reform. I wanted to draw a picture of a vinyl record with a big scratch on it, stuck on the refrain, *"Reforma Agraria, Agraria, Agraria, Agraria, Agraria . . ."* I was so tired of hearing about this Agrarian Reform. No one could watch television or listen to the radio without hearing about it. Sometimes we'd hear about it from Fidel himself, because every time he gave one of his six-hour speeches, it would be the only program carried on all the airwaves. When he spoke, all had to listen. Or turn off their radios and televisions. (The loudspeakers on street corners would show up about a year later and take care of the silence in some people's homes.) So, to me, this Reform deal was just one huge broken record. But vinyl records had too many lines, and my perfectionist tendencies stood in the way of drawing a record that didn't have the right number of lines.

I sold out, and I still hate myself for it. I'll never forgive myself.

I knew that our teacher liked Fidel, and that he was all in favor of the Agrarian Reform, whatever it was. I knew the teacher liked things his way, and his way alone. I knew that he had given us this assignment so he could send our posters to some other place outside our school where some special big deal would be made of schoolchildren's drawings in praise of the Agrarian Reform.

The catch for me was that I had already started to sour on Fidel. What I had come to loathe the most was the unrelenting barrage of information on the Revolution and its programs. It was like nothing else I had ever experienced, this saturation bombing of the mind. Even the worst of all things I despised—lessons on hell—lasted only a half hour now and then. Nothing had ever been rammed into my skull as persistently as the Agrarian Reform and all other things related to the Revolution. Even Mass lasted for only one hour once a week, tops.

I also didn't like the way Fidel hogged the airwaves. Something didn't seem right about it. And his speeches were incredibly boring, and rambling, and too full of promises and threats.

Anyway, I knew exactly what our teacher was looking for in these posters, and I gave it to him. I gave up on drawing a broken record, and instead turned my circle and its few lines into an archery target. And I drew three arrows, each with all their tail feathers drawn in painstaking detail, sticking right into the bull's eye on the target. Below the target I wrote, in the capital letters our teacher insisted upon, THE AGRARIAN REFORM HITS THE TARGET.

Dante was so wrong. At the lowest point, at the nadir of the ninth circle of hell, Satan will be sharing eternally cold space with treasonous brownnosers who abandon their principles and do what is wrong for the sake of a good grade, or applause. And these brownnosers will have to lick Satan's razor-studded butt forever and ever, with their tongues.

My infernal poster was awarded first prize by the teacher and sent on to some exhibition. And the worst part of all of this was that I didn't know whether to hate myself or be proud of my accomplishment.

To go back to counting the four days I remember from fourth grade:

day four was the day of the big explosion. There we were, going through the routine of another day in class, some afternoon in early 1960, when suddenly: *BOOOOOOOOOM!* The whole room shook. The window shutters rattled. The chalk on the little shelf under the blackboard jumped up. I especially remember feeling the force of the explosion entering through the soles of my feet and traveling through my body in what seemed to be an eternity, but was probably a mere fraction of a second.

If I hadn't heard the unmistakable sound of an explosion, I would have guessed it to be an earthquake. But you couldn't fool me when it came to explosions. And this was the biggest blast I'd ever heard or felt. I had no idea the big ones could be so nice. Yes, this was a great one! The best ever.

We all looked at one another and at the teacher in utter amazement. It sounded so close and far away at the same time. All of us knew instinctively that an explosion that big had to cause a lot of damage. I'm sure I wasn't the only one wondering what had been blown to pieces, and where.

About an hour after the explosion, we learned what had happened. Our teacher stepped out of the room for a few minutes, probably for the third time since the blast, and came back with the news: a ship full of weapons and explosives had been blown up in Havana's harbor. Same spot, almost, as the *Maine,* in 1898.

So this is what it had been like. All my life, I'd been hearing my aunt Lucía tell me about the *Maine* blowing up, and how she remembered the explosion, even though she had only been three years old at the time. I had always thought she was making up her memories of the sinking of the *Maine,* but now I understood. You don't ever forget an explosion like that.

And our school was miles from the harbor. I tried to imagine what it had been like closer up. It must have been incredible!

For the next few days after the blast, there was nothing but news about the ship, its crew, its cargo, and the likely suspects. It had been a ship loaded with armaments for the Revolution. Guns, ammunition, ordnance, military equipment of all sorts, purchased with contributions made by people in other countries who wanted to help the Revolution. An international show of support blown to pieces. A big ship, loaded with stuff that was made to explode. Stuff taken from Fidel and his glorious Revolution.

Not everyone was in favor of the Revolution, you see. And this was the biggest sign these counter-Revolutionaries had been able to send Fidel. It was also a huge strategic victory. That ship sank to the bottom of the harbor in pieces, along with its precious cargo.

What I didn't know at the time was that two of my relatives were involved with the people who blew up that ship. One was my cousin Fernando. The other was Fernando's cousin—his mother's nephew—who was no blood relation of mine, but still part of the family.

How I wish I had known.

Fernando's cousin was the son of a former cabinet minister, who had served other presidents, including Batista. Miguelito was a very nice guy, I hear. And he was also a serious bomber. My other cousin, Rafael, would tell me years later how Miguel would show up at his house in El Vedado, just one block from my fourth-grade classroom, at odd hours of the night, and ask for a drink. Then he'd sit in a comfortable chair, with his drink, looking at his watch.

"Twenty more seconds, and you'll hear a big one."

There was a *BOOOOOM!* somewhere off in the distance.

"Forty seconds, and you'll hear another."

BOOOOM! . . . . . . *BOOOOM!* again, off in the distance.

"*Muy bien!* Wait another twenty minutes. They'll sound closer."

Some conversation would follow, usually not about the bombs, but about those things that interested guys in their twenties in Havana back then. I can't fill in those details, sorry. I wasn't lucky enough to be in my twenties in Havana before the world changed. But my cousin Rafael tells me it was unbelievably wonderful.

Wonderful enough to plant bombs and blow up ships in Havana Harbor, just so it could stay that way.

BOOOOM! . . . *BOOOOM!* . . . *BOOOOM!* Twenty minutes later, definitely closer.

"Good. They worked. Now wait another ten minutes for the finale."

BOOOOOOOOOOM! Very close this time. Hard to tell, exactly, but close.

"Great! Wonderful! Such beautiful drumming. Perfect. That will show the bastards! Sons of whores! *Cabrones, hijos de puta!* Is it all right if I stay here until morning?"

Miguelito got caught one day. Most of them did, sooner or later. These fine boys who had once played with firecrackers and marbles and ridden their bikes around the block. These fine patriots, who drank Cuba Libres while waiting for their bombs to go off in the night, almost all of them ended up getting caught.

Fidel proved smarter than all of them. He won. And most of the world doesn't know or care how fiercely he was opposed. He's been there for so long now, he seems as permanent and inevitable as Mount Everest or the earth's two poles.

But, for about three years, he was not inevitable.

Fernando almost killed him. Almost. He came so painfully close, so awfully close. I'll tell you about that later. They didn't know about that when he was arrested and tried, and they never found out. If they'd known, he would have suffered the same fate as Miguelito.

Miguelito got the ultimate sentence, as did every bomber. *Paredón! Paredón! Paredón!* No suspense here; I've already told you about him. He's the guy who grabbed his crotch as he was about to get shot and said to his executioners: "Here, shoot this first, you queers!" I'm so glad he didn't shout "Long Live Free Cuba," or anything like that. Some messages are more beautiful when encoded in profanity, especially in the face of something as obscene as a firing squad that's working for a ruthless dictator masquerading as a humanitarian.

At the same time that he was sweeping the beggars off the streets, Fidel was silencing all opponents with an iron fist.

The long and short of it is that the legless woman disappeared from the church steps because begging became illegal. Did she receive enough to eat or get adequate care for her drooling boy? I don't know, but I suspect not. Nothing else I saw at that time, and nothing I've heard from those few relatives who still live there leads me to believe that the Revolution could give anyone anything adequate to meet their needs.

And if anyone received anything adequate from the Revolution, it was purchased with blood money.

I should have had a frank talk with my school bus driver. He looked like the sort of guy who would have benefited most from the Revolution. More so than Aulet's chauffeur, who wore a neatly pressed uniform all the time. Our driver on bus number two was a walking, talking tattoo museum. Both of his arms were totally covered in tattoos from the wrist up. Since he wore his short sleeves rolled up, and his shirt front open to mid-chest, we could also see that the tattoos were everywhere. Sometimes, when his pants were hitched up a bit too high, we could see tattoos on his legs too. Blue and red markings all over. Images of the Virgin Mary. Hearts entwined, pierced by one arrow. Women's names. Flowers. Diagrams and pictures of all sorts. Some animals. A Cuban flag.

I'd never seen tattoos before, except on cartoon characters.

Someday, maybe, I'll get up the nerve to get one. I came close to doing it a few weeks ago, but backed off. One of these days, a few beers too many might push me through the threshold, from this world to that. The world of the tattooed. The world of truth.

They are different, you know, tattooed people. Could liars or hypocrites ever etch anything permanently into their skin? I bet Fidel doesn't have any tattoos.

That's why I wish I had talked to our driver on bus number two. He would have told me everything I would have ever needed to know about the Revolution.

Bus number two made a wide circuit through Miramar, picking up most of us who were refugees from my former school. The very last stop was somewhere in a brand-new neighborhood, where the trees were still very small and the sunshine was blindingly bright. Our last passenger was a kid whose father owned a soft drink company. His family's name was on every bottle of soda they sold. Imagine that: having people call out your name when they ask for a soda.

"I'd like an orange Cawy, *por favor.*"

Would that make you feel special or totally ordinary?

Anyway, Cawy and all the other soft drinks went down the tubes soon enough. The Cawy boy and his family lost everything. Confiscated. Nationalized. Everything from Coca-Cola to Cawy and Materva and Ironbeer, everything taken over by the state. Excuse me. Taken over by the Cuban people.

And the soft drinks went to hell.

Che Guevara must have had a tattoo or two, I bet. Once, when asked on television about soft drink production in the newly nationalized bottling plants, he admitted that they had no clue as to what they were doing, that they didn't know how to get them to taste good. The owners had been forced to turn over their bottling plants but not their recipes.

"Forget about Coca-Cola and Pepsi-Cola," said Che. "Forget about them. We'll keep bottling something that looks like them, but we don't have the formulae. The Yankee Capitalists took them. You can keep drinking the stuff, if you want, but it's never going to taste the same."

Every one of those Che Cokes or Pepsis was an adventure. No two bottles ever tasted the same. Awful, every bottle, every sip. I stopped drinking them altogether and stuck to seltzer, which was very hard for the Revolution to screw up.

Bus number two made its rounds until June, the end of the school year. The route had shrunk a little by then, and there were more empty seats on the bus than there had been in September. Seats vacated by kids who suddenly vanished without saying good-bye. Not many, but enough to make me aware of an emerging pattern. People were beginning to leave the country.

And we were staying.

Louis XVI and Marie Antoinette never spoke about any of this. They had a way of keeping all conversations about the Revolution to themselves. They also had a way of surprising us with decisions about our future.

"You won't be going back to La Salle del Vedado next year. We think you kids need a change. Besides, we think you should go to a smaller school that's not directly affiliated with the Church. We don't know where we'll send you yet, but we'll take you to visit some schools and you can tell us which one you like best."

That was a big change. Asking for our opinion.

We visited four schools. One was just a few blocks from our home, and it was small enough to fit into a twelve-room house. It had very stupid-looking uniforms. One was a military academy that looked so awful, it made Tony and me pray out loud spontaneously for the very first time in our lives: "Please, God, no, no, not that school!" The third school I can't even remember. The fourth, however, was great.

A school with girls. Imagine that. I knew they existed but never dreamed I'd be going to one. Like death, or illness, it was something that always happened to other people, not to us.

But it happened. Our parents were shaken up enough to enroll us in Colegio del Salvador for the following year. It wasn't very far from our house, and we'd be allowed to ride our bikes back and forth. No Cadillacs, no chauffeurs, no buses. Just bikes. And there'd be girls, and women teachers, and no monks at all. All of this in a beautiful mansion on Fifth Avenue, with a very large tree-shaded yard. And, to top it off, I'd get to wear a different uniform, which included brown shoes. What a concept. Unbelievable.

This was worth every bad Che-Pepsi and Che-Coke I'd had that year. Maybe this Revolution wasn't all that bad.

I wasn't wrong about the school. It proved to be better than anything I could have ever imagined. But I was wrong about the Revolution.

That night of July 26, 1960, when I walked with my fellow fireflies down Fifth Avenue, I was so happy to be rid of my fourth-grade enemies, and so taken with the way in which Bat Masterson used his walking stick.

The palms swayed in the breeze that night, and the flames of our candles danced. They danced the cha-cha-cha, and laughed merrily, those flames. They threw a party, those candles, as they licked the slightly salty air and inhaled the perfume on those veiled ladies and the Brylcreem on those men.

Don't ask about the scent on those few boys and girls who were there, walking along with their parents. Maybe they smelled of hope and eternal distraction. I know I must have. And I know I swayed with the palms and danced with the flames, even though dancing was forbidden in my house, and I wielded my invisible walking stick like a stunted Quijote against all of my invisible enemies. I also know that I reveled in being a firefly for one night.

Fireflies were so much nicer than lizards.

Saint Anne, up in heaven, eyed this procession through the dancing flames with great curiosity and no small measure of delight. She always loves a good procession, as does every saint. Imagine that: perfect strangers out for a transcendent stroll in your honor, nearly two thousand years after your death. We should all be so lucky, and so good.

But these people down there in Havana were so odd. Saint Anne smiled and wrinkled her perfect, immortal brow. Flames never danced like that for other people. How did they get the flames to do that? The music didn't come from the doleful hymns these fireflies were singing, but from the atmosphere itself, and from their bodies. And why were the drums in that music so loud? Did the drumming have anything to do with those other flashes of light you could see around the city nearly every night? Those bright explosions set off by young men who also oozed that music from their pores?

Looking down from heaven, Saint Anne saw the lights. All the lights. And she heard the music. All the music. She saw, as one can do only in heaven, how the lights and the music were all of one piece, connected by love and zest for life itself.

The insects, the parties, the candles, the bombs. All connected.

And as she smiled she also wept, as one can do only in heaven.

25

VEINTICINCO

The sunlight slammed onto the front steps of the Miramar Theater with the same ferocity as ever and the same inaudible shriek. We bounded up the four terrazzo steps and into the air-conditioned lobby while Louis XVI flashed his I'm-a-judge-and-I-get-in-for-free card at the lady in the ticket booth.

A few months before, there had been a yo-yo demonstration in the theater, sponsored by Duncan Yo-Yo. They had interrupted the ritual, those Duncan iconoclasts, taken precious time out of the afternoon matinee intermission. They had thrown the switch on all the lights in the house, desecrating the hallowed darkness. Naked, revealed for us to see, the lush interior of the theater and the color of the velvet seats and the curtains in front: some kind of turquoise, like the sea. But worst of all, behind the large white screen that contained all of our important memories, a stage. A stage filled with talented children who could make their brightly colored yo-yos do wondrous tricks I could never hope to master. Children who had sold their souls to the devil, no doubt, in exchange for a walk-the-dog or an around-the-world.

I couldn't even get the yo-yo to go up and down three times before the string stopped working for me and the damn thing just hung there, like a horse thief on the gallows.

But those kids up on the stage, the traitorous stage that spoke of a secret past, those kids made me want to buy every yo-yo made at the Duncan factory. I pleaded with King Louis to buy them all for me, all the models, but he reminded me that I already had one and that it never obeyed my commands.

I understood envy fully for the first time that afternoon, and betrayal too. The Miramar Theater was for movies only, for darkness and a world beyond the flesh. That stage behind the screen, now crawling with yo-yo masters, had once harbored flesh-and-blood actors, traitors to the screen, enemies of truly otherworldly fantasies.

We were there to see a very special movie, and these yo-yo masters were keeping us from it. We were there to see Kirk Douglas, and the sea, and a very special machine.

You see, before he was a Viking, Kirk Douglas was a sailor. A sailor with a very tight striped shirt, trapped inside Captain Nemo's submarine, the *Nautilus,* in Walt Disney's *20,000 Leagues Under the Sea.*

So there we were at the Miramar Theater, as always, but this time we were waiting for the yo-yo demonstration to end. How we loved to watch Kirk harpoon that giant squid right in the eye, hitting him square in that evil, vacuous pupil, despite the huge waves washing over the *Nautilus,* and despite his tight shirt. (This scene probably made it necessary for Kirk to suffer some payback in *The Vikings,* with hawk's talons.)

And there we were at the Miramar again, about a year later, sitting in air-conditioned comfort, watching Kirk hack off one of the squid's tentacles so he could free Captain Nemo from its deadly grip.

And there we were at the Arenal Theater, watching Peter Lorre look goofy, no matter what he did. He wasn't a cretin in *20,000 Leagues,* only a nerd. There we were at the Ambassador Theater, watching the *Nautilus* ram a ship and sink it. There we were at the Maxim Theater, a few doors down from my grandmother's house, watching Captain Nemo get shot. James Mason really knew how to get hit by a bullet. You knew he'd been hit. No doubt about it. There we were at the elegant Trianon Theater, watching Kirk Douglas cavort with Captain Nemo's pet seal. There we were at the Roxy Theater, the stinking, stuffy, hot Roxy, watching Captain Nemo open that giant round window of the *Nautilus,* stunning Kirk Douglas, Peter

Lorre, and some other guy with the beauty of the undersea world. The world we all wanted to visit, to live in someday. I, for one, knew I'd be buying scuba gear as soon as my parents would let me. Maybe when I turned thirteen?

None of us ever got to scuba dive.

But we did get to see *20,000 Leagues Under the Sea* over and over again. Whenever any theater in Havana played it, we'd be there. Sometimes we even went to theaters that didn't let us in free. Such a shock, to see Louis XVI paying at the front booth. But it was always worth it.

By the age of eight I had learned to memorize the newspaper movie listings on a weekly basis. I once knew the names of all the theaters in Havana, even those to which we never went and never would go. I didn't memorize the times, just the bookings—even for Mexican cowboy films, the very worst kind of entertainment, as far as I was concerned. Even worse than stupid films about romance, with lots of kissing scenes.

I first started liking the kissing scenes while watching *Queen of Outer Space* at the Miramar Theater on a Saturday in early 1960. I remember that it was sunny and hot outside the theater that afternoon. But that's a cheap carnival trick: it's so easy to remember the Cuban weather. Much harder to remember what the weather was like for every movie you've seen in New York, Chicago, Minneapolis, Paris, or Madrid. But I can do it. I'm like the character of Mr. Memory in Hitchcock's second version of *The Thirty-Nine Steps* (which I first saw on a balmy, starlit summer night in July 1974, on a thirteen-inch black-and-white television set, in my apartment, about fifteen miles from where I am now sitting).

Anyway, *Queen of Outer Space* set my head spinning. It was a lousy science fiction movie about earthmen who end up on the planet Venus, which is peopled only by women and is led by its chief scientist, played by Zsa Zsa Gabor. There was a lot of kissing up on that screen, and the usual smooching sounds and loud cheers from the Cuban audience. *"Ay, dale, chupa! Chupa duro, mami!"* Hey, go to it! Kiss hard, baby! I walked out into the bright, blinding sunlight thinking more about the kissing in that movie than about the robots. It wasn't just that the actors who kissed seemed to be enjoying it so much, it was that the very idea of kissing a female on the lips for a long time suddenly seemed so appealing. I felt possessed by an alien spirit, but it was a good feeling. Very good. It made me want to take a rocket ship to Venus—a *cohete*, of course.

The *Nautilus* was so far from Venus, so different. No kissing between men and women; only between one man and a seal. Not one woman in the submarine, or the entire movie.

But Fidel saw something worse than kissing in that film, something awful. He must have, for he prevented all Cuban children from seeing it.

And so it was that one day in 1960 we went to see *20,000 Leagues* at the Roxy Theater and were told that it was not suitable for small children.

"You can't see this movie," said the woman in the ticket booth. *"Lo siento, prohibido a menores."* Sorry, forbidden to minors. You can't come in. Go away.

My dad was puzzled and asked a number of questions. But he didn't get very far with the woman. All she could do was recite the new rules to the old judge.

"*Lo siento.* This movie is forbidden to minors." Over and over, like some kind of automaton reciting a mantra.

I raised a fuss right there on the sidewalk outside the Roxy Theater. I must have asked a thousand and one questions, all of them variations on one theme: "Why?" Just like Dad. My brother and friends asked the same question.

I crossed the line, too. I told the lady at the booth what was on my mind. This was much worse than the Duncan Yo-Yo interruption of ages past. This was heart-crushing, mind-numbing betrayal.

"This is so stupid. So stupid. And . . . and . . . it's . . . it's unfair, too."

The lady looked at me with the oddest mixture of emotions I had ever seen. I couldn't tell if I had gotten myself into trouble or nearly brought her to tears.

Louis XVI, thinking maybe of the Paris mobs during the Reign of Terror, put his hand on my shoulder and said, "Don't bother. Don't argue with her."

So there we were, barred from seeing a movie we had all seen many times before. Expelled, banished from our own past. All that the lady in the ticket booth needed was a flaming sword. This was not Eden, though. Far from it. No, it was a crappy theater, the worst *cine* of all. No air-conditioning, just fans on the ceiling. Hard wooden seats. And a bathroom so filthy that my dad always told us never to sit on the toilet.

"All you can do at the Roxy is pee," he said. "You don't know what you might catch if you sit on the toilet."

I thought long and hard about what I could catch from the Roxy's toilet seat, especially any time I had to pee so badly as to risk a trip to the bathroom.

"You might catch parasites," Louis XVI revealed once. "If there are any parasite eggs in the toilet water and it splashes up at you, that's it. Forget it. *Lombrices.* Tapeworms. Worms in your intestines."

Needless to say, only the worst of stand-up emergencies would make me go to the bathroom at the Roxy.

Still, the Roxy holds a special place in my memory. It was there, on that sidewalk, standing next to a well-worn poster for *20,000 Leagues Under the Sea,* bathed in the light of the marquee, that I first felt that repulsive feeling of someone trying to invade my mind and soul. It was the first lancing. The blade of Fidel's scalpel had attempted the first incision, the first step towards the gradual head transplant.

"Sorry, you can't bring these children into the theater. Sorry, it's not suitable for minors. Sorry, the rules say I can't allow anyone under eighteen years old to see this movie. Sorry, I don't make the rules. Sorry, sorry, sorry . . . go home."

I know many non-Cubans won't believe me, but I swear to God this happened. May I be split in two by an evil lightning bolt if I am not telling the truth, as Cubans are wont to say. *Mal rayo me parta.*

And ever since that night I have given a lot of thought to why Fidel might have done such a thing.

Was it Captain Nemo? Was he so evil a character that we had to be protected from him? There he was, James Mason, sporting a beard, commanding the *Nautilus* to wreak havoc on the high seas. Seeking vengeance against those who had hurt him earlier in life, hell-bent on making the world's imperialist powers pay for their exploitation of the human race. Or was Nemo too much like Fidel? After all, there he was, Fidel, sporting a beard, commanding an island that looked a lot like the *Nautilus,* long and narrow, with a spear tip at one end.

Disney hadn't made Nemo a very likable character. Having no real food for his crew, he forces them to eat all sorts of disgusting things. He thinks nothing of killing people for the sake of his warped view of justice. And worst of all, Nemo sinks the *Nautilus* and forces his entire crew to die along with him.

Too close to home for Fidel. Too prophetic.

No. Too simple. Too obvious.

Was it the giant squid? Was it the seal? Was it Peter Lorre and his frog eyes? Was it Kirk Douglas and his constant desire to get off the *Nautilus* and escape from the clutches of Captain Nemo?

No, it couldn't have been any of these things. The only scenario I can come up with for what went on inside Fidel's mind is not very pretty. So brace yourself. I am about to think like Fidel—to think as if the head transplant he tried to give me had been completed.

I had no way of knowing this at the time, but Kirk played a gay man in that film. As gay as they come. There he was, Kirk/Ned, strumming his handmade turtle-shell ukelele in his small cabin aboard the *Nautilus,* flirting with a seal. Flirting with a fish-swallowing pinniped, kissing it, even. Could any straight macho man ever do that? Make a musical instrument from a turtle shell and then serenade a seal while wearing a shirt so tight that you wondered why it didn't burst at the biceps?

Never. Forget about it.

Walt Disney was gay, you know. Just take a look at *20,000 Leagues Under the Sea* if you have a chance. Disney was an evil genius, and gay.

If you doubt this, just take a closer look at Peter Pan. Gay. As gay as they come. Just look at his costume. Forget all this deception with Wendy. He had no real interest in her. The real reason Tinker Bell was so pissed at Peter was that she knew he was gay and could never be hers. All those Lost Boys . . . forget it. And Captain Hook? Take a close look at Hook and that pirate crew, especially his personal assistant, the limp-wristed guy with the striped shirt and the sandals. Good God. They call this a children's movie?

And why was Pinocchio's maker, Geppetto, that old man who lived alone, so interested in having a little boy in his house? Think about it.

Holy Moses. Jesus H. Straight-talking Christ.

I was oblivious to all this as a child. Of course, *20,000 Leagues* and *Peter Pan* were two of my favorite movies, and so was *Pinocchio.* I must have seen each at least seven times.

I was especially fond of *Peter Pan* because of Tinker Bell. She was my first love, really, long before I knew what love was, or began to like films with kissing scenes, or Marilyn Monroe and Kim Novak. How I loved that bitch Tinker Bell. And what a shrew she was. As bad as they come. But I loved her. She slew me, cut me to the quick, without my knowing why.

Anyway, there we were in Havana, all of us kids, before Fidel, watching gay films, oblivious to the fact that insidious Disney, that closet queen, lured us all to perversion so slyly. Those of us who were genuine macho men in the making, lusting after Tinker Bell and even Snow White, could have been subliminally corrupted by Disney if Saint Fidel had not come to the rescue. He rescued us all from gayness. Rescued us before we would lose our boy lust for Tinker Bell and be drawn hypnotically to Peter Pan, the Lost Boys, Hook, and all his gay pirates instead. *Maricones.*

Fidel saw so clearly the danger that lurked in the brains of the youngest generation of Cubans. He saw his island nation and his Revolution poised on the brink of sliding into gayness within one generation and raised an iron barrier as soon as he could.

That's what Fidel must have been thinking when he barred us from seeing the *Nautilus*. He hated gays with a passion, and still does. Fidel didn't want to perform the usual head transplant on gays. No, he despised gays so much, he would have much preferred to see them all drowned in the turquoise sea. They didn't necessarily plant bombs, but they definitely didn't conform to his image of what a genuine Cuban should be. They insisted on exercising their own will, and being different, and following their own impulses.

Which is the last thing one is supposed to do in Fidel's eternal Revolution.

Anyway, I woke up to the fact that something had gone awfully wrong with the world that day. We stood there for a while, all of us, asking questions, complaining. Incredulous, our gang of five: Manuel, Rafael, Eugenio, my brother, and I. It was the sheer shock of encountering a stupid rule that kept us there, loitering under the marquee. We couldn't bring ourselves to go home. We looked at one another in disbelief, feeling an extra tug from the earth's gravity. But eventually the awful truth sank in, despite the tug of the earth's pull. We weren't going to get in. We were screwed. Crushed under a giant thumb.

Sharing disbelief is quite an experience, and so is sharing a sense of doom. Though we had all been friends forever, we had never been so close, I fear.

No *20,000 Leagues Under the Sea* that night. No Ned, no Captain Nemo. No *Nautilus* plowing through the turquoise sea to ram helpless clipper ships. No men in diving suits collecting sponges on the sandy sea floor. Worst of all, no giant squid.

What was so bad about a giant squid?

We piled back in the car, crestfallen, rubbing our necks, all with the same look in our eyes.

"Come on, kids, let's go to Tropicream," said Louis XVI. "Let's go for a milk shake."

Those tropical shakes were out of this world, and they were about to disappear along with so many other things that could make a day special. So many different flavors that even I, Mr. Memory, can only remember a handful of names. *Ciruela. Frutabomba. Guanábana. Guayaba. Naranja. Piña. Plátano.* Mango. Mamey. I always went for the mamey, despite the fact that the name *frutabomba*—bomb fruit—was so appealing, so explosive. The color and taste of mamey were sublime. Some kind of bright red with an infusion of crazy pink that I have never seen duplicated in nature, except for a few tropical flowers. I won't even attempt to describe the taste: it would be as hard as trying to explain color to someone blind from birth. But now that I think about it, what drew me to those shakes must have been the hallucinogenic substance that is supposedly hidden deep within the mamey pits.

I think they used the pits in the mamey shakes at Tropicream. Those shakes always made me feel smarter. After one of them, I could fuse with almost any paradox, and I felt a special oneness with nature—all of it, except for lizards, of course.

But after my mamey shake that night I didn't feel any closer to understanding the riddle of Fidel, Ned, Nemo, *Nautilus,* and the giant squid. What had just happened? What had gone wrong? And am I any closer to an answer, so many years later?

Oh, for a mamey shake! Even better, a mamey pit! After a taste of mamey essence, I bet I'd be a lot closer to the truth.

To understand Fidel you have to be out of your mind. To live with the memories, too, it helps to have lucid moments that others mistake for delusions.

So, someone, please, get me a mamey with a big pit inside. One of those lustrous dark pits, as dark as the dots on dice, as dark as a stain on a pristine soul, almond shaped, about the size of a little boy's fist. Get me that pit. I need it. Badly.

And get me some mamey blossoms too: single blooms held between Tinker Bell's lips; bouquets pressed against the breasts of flamenco dancers; basketfuls, whole fleets of trucks, stadiums full of them, handled by laughing acolytes in turquoise vestments; and meteor craters, canyons, volcanoes, Great Lakes, deserts, oceans, continents, moons, and planets, and rings around planets, too, brimming over. All of Venus overflowing with mamey flowers.

But I suspect that just a single petal would be a gift beyond measure, and eternal, evanescent though its presence would be. Ridiculous the waste sad time before and after.

Yes, please. Here, now; quick, now. Evermore. I envy the rays of light that shine on these flowers, the insects that swill their nectar or doze on them, and the winds that make them flutter and waver. I envy the lizards that breathe on them, even.

I have no idea what they look like, mamey blossoms, or how they smell, or feel, or taste. Fidel drove me out of Eden before I could find out, and he stands there still, clutching a fiery sword, to keep me from reclaiming the knowledge that should be mine.

If you ever do get your hands on a mamey pit, or anything else like it, rush out immediately to any theater and watch any film your heart desires, and steel yourself for the awakening.

You'll see for yourself.

Stand in line for a ride at any Disney paradise, too, if you can. The long lines, the expense, and the sheer idiocy of the place will irk you to no end. But you will have entered into that vapid world of your own volition, without anyone standing in your way.

And maybe, as you stand in line, you will catch a whiff of Cuban cigar smoke, wafting at you from a faraway island where mamey plants are ever in bloom; a lizard-shaped isle where no one gets to choose freely and the only idiocy allowed is that which is sanctioned by Fidel.

26

VEINTISEIS

Seven guys in the car, plus you at the wheel. Damn it, it's so crowded in there that you can hardly steer the car or shift gears. It's not a luxury car, you know.

And the trunk. My God. The trunk.

And the clock, the clock. Ticking away. What if the G2, Fidel's secret police, pull up the street as you're backing out of the driveway?

Good. Thank God. You made it to the corner. Now you can turn onto the wide boulevard and fly. And if the G2 crosses your path, no big deal. They won't know who's in the car or what's in the trunk.

Two blocks. Five blocks. Good. But such a long way to go till you reach the next safe house, where you'll unload your cargo. Ten blocks. Great! But will you look suspicious to the police if they see your car with eight guys in it, packed tight like sardines? Hope not. Better not. No way in hell, dear God. No.

You're nervous. And you have every right to be. The trunk of your car is full of weapons, ammunition, and explosives.

Damn it all to hell. The traffic light is all you can focus on for the moment. No, please, don't let that light turn red. Not now. Every second counts.

The light turns yellow while you're still a few yards from the intersection. You think you can make it, so you step on the accelerator and shift into fourth gear. Your friends shout at you.

"Go for it, Fernando. Go!"

"We can't afford to sit still at this intersection."

"Still too close to the house we left. Hit it, bud!"

"Hit it!" *Dale, coño! Anda!*

Vrrrrrroooooooooooooooooooooooooooooooommmmm!

Coño! Qué mierda! Shit. Damn it. Won't make it. No.

Quickly, in one awful split second, the light goes red, just as the car's windshield hits the intersection. Bright, shining red.

Noooooooooo! No! God damn it all to hell. No! How you hope that no one saw you and your car full of men and munitions. There had better not be any cops close to that intersection.

No!

Hell! No! Hell! No! Sweet God in heaven! No! God damn it! No!

A cop car in the rearview mirror, with its red light flashing. No! Well, not cops, really. Militiamen. But they're the same thing. No! And the siren switches on, too. No! Cubans love to turn foul words into epic poetry when things go wrong, but in this case all that comes out of your mouth is a simple prayer: *"Dios mío, ayúdanos!"*

My God, help us!

If the trunk of your car is full of weapons, ammunition, and explosives, and your car is painted bright purple and lacks a muffler, and there are seven other grown men crammed into it, never, ever run a red traffic light. Especially not in a place where only the police and the militia are allowed to bear arms. And especially not in a place where the penalty for owning or transporting arms is death by firing squad.

It nearly cost Fernando his life to run that red light. He was lucky to walk away with a mere thirty-year sentence, and even luckier not to serve the whole three decades. God knows how many mistakes he'd made before that fateful instant when he decided not to stop for the traffic light. God knows how much he'd gotten away with. This time he didn't get away with anything.

I've often wondered how many times he must have replayed that moment in his mind as he sat in his cell and watched the days turn into months and the months into years and the years into decades, as his teeth dropped out of his gums like overripe breadfruit from a tree. Someday I should ask him. But he doesn't ever want to talk about it. No. He knows it was the biggest mistake he's ever made.

Does anyone ever really like to talk about their biggest mistake, even if it's just having worn bell-bottom pants, or having taken too many sedatives before one's own wedding?

He ran the red light, and the only reason the militia cops noticed, they told him later, was the roar made by his car. *Vrrrrrooooooooooooooooo-ooooooooooooooommmm!*

Fernando had failed to see that patrol car down the street he was crossing, past the red light. He didn't see it before he stepped on the gas pedal. No.

The militiamen weren't even looking at the intersection or the traffic light. But who would fail to notice a bright purple speeding car, especially one without a muffler, and jam-packed with men? It was so easy to spot Fernando and chase him down. It was almost as if he'd shouted out through a loudspeaker: "Here I am, come get me, I'm breeeeaaaaking the law!"

When the militia cops stopped him, the other guys quickly bolted, like clowns from a tiny car at the circus, spreading out in different directions.

"Gotta go, Fernando. Gotta make it to the wedding on time . . . *hasta luego.* See you later, buddy." "Hey, buddy, hang tough . . . bye!" *"Oye, chico, tú sabes . . . tenemos que echar un pie."* "Hey, buddy, you know, we've gotta run . . . Don't worry, we'll help you pay the fine."

And so on.

Many of those guys would be dead in a few months, killed during the Bay of Pigs invasion. But at the time all they knew was that they had to scram as fast as possible, before the militiamen asked Fernando to open the trunk. They knew what was coming, and how much they'd be needed. They were all working closely with the CIA and the exiles in Florida, trying to distribute weapons throughout Havana so that when the exiles landed, a mass uprising against Fidel could take place.

Fernando had been quietly summoned that day to a house full of guns, ammunition, and explosives that had to be moved somewhere else in a hurry. The message came in person. You never used the phone. Rumor had it that Fidel's secret police, the G2, had been tipped off by a traitorous informant, and that they were on the way to raid the house. So Fernando drove there as fast as possible, helped them load his car, and all eight of them headed for another house in another neighborhood.

Fernando's trunk wasn't all that large, so we're not talking about a huge stash of armaments. No. Just one trunkful. But all it took to earn the death sentence was possession of a single weapon. One.

"Open up the trunk, now."

"Hey, guys, come on. There's nothing in there."

"Open it. Now!"

"Hey, guys, how about just giving me a ticket for the red light? Deal? Huh? We were all late for a wedding, and I couldn't let all of us be late. One guy was the best man . . ."

"Then how come your friends all went in different directions just now?"

"Well, you know . . . weddings make us guys nervous and addled, don't they? Kind of like a death sentence, isn't it? Kind of like watching your friends being executed, one by one? No? . . . Either one of you guys married yet?"

Fernando delayed as much as possible so the other guys could get away. He marveled at the cops being so dumb as to let the other guys run. If they were dumb enough to let his friends get away, Fernando thought, maybe they could also be talked out of searching the trunk.

"Enough bullshit. Open the trunk!"

"I told you, there's nothing in there. I don't even have a spare tire."

He was telling the truth there. You don't think anyone who willfully removes his car's muffler, just for the sound effects, would carry a spare tire, do you?

"Open it. Now!"

Making sure that the last of his friends was out of sight, Fernando finally complied.

"*Qué mierda! Me cago en diez!* Those bastards, those sons of whores! Look what they put in here! And they didn't even tell me! Damn all of their mothers' wombs! *Cabrones. Hijos de puta!* How could they do this to me and not tell me?"

Fernando tried to blame it on his friends, who were now out of sight, but the cops didn't buy it. They took him immediately to G2 headquarters, where he was horribly tortured for days on end. And he never gave them any information.

They combed Havana for his friends but failed to find a single one. At least for a while. They'd find many of them later, and kill them, when they tried to start the uprising that never happened.

Fernando won't show you the scars or talk about what they did to him at G2 headquarters. All he'll say is that he thought he had died and gone to hell.

The headquarters for the G2 police was in a mansion on Fifth Avenue, not far from our house. It was a beautiful house with a lovely garden. We drove by often, to see if Fernando's car was still parked outside. It was there for several weeks, his purple car, outside that pretty house, parked in the shade, under a big tree, and then one day it was gone.

Gone. Who knew where? That beautiful, deadly car, gone. And Fernando gone, too. We were all sure he'd be executed.

But he was saved by a fluke. Or call it Divine Providence. Fernando hadn't been born in Cuba, but in Seville, Spain, while his father, my uncle Filo, was stationed there at the Cuban consulate in the early 1930s. This meant that he was legally a foreigner. And since his father was a career diplomat, he knew who could help him at the Spanish embassy in Havana. He went to work on this as furiously as any father would, and the Spanish embassy staff ended up saving Fernando's life.

At his trial, the fact that Fernando wasn't born in Cuba, coupled with pressure from the Spanish government, earned him a lesser sentence than what the law required: thirty years in prison.

That's not to say that Fernando was spared from the firing squad, once he was jailed. No. Prisoners such as Fernando were often prepared for execution, led to the *paredón,* and shot at. Prior warnings were not considered necessary. Too formal.

Preparen! Apunten! Fuego!

Blam! Blam! Blam! Blam! Blam! Blam!

Silence.

Laughter. Loud, raucous laughter.

"Look, the bastard crapped in his pants!"

"Bet you thought this would be it, huh?"

"Bet you liked our aim, didn't you? We're such bad marksmen. Ha!"

"Just fooling. These weren't blanks at all. We just aimed above your head. Ha, ha! Fooled you, ha! But this one coming up now is for real!"

"Okay, men: *Preparen! Apunten! Fuego!*"

Blam! Blam! Blam! Blam! Blam! Blam!

"Ha, ha, ha!"

"Look, he had even more crap left in him, and more piss too!"

"Ha, ha, ha!"

Fidel's men sometimes shot prisoners with blanks, just for the thrill of it, as a way of driving the prisoners mad and breaking them. And sometimes they shot over their heads once or twice before shooting to kill, or shooting to maim horribly.

You see, one never knew whether the rifles were loaded with real bullets or with blanks, whether they were aiming high or at your body. One could be roused out of bed before dawn, or snatched from the cell at noon, or at three in the afternoon, or eight at night, without any warning or any real death sentence having been passed, and led to the wall, and shot at. Most of the time it was with real bullets, but sometimes it wasn't.

Prisoners such as Fernando, who refused to talk, or showed no sign of remorse for their counter-Revolutionary sins were shot at more often. It was a kind of perverse Russian roulette.

He won't talk about that either—about what it feels like to stand in front of a firing squad over and over and over again, not knowing if *this* time, *this* time, *this* time, it's for real.

You see, prisoners were also often forced to watch one another's executions. So Fernando knew about the blanks, and about the shooting into the air, and the shooting to kill. He also knew about the real ammunition, and what really happened when someone was riddled with bullets. He knew that much too often the firing squad aimed to maim, not to kill, and that they'd make the condemned suffer as much as possible before blowing out his brains, with the so-called *coup de grâce*.

Blam!

"Thank you very much, comrade, I must have deserved it."

Through all of this, and even more, Fernando remained as tight-lipped as a corpse. Never revealed any information about his companions or what they were up to. And he reserved his deepest silence for what could have been his greatest boast.

What would you have said or not said, if you'd almost killed Fidel?

You had it all planned. You'd been so careful. You had it timed down to the minutes and seconds. You'd risked your life to approach a couple of guys you weren't too sure about. You'd rehearsed it so many times.

But where the hell was that guy with the key to the hangar? He was already seven minutes late. Seven precious minutes.

The guys who were busy distracting the guards, and those other guys who were distracting the controllers at the tower couldn't keep up their bullshit much longer. No. And that jet in the hangar was so full of the stuff you needed. Loaded. Ready to go. But locked tight. There, behind that hangar door. So close and yet so far.

Eight minutes. Damn it all to hell, where was he?

Nine minutes. Shit. *Qué mierda*. Where's that guy?

You need to get into that jet and fly low over the western end of Havana. You need to fly right over the cemetery, right over the family pantheon, and swoop right towards the Castillo del Príncipe, and beyond that, to the Plaza of the Revolution, where Fidel is giving his speech. They won't expect a plane from that direction.

No doubt, he'll talk for hours. But here at the airport the time is slipping away. If the guy with the key gets here any later than this, the risks will be enormous, the chance for success minimal. They'll catch on and shoot you all dead on the spot for trying to take that plane out without authorization.

Ten minutes! Where's the bastard? And what if a guard shows up now? What will you say? Maybe you should just tell him the truth? Tell him that you intend to fly the jet that's inside that hangar right over the Plaza of the Revolution and unload all of its bombs and all of its ammunition on the speaker's platform under the monument to José Martí, right on Fidel and his brother Raúl and Che Guevara and all the other bastards who sit up there with him every single time, licking his butt. And the beauty of it is that Fidel's pulpit is so far removed from the crowd, so high above them, and so far back. It's so easy to see and easy to hit, with little chance of civilian casualties.

Drop the bombs, let them fly. Down, down, down, right on Fidel's head. Nice big bombs. What a nice sound they'll make. What a sight, too.

Maybe if you describe how nice the explosions will be, any guard who shows up will join your team?

Twelve minutes! Forget it . . . so close, so close, and it's slipping away.

Qué mierda. Coño. Carajo.

The guy who was supposed to open the hangar—the only guy who could—never made it to the airport on time. His alternator belt snapped off on his way to the airport, and he had no replacement, and couldn't rig up a substitute fast enough.

Or at least that's what he said. Maybe he had chickened out. Who knows?

When your life's on the line, it's easy to choke. It happens to the best of men. So, even if they make up a story, you take them at their word.

Fernando and the other men waited and waited, ready and willing to take even greater risks if he showed up late. But by the time he showed up, it was way, way too late.

I bet Fidel doesn't know how close he came to dying that day.

Flash forward, five years.

Fernando sits in his cell at the Isle of Pines penitentiary as he always does, day after day. He thinks about the visit he had the day before from his sister Maria Luisa. He shakes his head and wonders how it is that she could fall in love with the guy a few cells down from him. How can a man and a woman fall in love during these brief, closely watched visits? Amazing. He wonders if he'll ever spend time with a woman again, before he's too old to really enjoy it. He cracks jokes that the other prisoners can hear in their cells, and they all laugh.

Flash forward ten years.

Fernando sits in his cell at the Isle of Pines penitentiary as he always does, day after day. On this particular day, he's been offered a chance at freedom. As they've done more times than he cares to remember, the prison authorities have asked him to undergo a "rehabilitation" program in exchange for freedom. If he will only sign an oath of loyalty to the Revolution and allow himself to be properly educated in its glories, then he can walk out a free man. Marked and stained and always closely watched, but free. As he has done more times than he cares to remember, he's told them all to go to hell. He thinks about that cruel ritual he has witnessed so many times, where the guards strip all the prisoners naked and parade the most handsome of them in front of the newly arrived inmates to find out who among them is gay. He thinks about how anyone who gets aroused is taken away for a special mandatory "rehabilitation" program that includes the application of electrical currents to the genitals. He thinks of all the other unmentionable tortures he has witnessed. He thinks about his own pain and the time lost. Fernando cracks jokes that the other prisoners can hear in their cells, and they all laugh, even those who have been through rehabilitational electrocution.

Flash forward, fifteen years.

Fernando sits in his cell at the Isle of Pines penitentiary as he always does, day after day. One of his remaining teeth hurts like hell today, and he feels feverish. His back hurts, too, where he has that large lump over his spine, right there, where the prison guards beat him with their rifle butts years ago. He keeps thinking about the letter he received from Uncle Amado in far-off Bloomington, Illinois, and what he had to say about a Spanish admiral named Nieto who was pressing for his release. Lucky thing Uncle Amado saw the man's name mentioned in the Bloomington *Pantagraph* and had the nerve to write him and ask if he might be related to us. Lucky thing our family has been obsessed with genealogy for so long, and the admiral can easily find out that he *is* related to us. Lucky thing this admiral takes up the cause of pressing for one Spanish citizen's freedom from a Cuban prison. In the long run, the painfully slow process set in motion by the admiral will set him free before his thirty-year sentence is complete. In the meantime, Fernando cracks jokes that the other prisoners can hear, and they all laugh.

Flash forward, twenty years.

Fernando sits in his cell at the Isle of Pines penitentiary as he always does, day after day. Once again, those bastards have urged him to accept "rehabilitation" in exchange for his freedom. Today they rattled off a long list of former inmates who swore loyalty to the Revolution and are now back with their families—many of them in the United States. All of the names belong to men he knows and respects. Once again, Fernando has told them to go to hell. Unknown to Fernando, in far-off Chicago, one of the men whose name was on that list is talking to his cousin Tony at O'Hare Airport. The man has just arrived in the States and taken a job at the airport, where he'll be working for Tony every day. The man tells Tony that Fernando was the funniest inmate at the Isle of Pines, and always kept everyone in stitches. He also tells him that Fernando is holding fast, refusing to undergo "rehabilitation." Back at the Isle of Pines, Fernando cracks jokes that the other prisoners can hear in their cells, and they all laugh.

Flash forward, twenty-three years.

Fernando is free at last, standing on Spanish soil. His father, my Uncle Filo, lays in a heap at the feet of King Juan Carlos of Spain, and Fernando is right next to him, wondering what to do or say. Filo has tripped and fallen at the feet of the King of Spain, at an airport outside Madrid. He's a much smaller man than he used to be, Filo Nieto, and he looks a lot less distinguished. His suit is as wrinkled as his soul, and his eyes have a peculiar look to them. He has a look in his eye like that of a father who has heard the sound of rifles shooting at his son over and over.

Filo has fallen down and has trouble raising himself off the ground because he is drunk. Dead drunk. He is dead drunk because he did see and hear firing squads shooting at Fernando more times than he wishes to remember, and he is now a crushed, thoroughly wrecked man. You see, Filo would eventually also be arrested and imprisoned, and subjected to watching or listening to the shooting charades staged by Fidel's firing squads.

"Hey, Nieto, wake up. *Buenos días!* We're about to shoot your son in five minutes. When you hear shooting outside, that'll be your son getting shot. Enjoy your breakfast."

He would also see and hear other things in prison that made him lose his mind completely for a while. But that's another story.

Fernando laughs and laughs, inwardly, at the sight of his father, who has spent most of his life trying to discover some family ties to royalty, lying there drunk at the feet of the King of Spain. He helps his father up, whispers in his ear, and encourages him to muster as much composure as he can.

Fernando searches for words. *Straighten up, Dad. Fix your tie. This is the King of Spain, right here . . . Oh . . . so sorry, Your Majesty, excuse us, please . . . Your Highness, we're all a little worn out. You have my word, next time I'm released from prison, and you help me get out, we'll all try to be more poised and well-mannered.*

Flash forward, thirty-one years.

Fernando sneaks up behind me at my cousin Rafael's house in San Juan, Puerto Rico, and taps me on the shoulder. I turn around and see a thin, graying, bald guy with a moustache who is much shorter than me. I don't recognize him at all. He realizes I am clueless.

"Carlos . . . *soy* Fernando!"

I recognize him, probably with the same look on my face that Jesus' disciples had when they saw him after the Resurrection. I hug this guy who used to toss me into the air.

"Fernando! . . . *Oye, qué maravilla, esto!*" I say in my rusty Spanish.

"Here, Carlos, I want you to meet my wife and son . . . . And, by the way, how'd you get so tall so fast? The last time I saw you, you were just a shrimp."

I laugh, then remain speechless for a while. As silent as a lizard basking in the sun.

27

VEINTISIETE

She was so unbelievably beautiful. It hurt, sometimes, just to look at her. And she was so, so nice. Never ever had I thought it possible for any teacher to be so wonderful.

She was young: still under thirty, I'm sure.

And she liked me so much. It hurt, sometimes, just to feel her affection. I thought the other kids in my fifth-grade class could tell that there was something going on between me and our teacher. Whenever one of my parents would show up, she'd start gushing about how good a student I was, and how courteous, and so on. It was so awkward and embarrassing for me to have to stand there and listen to all this, especially when other kids were within earshot.

She actually told my mom once that I had the nicest skin, and that she loved to feel my arm. And she ran her fingertips back and forth over my forearm right then, slowly, as always, just to show Marie Antoinette how she did it. Good God! I wanted the earth to swallow me whole. But I also felt good about it. It puzzled and sickened and thrilled me, all of this.

Even I, a snot-nosed fifth grader with black dirt under all his fingernails, could tell that her soul sparkled.

She was bright, too. Smarter than any teacher I'd ever had before. And she never made you feel dumb for not knowing as much as she did. Any-time she told you something you didn't know, it was as if she were opening a golden door to a room full of treasure.

It didn't matter which subject she taught: she had a way of making you like them all. In math, you'd actually care about the trains rushing towards each other at different speeds; in English, you'd be eager to learn more about the seemingly insane rules of pronunciation; in poetry, you'd long to write poems yourself, or even to die in a hail of bullets while charging the enemy, just like the Cuban poet José Martí; in history, you'd be transported to the past as if in a time machine.

And she didn't call any of us by our last names. No. She used our first names or our nicknames. She was intimate with each and every one of us.

This school, El Salvador, was great, and I loved every fraction of a second I spent there. The name was perfect—the Savior—for I had been redeemed, set free from the hell that was La Salle del Vedado. When I was there, it was as if time stood still. Even then, I knew that, somehow, I was already enjoying eternity, in some weird way. Everything was a great surprise and a wondrous homecoming all at once.

Plato would have been so proud of that classroom. The teacher led us to behold the eternal forms, and we uttered sighs of recognition each and every day. Truth, goodness, and beauty were all of one piece, and my teacher was living proof of that. I'm sure if Plato had been there, he would have fallen in love with her. And not in a platonic sort of way. No, I'm willing to wager that he would have wanted more than words to pass between them.

Who knows? Plato might even have boasted to his disciples about the hickeys on his philosopher's neck and the perfume that had rubbed off on him. He might even have sought advice from much younger men about the ways of the world, bought himself some loud shirts, or taken up smoking.

Immanuel Kant, on the other hand, wouldn't have noticed her at all. He would only have worried about whether or not it was time to go for a walk yet, and whether or not the teacher was being thorough enough in finding ways to make the obvious seem complicated and profound. That school, in fact, might actually have unnerved him and led him to use three pairs of garters, or four, in place of the usual two. Kant wouldn't have looked out the window at the beautiful foliage and the sunshine that bathed it. He wouldn't have noticed the clouds either, I'm sure, or the girls in the classroom.

I noticed all these things, of course.

Beautiful plants, sunshine, and clouds were not new to me. But they seemed so different—so much nicer—when viewed from a classroom full of girls.

Even the *Caballero de París* looked good from our classroom window. The *Caballero*—the Gentleman from Paris—was a crazy man who dressed in a tuxedo and wore a flowing black cape and a top hat, even on the hottest days. He had shoulder-length gray hair and a beard as full as that of an Orthodox priest. He walked up and down the streets of Havana, especially Fifth Avenue in Miramar, always looking as if he were making his way to an awesome party. I'm told he was fond of reciting poems to women on the street and that he sometimes gave them flowers.

My brother and I made fun of him whenever we saw him, naturally, and so did our friends. Whenever we saw him while riding in the car, though, our dad would stop us dead in our tracks.

"He's a very wise man. He may be crazy, but he's infinitely wise. Treat him with respect."

"But he's nuts!"

"Yeah, *Papa,* you're just saying that because he's from Paris."

"You can be crazy and wise all at once. The two usually go together, because wisdom makes you see things others don't," said Louis XVI.

In our classroom it was a very different story, however.

"El Caballero!" someone would shout. "He's here, look! There he goes!"

Everyone would rush to the windows, gawk, and make fun of the guy. Our teacher was unable or unwilling to stop us. That would have never happened at either of my former schools.

The truth was that the *Caballero* looked more dignified when viewed through a window in a classroom with as many girls as boys. He almost made sense, even though we loved to laugh at him. Especially the boys. We laughed, maybe, because we wanted to dress like the *Caballero* and spout poetry. Maybe we knew we'd end up like the *Caballero* someday, looking and acting ridiculously insane for the sake of love, driven by some inner music that would never stop. He was a bearded prophet: our Isaiah, our Jeremiah, heralding our joyous doom in top hat and cape.

Maybe the girls laughed because they too saw their future in the *Caballero*. Maybe they saw themselves being courted by avatars of the Absurd and loving it without knowing why.

Girls. Too many words for them in Spanish, because the Spanish are infinitely wise about such things. *Niñas. Niñitas. Muchachas. Muchachitas. Hembras. Jevas.* Their presence made everything so much less hard-edged that it changed the way we boys behaved towards one another. There was less teasing, less wanton cruelty. Far fewer fights, too.

In that school there was a constant buzzing, as though some kind of current flowed through the room, effecting a slow electrocution that made your senses come alive. Even a huge box of a hundred different Prismacolor pencils made sense. Before, I'd considered any box containing more than twenty pencils a useless extravagance, something Sugar Boy would buy just to show off. How many shades of the same color did anyone need, anyway? Now, in fifth grade, one hundred different colors didn't seem enough. I wanted the biggest box of Prismacolors ever made. Five hundred pencils, a thousand, ten thousand, each a different hue. More pencils than could fit into my entire school.

Not enough.

I was alive for the first time, or so it seemed, because of the girls. We remained two different species from different planets most of the time, but every now and then we'd interact.

It was nice to laugh with girls. Nice to sit near them. Nice to look at them. Nice to listen to them talk. Nice to talk to them on those rare occasions when we crossed the gulf that separated us. Nice to smell them, too.

But it wasn't the least bit nice to get caught liking one of them. Not at all. No way.

You'd have to go through the mating ritual. It seemed to happen at least once a week. It was horrible, infinitely worse than seeing men get shot on live television.

Whenever the word got out that some boy liked a girl, or vice-versa, their classmates would gang up on them at recess. They'd sneak up on their victims. Usually, it was their closest friends who got close to them, acting innocent, and then jumped on them and hugged them tightly. (Usually, it was this very same Judas who had spilled the beans and let everyone know about the romance.) Then all the others in their class would gang up on the victims, like a phalanx of Spartan warriors, and push them slowly towards the center of the playground. Boys at one end, pushing one of theirs; girls at the other end, pushing one of theirs towards the same point.

Screaming, shouting, taunting, such as you should never wish to hear. And that awful chant from hell, composed by demons, no doubt.

"Ricardo ama a Marta . . . Ricardo ama a Marta . . . Ricardo ama a Marta . . ."

Ricardo loves Marta . . . Ricardo loves Marta . . . Ricardo loves Marta . . .

"Marta ama a Ricardo . . . Marta ama a Ricardo . . . Marta ama a Ricardo . . ."

Usually, Marta and Ricardo, or whoever was being pushed, would squirm and try to drag their feet. But it was as useless as struggling against prison guards leading you to the *paredón*. The chanting always grew louder as the two groups got closer and closer. And the shouting and laughing from all the other kids assembled in the playground usually turned into a roar.

The teachers did nothing to stop the torture.

Keep in mind that in most cases, only one of the parties being pushed towards the center felt any attraction or "love." For the other party, it was usually a total surprise.

Imagine revealing your deepest secret to your best friend and having your crush announced to the entire school. And imagine being forced to hug and kiss the object of your affections for the first time in front of the whole school—or worse, imagine being forced to hug and kiss someone you weren't the least bit interested in, or didn't like at all.

That's what happened at the center of the playground, when the two phalanxes finally met: the boy and the girl would be pushed into each other's arms and taunted until they embraced and kissed. And then the roar from the playground would be deafening. Maybe the Colosseum in Rome sounded like that sometimes.

Little did I know in September, as I laughed at all this, that by February I'd be the one being led to my execution.

It happened so suddenly, and without warning. Funny how it always sneaks up on you, just like Cuba clouds.

One day I was fine. The next day I was in love, transfixed, pierced right through. Ablaze but not consumed, like the burning bush on Mount Sinai. What a shock. I'd been in love before, sure, but it had always been some actress on a movie screen or on television, and the flames had burned low. This time it was a girl my age, someone I could actually have touched, if I'd had the nerve. And the flames were like solar flares.

She sat to my right, across a narrow aisle. Forget those blondes, Marilyn and Kim. Forget all blondes. She had brown hair, cropped straight across her wondrous neck. Her eyes were brown, too, and she had very thin, very fine eyebrows.

Jesus H. Soul-searching Christ, how could everything about her be so wonderful? Each and every hair on her head. The bridge of her nose. The bones in her wrist. The feet inside those brown shoes. The fine, fine hairs on her legs, the way she rested her hands on the desk, the way she sharpened a pencil, the way she laughed, the way she ran on the playground, the way she clipped her syllables.

Her voice.

Forget Odysseus tied to the mast, and the song of the Sirens. Rank amateurs, the Sirens. Her sound waves were keyed in to all five senses, not just one. You could have plugged my ears with hot molten lead and the sound would still have invaded the core of my soul. I believe there was also some sixth sense involved, maybe a seventh and eighth, too.

That space between us couldn't have been more than a foot and a half, but it was as vast as the entire universe and as null as zero itself. It was a space I dared not cross, though she already dwelt within me. It was sacred space. Numinous.

I never dared to approach her outside the classroom. And inside the classroom, of course, all of our paltry conversations were hemmed in by our lessons and the everyday events that took place within those four walls.

Of course, I would no more have revealed my feelings to her than I would have stretched my ten-year-old hand across the aisle to touch her. But I do know that I made her laugh a couple of times.

How I wanted her to notice me. So, inspired by the *Caballero de París,* I went on a grooming crusade. There had always been this dark ring around my neck and all this dirt under my fingernails. My teeth were always kind of green. And though my hair was always cropped short, it was always messy. I never bothered to tuck in my shirt, either, when it spilled out of my pants, which was every day. All of these faults I attacked with the zeal only a novice can muster.

I began taking showers at noon, when I went home for lunch break, and even using deodorant. I insisted on more frequent haircuts. And whenever my shirt began to spill out of my pants, I'd ram it down into my waistband, furiously. I let my mom know that my shoes needed to be polished every day. And I brushed my teeth at least twice a day.

I tried to talk to her, but only in class. She'd talk back to me, but that was the full extent of our relationship. Still, I thought everything was moving along very nicely, what with my sprucing up and the joking around. Until the day I spoiled it all.

One day, at recess, I couldn't hold it in any longer. It just sort of jumped out of my mouth, like a toad.

"You know, Ciro, I think I'm in love with my right-hand neighbor. You know who."

"Yeah, I can see why," he nodded. Ciro was my best friend.

He could see all right. He could see himself playing Judas.

A couple of days later at recess, it happened. Ciro got close to me and gave me a bear hug, and all the other boys in the class descended on me. I was besieged, captured, and pushed towards the center of the playground. I resisted as much as possible, keeping my eyes closed. I didn't want to know how close we were getting to the awful moment.

Finally, I peeked through half-closed eyelids at the approaching doom. She looked so terrified on the other side. So utterly scared.

We were pulled and pushed to the center of the playground, my first love and I, and God knows what happened there at the center. I can't recall the full horror.

All I can remember is that within four weeks she was gone. Gone forever, just like all the other kids. One by one they disappeared.

It was early 1961. March, to be exact. About one half of my classmates had vanished without saying a word. One day they'd be there, and the next day they'd be gone. Teachers vanished too. Off to the United States or some other country. The rest of us knew why they were vanishing and why they couldn't say good-bye, but it hurt all the same to see the empty desks.

By April the school had to close because there were too few students and teachers, and because so much had changed for the worse.

We children of the Revolution had much to learn when I was in fifth grade. Everything changed. I will tell you all about that soon enough. And as bombs fell from the sky, and bullets flew, and money evaporated, and

Fidel laid claim to our souls, and everyone I knew and cared about vanished quietly, and I began to face the prospect of my own vanishing, what do I remember most vividly?

Her beautiful brown hair brushing against her neck. It was cut in such a straight, straight line.

28

VEINTIOCHO

They say when you die your entire life passes before your eyes in a split second. But even if it's more like an ocean of time than a split second, I'm willing to bet that when my turn comes, I'll see one whole section that is nothing but fragmentary images.

Sometimes, when I least expect it, they'll pop out, these fragments of a world turned upside down. Like flashbacks from a bad trip.

Bummer, man.

Here we go. Hold on . . . *Aguántate* . . . I feel one coming . . . .

There are Pioneers marching down our street. Kids our age, all dressed alike, wearing red berets and red neckerchiefs, marching like little soldiers.

"Uno, dos, tres, cuatro . . ."

Soldiers in the making. Militiamen and women of the future. Spies. Informers. Obedient servants of the Revolution.

The marching is relentless. Every single day, and always at the same time.

Little copies of Immanuel Kant, taking his stupid walk at the same time every day. Dozens and dozens of them, marching down our street. Always in the same direction, too.

How I long for the pesticide Jeep to show up and spray them all. Maybe they'll all get tripped up in the fog and march into one another. A heap of Pioneers left behind, all coughing. We all know they probably couldn't take the poison the way we can.

Stupid red berets and red neckerchiefs. Stupid marching slogans.

"Uno, dos, tres, cuatro, Cuba sí, Yanquis no, Cuba sí, Yanquis no . . ."

"Fidel, seguro, a los Yanquis dale duro . . ." Fidel, undaunted, hit those Yankees hard . . .

But there's no more pesticide Jeep. No pesticide to spray. Like everything else, none to be had.

Tony and I had been Cub Scouts for a while, a couple of years earlier, but had given up in disgust. Too many petty rules masquerading as important stuff. Stupid merit badges. Stupid salutes. Stupid uniforms. I don't think we lasted more than three months. Our troop leader, Fred, was French and had served in the Foreign Legion. What the hell was he doing in Havana, running a Cub Scout troop, and trying to turn us all into little Legionnaires?

We didn't stay with the Scouts long enough to find out.

And now those creeps next door want us to be Pioneers. They badger our parents about it, those creeps who run the Committee for the Defense of the Revolution. They want us to be just like all those kids marching in lockstep down our street, and all around the neighborhood.

They moved into Chachi's house, these neighborhood spies and busybodies. Chachi's family had moved to that gorgeous house by the seaside, only to leave it behind a few months later. Off to the United States, their new house left for someone else. Their old house left behind for spies and meddlers.

Every block in Havana has one of these houses. They're everywhere. Watching. Listening. Prodding. Intruding. Threatening. Controlling. We're unlucky enough to have them next door, and to live in a climate that forces us to keep the windows open all the time.

Manuel comes up with the perfect counter-slogan for the pioneers:

"Uno, dos, tres, cuatro, comiendo mierda y gastando zapatos . . ." One, two, three, four, eating shit and wasting shoes . . .

I must explain: for Cubans, anything that's dumb or a waste of time can be called "eating shit." A chump or a fool is a *comemierda,* or shit eater.

Anyway, after our resident genius Manuel comes up with his counter-slogan, we can't refrain from using it. We hide on the porches, or up in the trees, or behind the shrubs, and shout out as they walk by:

"Uno, dos, tres, cuatro, comiendo mierda y gastando zapatos . . ."

They're all so busy marching in lockstep and shouting out their stupid slogans that they don't hear us.

Or can they hear us? Maybe they can. Every now and then we see a head or two turn and look around, at their own peril. Looking in any direction but forward is wrong. For a Pioneer, that is. Che Guevara has a slogan they also chant, ad nauseam:

"Marcha atrás nunca, ni para coger impulso." Not one step back, not even to gain momentum.

It's dangerous for us to call the Pioneers shit eaters and to accuse them of wasting shoes, especially since shoes are scarce and rationed nowadays. About three or four months ago shoe repair shops started using old tire treads as heels and soles. I see them every day on my dad's wingtip shoes.

And I yell at Pioneers from my hiding place and call them shoe wasters. I wonder how different my life would have been if my mother hadn't caught us doing it.

It frightens her to the core. She has visions, the kind mothers get. Flash-forwards rather than flashbacks. Ugly, tormenting visions of my brother and me being hauled away by militiamen, never to be seen again. Visions of our Defense Committee neighbors overhearing us. Visions of us in some juvenile prison camp way out in the provinces, where all we'd do for the rest of our lives is cut sugarcane. Or even worse, visions of us being packed off to Russia or East Germany or Czechoslovakia, of us disappearing to some foreign land and never returning.

Someday I'll lose count of how many times she's told me about how much we frightened her that day she caught us yelling at the Pioneers, and how much that awful moment weighed in her decision to get us out of the country as soon as possible, in any way possible.

She sees us as little Fernandos, I guess. Next thing you know, we'll be planting bombs and hauling weapons. She knows about our love of fire-crackers, so I guess she's not entirely wrong to worry.

And the rumor begins to circulate. The rumor of all rumors.

The Revolution is going to take all the children away from their parents, and soon. Something in the new Cuban constitution allows for it: *Patria Potestad*. My mother is now convinced that the state is going to herd us into trucks and ship us off to parts unknown. Maybe even to Russia. After all, it happened during the Spanish Civil War in the 1930s, in some areas controlled by the Communists, and everyone knew someone who had known someone who had known someone whose kid had been sent to Russia, never to be seen again.

There are so many Spaniards in Havana, and so many children of Spaniards. The memories are fresh. My mom and many others know it's possible.

Communists? I am hearing the word for the first time. Batista is still president. I am about five years old, and I'm in our car on the way to my grandparents' house, just as we pass what will become the Plaza of the Revolution. It's still under construction. Tony and I are in the backseat, as always, and I hear my parents talking about Communists in the front seat.

"Hey, those Communists must be good guys," I chime in.

"Why do you say that?" asks Louis XVI, with a tone that can only mean I've made a mistake.

"Because they must help people communicate . . ."

Prolonged laughter from the front seat. "How cute," says my mom.

"What's so funny?"

"Oh, never mind, you're too young to understand. But Communists aren't good. Not at all. They're very bad."

Now I am a few years older, passing the same spot, staring at a hammer and sickle on a billboard from the backseat of the car, and we're all supposed to become Communists.

Fidel has declared himself a Marxist-Leninist and proclaimed the Revolution and the country Communist. No more private property. No more mine and thine. No more exploitation of the masses by capitalists. Share and share equally. And if anyone fails to work, then he or she will have nothing to eat. And you can't work just for yourself or for your family. Everyone has to work for everyone else. And everyone owns everything, all together.

So he says.

The Chinese hot dog man has lost his hot dog stand. The Revolution won't tolerate anyone claiming a business for himself. Not even a hot dog stand. The hot dogs have vanished along with a lot of other stuff. Like Coke and Pepsi.

My uncle Mario has lost his two businesses to the Revolution. The last thing he did at his furniture store was to burn all the accounting records so that those who still owed money on their furniture wouldn't have to pay the state. The Revolution wanted to keep collecting the money they owed. The money they owed to themselves, I guess, according to the logic of the Revolution.

My uncle is almost sent to prison for that subversive act.

Fernando Chan has lost his store, too. He can still work there if he wants, but he won't be the owner any longer. He can't give kids raisins and olives, either, since they're not his to give away anymore.

Everyone has lost whatever real estate they owned.

The state has compensated them, but with such paltry sums as to make the whole deal stink.

Besides, one fine morning, recently, Che came up with the great idea of doing away with money altogether. I've had it a few times myself, especially when short on cash. No money at all. Let everyone share and share alike. To each according to his or her needs. So all the banks have been closed, and all accounts have been seized. This is the first step. Everyone who had a bank account can keep some arbitrary low sum—a few hundred pesos, I think. All else is gone, obliterated.

My grandfather cries for a while about that.

The second step is to change all the currency so that the bills and coins that people have will be worthless and all Cubans can start on a completely level playing field. Each person is allowed to change a set amount of money, maybe fifty pesos.

It's a fine Sunday morning and everyone in the country has lined up at appointed places to change whatever money they can. If you haven't changed your money by the end of the day, tough luck. From that day forward, all the old currency will be worthless.

The lines are very long, but they move fast because you are allowed to change so very little. I'm standing in line, and so is my brother Tony, and everyone else I know. No one is sure about the rules, but the money changers don't ask very many questions. When you finally make it to the changing table with bills and coins in your hand, they take them from you and give you new colorful bills with pictures of Fidel and Che and Raúl and Camilo and all the other heroes of the Revolution. The new coins are so flimsy that we take turns trying to blow them off one another's hands.

No one panics, but it's still nothing more than controlled chaos. Very quickly, people discover that they can go to more than one changing center. So everyone is trying to hit as many lines as possible.

I don't think I have ever heard people talk more loudly or faster than on this Sunday morning. And that's saying a lot for Cubans.

"Did you hear that there's another changing center five blocks down, on Twenty-seventh Street?"

"Yeah, and there's another one ten blocks in the other direction, on Ninth Avenue."

Those who don't have enough money to change hire themselves out as changers, for a fee. Some of the fees are pretty high. And there is a lot of thievery going on. You hand your money to perfect strangers who promise to change it for you for a twenty-five-percent cut and you never see them again.

There are plenty of stories about heart attacks.

Four decades later, I am staring at my troubled bank account, meditating on the numbers I see before me. Suddenly I see them all turn to zero. I am back in line that Sunday morning and I don't know whether to laugh or cry. I still expect all the money in America to disappear someday, the same way. It's all an illusion, mere figures on paper. Retirement account? Stocks? Bonds? Savings accounts? Forget it. I don't put away one cent. I don't have any money in any bank, save for the little I have in my checking account, which is always fully depleted by the end of every month. I spend every cent I earn and then some. I'm always in debt, always ready for the day when everyone else will lose their money. On that day, thanks to my advance planning, I won't have any to lose. I'll only have debts to wipe out, like my uncle's customers, come the Revolution.

Ha.

I don't count on my retirement account at all, because I don't expect to see a penny of the money my employer has forced me to put into the hands of professional investors.

College funds for the kids? Ha. Dream on. What's the point? The Revolution will make sure they're educated for free.

Not one penny put away. Not one penny to lose.

I think of my relative Pepito Abeillé, who helped me see the futility of saving money. He was one of those who hired himself out as a changer that Sunday morning. He hustled that day as he had never hustled in his entire life. His problem and his salvation were one and the same. He had never worked a day in his life. His father had lost his entire fortune back in 1929 and he'd been poor since then. But, like some deranged Spanish hidalgo from a picaresque novel, Pepito always dressed in a white silk suit and refused to work, insisting that he was too dignified for any job. He and his mother lived in a tiny apartment in Old Havana that was full of old newspapers and reeked of cat piss. I think the rest of the family kept them alive with small contributions. He was a smart guy, Pepito, and always very proper. But he wouldn't work. He'd come to our house a few times a year, in his white suit, sometimes with his old mother in tow, and visit for a few hours. He had it all figured out. He paid visits to every relative, no matter how distant.

On that Sunday, Pepito made more money than he had in his entire life, changing currency for the family that had supported him for so long. He was doing everyone a favor, and everyone felt obliged to let him take his percentage.

I am back in that line again, getting close to the money changers. I see Pepito coming towards us, walking briskly. I've never seen him move so fast. He's walking all over Havana in his white suit, changing bills and coins for everyone he knows—for a fee, of course. On this day he's lost nothing and gained much.

My hero, Pepito.

I see another hero of the day, my grandfather Amador. He has lost a lot and is weeping, but he hasn't lost everything. For years, he's been stashing away jars of silver coins inside his living room wall. Yes, he opened holes in his wall, put the jars in, one by one, sealed up the wall with plaster, and repainted it. He had lost it all in 1929 and no longer entrusted all of his savings to banks.

He has a wall full of silver on the day the currency changes. He stares at the wall and thinks of the hidden silver that he will mine, little by little, until the day he drops dead. He knows that silver always buys you more stuff than your neighbor, if your neighbor doesn't happen to have any. Even in a Communist paradise. He knows instinctively that ration cards are a scam, just another way of making unfairness seem fair.

Almost everything is rationed now. Every now and then the stores get a huge shipment of rice, or black beans, or beef, or whatever, and the word spreads like wildfire. Everyone rushes down to the store and stands in line forever. Sometimes if the line is too long, by the time your turn is near, they run out of the beans, or the garbanzos, or the chickens, or whatever.

But the greatest scam of all is the black market. People sell you their rations for more than they paid for them, or trade them for whatever they need more. And there are plenty of people like my grandfather, who have silver to mine, or whatever. There is always some whatever in rationing and in Revolutions.

I've been standing in line a lot these past few months. I stand in line with old people, housewives, children, bankers, lawyers, doctors, and former capitalists. Aulet, the man with his own zoo, has to stand in line, too. You have to show up in person, with your card, and stand in line, or you don't get your food.

Everyone has to stand in line, except the leaders of the Revolution. No one ever sees them or their servants standing in line. Yes, they have servants.

Medicines are disappearing too. And clothing. And appliances. And cars. And hardware. And toys. Everything is disappearing.

No more comic books. No more American films. No more American television programs. No more ice-cream man. No more shaved-ice man. No more fruit man. No more vegetable man. No more coal man. No more *guarapo* man. No more Jamaican pastry man, and no pastry man song.

"Pasteles . . . pastelitos . . . Pasteeeles, paaasteliitos . . . Frecos, fresquitos . . . Dulces . . . buenitos." Pastries, little pastries, fresh and sweet and good . . .

I am standing on my porch, listening to his *pregón*—his selling chant. Man, oh man, that tall, tall Jamaican has the best pastries I have ever eaten. He comes around the neighborhood about once a week, on foot, lugging a huge metal container. Always at evening time, after dinner. His bin is a marvel of engineering. I think he built it himself. It's full of little doors that open and drawers that pull out to reveal special surprises. Jamaican guy works the doors and drawers with flair, then holds up the pastry with a pair of tongs for you to examine. You can tell by the way he handles them that he loves his pastries. He is as reverent as a priest at the altar, and even more graceful.

I love the chocolate eclairs that are the same color as his arms. And I love the way he speaks Spanish.

But now there is no more pastry man.

No more avocado man either.

I can hear him still. The avocado man has one of the prettiest chants I've ever heard.

Aguacate maduro, aguacate. Aguaaacate maaaduuuuro, aaaaguuuuaaacaaateee! Avocados, ripe avocados.

We have some good counter-jingles for that guy.

Aguacate maduro, peo seguro. Ripe avocados, fart for sure . . .

Aguacate verdoso, peo apestoso. Greenish avocados, stinky farts . . .

Aguacate amarilloso, peo ruidoso. Yellowish avocados, noisy farts . . .

And so on. We have dozens of them. Even my dad has pitched in with a few counter-jingles of his own.

Aguacate podrido, peo mordido. Rotten avocados, a fart bitten into.

One of his crown jewels.

And there are those damn Pioneers marching again, droning on with their stupid slogans. I think of the avocado man and our counter-chants. Good thing we've had plenty of practice at such things. Stupid Pioneers, reminding us that it is all gone, gone, gone.

A lifetime of memories gone in less than a year. An entire culture pulled up by the roots. It is a Revolution, after all.

The priests have vanished too, along with the monks and the nuns. All religious orders have been banished from Cuba. Gone are the Jesuits who had educated Fidel and my father and grandfather and great-grandfather. Gone are the Dominicans, and the Franciscans, and the Carmelites, and the Christian Brothers, and the Ursulines. Gone are the Italian priests who lived across the street from us. All foreign clergy have been expelled from the island.

I am standing in the front parlor of the priests' house. It is a dark room, the windows shrouded in dark velvet curtains. A confessional booth looms large at the foot of the stairs. These priests are pretty nice, for priests. My mom has sent me to have a chat with the older one because I'm starting to worry about death too much, like everyone in my father's family. He tells me I have nothing to fear, that death is the doorway to something much better, and that, anyway, it is so, so far away for me. He admits that he is much closer to death than me because he's old, but he isn't the least bit scared. He says that when you get to be his age, it doesn't scare you much at all, especially if you've tried to be a good person. I went home feeling so much better.

The younger guy is also very nice. Sometimes he comes over to our house with his tape recorder and asks all of us kids to talk into the microphone and send messages to people in Italy.

"Go ahead and say something. Italians can understand Spanish." And he shows us how close the two languages are by speaking Italian into the microphone himself. Amazing! We can understand him.

So we speak into the microphone and are all surprised when he plays back the tape. Our voices all sound so high-pitched. We accuse one another of sounding like girls. And the priest laughs a lot at the way in which we all seem so offended by one another's accusations.

Every now and then the Italian priests would set up a movie projector outdoors, with a large screen, and show movies for the whole neighborhood. *The Teahouse of the August Moon* was the worst of them all, but we kids had so much fun that night sticking our arms and hands right in front of the projector's lens and making the grown-ups scream at us. Especially when Manuel gave everyone the finger. A giant finger on the screen, blotting out Glenn Ford. I think I heard the priests laugh, in the darkness.

But they are crying, those priests, on the day they say good-bye to us.

Bang, bang, bang, bang, bang, bang, bang, bang, bang . . .

It seems to go on all day long, for all time. It's the sound of sledgehammers pounding on sacred symbols at the former convent and school of the Ursulines, one block away from us. The school where Tony had attended preschool and kindergarten. Sledgehammers demolishing crosses. Sledgehammers pulverizing images of Jesus and Mary and the angels and other saints. Sledgehammers demolishing Gothic spires, too, just because they are Gothic and look religious.

Bang, bang, bang, bang, bang, bang, bang, bang, bang . . .

There is nothing else in the world like the sound of sacred symbols being pulverized, little by little.

You can see the workmen on the roof and the towers. I watch the crosses fall, piece by piece, from a block away. The sound waves take a few seconds to travel the distance from the former convent, so the whole process seems unreal. I hear the sound of the hammers striking the stone as the workmen draw back their tools, gaining momentum for the next blow. A little time lag that makes it seem as if past, present, and future are all askew.

Bang, bang, bang, bang, bang, bang, bang, bang, bang . . .

As we ride our bikes to Che Guevara's palace, we can hear the pounding getting louder and louder. We have to ride past the former Ursuline convent to get to Che's mansion, which is two blocks farther down the street. Only three or four blocks from my house.

We like to ride down there and ask the guards stationed outside about their guns and beg for bullets. We also like to keep an eye out for Che. Sometimes we can see him pulling in and out of the giant mansion in his Mercedes-Benz. He's always dressed in his military uniform with the beret, the man who wants to do away with money. So is his chauffeur.

Such a beautiful house. So huge. Such beautiful grounds. Such great palm trees. Such a fabulous set of wrought-iron gates. Such a nice Mercedes. It looks bulletproof.

Bang, bang, bang, bang, bang, bang, bang, bang, bang . . .

We don't know who owned this house before and we don't care. The number-two guy in Cuba lives down the street from us. He might have done some terrible things, like wiping out everyone's money, but he is famous. And kids always like to say they've seen someone famous. And they like to see their limousines. And their chauffeurs. And their mansions. Even if they realize what big fat hypocrites they are.

Bang, bang, bang, bang, bang, bang, bang, bang, bang . . .

"Not one step back, not even to gain momentum."

"Uno, dos, tres, cuatro, Cuba sí, Yanquis no, Cuba sí, Yanquis no . . ."

"Fidel, seguro, a los Yanquis dale duro . . ."

Bang, bang, bang, bang, bang, bang, bang, bang, bang . . .

Always dressed in his military uniform with the beret, the man who wants to do away with money. So is his chauffeur. I wonder if the chauffeur, a good Revolutionary, has dirty magazines. I'll wonder about it till the day I die.

Aguacate maduro, aguacate. Aguacate maaaduuuuro, aaaaguuuuaaacaaateee!

Aguacate podrido, peo mordido . . .

Bang, bang, bang, bang, bang, bang, bang, bang, bang . . .

"Uno, dos, tres, cuatro, comiendo mierda y gastando zapatos . . ."

Pasteles . . . pastelitos . . . Pasteeeles, paaasteliitos . . . Frecos, fresquitos . . . Dulces . . . buenitos.

"Not one step back, not even to gain momentum."

A giant finger on the screen and priests laughing in the dark.

And they are crying, those priests, as they say good-bye to us. And my grandfather is crying, as he stands in line to change his currency. And the Jamaican pastry guy is crying for his pastries. He loves them so.

And Pepito Abeillé is counting the bills in the pocket of his white slacks.

Whatever. There's always a whatever in Revolutions.

And I wonder if the chauffeur, a good Revolutionary, has dirty magazines.

Aguacate maduro, aguacate. Aguacate maaaduuuuro, aaaaguuuuaaacaaateee!

Aguacate podrido, peo mordido . . .

Bang, bang, bang, bang, bang, bang, bang, bang, bang . . .

But wait, where are the lizards? Can Fidel and Che make them disappear too? So long as everything else evaporates into memories, why not them, too?

Bad acid, and too much of it. Killer flashbacks.

Bang!

Bummer, man.

Ba . . . nG . . . bAnG . . . baNG . . . BA . . . bA . . . bababababa . . . nnnnG . . . gG . . . nNGB . . .

Gnab bing? BanG!

Bgan . . . gban . . . BNaG . . . banbanbanbanG!

Abng . . . B . . . Nn nN . . . . . . NNNgggg . . . b . . . b . . . b . . . . . . n

baa? BbBbB . . . bb . . . N n Ng? . . . . . .

Gg . . . gG . . . gg . . . GG NoNoNoNo . . . no

AaaaaaaaaaA . . . sí . . .

Bang!

<*#!!%$+!>

QUE CARAJO

Some chapters just can't be numbered.
Not at all.
I'm sure you have chapters like that in your life.
They're not safely tucked away in some vault of oblivion, if you have one.
No.
Just the opposite.
The memories are there.
And you wish you could make them go away.
You wish they didn't exist at all.
Ugly as hell.
Hell itself.
The very essence of pain.
You can't assign numbers to these chapters.
Not even zero.
Not even a zero ringed with thorns.
You can't write them the same way as all the others.
They can't look the same either.
No.

If you were to write them, you could only begin to do it at 2:30 a.m., after a horrible day.

Only when your every nerve is on the point of exploding.

Only on a day in which, several times, you thought you'd be better off dead.

Only on a day in which you spoke out loud to the Prince of Darkness in your basement, and told him to stay in hell and leave you alone.

Only after a day in which you were so lucid about your own plight that it hurt to look at your own hands.

Only after a day in which your powers of denial were at their weakest.

This is one of those chapters.

It's about Ernesto.

It is about the boy I can hardly mention.

The boy I can only hint at.

The boy my father brought into our house.

The boy no one liked but my father.

The boy whose soul was twisted beyond belief.

The boy whose own childhood must have been hell.

The boy who came from a very poor family.

The boy who sold lottery tickets all day long instead of going to school.

The boy who saw my father trip over a curb and lose his eyeglasses.

The boy who picked up Louis XVI's glasses and handed them back to him.

The boy my father instantly recognized as his son in a previous life.

The heir to the French throne.

The Dauphin.

The Dauphin, selling lottery tickets on the streets of Havana.

The Dauphin with the blue eyes.

The blue eyes that matched those of Eye Jesus in color.

The blue eyes that always looked so unlike those of Eye Jesus.

The blue eyes in which danced the flames of hell.

He continually betrayed my father's trust of him, unseen.

He was sly and deceitful, and full of rage against all of us.

But I saw, I knew.

Pervert.

He tried.

Repeatedly, for a while.

He tried to hug me the wrong way.

Even when I was so young I didn't understand what he was up to.

Just a few inches away from Eye Jesus.

Jesus H. All-seeing Christ!

Thank you, Eye Jesus, for keeping an eye on me.

You did not allow the worst to happen.

I fought him off, many times.

And he wouldn't stop trying.

Until I got big enough to punch him hard enough.

I remember the day he stopped.

I remember punching and kicking so hard that it hurt me, too.

But just the fact that I had to do that brought me down to hell with him.

He was evil, through and through.

Evil, say the Platonists, is simply the absence of good.

Wrong.

Evil is a presence, real and cunning.

Evil is a spiteful wretch in your own house.

A clever pervert who could twist everything around if you were to speak out.

A pervert smart enough to know that what he was doing could make you look awful.

A pervert you know is capable of poisoning your relationship with your father.

A pervert who knows your mother would believe you, but your father might not.

A pervert smart enough to know that his lies could drive a wedge between your parents.

This is how he paid back my father for all his kindness.

If only I'd trusted in my father more, and in my mother.

If only I hadn't been so awfully young, and so afraid of having my father believe him.

I know now he'd have been kicked out of the house faster than the shoe Tony slid down the hall at me—the one that bounced off my toe and landed in the cup.

The one that earned me such an unjust beating.

I know that now.

I know King Louis would have believed me and sent him back to selling lottery tickets.

Too late, too bad.

I was just a dumb kid, who didn't have a good track record of being believed.

Worst thing of all was that I didn't know the full extent of his perversity.

Tony had to fight him off, too.

I had no idea.

He was very clever, the pervert.

I didn't find out about the full horror until I was forty years old.

Tony was afraid to tell, too.

Jesus H. All-forgiving Christ.

He repaid our father for all his kindness by betraying him thoroughly in secret.

Perhaps he did even worse things I still don't know about.

And our father had to go and adopt him.

Dark day when Louis XVI broke the news to us.

Dark, dark day.

He never asked for our opinion.

He didn't even warn us it was going to happen.

One day he simply said something I never thought I'd hear.

"You know, from this day forward Ernesto will be your brother."

"His surname is now the same as yours."

Louis XVI was able to do this without my mother's consent because he was a judge.

And a judge in Cuba could do just about anything he wanted.

It was legal.

Things were never the same.

Louis XVI and Marie Antoinette didn't get along too well after that.

My brother and I trusted our father a lot less after that.

Ernesto seemed very pleased with himself after that.

Pervert.

Canalla.

Sinvergüenza.

Lizard.

I expect you to call me a liar and to twist everything until the day you die.

Chances are when this is all in print, you will lie and lie and lie.

But I know the truth, and so does God.

I won't send you to hell, though, where you sent me.

Hell is too good for you.

I was just there today, checking it out.

Nope.

Won't do.

I've toyed with the idea of sending you to the same corner of heaven as Immanuel Kant and Mel Blanc and Airport guy, but that's too good for you, too.

Besides, I couldn't do that to Immanuel, no matter how deep his faults.

You might try to hug Kant the wrong way and turn heaven into hell for him.

Instead, I'll send you to another spot in heaven.

The very best spot.

I think you should go straight before the throne of Jesus and spend eternity under his gaze.

I think you should see him staring at you forever.

Staring with rainbow eyes into your blue eyes.

Forgiving you over and over and over.

Embracing you.

Eternally.

29

VEINTINUEVE

Thunder, in my dream. It's a rumble that comes from deep within the earth and also from the sky at the same time. Weird thunder, like I've never heard before. My bed is shaking, and I can see the sound, in my dream. It looks like a giant cloud, big and black, expanding over my house. It gets bigger and bigger, and louder and louder, and darker and darker. And I see flashes of lightning, too. But these aren't real lightning bolts, all snaky and wiggly and forking and diamond white. No. These bolts of lightning look just like the ones in comic books. They zigzag in nice, straight angles, and they're thick and sulphur yellow.

So very odd this thunder. It makes my whole body shake and vibrate.

Am I awake?

No. I don't think so. Wait, maybe I am. Maybe. And what's that rumble within the thunder, the rumble that comes from the giant black cloud? It's more of a whirring than a rumble.

Airplanes. Airplanes, and I'm awake, for sure. Where did these planes come from and why are they flying so low in the middle of the night? Why are they buzzing our house? Are they flying low to escape the lightning?

Booooooomm! Ka-boooooom! Booom-baroooom! Ka-boooooom-boooom!

Whoa, that thunder is so loud! It's even drowning out my mother's voice as she approaches down the hallway. And she's screaming. Yes, she's burst into our room, still dressed in her nightgown, and she's screaming louder than I thought it possible for her to scream.

And I still have some trouble hearing her over the roar of the thunder.

"*Ay Dios mío!* Oh, my God, they're going to kill us all! We're all going to die! *Ay, Dios mío, ay Dios mío!* We're going to die! Quick, get under your beds! Now!"

"What's happening, Mom? It's just a thunderstorm."

"Yeah, Mom, we never have to get under our beds for thunderstorms—"

Boooooomm! Kla-boooooom! Boooom-Bar-oooom-Boom! Ka-booom-ba-boooom!

"Oh my God, it's not thunder, kids! We're being bombed! The planes are dropping bombs all around us! And we're all going to die, we're all going to die! *Ay Dios mío!* Under your beds, NOW! *Nos vamos a morir!* We're going to die, we're going to die, We're going to die! Aaaaaaaaaaaaayyyyyyyyyy!"

The noise outside is deafening. My entire body feels the sound waves, along with the house and everything in it. And it's so dark, outside and inside.

"Aaaaaaaaaaaaayyyyyyyyy! We're going to die! Aaaaaaaaaaaayyyyyyyyy!"

Bombs falling from the sky! I'm finally inside a war movie. But wait, I don't have a helmet or a weapon. Wait a minute, I'm one of those stupid civilians. A child, in a war movie. And what happens to kids in war movies? Hey, I don't like this. The kids often get shot or blown to pieces or turned into very dirty, ragged orphans. They're just there to add pathos to a tragic story. Pathetic props, that's all.

KaarrroooomBoooomBabooom! Booooom! Kaabooooooom!

"Aaaaaaaaaaaaayyyyyyyyy, Dios mío!"

Louis XVI enters the room, still in his boxer shorts, which are as baggy as his trousers. I've never seen him put them on, but I bet that sometimes he puts on his shoes first.

"Calm down! We'll be okay. But get under your beds, anyway."

So I dive under my bed, and I see Tony do the same. Neither one of us says a word.

The planes buzz overhead, flying very low. I don't remember ever hearing airplane engines that near. Are they grazing our roof? Maybe.

Ka-blam, ka-blam, ka-blam, ka-blam . . .

Wait, what's that? Gunfire. Very close, too. Gunfire next door, where

Chachi used to live, now home to the Committee for the Defense of the Revolution. It's hard to make it out through the sound of the explosions, but it's unmistakable. Our new next-door neighbor, the government informant and spy for the entire block, has gone up onto his flat roof and started firing at the low-flying planes.

What if Marie Antoinette is right? What if one of the bombs lands on our house? These explosions are so awesome, and they sound so close. Naaah. Won't happen. Or maybe it will. Funny, I don't hear the bombs whistling when they hurtle towards earth, as they do in war movies. But what if a bomb falls on us?

I start to shake and I plug up my ears with my index fingers. It's not the bombs but the sounds being made by my mom that I'm trying to block out. *Stop it, Mom. You're scaring me.* I don't say this out loud, of course. I'm shaking too much to talk. This fear, what is it? Is that death out there, calling me, calling all of us? I thought I'd live longer than this. No it can't be.

Why can't I stop shaking? Am I really crying? How can I cry about explosions?

Because we're all going to die, that's why. My mother is never wrong. And listen to her.

"Aaaaaaaaaaayyyyyyyyyyyyyyy!"

The noise begins to die down outside the house. I can hear the sound of the engines receding. No more bombs, no more explosions, no more gunfire from next door. Inside the house, it's another story. Marie Antoinette can't stop screaming and crying.

I come out from under my bed and Tony comes out from under his. I'm shaking like some kind of possessed voodoo guy.

Louis XVI is actually hugging Marie Antoinette, something I've never seen before. Now I know for sure that this must have been something really bad.

Two days later we get an even bigger surprise. The Invasion has begun. Armed exiles from Florida have come back to reclaim the island. They've landed in an unlikely place, the Bay of Pigs, which borders the largest swamp in Cuba. And all of us watch this war live on television. We find out about the bombing. It was the prelude to this Invasion. Airplanes piloted by Cuban exiles—some of them Fernando's friends—tried to bomb and strafe Fidel's planes at the Columbia military airfield, not far from my house. Aircraft from the United States, provided by the Central Intelligence Agency, carefully disguised as Cuban Air Force planes. Their goal was to cripple Fidel's air force, so that when the men landed, there would be no planes left to bomb them on the beaches. No such luck. God willed differently that morning and for the next week or so.

The men landed. Around one thousand five hundred of them. And they failed.

They were mowed down like wheat in a sickle's arc, pinned down like bug samples in an entomologist's lab, blown up like lizards in the hands of boys with firecrackers, herded into prisons like cattle at the Chicago stockyards. Many died fighting. Most of them surrendered.

They had no choice. Their backs to the sea, nothing but swamps all around them. No artillery. No air cover. No tanks. And outnumbered, with Fidel's planes bombing the hell out of them.

We saw it all on television, in living black-and-white. The exiles on the beaches, where they were dumped without the air cover they'd been promised. The exiles in the swamps, where they were unloaded by mistake. Fidel's army descending upon them. Fidel's planes, intact, strafing them on the beaches. Fidel firing a cannon at them, smiling, laughing, patting his soldiers on the back, waving his cigar like a scepter, tapping his olive green cap as if it were a crown. Fidel giving speeches for days on end. Speeches in which he used his arms as much as his tongue. He was so excited, the Maximum Leader of the Revolution.

We also saw the exile invaders surrendering in droves, their hands behind their heads.

It took only three days: April 17, April 18, and April 19. The future—my future—defeated, captured. All hope lost.

We couldn't believe it. Couldn't understand how it could all go so wrong.

In the meantime, the uprising that was supposed to happen never did. Fidel acted quickly to make sure there would be no support for the invaders. From end to end of the island, men and women were rounded up by the thousands and herded into theaters, stadiums, military bases, and any place that could hold them. Anyone who had been fingered by the Committee for the Defense of the Revolution, anyone who looked the least bit suspicious—all of them, rounded up, before they could do anything. Anyone with a son in prison, too.

Including my uncle Filo, Fernando's father.

They came in the night, pounded on the door, hauled him away, and he was gone. No one knew where he'd been taken, or what had happened to him.

I find out about my uncle's arrest while I'm watching the war on television with my favorite empress, as ever. She is silent, as she always is in the daytime. Her hand rests demurely on her breast. Tony is there, too. It just isn't as interesting as a war movie, to tell the truth. Much slower pace, no discernible plot, no heroes to identify with. And who ever heard of the good guys losing?

Anyway, there we are, sitting in our usual spots in the living room, guarded by Maria Theresa and Shepherd Boy Jesus, glued to the screen. And our mother and father rush through the room on their way to the front door, pausing briefly like sprinters out of breath. Marie Antoinette says to both of us:

"Your uncle Filo has just been arrested. They came and took him away last night, and the same thing might happen to us. So, if we don't return, or they come for us later, and you don't see us again for a while, don't worry. We'll be in prison. And don't worry, they're not arresting any children yet. Bye."

Louis XVI tells us not to worry, too, and that's it. *Whoosh.* Out the front door they go, in a great rush. They close the door quietly, but it seems as if they're slamming it louder than ever.

Jesus H. Bomb-dropping Christ.

Tony and I look at each other. I suppose my face looks a lot like his. It's a weird look, one that will be hard to forget. I'll only see it a few more times in the next forty years or so, and I'll learn soon enough that it's never good news.

King Louis and Marie Antoinette zip down to Filo's house to comfort his wife and daughter, and to do whatever it is you do in a situation like that. But what *do* you do? There were no greeting cards for such occasions then, and there are none now. Imagine having to come up with the text for such a card:

> *So sorry to learn of your dear one's arrest. Our thoughts are with you as you await word of their fate. May God smile on your worries and grant you the courage to bear the suspense.*

And what would one do for an illustration? An empty armchair with a cigar still burning in the ashtray? A face with a huge question mark over it? An anxious-looking person sitting by a phone?

A few tense, doleful days pass. We hear nothing about Filo and don't know whether he's dead or alive. My mom and dad go to Filo's house every day and return home unharmed. They wait for their turn to be arrested, but no one comes to take them away. Maybe the Committee for the Defense of the Revolution next door is more lenient than we thought. Or more stupid.

The crushing defeat of the exile invaders is beyond belief. How could they fail so miserably? Was God asleep? Or infinitely angry?

We find out where Filo has been taken several days later, and my dad goes to visit his brother. No war movie I'd ever seen had a scene like the one painted by my dad that day when he returned.

"Filo is packed into an auditorium along with hundreds of others. They have nothing to eat, and no clean clothes to change into. The only water they have to drink is from the bathroom faucets. There are only a few toilets, which have clogged up from overuse, and no showers at all, so these hundreds of prisoners have to make do without them. The stench is unbearable and so is the heat. Some of the prisoners have gotten sick and receive no attention. There are some doctors in there, but they can't do much without medicines or equipment. There are people moaning and groaning, people crying and screaming madly. A few women seem to have lost their minds completely and they wail constantly. And the worst part of it is that the guards keep threatening to kill them all. No one in there knows what will happen next. They're all terrorized. The guards have already beat up quite a few people and hurt them badly."

I ask the most important question: "If the toilets don't work, what do those people do?"

"They make do without them."

"What does that mean?"

"It means they have to use the floor . . . and also make do without toilet paper."

"Yecchhh! How could you stand going there?" asks Tony.

"Hard to take, but I'm glad I got to see him. The guards told me I could bring Filo some food. It's the only way he'll get anything to eat."

For a couple of weeks or so my dad brought food for his brother. Then, one day, Filo was taken from the auditorium to another prison in Havana, the Castillo del Príncipe. The same prison from which the man who begged us to help him a couple of years earlier had escaped. As it turned out, Filo's son Fernando was there, too.

I have no idea how long he was there. All I know is that we didn't have to bring him food anymore. I don't think there was any kind of trial or a hearing or anything like that. There were far too many suspects in the same fix, and those in power saw no need to try them anyway. They were guilty of being suspect, one of the worst crimes of all.

Some never came home from that prison, or from the others to which they were dispersed. Uncle Filo was one of the lucky ones. He actually came home several months later. The bad news was that he'd lost his mind in prison.

My father wouldn't give us the details even though Tony and I begged for them. We wanted to know what it was like to be totally insane—*completamente loco*. It sounded so interesting to have a crazy uncle. But Louis XVI wouldn't budge.

"You don't want to know, believe me."

One day, however, my father slipped and mentioned that the electric shock treatments weren't really doing much for his brother. He went on to describe the shock treatments in some detail. It sounded a lot like the electric chair to me.

Eventually, the shock treatments did something. Or maybe it was just the passage of time. Filo gradually regained some measure of sanity. But although he began to interact with others, he couldn't talk about what he had lived through for a very long time. Eventually, he told a few stories, but my parents kept most of them to themselves. They only spoke about the firing squad trick played on Filo day after day.

"Hey, Nieto, when you hear firing outside, that'll be your son we're shooting today."

I remember visiting him at his house about ten months after his arrest, just before I left Cuba for good. He spoke in a whisper, warning us that there were listening devices everywhere. He also constantly checked the window shutters to make sure they were closed.

"They're always listening, you know. Always. And they're everywhere.

Where you least expect them, when you least expect them, there they are. Always. *Siempre. Siempre. Siempre.*"

Most of the time he just sat there like some kind of living mummy, with a strange look in his eyes. There's really so little to talk about when you think someone is always listening to you. Especially when those who are listening might throw you back in prison for saying the wrong thing.

How beautiful, those Committees for the Defense of the Revolution! How utterly beautiful an instrument of fear and intimidation. Because we had one right next door to our house, we always had to watch what we said inside our own house. The walls had ears. Voices carried.

Too bad we didn't have greeting cards for the CDRs, as they came to be known. If only someone had thought of it, or if there had been enough paper and ink to produce them. You'd need a lot of these cards in Havana alone, given the fact that every single block had a CDR—and still does, even as I write this.

Imagine writing the text for such cards.

> *Comrades, thanks! So glad you insisted on my presence*
> *at the latest rally. It really bolstered my Revolutionary spirit*
> *and gave me a sense of purpose in life. I will remain forever*
> *grateful. Keep it up, please! Not one step back,*
> *not even to gain momentum!*

> *Silly me! Sorry I forgot to volunteer to cut sugarcane.*
> *So sorry. Thanks for reminding me. Love the work*
> *you're doing, comrades. I also love hacking cane*
> *with a machete. Long live the Revolution.*

> *Thanks a million, comrades, for reminding me that you control*
> *the ration cards I need for my survival. I am so, so sorry for*
> *whatever it is that you think I've been doing wrong lately. If*
> *you have the chance, please point out to me what that might be,*
> *so I can stop doing it. Or not doing it. Whatever.* Venceremos!

With the deepest, heartfelt gratitude I wish to thank you for denouncing my loved one to the authorities and seeing to it that the worm was sent to prison. It is my fondest hope that this scumbag will be rehabilitated sometime. Should this worm ever return home, I promise to keep an eye out for anti-Revolutionary thinking and tell you about it.
Ever yours. Ever forwards, never backwards.

Worms. I should explain. That was the new name for counter-Revolutionaries. Fidel called the invaders and all who supported them *gusanos.* Worms. Maggots. The lowest of the low. Crawling vermin. Vile insects seeking to destroy the Revolution.

And Fidel made all of the captured invaders wear yellow T-shirts, so they would look wormlike. How he was able to come up with thousands of yellow T-shirts for the prisoners when all clothing was in short supply was one of those miracles made possible by the Revolutionary will to power. Then the men in the yellow T-shirts were interrogated on live television for days on end. Since all television sets back then were black-and-white, and newspapers and magazines didn't carry color photographs, and very few Cubans got to see the prisoners in person, the yellow T-shirts were also a fitting symbol of the genius of Revolutionary thinking.

Somehow, though, we found out that the T-shirts were yellow. And, like the ancient insult "Christian," the name "Worm" was proudly taken up by those of us who had wanted the invaders to triumph.

But those men didn't inspire much pride. There they were, being interrogated on television, one by one. Fidel made sure that those who were the sons of the "finest" families were given the greatest exposure. Worms. Crawling vermin, returning to reclaim their property and privilege, returning to enslave all other Cubans once again. Fidel wanted everyone to think that all of the invaders were the sons of the rich and powerful.

One of them was the son of one of my father's closest friends. He was a funny guy, about ten years older than most of us kids. He had one of the nicest rooms I had ever seen. It was full of model airplanes hanging from the ceiling. I liked visiting his house, just so I could see the room. And it was a dangerous house, so that's saying a lot. His patio had more lizards than I had ever seen in any one place. They were everywhere, crawling, darting, jumping, basking in the sun. My dad would sit out there with his friend and talk, ignoring their presence. I couldn't. I tried to spend as much time as possible away from that patio.

And there was something else scary about that house. The guy with the airplanes hanging from the ceiling was a hypnotist, and he loved to terrorize us.

"Watch out, kids, here I come. All I have to do is look at you and you shall turn into my slaves. Here I go . . . Ommmmmm . . . you are under my command . . . you shall do as I say."

We believed him, of course, and we ran away from him, and he chased us. One day, at the beach, we spent an entire afternoon running away from him and avoiding his gaze.

Now, there he was, on television, looking totally submissive, his eyes lowered in shame and disgust. He wasn't hypnotizing anyone. No. Just the opposite: he looked as if *he* had been hypnotized. Or brainwashed. In reply to the question "What did the Americans do for you?" he was saying the same thing as all the other men.

"Nos embarcaron." They shipped us off. They left us hanging. They screwed us.

This was hard to believe. Inconceivable. The hypnotist and all the other yellow-shirted Worms, each and every one of them, said on television that the Americans, who had planned and funded the Invasion, had dumped them at the Bay of Pigs and left them stranded without any of the support they'd been promised. None of us watching our televisions believed them. They must have been drugged, or brainwashed, or hypnotized.

Americans didn't break promises or screw freedom fighters. No way. These men were all lying. They were lying so they could be treated well in prison, or released maybe.

Desengaño. Hard to take.

Years later, the truth would emerge. They did get screwed, after all. Those damn Kennedy brothers, John and Bobby, pulled the plug on the Invasion when it was much too late to do so. Pulled the plug and left the men there to be mowed down, as the dogwoods and azaleas bloomed in Washington. They were only Cubans, after all.

Fast-forward, two years or so.

The Orange Bowl is packed. People are lined up outside, unable to get in, but we have great seats behind one of the goalposts. We live only five blocks away and have hung around the small baseball stadium outside the Bowl countless times, waiting for home run balls to sail over the fence and into our hands. But we've never been inside the Bowl. What a thrill.

We're there to see President Kennedy welcome the returning heroes of the Bay of Pigs Invasion. Imagine that! We'll get to see all the Worms and the president of the United States, in person. This is history in the making, and we're there. We'll be able to tell our kids and their kids all about this day. We're so lucky to live only five blocks away, in that orphanage.

The Worms have been exchanged for fifty-three million dollars worth of medicine and food. A fair trade. Fidel suddenly has a thousand fewer mouths to feed and he gets good American stuff in return for looking benevolent. Good riddance. Jack Kennedy gets to play the hero, rescuing the freedom fighters he screwed.

Jackie Kennedy is there, too. The Queen of America gives a speech in nearly flawless Spanish. She and her husband speak of the great sacrifice made by these men, and they promise that the flag of their Brigade 2506 will soon wave over a free Cuba.

I am still dumb enough to believe them, and I cheer and clap along with all the other Cubans at the Orange Bowl.

We return to our orphanage filled with hope. Cod for dinner that afternoon. The house stinks. And it's my turn to wash the dishes that day. I'm so hungry I try to eat the fish, even though it smells and tastes like putrid demon testicles from hell. But I can't; I just can't. I run to the bathroom, gagging, and I puke. Tony is brave enough to eat three or four mouthfuls. I come back to the table, scrape the cod off the rice, and eat what remains below the top layer, unpolluted by the fish. The other boys stare at me as if I'm insane. When everyone's done, I go into the kitchen to wash the dishes. The codfish pot has a thick crust on the bottom, which I have to scrape off.

Later that evening, around sunset, Tony and I make our way to the public library on Seventh Avenue. God bless my brother, he has found a place where we can read in air-conditioned comfort, away from the thugs at our orphanage. We go there several nights a week and stay until closing. I scour the history section. So few books left to read. I've read almost all of them. What will I do when there are no more history books left to read in this library?

The librarian announces that the library is about to close. We each check out a couple of books and head back to the orphanage. On the way back we catch sight of a dead possum, flattened and rotting on the curbside. We've never seen anything like it. I say it's a giant rat.

"Look at the tail, Tony. Only rats have tails like that."

"Don't be stupid. Rats never get that big. It's some kind of porcupine."

"You're wrong. Porcupines have quills, not fur. It's a rat."

"What do you know about rats, anyway? I say it's a porcupine."

"And, hey, what are all those worms crawling all over it? They look like moving grains of rice. Look at them."

"Disgusting. Yecchh. I've never seen so many worms eating a dead animal. I think they're maggots."

"Heeew, I don't know if I'll ever be able to eat rice again. And it's about all I can eat at that house. What will I do if I can't eat the rice? Eat nothing but toast and guava paste?"

"Don't think about it. Let's go. Let's see if we can find some empty soda bottles."

We scour the sidewalks, curbs, lawns, and empty lots for bottles we can cash in. Each is worth two cents. It's a good night tonight. We find enough bottles to trade for two ice-cream sandwiches. We talk as we walk and eat.

"Hey, we got to see President Kennedy today, and all the Worms too."

"Yeah, that was great. But do you think he's right? Will Fidel be defeated soon?"

"You bet. We'll be going home any day now. Any day. Soon. Very soon, you'll see."

"I hope you're right. I can't wait to go home."

Flash forward thirty-seven years to the present day.

As my loved ones slumber all around me in air-conditioned comfort in our house in the woods, I imagine what might have been. What if the Invasion had gone as planned? What if Fidel's airplanes had been bombed to smithereens that April morning? I picture the uprising. I see thousands of ordinary Cubans reaching for the weapons Fernando and his friends had stashed away, fighting the militiamen, house to house. I visualize the United States Air Force joining in the fight, defending the men on the beaches.

I close one eye and see nuclear warfare between America and Russia. No good. Wait. I close the other eye and see the Worms victorious. That's much better. I see Fidel vanquished, lined up against a wall and shot with blanks for days on end before finally being sent to live for the rest of his life in Trenton, New Jersey, sentenced to a lifetime job as janitor at the train station, his mouth permanently gagged, a paperback copy of Kant's *Metaphysische Anfangsgrunde der Naturwissenschaft* in one pocket and one of *Kritik der Reinen Vernunft* in the other. I see Fidel being forced to read these two books at night, constantly, as he lies on a hard table wired for electric shock treatments. If he dozes off, or takes his eyes off the text, or fails to turn the pages in a timely fashion, or fails to answer correctly when quizzed on his reading of Kant by volunteers from the Princeton philosophy faculty, I see him being shocked. I see myself staying at home in Havana, with no Revolution left to chase me away, free to apply Brylcreem to my hair and dance the night away at a thousand and one nightclubs.

I see myself leading a better, sweeter life than the one God has graced me with.

Forget about it. Nothing is that simple. Not even when you're a hypnotized Worm.

I loved my walks to the library with Tony, and our search for bottles, and that dead maggoty possum as much as I loved the bombs that fell from the sky and nearly killed us.

I swear it. May I be cleft in two by a wicked lightning bolt if I'm not telling the truth—preferably one that zigzags in nice, straight angles, and is thick and sulphur yellow.

Lo juro. Mal rayo me parta.

30

TREINTA

Another day in Limbo. No school. No place in particular to go. No plans for the day, except to play, soak up the sunshine, deny the present, and wait for the exit permit.

Shafts of light streamed through the shutters, as always, knifing through the swirling galaxies of dust. On this day, there was also a mosquito net in view when I opened my eyes. The shafts of light poured through the net as if it weren't there at all, filling the space around me, defining it. Each and every thread in the net was aglow.

Sweet world, I thought. Safe sweet world, in the light. It felt as if I were inside a cloud, floating above the earth, far removed from all trouble. No mosquitoes trapped in the net this morning.

I was waking up in my parents' bed that morning, not my own. I'd had the terrors in the middle of the night and had asked to sleep there. I'd been doing that a lot lately. Louis XVI was a very large man, and there really wasn't enough room in the bed for three of us, so he got up patiently, as always, and shuffled off to my bed in his baggy boxer shorts. I was ashamed of my night terrors but couldn't do much about them.

I was fine during the day. The sunlight was grace itself, and I could ignore everything that troubled me.

But nighttime was different. At night, it was hard to keep evil at bay. That choking darkness, full of lizards you couldn't see. The shadows you didn't want to see. The fears. The awful dreams. Not about Marilyn Monroe, Kim Novak, or my fifth-grade love. These were dreams that allowed the hidden lizards to escape. Like the one about the voodoo witch.

It was that dream that started the terrors. In it I was chased by a large African woman who looked a lot like the legless lady who had begged outside of church for so many years. She chased me in the same way that Torso Lady and Candlestick Lady had done when I was younger, but she was much worse. For one thing, she had legs and could use them. Worse than that, she was evil incarnate, seeking me out, longing to capture me and annihilate me slowly and painfully. And she wasn't just after my body. No, she craved my soul. She wanted to possess me totally and bring me down to hell. In the dream, she would almost catch me, but just as she'd be about to grab me, I'd find myself in bed, awake, and see her clinging to the iron grillwork that covered my bedroom window, giving me the evil eye and laughing madly. She didn't have to speak. I knew exactly what she wished to do to me. And she knew I knew, and she loved it.

Of course, I had plenty of facts from which to spin this dream. We'd recently had a maid, Caridad, who threatened me with voodoo curses. I knew she hated me. I knew her daughter, who often came to the house with her, hated me even more. Both of them taunted me whenever my parents were out of earshot. They'd tell me how much they were going to enjoy the day when I'd be cleaning their house and shining their shoes, and then they'd threaten to fill my life with voodoo curses if I ever told my parents about what they had said. I thought maybe Caridad had sent this witch to plague my dreams because my parents had fired her for stealing.

Maybe she had.

Then there were the dreams about all the things that had actually happened to me, or were about to happen. Those were bad enough to compete with Voodoo Woman.

Some kind of indescribable terror possessed me totally, smothering the life out of me. I now know it was fear of death. In so many ways, I was about to die, and I knew it, at least at night. Marie Antoinette had decided that she had to get us out of Cuba as quickly as possible. My father didn't agree with her, but somehow he was persuaded to agree with her plan. We were to be sent to the United States on our own.

It was the only way to get us out quickly. Children didn't need security clearances to enter the States and were given visa waivers. The parents had to wait many months for their visas, sometimes a year or more.

Thousands of families were doing this. By the time Fidel and John Kennedy put a stop to it in October 1962, fourteen thousand children had been sent to the States all alone. So it wasn't too weird, as far as these things go. But, of course, when a world falls apart, everything is so strange that nothing is strange. So two pampered boys who have never spent a night away from home can be sent to live in another country, where they don't know a soul.

I was ten years old, but I had just learned how to tie my own shoelaces, and I had never cut my own steak or buttered my own toast. I'd never lifted a finger to do anything around the house. No chores. No responsibilities. No clue about what it took to survive.

All of my friends were in the same fix, and all of them were being shipped off too. *Niños bitongos,* Fidel called us. A bunch of pampered boys. He loved to make fun of us in his speeches. Manuel and Rafael, Eugenio, Gerardito, my new friend Ciro and his sisters, my other new friend Daniel, Jorge, and Julio. Each and every one of us, *niños bitongos* on our way to the United States, to enroll in the school of hard knocks.

And in the meantime none of us were attending school, despite all the pressure our parents received from the busybodies at the Committee for the Defense of the Revolution. Not since the Bay of Pigs, when all private schools were closed down. I didn't go to school for an entire year.

As we waited for our exit permits, we spent our days playing furiously. We knew the end was around the corner.

But what a year that was! In so many ways it was every child's dream come true. No school. No tutors. No attempt by any adult to educate us in any way. No books. No lessons of any kind. Not even English language lessons.

Well, I take that back. I should say no formal lessons.

We learned how quickly you can get drunk on Scotch whiskey one day at Eugenio's house, when Manuel downed a small bottle on a dare. He got so drunk that he couldn't get up off his chair and babbled nonsense. We thought it was one of the funniest things we'd ever seen. But when he passed out, we began to worry and had to ask for help. His dad had to come get him, and we all got into trouble. Eugenio's dad wasn't too mad about the whiskey he lost that afternoon, even though it was now as rare and precious as gold. He knew he'd have to leave it behind anyway. He was mad because we were far too young to be getting drunk.

We learned to thank our parents for keeping us out of school by looking at the books of an unlucky friend who wasn't in limbo, like us. One math problem will remain forever burned in my memory: "Before our great Revolution Ramiro Gómez used to pay his scumbag capitalist landlord thirty pesos a month for rent. Now that our Maximum Leader Fidel Castro has made the Urban Reform possible, Comrade Gómez only has to pay twenty-five pesos. What percent reduction in rent has the Revolution granted him?"

We also learned how to break windows in all of those houses that had been abandoned, and to cruise through them, looking for treasure. But all we ever found of value was a huge box of fluorescent lightbulbs and a set of old *National Geographic* magazines (which everyone knew were highly valued by chauffeurs and teenage boys).

The houses were stripped bare, for the most part. Cleaned out. Trucks would pull up and clean house, literally. And there were so many of them in our neighborhood. Everyone was leaving, or so it seemed. The world was being emptied of people and filled up again with replacements. Some of the houses were filled with poor children from the provinces. Most were filled with new families, all members of the Communist Party, who brought along furnishings taken from other houses. Very, very few of these new families were African Cubans. None were Chinese. Very, very few were dark-skinned.

Before anyone left, government officials would come to the house and inventory all of their belongings. This could take days. Then, shortly before leaving, these inventory takers would show up again and make sure that every single item was still there. If anything was missing, the exit permit would be revoked. No one was allowed to take any belongings out of the country, you see, save two changes of clothing, three pairs of underwear, a hat, and one book.

The books were the only hint of mercy. When my turn came, I got to take with me a copy of Thomas à Kempis' *Imitation of Christ*. Not my choice, of course. What normal boy would choose a devotional manual from the fifteenth century as his only reading material? It made me think of Eye Jesus and Window Jesus. My parents insisted I take it along, and I grumbled. But five years later, it would change my life, perhaps even save it. Wait, I'll take back the "perhaps." I know it saved my life. Why deny it?

Anyway, we amused ourselves the way we always had. Those fluorescent lightbulbs, for instance, were wonderful. We took dozens of them to a vacant lot and hurled them like spears or javelins. We watched them fly, fall, and explode with a loud bang—a good substitute for firecrackers, which had become extinct on our island.

The bombs had stopped since the Bay of Pigs. Every now and then something would happen, but there were very few active dissenters who were not already in jail, and those who were still at large had little to work with. A bomb here and there. Some shooting here and there, but not much.

Well, not much if you're not one of those involved. If you happen to be there when the shooting starts, then it might seem like too much. Why deny it?

A boy who lived across the street from my grandmother was just standing around outside his house when he was hit by a stray bullet. He almost died. I heard that he didn't know he'd been hit by a bullet and that he kept asking "Who pushed me?" as they rushed him to the hospital. Some militiamen had been chasing a guy and shooting at him. Too bad for the boy. He lost part of his stomach.

And I almost lost my life. Yes, once again, I came close. Why deny that too? I remember it better than so many other things.

There I am at the park with my friend Jorge. At almost exactly the same spot where we'd tried to launch our lizard satellite years earlier. Both of us are collecting plants and flowers for our moms. There are all these flowers at the park, and since they belong to everyone, we take them with glee. Anyway, there we are, minding our own business, when suddenly a big black car stops at the curb about twenty feet away. I pay no attention. Then another car comes along, moving very slowly. And then a guy in the first car pulls out a machine gun and points it out the window at the oncoming car.

Rat-tat-tat-tat-tat-tat . . .

The guys in the second car pull out their guns and start firing back. And another gun comes out of the first car, and more from the second one. And a small war erupts a few feet from us. Jorge and I look at each other with that look I've already told you about, the one you're better off not seeing.

I'll spare you the sound effects this time.

Bullets are flying all over the park. That whizzing is hard to forget, and

I'd heard it before. Jorge and I drop our flowers rudely and start running away from the cars as fast as possible.

In the bright, cell-soaking sunlight I run for my life, bullets whizzing past. With every step I think of the boy who got shot near my grandmother's house. I wait for the feeling of being pushed. I cross the street without looking in any direction. Better to be hit by a car than a bullet, no matter how much my family has warned me of the perils of being run over.

I see the garden wall ahead of me. The wall with the hedge behind it, at the house on the corner at the end of my street, the house where the medical student used to keep a real skeleton in his room. I keep my eye on the light green wall. Details jump out at me. The nubs of the stucco on the wall. The ledge on the wall. The hedge behind the wall. The leaves on the hibiscus plants, so dark green. The serrations on the edges of the leaves. The blood red hibiscus blossoms, fully open, partly open, and not yet open. The sound of the gunfire, still going on behind me. The strange sensation of my legs moving so fast. I can't believe it's possible to move this quickly.

I've taken off. I'm flying, head first, over the green wall and the hibiscus hedge. I'm Superman, at last. I've outrun bullets, and I'm staying aloft forever. I clear the wall and the hedge. I'm descending now. I see the lawn approaching my face. I can count every blade of that coarse grass. I see an anthill. Looks like fire ants—better stay away from them. My hands hit the ground and I roll over. Nice somersault. Didn't know it was in me.

I'm still alive. And I missed the fire ants! I'm Superman! But where's Jorge? He runs into the garden through the gate, huffing and puffing. I'm relieved to see him.

Immediately, all sorts of people show up. The people inside the skeleton house come out. Other neighbors. They begin to ask us questions, all of them stupid.

"Are you all right?"

"What happened?"

What's the matter with them? Can't they see we're in one piece and that the shooting is over? We can still hear a few shots in the distance, getting fainter and fainter. I'm not the least bit scared by any of this. No way. I'm a veteran bullet dodger.

I remember thinking that those two cars must have had a lot of ammunition. And that none of the men firing the guns knew how to aim. I also remember wanting to ask if they still had the skeleton in the house, and whether I could go in and see it.

A militiaman shows up about the same time as my father. He begins to ask us questions, less stupid ones, and I do most of the talking. Louis XVI, I notice, has his arm around me and is listening to me very attentively. He's letting the militiaman ask the questions, which I think is strange. Then Marie Antoinette shows up. Her limp makes it difficult for her to walk very fast, so it's taken her longer than everyone else to get there. The garden is quite crowded by now.

And I'm talking a mile a minute, showering the militiaman with all the details I can remember. The color of the cars. The number of people inside. The guns. What the men looked like. What the guns looked like. Even what we were doing at the park.

The militiaman takes down my name, address, and phone number. I also point down the street and say I live just a half a block away.

I go home with my parents. Jorge walks along with us. I get home, drink a glass of iced water, and start to cry.

I don't know why I'm crying. I can't explain it. But the tears and the sobbing bubble up like some unstoppable geyser. My dad hugs me tightly. I feel the stubble on his face, and I remember how he used to rub my face into it when I was smaller, and that makes me cry even harder.

"It's okay now. You're okay."

"But I'm afraid of the militiaman . . ."

"Why?"

"What if he comes back and asks more questions and arrests me for stealing flowers?"

"No, no, don't worry, that won't happen."

But I *am* worried, and in shock, and nothing he says can keep me from crying. I am scared about having confessed my crime to a militiaman. Maybe I'll end up like Uncle Filo or Cousin Fernando. I was, after all, taking the people's flowers. Foliage of the Revolution, which belonged to all and could never be owned by any one person or family. I had stolen from the Cuban People. It doesn't cross my mind at the time that the bullets had anything to do with my crying.

Denial has always been one of my greatest talents. But there are some things that just can't be denied. For instance, I can't deny Cousin Addison's iguanas. He has so many of them in the backyard of Aunt Carmela's house, and they are all so huge. It would be impossible to deny the existence of those monsters, or of Addison's bizarre garden.

Dozens upon dozens of banana trees, evenly spaced. Ponds in all shapes and sizes, stocked with exotic Cuban fish. Cages and cages full of iguanas. Addison catches them with his bare hands on the seashore east of Havana and brings them home to the cages that wait for them, cages he has built himself. Every now and then one escapes, as iguanas are wont to do when they're in small hand-built cages, and Addison has to go looking for it. Sometimes they show up on someone's porch, or kitchen, or living room, and Addison has to answer to his angry neighbors.

There, in the back of this gracious mansion, just a few feet from the giant Saint Lazarus statue near the kitchen, in one of the most elegant houses in Miramar, Addison, the half-Cuban, half-American former denizen of Hollywood, has built himself a banana plantation. He always acts as if it makes perfect sense. He sits back there in his comfortable wicker chair, sipping frosty drinks under the shade of the banana trees, looking very satisfied and immensely proud.

His iguanas are brown, not green. He says they are that color because they're seashore iguanas, from a rocky place. They are camouflaged to blend in with the rocks, not with foliage.

Lizards are bad enough, but these monstrosities are beyond belief. They are so unbelievably large. And so ugly. So hideous, in fact, that I soon realize they could be an argument against the existence of God. And that frightens me more than the iguanas themselves, though I, of course, deny it.

The scales, the folds on the skin, the mouth, the tongue, the claws, the spikes, the tail. And those eyes, those horrible eyes from hell. Everything about them is pure evil. I imagine that Ernesto's soul must look like that.

I have some trouble sitting in Addison's banana plantation because of the iguanas, but he has a way of making you trust him, and he has convinced me that in his Eden the reptiles are trapped in the prisons they deserve. He doesn't exactly trust those lizards, so I have to trust the guy.

Or maybe it's his weirdness that makes me trust him. Maybe it's because he is only half Cuban. Not many Cuban men are only half Cuban. Maybe it's because he looks a lot like Jimmy Stewart. Not too many Cuban men resemble an actor who has kissed Kim Novak and Grace Kelly. Maybe it's because he can talk about early Christian martyrs whose severed heads were used as balls in games at the Colosseum. No other Cuban man tells stories like that. Maybe it's because he once lived in Hollywood and went to parties with Charlie Chaplin. Very few Cuban men have done that. Maybe it's because he rides a bicycle everywhere. Cuban men don't do that, for sure. Maybe it's because he goes scuba diving and swims with sharks on purpose. Most Cuban men don't trust sharks. Maybe it's because he lives at his mother's house and shares it with a very young, funny guy who is an acrobat. He might be the only man in Cuba who does that.

The acrobat is about eight years older than me, the same age as Ernesto. He has lived at Aunt Carmela's house with Addison for a while and goes everywhere with him. He helps him catch iguanas and tends his banana garden. He brings us drinks from the kitchen when we sit out in the garden and shows me how to do all sorts of somersaults and cartwheels. Once I saw him leap over a very wide pit about thirty feet deep. I thought he would fall into the abyss, but he managed it with all the finesse of a jaguar.

I think that he and Addison are just good friends. Or maybe I deny some other thoughts.

Addison and my aunt Lucía have been spending a lot of time together at his house, along with the acrobat. Recently, Lucía, the woman without desires, has visited him almost every day. I think that maybe they are getting romantically involved. Maybe my aunt is harboring some faint, smoldering desire. Sometimes she brings me along to see Addison. By now I've lost my fear of Carmela's driveway. But I still haven't lost my fear of the inside of her house. Even a banana garden full of iguanas is preferable.

I've gotten to know Addison pretty well this year, not just because he comes to visit Lucía at our house often, but also because he and Lucía have invited me to join them on some of their outings. I've seen movies I'd never seen before, most of them from the silent era. Addison knew some of the people who made them. I've also seen my very first live staged play with them: *El robo del cochino. The Theft of the Pig.* It was a brand-new play written by a Cuban, and it was set in the countryside. I'd never seen live actors before, or seen a story written by a Cuban, and I sat there, stunned, wondering how it was that they had memorized all that dialogue. Or maybe they were making it up? Every bad word in the book was uttered in that theater that evening, and some I'd never heard before. No one ever used bad words in movies. How could they get away with this on stage? No one would dare write a script like this, not even a Cuban.

It was a boring story, but an ear-opening and eye-opening experience. The whole play was about the exploitation of laborers, and the evil lives of the landowners, and the injustice of claiming ownership over anything. At the end of the play, of course, the pig got slaughtered. But since it was an invisible pig, there was no blood shed on the stage, and no squealing.

I may be missing a lot of school this year, but the play alone is worth about two months of formal education. The banana plantation, the ponds, the iguanas, and the circus acrobat are worth about another month. Addison's stories about Hollywood are also worth another month or so. That's about half a school year right there.

The shoot-out at the park is worth the other half, all by itself.

The fights between my mother and father aren't worth anything. Every now and then they scream at each other. Half of the time I don't know why, exactly. But the other half of the time I know exactly what they are arguing about: what to do with Tony and me.

Somehow Marie Antoinette has managed to wear down Louis XVI. She's gotten him to agree to send us to the United States. The catch seems to be that she is handling the whole thing by herself. He wants no part of it, and carries on with his life as if none of this were happening, collecting art and antiques by the truckload as other collectors flee the country.

So Marie Antoinette has set herself to the task of shipping Tony and me to the States. And somehow she is managing to do it, all by herself. She has stood in line for our visa waivers at the Swiss embassy. She has stood in line for our passports. She has stood in line to request our exit permits. She has hired a lawyer to draw up all the necessary papers, even though her own husband is a judge and attorney. She has talked to a thousand and one people on the phone and in person. She has taken buses and taxicabs everywhere.

One day she calls my father's friend Puentes Pi, the crime scene photographer, and arranges for our passport pictures to be taken. Puentes Pi shows up after dinner one evening with that old camera of his, the same one he uses to photograph corpses. His camera has captured a thousand images of people who've been murdered or run over by cars. It has also captured hundreds of images of Tony and me growing up. He is always there, it seems, taking pictures. Not just on birthdays, but throughout the entire year. He has the nicest old camera, with flashbulbs that explode like small firecrackers. He is a determined enemy of the candid photo, too. He makes us pose and pose and pose, as if he were painting a portrait. Maybe it's because he is so used to photographing corpses, which are always in their ultimate pose.

Nearly all the photographs I have from my childhood were taken by Puentes Pi and his crime scene camera.

Now he makes us pose for the very last time, at one of my eternal crime scene locations, under the portrait of Maria Theresa. I think he knows this is his farewell to us. We have to dress in a tie and jacket for our passports, since it is the ultimately serious document, but he's told us we don't have to put on the suit pants for the picture.

"No one will know what you're wearing below the waist. If you want, you can pose in your underwear, or your pajamas."

So that's what Tony and I do. We put on our suit jackets, white shirts, and ties on top, and our pajama pants on the bottom. And our mom lets us do it, and it surprises both of us very much. You have to understand, this mixing of categories was unthinkable in my family. It could cause you to catch pneumonia and die of an *embolia,* or worse, maybe even land in hell for eternity.

We laugh so much about this, it forces Puentes Pi to work harder. We don't look very serious, knowing that we are wearing pajamas for our passport photos. But he finally manages to snap the perfect pictures, in which Tony and I look serious, amused, angry, and terrified, all at the same time. Absolutely perfect pictures.

Years later I still have that passport. It's in my desk drawer, right here, no more than eight inches from my elbow. I look at that photo whenever I think I am hitting bottom.

When I finally get to show that passport at the airport, on the day I leave Cuba for good, I feel a strong urge to laugh. There I am, about to be strip searched, and I'm showing these very important guys a picture that is a joke of sorts. I am not what I seem to be.

I'm turning into a chameleon, or into one of Addison's brown iguanas. I'm camouflaged. I blend in so well as a respectable Cuban boy from a good family, but underneath I am a rebel, a worm, and a refugee in the making. I'm wearing my God-damned pajamas.

If I'd been able to use swear words back then, I might have said to all the airport guys that day: "Go to hell, I'm wearing pajamas below the belt in this picture. Up yours, I'm not even wearing a belt, or socks, or shoes."

But I don't say anything like that at all. Instead I say something stupid about my luggage. Why deny it?

It is very special, my bag. Marie Antoinette took a bus to the heart of Old Havana to find a woman who made luggage for kids such as us. Special canvas luggage, handmade from fabric once used for awnings. It's the only durable cloth available that is light enough. The bags are a special size. Just large enough to carry the only items we are allowed to bring with us: two shirts, two pairs of pants, three socks, three pairs of underwear, one sweater, one hat, one set of pajamas, and one book. The bags have to be that size and no other because there is a weight limit to what you can take too, and if you are one measly ounce over the limit, they make you take out one whole item. Or they seize your entire bag, we've heard.

That's what a Revolution is all about, you know. Ounces.

Although my mom could have made these bags herself in one afternoon, she didn't. Instead she took the bus to the bag maker's house, and even made several trips, because the woman didn't have a phone and didn't finish them on time. She was making hundreds of bags, this woman. She had so many requests she could barely keep up. We went right down to the wire on those bags. I think we got them about one week before we left.

I remember riding the bus with my mom and brother all the way to that house, climbing the steps to the sun-drenched rooftop apartment where this black woman made the bags. And I remember marveling at the finished product. Why had it taken her so long to make this tiny thing? It was so small. So small, and thin, my duffle bag. My *gusano,* my worm.

The bags looked like worms. *Gusanos* for the *gusanos.*

Very funny. Especially when you know that caterpillars are also *gusanos.* Everyone knows what happens to caterpillars.

But Louis XVI wouldn't laugh at this pun, or get involved in any of the things that needed to be done to get us out of Cuba. He did nothing except open his hands and let us fly away. Nothing. He did nothing. There's no denying that, no.

Nada.

And we flew away from Limbo, *gusanos* in hand, and he stood there with his hands in his pockets, and we never saw each other again.

And sixteen years after that farewell, after he had already been buried for two years, I turned his surname into a middle initial, N, and began using my mother's surname, Eire, so that it could be the name I would pass on to my children, none of whom had been born yet. I knew he would be proud of me for doing it.

It was the correct thing to do. As right as putting on your shoes before your pants. As right as always wearing socks, no matter what. As right as defending Empress Maria Theresa's reputation. As right as taking an urchin off the street and adopting him.

As right as letting us go.

31

TREINTA Y UNO

Sharks. In the swimming pool. Sharks, and plenty of them, swarming. It's a kidney-shaped pool, large and deep and turquoise blue, nearly the same shade as the sea. The sharks are densely packed, swimming in tight circles, looking for something to kill and devour. It's a large pool for a house, but not as big as one you might find at a swim club.

The diving board is still there, poised over the lethal brink, rudely shouting, "Suicide, anyone?"

And the sea is no more than a few feet away, full of sharks that swim freely. It's a windy day, and the waves are decent. They crash against the sharp-edged rocks and the concrete seawall, as if to remind the sharks in the pool that they've lost their freedom, just like all the humans on the island. I ask myself: can they hear the waves pounding against the shore?

The sharks are looking for blood and freedom, circling furiously. There's nothing calm about them. All kinds of sharks in there, including a couple of hammerheads. I don't know all their names, but most of them are large enough to eat me, for sure. Some could even eat Louis XVI and Ernesto with just a few bites.

I ask myself: do they sense that the pool is kidney shaped? Do they know that Ernesto is here, looking at them, so close to the diving board?

Lizard. Iguana-souled wretch.

The diving board shouts at me: "Justifiable homicide!"

I ignore the shouting. The sharks remain as silent as a woman who's trying to hide her thoughts in order to spare your feelings.

I'm at the Aquarium of the Revolution. It looks like a tureen from hell, that swimming pool, a giant soup bowl teeming with deadly squirming noodles.

I've come here with Louis XVI, Tony, Ernesto, Manuel, and Rafael. We've just found a beautiful parrot fish stranded in one of the tidal pools at La Puntilla and rushed him here in a pail full of saltwater. I've never seen a fish as beautiful as this. Good God, it's a living rainbow. Too much. If I were God, I wouldn't let anything so beautiful die. The director of the Aquarium has identified the fish, thanked us for bringing him, and dropped him into a large glass tank on the rear porch of the mansion.

The Aquarium of the Revolution has been set up at a splendid seaside house in Miramar, not far from where we live. The pink house is right up against the sea, and the pool is filled with saltwater. Huge upright glass tanks dot the backyard, which faces the Gulf of Mexico. And these tanks contain wonders. Gorgeous, incredible fish. This is too much to take in all at once. The parrot fish we rescued seems smaller and duller when viewed in the company of the others. These fish are unreal. Colors I've never seen. Patterns and shapes I'd never imagine, not even in an eternity. And all these fish are out there, all the time, along with the sharks and the moray eels and the stingrays and lobsters and crabs. All the time, swimming with sharks.

I ask myself: who owned this house? What was it like to live here, day in and day out, with your own pool, right by the turquoise sea? What was it like to give up all of this? What would the former owners of this house think of the Aquarium of the Revolution? What would they think of the sharks in their pool? What would it be like for them to come back right now, with their memories still intact? Would the sight of the shark pool dissolve all their memories, like acid?

Not that long ago, I tell myself, children surely must have used the pool. Not that long ago, a man and a woman must have kissed in that pool. Someone must have. Who wouldn't kiss, right there, at the edge of the turquoise sea?

The director of the Aquarium tells us of their plans to expand, to turn this into a huge showcase for all the world to admire. All you need is the will to do it, he says. This mansion shall be transformed into one of the world's greatest aquariums. That's what the Revolution is all about. Poor guy, he really believed it.

He thanks us once again for bringing in such a beautiful parrot fish.

And I tell myself that this is the first thing I've seen that makes the Revolution look halfway good. The sharks in the pool are a weird touch, but the Aquarium is a great idea.

Meanwhile, the sharks are like sardines in a can, with nothing to eat except one another. And I can't stop staring at them. Every few seconds I look up from the sharks in the water and eye the diving board and Ernesto standing near it. How I wish that the sharks could swallow Ernesto whole. No, wait, why deny it? How I wish they'd chew him up, slowly. How much I'd love to see his blood turning the pool a deep, bright, joyous crimson.

Too much, for sure. Far too much.

I remember, suddenly, that I'm in Limbo. This is all here now, and I'm here now, but it won't be like this for very long. No, it's as good as gone, along with all that's past, and the future is a giant, gray, shapeless blank. I'm due to leave any time now. One of these days, we'll get a letter in the mail telling us when we can leave for the States. Rafael and Manuel are waiting for theirs, too. In the meantime, we wait.

Ernesto is waiting for us to leave.

And I watch the sharks circle and circle.

Why do they all stay so close to the bottom of the pool? What are they fed, and when, and how? Do they ever sleep? Do they ever fall in love? Do they ever worry about the future? Are they really as selfish as they seem? How did anyone catch them and get them into the pool? The Aquarium of the Revolution elicits a thousand and one questions and yields very few answers.

Flash forward seventeen years.

I'm swimming laps in an Olympic-size swimming pool in Minnesota—indoors, naturally. Outdoors, it's about twenty degrees below zero, Fahrenheit. At that temperature, your tears freeze in an instant. I'm about fifteen hundred miles from the nearest ocean. I have the pool all to myself, and it's lunchtime. I've just eaten a large lunch to taunt the god of *embolias,* and I've already completed about thirty laps when, suddenly, I'm seized by an irrational panic. I've just crossed from the shallow end to the deep end. This is also a diving pool, and it's very deep. I look down at the bottom, so far from me. It's green down there. Kind of blue-green. But I see turquoise, I see sharks circling. I feel them coming up from the bottom of the pool, from behind me, from the right and left. I see them. I'm still very far from the end of the pool, far from safety.

Stupid imagination. Stupid Aquarium of the Revolution. Wish I could banish it from my mind, this crazy fear. But the fear is so intense, the sharks so real. I can feel their jaws approaching. I can see my blood streaming into the pool, mingling with the chlorine. I see my femur sticking out of my severed leg. I feel the pain.

Stop it! Stop it! *Coño.* Too much.

I reach the end of the pool and leap out, shaking like Jell-O. I look at the water. Blue-green. Calm. Not one shark in sight. I'm in Minnesota, God damn it. God forgive me for swearing, but it's hard not to when I think about Minnesota.

Damn it. When will someone else show up? I'll be all right if someone else is in there to attract the sharks.

Five minutes later, someone opens the door from the locker room, walks over, and dives in. Thank God. Now the sharks in my mind will go for him instead. Now I can finish up. Thirty more laps to go. I hope this other guy stays in here that long. He does. I finish up, shower, and go back to work.

Believe me, if you ever see a swimming pool full of sharks, you'll never be the same again. I guarantee it.

You might even find a wife because of it.

Flash forward another two years.

I'm now living in the former Confederate States of America. I've only been at this job in this new town for about a week. I've driven into town in my Karmann Ghia, with all of my possessions crammed into it, Rolling Stones blasting "Can't You Hear Me Knocking" as I descend the eastern slope of the Blue Ridge Mountains. It's September, but it's still brutally hot. Hotter than Cuba, and much, much stickier. I meet a nice woman named Jane in the hallway outside my office. She strikes up a conversation. We talk. We go out for dinner. Somehow, out of the blue, I start telling her about a pool I once saw full of sharks. It's one of my worst flaws, bringing up odd subjects with women I like. Odd subjects are so much safer to talk about than your feelings. She tells me that she's never seen a pool full of sharks but has been haunted all her life by that image, and by a very real fear of finding sharks in every pool. I believe her and confess that the image and the fear both haunt me still.

Both of us smile in an odd way, and I change the subject. I can't help thinking I've known this woman for a very long time, maybe even forever.

Flash forward another two years.

The shark pool woman and I get married across the street from the biggest pool in town.

Flash forward another sixteen years.

Deep into the night, close to dawn, as the bullfrogs croak in my swamp, I fret about Saint Thomas Aquinas and his five proofs for the existence of God. I've only come up with four thus far, after covering so much ground. The Angelic Doctor has me beat. I'm close to the end of the race, and he's still ahead. He died when he was about my age. How long will I have to come up with five?

But, wait! What's this?

Yes . . . why didn't I see it before? Fool. Good God. Why, why didn't I see it?

Too much.

Like the burning bush, or the stillness in the midst of the whirlwind, or the water changed into wine, or the nets ripping from the weight of the catch.

Shoeless Moses. Jesus H. Fish-eating Christ.

A Cuban refugee catches up with Thomas Aquinas near the finish line, and offers up his fifth proof of the existence of God: a pool full of sharks.

32

TREINTA Y DOS

Two things. Two goddamned things in this world that are too hard to take, always.

One is knowing that you will never have something that *should* be yours. Knowing that what you love and need and crave with every fiber of your being will be forever beyond reach. Never, ever will it be yours, not in this life or any other life or in a parallel universe.

The other is knowing that something that *shouldn't* be yours is yours to keep. Knowing that something you don't want at all and hate and know is all wrong is yours eternally, without reprieve. Eternally yours, the stinking evil, because it's who you are, forever, even after forgiveness is released from its cage.

I'm sure you know what I'm talking about. Everyone's an expert on this subject.

Don't get me wrong. I'm not complaining. I wouldn't trade my life story for anyone else's, not for a minute. I'm just boasting, that's all. I can take it. I'm tougher than the hide on the oldest, meanest devil in hell.

Don't ask me which of the two things is worse, though. Both are ungodly. All I can say is: don't wish either situation on anyone, not even on your enemies. You're supposed to forgive your enemies, you know. Turn the other cheek. If they ask for a shirt, give them your coat. If they strike you on the right cheek, offer them the left cheek. If they try to kill and rape you, say thank you very much, I deserve it.

Tough commandments, especially if your enemies have hurt you deeply. Too tough, even for someone who's tougher than the hide on the oldest, meanest devil in hell.

Around the time the planes bombed my neighborhood and the cars had their shoot-out right next to me, sometime during that year I didn't go to school, just as I was getting ready to leave everything and everyone I knew, an enemy appeared. And he left me a gift I didn't want at all.

He came from nowhere. Or seemed to. Suddenly he was just there, wearing a ship captain's cap, with a black dog at his side. Or was that a chauffeur's cap on his head? It could have been. He was very young. Maybe nineteen or twenty. He was thin and dark-skinned and had curly black hair under his cap, the same color hair as his dog.

Jorge and I were no more than twelve or fourteen feet from the front door of my house, under the shade of the ficus tree, getting ready to climb into its upper reaches to look for lizards we could kill.

"Hi, kids, how are you?" he said. Then banter about how we were and what we were doing.

He seemed normal enough. He was just a guy with a stupid hat and a dog. The dog seemed nice enough. He told us he was trying to sell it. We didn't ask where he'd gotten it, or how long he'd had it, or anything like that. We didn't care. We didn't even ask if the dog was really his to sell. We just said we didn't know anyone who was looking to buy a dog.

"Hey, kids, I really need to pee. Do you know where I might be able to take a leak?"

"Right here," I said, pointing to my house. "You can use our bathroom."

"Oh, no, I couldn't do that. I wouldn't impose on you and your family that way."

"Sure, no problem. Go on. It's fine."

"Oh no. No. No. No way, I couldn't do that. I'm too shy."

That should have made some alarm go off, but it didn't.

"Well, we have a bathroom in the back of the house. It's our maid's bathroom. You can go around the side of the house to the rear patio and use that. You won't even have to enter our house."

"Oh no. No. No, that won't do either. No way, I couldn't do that. I couldn't impose; I'm too shy. What I'm looking for is just a place where I can pee outdoors, out of sight."

Why didn't the bells go off? I thought his self-professed shyness was weird, but I had no clue that he had crossed some line.

So Jorge offered him an alternative.

"Well, there's a vacant lot around the corner. Someone started to build a clinic there, but they never finished."

"Yeah, that's it! Could you kids show me how to get there? I don't know this neighborhood at all."

"It's very easy to find," I said. "You just walk to that corner over there, and turn right. You can't miss the vacant lot. It's three houses down from that corner, right there. And it's big, and it has an empty-looking building next to it."

"Oh, but I'm afraid I'll get lost. Could you please show me how to get there?"

"Sure," said Jorge.

The bells were ringing faintly, very faintly. How could he get lost on the way to the vacant lot? Even the dumbest kid could find it. Something was fishy. But Jorge had spoken up and agreed to show him the way. Now we had to do it.

So we walked him there. He walked with the dog tailing him. He didn't have a leash; the dog simply kept pace with us, staying close to him. I thought he was a little strange, and too childish, but it never crossed my mind that he meant harm in any way. He was just goofy, I thought.

When we reached the empty building and the vacant lot he had another request.

"Looks great, kids. But what will the neighbors around here think if they see me going back there? I'm a stranger here. And it looks kind of scary back there. Could one of you please come with me, so I can pee behind the building, out of sight. Please? I'm scared to go back there. Those trees back there are so big and the shade is so dark. Do you know what it's like to be scared? Haven't you ever been scared? Huh?"

I certainly knew what it was like to be scared to go into dark, strange places, but something didn't seem right. Why was this older guy so scared?

"What about your dog?" I asked. "Can't your dog keep you company?"

"Oh, no. He's a good dog, but I need human company. How about it? Please? Won't one of you come back with me?"

I looked at Jorge and he looked at me. He looked a little puzzled too. The guy with the cap and the dog looked at me."

"How about it, huh? How about you? You're older and bigger, and would help keep me company much better. Yeah. Please? Come on, please, I'm about to pee in my pants. I really have to go, now. Please?"

I felt sorry for the guy and annoyed by him all at once. *Grow up,* I thought.

"Okay," I said.

"And you," he said to Jorge, "stay here and keep an eye out. Make sure no one else comes back there. I'm so shy."

He pulled a knife on me the instant we stepped into the passageway. Since the passageway was L-shaped, we turned a corner and went out of sight. Jorge had no clue. It was a switchblade, with a white pearled handle and a long blade. It had a button on it that made the blade pop out. He opened and closed it, opened and closed it, and when we reached the rear of the building, past the shade of the trees he had claimed to fear so much, he kept it open for good.

The sunlight hit the blade and bounced off with all the ferocious indifference stored up in the universe. It blinded me. The light hit the blade and turned it into a flaming sword.

He grabbed me with the arm he wasn't using to hold the knife, roughly, and pulled me up against him. He held me tightly.

"Help me pee."

The dog, who had been calm until then, began to leap around. Was he all too familiar with this? He was leaping up to the knife, and the guy told him to calm down. He called the dog by name for the first time. It seemed like a very dumb name, but I can't remember it. My mind was on other details.

Like the knife. And the way he was holding me so tightly, so as to make it hard for me to get away. And the sight of his knife hand pulling down the zipper. It must be hard to pull down a zipper while holding a knife, but he managed to do it. It seemed as if he'd had a lot of practice.

I don't think he really needed to pee. He was much too excited. I'd never seen anyone so excited in all my life.

"Here, help me pee. Put your hand right here."

Jesus, no.

And he pulled the knife up to my face, tightened his grip on me, and he told me how I should help him. He was very strong for a skinny guy. The blade felt cold, despite the sunlight it reflected.

My choices were painfully simple: do his bidding or get knifed.

Then, as I was being dragged down to hell, came that voice from heaven, shouting obscenities nearby. *"Coño, carajo, hijo de puta, cabrón, qué mierda, puñetera madre que te parió, mal rayo te parta, mojón del diablo . . ."*

El Loco. The neighborhood wino we had tormented so often, screaming at the top of his lungs, stringing unconnected swear words together like beads in a rosary. He screamed as he always did, but this time he sounded like an entire choir of angels.

The pervert jumped at the sound of *El Loco*'s voice, and his grip on me loosened a little. Just then Jorge started yelling, "*El Loco,* it's *El Loco,* he's here, *El Loco*!" We were all scared of the guy, especially because we teased him so much and had been chased by him so many times. Jorge, especially, was terrified by him, and ran away screaming.

Jorge's cries startled the pervert enough to make him loosen his grip a little more. Enough to allow me to wriggle free and run like the wind. The dog barked and jumped up at me, but I couldn't have cared less. I sprinted out of the passageway. I ran down the block, and around the corner, and down my block, and into my house without looking back. I ran past the blood red hibiscus blossoms, oblivious to them and their desires. I never even caught a glimpse of *El Loco,* even though his shouting rang in my ears nearly all the way home. Maybe he even chased me and I didn't know it.

But I wasn't worried about *El Loco*. He'd saved me from shame, maybe even saved my life. I had another crazy guy to worry about, one with a knife.

On the porch, at my house, there was the rest of the gang. Why hadn't they been there a few minutes before?

I ran back to the bathroom. I felt like vomiting, but nothing came up. I was shaking and sweating and cold all at once. My hands trembled. I started worrying about the pervert. What if he came after me? He knew where I lived. What if he was out there at that very moment, waiting for me, his switchblade in his pocket? What about tomorrow or the next day? Or the day after that? Or next month?

I stayed inside the house for the rest of the day.

Jorge came by and asked me why it had taken that guy so long to pee.

"I don't know. He was such a goofy guy. I don't know . . ."

"Hey, *El Loco* got really close to us. He just kind of snuck up. That was scary, wasn't it?"

"Yeah, really scary," I lied.

I didn't tell my parents or anyone else about what had happened. It was all too embarrassing. I felt stupid for having fallen for the guy's deception, especially since I'd been warned many times not to talk to strangers or go places with them. *I've been really stupid,* I thought. I can't tell anyone. And I certainly can't tell anyone that the guy asked me to help him pee. No way.

I did tell my mom several months later, but by then it was too late to chase down the guy. I told her because I couldn't stop worrying that he would show up at our front door again. I was staying indoors as much as possible, trapped in my house by fear of him.

Then I had an even worse thought. What if Ernesto had sent him? After all, why had the guy come to our house? He admitted that it was the first time he'd been in our neighborhood. Why was he there then? Why had he insisted that I, and I alone, follow him to the back of that abandoned building? I couldn't ask Ernesto, because that would have meant revealing the incident to him. Besides, I knew he'd lie if he'd really put the guy up to it.

I became as paranoid as my uncle Filo. I even began to fear that I'd run into the guy in the United States. The thought of being alone in the States, with no one to protect me from that creep, was more than I could bear.

So I told my mom. And she hugged me and said all the things a mom should say and scolded me mildly for not having told her sooner.

"Your father is a judge, don't forget. If you'd told me earlier we could have found the guy and your dad could have put him in prison, where he deserves to be. Maybe he's still out there, hurting other little boys."

So now it was also my fault that he was still out there, somewhere, being himself, excited in the presence of little boys. But she was right, and I knew it. If I had blurted out the awful truth the minute I set foot in my house that day, we could have probably chased him down. I know that because two or three days later, when I finally ventured beyond my house, I ran into his dog.

There he was, the leaping pervert of a dog. Reminding me.

One of our neighbors now owned him. After he tried to knife me, the bastard had gone door to door and sold the dog to the Basque family whose backyard was adjacent to ours.

I had to hear that demon hound barking every day. I had to see the accursed dog all the time, too. I told my mom about the dog when I told her about the pervert, but when she asked the neighbors about it, they said they didn't know the name or address of the guy who had sold them the dog.

Too late, too bad.

Glorious Revolution. We were all supposed to be transformed overnight, saved from self-love. And were we transfigured yet?

Yeah, sure. We had changed as much as the lizards had.

The lizards stared, as always, indifferent to what humans did, back in the Garden of Eden and back behind that abandoned building.

Lucky bastards.

33

TREINTA Y TRES

If you've never seen a ripe breadfruit, you haven't really lived.

They are so unbelievably spongy when ripe. Years later, when I saw the film *Mutiny on the Bounty,* I immediately understood why the good ship H.M.S. *Bounty* was so full of breadfruit, and why the British were so determined to spread breadfruit to all tropical corners of their empire, including the Caribbean. Ripe breadfruit explodes so nicely on impact. So thoroughly. So messily. What is an empire without breadfruit? A sham.

The giant breadfruit tree in the yard next to my house stood as tall as the monument to the U.S.S. *Maine* on the Malecón. And it was always loaded with huge green round breadfruits, each about the size of a small melon. So round, so pocked, their surface covered with little square mounds, each blessed in its center with the slightest hint of a nipple. Hundreds of little breasts, arranged in beautiful intricate whorls: little teats, which, when pricked or shot with BBs, would ooze a white milky liquid. Those huge green balls of soft milky pulp with a firm brown stem on their crown, a stem you could grab like the handle and use so well for throwing. They were just like the German grenades the Nazis used in war movies, only round instead of tubular.

We had heard that breadfruit was edible. We knew this because we had often seen the Jamaican man collect the breadfruits and go home with a burlap bag full of them. He told us it was delicious, in a very strange accent. We laughed at him and thought him crazy. Breadfruit was not for eating. It was for shooting at with BB guns or for throwing.

Years later, after Tony and I had left, and after my mother had left, and our uncle Filo had gone *loco,* my father and Ernesto would eat breadfruit. That's what can happen after a Revolution, especially one with a capital *R.*

But years before Louis XVI ate breadfruit, during one of our days in Limbo, we suddenly woke up to the fact that the crop next door was bountiful. The huge tree groaned under the weight. The ground was covered with them. The shade under the tree, so dark, so cool, must have preserved the fallen fruit. Our neighbor's gardener had even started to pile up some of the fruit in the corner of the yard nearest the entrance to our house. One hop over the iron fence, taking care not to impale yourself, and you were in breadfruit paradise. We didn't worry about damaging the hibiscus bushes right under the fence. They were expendable.

We had tossed breadfruit before that day. We knew its potential. But we had never before been inspired to throw more than a few. How we got started, I can't remember. All I know is that we threw one or two and then couldn't stop.

These breadfruit were absolutely perfect.

Such beautiful detonations when they hit something, anything. Such a splat, such a reverberating, satisfying concussion. A faint yet true echo that touched each of us deep in our souls. And what a feast for the eyes as well: all that gooey pulp hurtling through space, adhering to whatever stood in its way or falling to the ground in perfect arcs, so obedient to the law of gravity. And that smell, that primal scent, that musk, that fifth dimension. It spoke of swamps, ooze, eggs and sperm, and infinite reproduction. We didn't know about that stuff yet, at least some of us didn't. All we knew was that it was a fine smell, as fine as they come, giddily perched on that elusive boundary that stands between right and wrong.

We hopped over that spear-point fence, raided the pile of breadfruit the neighbor's gardener had left for us, and threw and threw and threw. Most of our shots missed their intended targets, but some were bull's-eyes. The sound of ripe breadfruit exploding on the chest of a ten-year-old boy is like nothing else in the world. Except for maybe the sound of ripe breadfruit exploding on the head of a ten-year-old boy. The sight of it, too. The pulp smeared on the shirt, the forearms, and especially the chin and neck. The strands of pulp falling off someone else's chin, as you laugh so hard that you think you'll lose your mind. The strands on the eyelashes, and those up the nostrils. Even funnier. Especially when the target is your own brother.

We didn't break up into teams as we usually did, the older guys against the younger—always a guaranteed loss for Rafa and me. This was the ultimate free-for-all. Each for himself and God against all. This was our own World War, which we knew so well from movies. It was the fall of Berlin, the fall of Rome, the fall of Havana. It was the beginning and the end rolled into one. The Alpha and Omega. Emanation and Remanation. The Big Bang, coming and going. The Big Whimper, too.

The five of us knew our world had come to an end. The Apocalypse had arrived. We all knew that our parents were making plans to send us to the United States. We knew our days under the breadfruit tree were numbered.

So we threw those smelly, gooey breadfruits, hurled them with absolute abandon, with fury. We tried to inflict as much damage as possible. We laughed our heads off, even when we got hit. Those breadfruit hurt, but we didn't feel pain. We laughed and kept throwing, more and more.

I think it was *El Alocado* Eugenio, as always, who found a way to open the gate that led from the neighbor's yard to the street. It doesn't matter who opened the gate, really. What matters is that the breadfruit war, at first safely contained, spilled out onto the street. This being a free-for-all, each of us had to gather ammunition and throw on our own. Raiding the breadfruit pile, or gathering fruit from the ground once the pile vanished, while keeping an eye on four opponents wasn't easy. Carrying an armload of mushy fruit out onto the street while being pelted from four directions was even harder. But somehow we managed to do this, each of us fighting against the other.

Then the rules of war changed. Many of the houses on my street had masonry or cement walls right up against the sidewalk, most of them about four feet tall, and we quickly figured out that these barriers could serve as fortresses. Someone called a time-out, and we each gathered a pile of ammunition to bring behind our respective ramparts.

I don't know how long the truce lasted. But each of us gathered enough breadfruit to cover one entire suburban street in the tropics with breadfruit slime. And that's what we did. We were five boys throwing breadfruit from one side of the street to the other, with a no-man's land in between, just like soldiers in their trenches at Verdun. Five boys seeking shelter from gooey projectiles behind five walls on opposite sides of the street, lobbing, hurling, tossing, seeking to maim one another, or at least to smother their world with sticky, stinky pulp. We couldn't throw to anyone on our own side of the street due to shrubbery. So it was three on one side of the street, two on the other side, and the breadfruit flying across.

This is what it must be like to have a snowball fight, I thought.

The breadfruit flew that day as never before or since. Never, ever, anywhere on this earth, I'm sure, will breadfruit be hurled with such rage, delight, and courage. And as happens in any war, or any game, there came one moment of blinding, awe-inspiring bravery, of grace, brilliance, and heroism.

As our ammunition piles dwindled, Manuel made a daring raid on my brother Tony's bunker. Armed with a single breadfruit, Manuel dashed out from behind his wall and entered no-man's land, opening himself up to fire from all sides. Then, summoning all of his strength, Manuel launched his green missile at Tony the instant he saw his crew-cut head peering over the edge of the wall. The trajectory of that breadfruit was a perfectly straight line: good and beautiful, but not exactly true. Instead of hitting my brother's head, the breadfruit hit the wall. And it hit it with such force as to make the entire wall move. I know it moved. I saw it move. The sound made by that impact was by far the most sublime of the day. This was no mere splat, it was a peal of thunder, an earthquake's rumble. I can still hear it and feel it. I think I shall always hear it and feel it shake. Such a beautiful sound, so much like the pounding of a human heart. I shall always see that wall move, too. Such a miracle, a wall shaken by fruit, fruit thrown by a child about to be expelled from paradise.

A child who would end up fighting in a real war in Vietnam a few years later.

Instead of pouncing on Manuel, the four of us simply froze, standing or crouching, transfixed. Then we laughed, and the laughing couldn't stop, wouldn't stop. And we looked around and saw what we had done. Breadfruit pulp everywhere. On walls, on tree trunks, on the sidewalks, on the street, on our neighbors' porches, on their porch furniture and light fixtures. On ourselves. Then we realized we had used up nearly every available missile. And the laughing stopped. We dashed to our respective houses, cleaned ourselves up, and pretended nothing had happened.

Then the phone calls began to come in from neighbors. Complaints. It seemed the phone would never stop ringing. Since it was our street, it was my brother and I, and our parents, who shouldered the responsibility for our Apocalypse. My father went out the door, took a look at the street, and made two phone calls of his own, one to the parents of Manuel and Rafael, the other to Eugenio's parents. Within a half hour or so, there we were, the five of us, cleaning up the mess with hoses, brooms, mops, and shovels. It took the rest of that afternoon to remove every trace of our glorious breadfruit war.

We worked harder than we ever had. We toiled even harder than the school janitor who cleaned up pee puddles. We had been undone by our own war, our version of a counter-revolution. Transformed from worms into worker bees by glorious stinking breadfruit. Funny, I don't remember complaining about working really hard for the first time in my life. I only remember inhaling deeply and laughing.

And now, whenever I feel the rage rising within me, I force myself to smile and breathe deeply. Nine times out of ten I smell breadfruit. Nice and ripe.

34

TREINTA Y CUATRO

I was the first to lay eyes on the woman with the big butt. Her rear end was monumental, large enough to contain all of the world, and all of human experience.

Thinly, very thinly veiled by red fabric, it spoke of many things without speaking. Fertile fields, sunlight, water, earthworms, hard labor, sweat, roots, greens, fruit, udders, milk, flies, muddy hooves, feathers, trucks full of produce, market stalls, blood, meat, money, canvas shopping bags bursting at the seams, kitchens with banged-up pots, crusty kerosene stoves, lard wrapped in wax paper, dripping tins of olive oil from Spain, diced onions hissing in black pans, garlic fumes, knives that gave off sparks when sharpened on pedal-driven wheels lined with flint, sparks that flew like planets being born, Band-Aids, iodine, aprons stained with memories, ladles, spatulas, spoons, forks, dishes, glasses stained with lipstick, cups, napkins, tablecloths folded by grandmothers, dishes steaming on the table, thinly sliced avocados, fried plantains, *malanga,* yucca, *carne asada, arroz con pollo, picadillo, ropa vieja, tasajo, papas rellenas,* tons of rice, black beans, garbanzos, red beans, paella, beer, wine, rum, coffee, flan made in old chorizo tins, custard with vanilla wafers stuck inside, guava paste and cream cheese on crackers, lots of sugar, sunsets, endless talk, whispers, shouts, gossip, songs, music on the radio, dancing in place, hands around the waist, hands on the back, familiar bones felt under the flesh, new ones discovered, heat within, heat in the air, kisses, joy, disappointment, betrayal, sorrow, arguments, prayer, sex, birth, ration cards, firing squads, illness, and death.

And eggplants, of course.

And oh, yeah, love, too. I'm sure love had a lot to do with making that butt so big.

Anyway, the woman with the world's largest rear end was standing under a palm tree, near a drinking fountain, talking to some friends. I fingered the peas in my pocket and tapped Rafael on the shoulder.

"Look, over there, the perfect target."

"Good one!"

"Let's find the others. We have to tell them!"

We were roaming the new park on the banks of the Almendares River, attacking people with our blowguns. It was none other than Louis XVI who had made the peashooters for us by cutting up an old television antenna. A simple enough weapon to make and use. Thin, hollow metal cylinders, about ten or twelve inches long. All you needed was something hard to shoot out with your tongue and air from your lungs. Aiming was a snap, especially at close range, and with a projectile as hard as a dried pea.

We had just seen a documentary on the Indian tribes of the Amazon River basin, which must have been deemed acceptable by the Revolutionary authorities, and we had fallen in love with their blowguns. And King Louis, ever eager to amuse us and our friends, had said: "I can make even better blowguns for you out of metal." So he took out his hacksaw and cut into pieces the rods of an old antenna he just happened to have on hand. Then he carefully sanded and polished both ends of each of the resulting cylinders and gave all of us sturdy, nearly indestructible blowguns.

"I can't make you any poisoned darts, though," he said as he handed us our weapons. "I might be able to make the darts, but I don't think I could come up with the poison." He looked sort of crestfallen as he said it.

"But you can use peas," he said, his face brightening. "They're not being rationed right now. I can get you each your own bag of peas."

We piled into the '51 blue-and-cream Plymouth and headed for the nearest food store. On the way there we practiced shooting spitballs out of the car's windows or at each other, at close range. Those spitballs stung. And they stuck to anything we hit with them. Parked cars, telephone poles, street signs, pedestrians, and what not. We made the spitballs from the pages we'd ripped out of an old *Bohemia* magazine.

The peas were so much better than the spitballs, though. No comparison. They'd come barreling out of our blowguns like torpedoes from a submarine. And they made such a nice noise as you fired them, snapping back your tongue from your lips. But that soft *thhhhpp* was nothing compared to the loud *thhhwack* you'd hear when you hit your target. Such a sublime sound.

We had practiced with our peas for a day or two before going to the new park and were actually working on our second bags of ammunition, grateful that they weren't being rationed.

The new park was one of the first urban projects completed by the Revolution. The Almendares River flowed between Vedado and Miramar, forming a natural boundary between the two suburbs. It also flowed past one of the last remaining slivers of forest in Havana, *El Bosque de la Habana,* which was high above it on a bluff. The woods there had previously been accessible only to those who wanted to brave the wilds. Now the wilderness was open to the People.

We'd braved the wilds in the Bosque many times before the park was built. Louis XVI loved taking us there. We'd hike the rough trails and marvel at the trees and the bluffs. One cliff in particular was very scary. You had to inch your way along a very narrow ledge, clinging with your hands to the chalky stone face. It must have been at least a two-hundred-foot drop. One false step and you'd be dead.

We walked that ledge so many times I lost count.

I can still close my eyes and see the green water far below and my overweight father struggling to flatten his stomach against the cliff face as he inched along the ledge. I can also see my own feet creeping along the ledge and hear my dad urging me on.

"Keep moving, keep moving. If you stop moving and look down, you'll get vertigo. So move, move, move."

"What's vertigo?"

"What you're feeling right now."

Louis XVI must have been one of the least safety-conscious men in Cuba. Or the world, I think. I still remember the sound the pebbles made on that thin ledge as we dislodged them with our feet and they tumbled down the cliff face. The ledge wasn't exactly firm. And my dad's two-hundred-plus pounds made the pebbles rain down.

"Listen to those pebbles," my dad would say as he clung precariously to the chalky rock face, "and try to imagine what sound a body might make if it were to fall down the cliff. Imagine how the screams would get fainter on the way down, and how they might echo. Imagine how the splash would sound as the body hit the water."

Louis XVI was right about that. There was a wonderful echo in the Bosque. Even the falling pebbles produced an echo. And there was one great spot where we could really play with the echo, shouting and waiting for our voices to return. When all of us shouted within split seconds of one another, the barrage of voices that would return was spectacular. Every voice obeyed its appointed time delay.

Louis XVI was probably wrong about something else, though. "You know, those ruins are just waiting to be discovered," he'd say, pointing to a spot across the river. "They're older than the sunken continent of Atlantis. It was a civilization much more advanced than our own. But only the right person will be able to really see them, and read their documents, and pass on their great secrets to the world. They await a Messiah of the Ruins. Do you see them? Right over there? Maybe one of you will discover them. Maybe one of you is their Messiah."

We thought we saw them. And we begged him to take us there, to the other side of the river.

"No, you have to get there all on your own. Maybe when you're older."

I think I began to take an interest in the past right there, looking across the river to those mysterious shapes on the opposite bluff.

But all those trips to the Bosque had been long ago, in the past, before the world changed, or shortly thereafter. The Bosque was being civilized now, opened up to the Cuban People. It was a very pretty park they'd made, you had to admit it. Nice walkways, benches, kiosks, and lights. Beautiful views. And it was all so safe, so close to the river. The trails we had walked so many times before were still above us, untouched by the park.

We were there on the day it first opened to the public. And Inaugural Day for the Park of the Revolution had brought out a huge crowd. The place was teeming with people, as packed as the shark pool at the Aquarium of the Revolution. Which is why we could shoot our peas with impunity. *Thhhhp! . . . thhhwack!*

It was so easy to hide behind other people or behind trees. We had shot dozens of people and slipped away without any trouble. It was so much fun to see their reactions. I aimed for their heads. My brother aimed for their backs and butts. The others aimed at different parts of their victims' bodies.

Every now and then, when the other guy least expected it, we'd shoot at each other, too.

It was the most fun I'd had since our breadfruit war. It was almost as if nothing had changed and we were back in our old world. But there was a certain kind of ferocity to our play that evening, in that new park by the river. We knew our days were numbered. And in so many different ways we were all pissed as hell.

What we didn't know was that it would be our last adventure together. If we had known that, we might have actually shoved people into the river, I think.

Louis XVI had brought Ernesto along, but Ernesto said he was too grown-up for such hijinks. King Louis himself made no effort to supervise the small guerilla squad he'd brought to the park. He seemed to derive great pleasure from knowing that we were all out there, shooting peas with abandon. So King Louis and Ernesto walked along the paved paths that we stalked, paying little attention to what the rest of us were doing.

Eugenio, Manuel, and Tony, all of them thirteen or fourteen years old, were far ahead of me and Rafael in terms of their aggressiveness and risk taking. Rafa and I were only eleven, and still more cautious.

Before long, *El Alocado,* Eugenio, began to get careless. He'd shoot people and barely make an effort to hide. He'd just put the blowgun behind his back, stare directly at his victims, and laugh. We all warned him to be more careful, but he wouldn't listen. Then Manuel and Tony dropped their warnings, and joined him.

Thhhhp! . . . thhhwack! Ha, ha, ha!

You can understand why I had to tell them about the lady with The Butt. We were one soul with five bodies. Something like that had to be shared. All for one, and one for all. For the last time.

So we decided to shoot The Butt in unison. What else would anyone in their right mind do?

It was an act of pure love, what we did.

"Caritas," Saint Augustine would have said, pure love directed towards God and others, rather than towards the self.

We lined up like a firing squad about ten feet from The Butt. She had her back turned to us, and the people with her were so busy talking that they didn't notice us either. We couldn't say "ready, aim, fire" because we needed our mouths and tongues to fire the peas, so we cued one another with our eyes and other subtle signals and aimed our blowguns in unison.

Thhhhp! . . . thhhwack! Multiplied by five!

Every one of us, I'm proud to say, hit the target. It would have been a disgrace to miss. It was like hitting the side of a barn, as they say in the Midwest.

"Aaaaaaay! Qué fue eso?" What was that? She wheeled around faster than we thought she would, and, of course, she saw us. *"Aaaaaaay!* What are you doing? Degenerates. They've shot me up! Militiamen! Militiamen! Please help, do something."

She lunged at us. Well, sort of. When you're that large it's hard to lunge. She came towards us, yelling at the top of her lungs. People stopped dead in their tracks and stared. We, of course, ran away as fast as we could.

Louis XVI was nearby, and we ran through the crowd to him.

"What's all the noise, kids?"

"I don't know, some lady just went nuts over there."

"Really? Maybe I'll go take a look."

"No, don't . . . let's get out of here."

In the meantime, Butt Lady had worked her way through the crowd and found us talking to the King. She started shouting at my dad, very loudly, waving her arms wildly. The fat under her upper arms swayed like walrus blubber as she shook her index finger near his face.

"Hey, you, *señor,* what are your boys up to? This is a total disgrace! They shot me! What kind of kids are you raising? I should report you and those kids. Criminals! That's what they are: criminals! They belong in jail, or a work camp."

"I'm so sorry, *señora,* but I don't know what you're talking about."

We left the judge in charge and snuck away silently, on cats' feet. I didn't want to know how he would handle this, and neither did any of the rest of us. We exited the park and waited for him at the car. Of course, we assumed he'd survive the fat lady's attack. And he did. A few minutes later, he found us standing around the Plymouth.

"Hey, you guys got carried away back there, didn't you? What were you thinking? Shooting up people like that. Are you crazy? I didn't make those blowguns so you could do something like that. That lady was ready to call the militiamen on you. You know how serious that is?"

He didn't sound the least bit angry. Instead, he sounded worried and sad.

We stood there as silent as the peas in our pockets.

Ernesto stood off to the side, behind my dad, with a smug look on his face. Near the end he often had that look.

"I got you off the hook, you know, but it wasn't easy," Louis XVI said. "You guys put me in a very tight spot. Don't ever do that again, you hear?"

We said okay and got into the Plymouth. We knew there wouldn't be a next time. And I guess he did, too.

35

TREINTA Y CINCO

It was a miracle. It had to be. You can't doubt what you see. If this wasn't a miracle, then nothing else could be.

The color of the sea was changing, as if some giant brush were being applied from beneath. Or was it from above? I stared long and hard at the wild cloud-shaped rainbow in the water. There were splashes of tangerine in there too, little bits of sunset at midday, along with splashes of blood red hibiscus blossoms.

And it *moved*. The colored cloud inside the water kept moving to and fro, twisting and turning with great speed.

It was the most extraordinary thing I had ever seen, and perhaps the most beautiful. I stood there on the dock of a formerly private beach club, under the sun and the clouds, transfixed. I thought surely this was a vision sent directly from heaven—one that spoke to me without scaring me to death. All the visions I'd heard until then had been frightening: Jesus and Mary and the saints appearing to children and giving them messages that none of the adults around them would believe. I'd heard of statues in churches moving, or breathing, or talking. I'd also seen a very scary movie about a boy named Marcelino who struck up a friendship with a crucifix that came alive. The Italian priests across the street had screened that movie outdoors one night, but none of us kids dared to put our hands in front of the camera for that one, much less a middle finger. Talk about scary! The thought of Jesus coming to life on his cross and speaking to me seemed worse than Frankenstein, Wolf Man, Dracula, the Mummy, and the Creature from the Black Lagoon put together.

Twenty years later, in Lugo, not far from where my grandparents had been born, I would almost end up locked into a chapel with a similar crucifix for an entire night. The sacristan didn't see me and locked the gates while I was looking at the altarpiece. The thought of spending the whole night in there with a life-size crucifix, in total darkness, was too much for me to bear. I started yelling for someone to open the gate and get me out. My Spanish cousins laughed for days about that.

I explained to them that I had a fear of bleeding Christ figures, but that only made them laugh harder. They're probably still laughing. "Watch out, don't run into a bleeding Christ on the way," one of them said to me as I boarded a train bound for Madrid.

But this fast-moving storm of shapes and colors within the turquoise water was a good miracle. It moved and moved without stopping. Sometimes it split into two and the halves circled around to form a whole again. And in the meantime, as the halves danced with each other, the contrast between the cloud and the turquoise sea grew even more intense.

Truth, beauty, goodness, and eternity were out there dancing with the sharks and all the other creatures that feed upon one another—and sometimes upon humans—with sharp teeth or stinging venom. Love was there too, unencumbered by self-centeredness, possessiveness, doubts, or jealousy. Trouble-free love, squirming inside a wondrous sea—a sea already too beautiful to take in.

Was this a farewell vision of everything that was beautiful in my birthplace, all wrapped into one?

This was so much nicer than Window Jesus or Eye Jesus coming to life. This was grace, pure grace, out there, embodied amidst the sharks.

I don't know how long I stood there, or what I said. I had the strangest sensation of not having my feet planted on the ground. Then my brother and my friends Rafael and Manuel showed up. Eugenio was already beyond the horizon, in the United States. We all wondered out loud as to what it could be, and what *El Alocado* might have said.

Tony called out to our dad, and he came over, accompanied by Ernesto. With all of his years of experience in this life and in previous ones, Louis XVI, too, was stumped.

"That is truly amazing. *Que maravilla!*"

The miracle was not just for me, for sure. That made it even nicer.

Our noise attracted several other people.

"Parrot fish. It's a whole school of them," said the man behind me. "Hundreds and hundreds of them. Maybe thousands. I've never seen that many all at once." He explained to us all how parrot fish swam in groups and how they swarmed sometimes.

I thought of the shark pool at the aquarium and the parrot fish we had rescued. We went back about once a week, just to see him. Of course, each time we went we also stared at the shark pool. It kept getting more and more crowded.

And the diving board never shut up about Ernesto. Never. "Do it now. Push him in. Sneak up on him from behind. You'll feel so much better after you do it. Push him in. Now!"

We all stood there on that dock, watching the miracle unfold for a long, long time. It was as if we were glued to the dock and aloft at the same time. Ernesto stood there too, totally silent.

Eventually, the miracle vanished just as it had arrived. The colors moved farther and farther away, towards the horizon, northwards, riding the Gulf Stream, towards the United States. And then, suddenly, we could no longer see them.

Something else to leave behind, I thought.

No amount of wishing on our part brought them back that day or any other day, and no memory has ever come close to the real thing. After staring at the sea for a while, we went home to await the *desengaño* that was sure to follow.

36

TREINTA Y SEIS

It was a grand staircase all right. I'd never seen one so grand or so impressive or so modern. It looked like a giant, graceful corkscrew, or one of the paper streamers Cubans used to throw into the air at Carnival and at birthday parties.

And it seemed to float in the air.

It had a handrail, I think. It must have had one. Cubans were careless about safety—except when it came to swimming after eating or catching pneumonia—but I don't think they would have been so reckless as to build a freestanding staircase without a handrail.

The staircase was inside a beautiful house not very far from my own in Miramar. The house had a swimming pool outside, free of sharks, and five marble statues around the pool. The five statues represented the five girls in the family, now fully grown.

The family that lived in the house were friends of my mother and her family and had owned a chain of bedding stores. All of the money used to build that house came from something as prosaic as mattresses and beds.

My aunt Lily had been engaged to an uncle of the five girls. But he had died very young, and my aunt never got to marry him. I have his sapphire ring, which my mother snuck out of Cuba inside a sanitary napkin, but I don't wear it. It's much too small for me, so my wife wears it. Better that it be on a woman's finger, anyway. Whenever I think of that family, only women come to mind.

The house was inhabited by women only. The widowed matriarch, Pilar, and four of her five daughters. Three were unmarried, one was divorced. Another one was married and lived nearby.

They were all very beautiful, these five women. Their mother had almost become a nun, and their father had studied for the priesthood. The almost-nun and the almost-priest were appropriately blessed with five enchanting daughters.

One balmy evening, Fidel met one of the daughters at a restaurant. At that time, fairly early in the Revolution, he would show up at restaurants now and then with his retinue of guards. One thing led to another, and Fidel ended up going home with that one daughter, whose nickname was Kika. He got into her car and let her drive. He told her that he was testing the Revolutionary merits of the People's Car for the first time, and that it was too small for him. He had discovered that the People's Car, a Volkswagen, was uncomfortable for anyone over six feet tall. That's what he told her anyway.

They drove to Miramar in a caravan, front, rear, and sides protected by other vehicles full of guards.

"You're a very good driver," Fidel told her.

When they got to her house, the guards surrounded the entire block. Fidel and Kika walked into the house, along with a bunch of other men. Fidel sat by the pool talking to this woman for a while, drinking a whole liter of milk from a bottle. He made a point of asking for a liter that hadn't yet been opened. Back in those days, milk bottles had a seal that was held in place by a thin wire—wires we sometimes used to tie up hibiscus blossoms. Fidel wanted to make sure the milk hadn't been tampered with. The great burden of every despot since ancient times: fear of poisoning. He didn't even pour the milk into a glass; he just drank it straight from the bottle.

And he made small talk with Kika while a retinue of guards surrounded him and the entire house. "Where's the rest of the family?" he asked.

She hemmed and hawed. She said they were all in bed with colds. The truth was that the matriarch and the other three daughters didn't like Fidel at all and had stayed upstairs in their bedrooms.

Fidel knew exactly where the rest of the family was, and why. He knew that the matriarch and the other sisters were not good Revolutionaries. Perhaps he knew exactly where their five stores were and what they looked like: they'd been confiscated, along with every other business. And the daughters now had to work as employees of the state at the stores they had once owned. Everyone had to work, you know. *El que no trabaja, no come.* If you don't work, you don't eat. It was one of Fidel's favorite slogans.

He raised the milk bottle above his head and faced the upper-story windows that looked over the pool.

"Here's to you, ladies! Hope your health improves. Thanks for the milk! I know it's hard to come by."

They tell me he laughed after he said that. He knew, of course, that milk was rationed.

I heard this story from Pilar herself, who said that she'd been standing at her window, behind closed shutters, when Fidel toasted her with a liter of her own rationed milk. Only so many ounces per week.

Pilar also told me that this knocked the wind out of her, literally, and that she couldn't catch her breath for quite some time afterwards. When Fidel left the house along with his retinue, she said, she was still having trouble breathing.

Fidel never returned. No more dates with Kika. Maybe it was something she said, or something she didn't say. Or maybe it was all those other women peeking through the shutters. Or maybe it was the poolside statues that turned him off. So bourgeois. Too bourgeois, even for a one-night stand and the chance to sire yet another child.

Anyway, Pilar and her daughters loved to throw movie parties on Saturday nights. They had access to Hollywood films, some now banned from Cuban theaters, and screened them in their palatial living room with the same kind of projector that was used in a movie theater. Most of the time, I watched from the spiral staircase, the stairway to heaven.

Movies in a house! A house large enough to accommodate an audience of twenty or so. Drinks. Rationed drinks, but still drinks. No popcorn, though. That wasn't available. But it wasn't the refreshments that made the evening, it was the event itself. And the fact that I got to stay up until way past midnight.

The grown-ups joked out loud as the movie played on the screen. No middle-finger shadows blacking out the actors, but the gist of the jokes was not much more advanced than that. We children just sat back and watched and listened.

Whenever I think of what my adult life in Cuba might have been, if the world hadn't changed, it's those movie parties that come to mind. The lights turned off, the hum and whirr of the projector, the pool glowing outside through the French doors, the jokes.

"Hey, Demetrius, you need a bra!"

We were watching Victor Mature in *Demetrius and the Gladiators,* the sequel to *The Robe.* They'd spent so much on the sets for *The Robe* that the producers had decided to spin off a sequel. It told the story of the Greek slave who had served the Roman centurion who ended up with the robe of Jesus at the crucifixion, and it was pure Hollywood fluff. Since Richard Burton and Jean Simmons had been killed in *The Robe,* martyred by the mad Emperor Caligula, someone wrote a lame story about what happened to Richard Burton's slave. And since Victor Mature had played that slave before, he landed the starring role. And we were watching Victor Mature's very large pectoral muscles convulse.

"Hey, Demetrius, I think you'd take a C cup!"

It seemed like sharp humor at the time. No one in my house would ever think to shout out anything like that, especially during a religious movie. I might have been slapped for blasphemy or bad manners or poor taste.

So we watched *Demetrius and the Gladiators,* and *How to Marry a Millionaire,* and *Three Coins in the Fountain,* and a few other movies, over the space of a few months. The last months I would spend in Cuba.

Louis XVI never came with us to these parties. These were my mother's friends, and he didn't really like them much. Anyway, King Louis and Marie Antoinette never did anything together anymore.

They weren't even planning to join us together in the States. Nope. They'd already agreed that Marie Antoinette would be the only one to follow us. She was handicapped, knew no English, and had no job skills of any kind, save sewing. Still, she would be the one to join us and take care of us in the United States until we could return to Cuba. It wouldn't be that long, two or three years at most. Fidel couldn't possibly last longer than that. The plan called for King Louis to stay home to guard the precious art collection from the Cuban People. He wouldn't give that up, not even to be with his real sons. He did keep us in mind, though: he repeatedly said, as the years dragged on and we all got older, and Fidel got more deeply entrenched in power, that he was staying behind so we wouldn't lose our inheritance.

And one fine day his heart burst, and Ernesto got to keep everything.

We'd be given a ride home from the movie parties by Kika, the daughter who had attracted Fidel's attention. We'd ride through Miramar at one or two in the morning, in the car that had once given a lift to Fidel, through utter dark and utter silence. *La madrugada,* that magic time before sunrise when the entire world seems asleep and you think you are the only one who's truly awake. The best time in the world. The only time that truth appears, uninvited. Still, you have to be careful; you musn't let truth overtake you. Some truths are best left buried.

If you don't bury some truths, they'll have a chance at burying you.

I confess to being an idolater, and to performing sacrifices daily, even hourly, at the altar of the god of denial. I sacrifice painful truths constantly, especially about myself, and bury them without reading their entrails first. It's a means of survival I learned on the fly, when my world was stripped away, bit by bit. Somehow I learned to cling to one piece of fiction that floated calmly above the wreckage, undisturbed: I am still the same.

I'm still the same even though my friends have all vanished.

I'm still the same even though my favorite school will never exist again.

I'm still the same even though my first childish love vanished overnight.

I'm still the same even though I have no comic books, ice cream, baseball cards, Coca-Cola, chewing gum, toys, good movies, or decent shoes.

I'm still the same even though I don't have the right to say what's on my mind inside my own house, let alone in public.

I'm still the same even though my father has adopted a pervert who is now my brother.

I'm still the same even though another pervert has tried to drag me down to hell.

I'm still the same even though I've been shot at and bombed.

I'm still the same even though my parents have decided to send me away.

Still the same. I can't change. I'm like Victor Mature's pectoral muscles in *Demetrius and the Gladiators*. He'll be dead and buried someday, but he'll always need a bra in that movie. I'm like Kirk Douglas' dead eye in *The Vikings*. No matter how old or how dead Kirk and Janet are, that eye will always come to life when Janet Leigh comes into view on the screen, and it will burn, burn, burn.

I'll always be who I am.

Denial is wonderful. Try it sometime, if you haven't already. But don't count on it too much. Sooner or later, denial denies even itself.

Flash forward two months from my last Saturday night movie party at the house of the pool with the five statues, in Miramar.

I'm sitting on a very modern-looking chair in a sparsely furnished and bright living room in a small house in Miami, South West, two blocks north of Coral Way, in the 7900 block. I'm in Paradise, where everything is perfect. There's no religious art to be seen anywhere, only reproductions of Picasso and Miró. I don't recognize the art as art, and don't even know that the artists are Spanish. It's strange, this house, and wonderful. Nothing original inside a frame. Nothing old, anywhere in this house. The floor is wood, not marble. The living room and dining room are actually one large room, and there's an air conditioner sticking out of the wall above the living room couch. Beyond the dining room, through clear glass sliding doors, I see a patio like none I've ever seen. There's actually a huge cube of a frame enclosing it all, even on top.

What genius stole that idea from me? I'd longed for such an enclosure and planned it down to the smallest details while lying in bed under my mosquito tent in Havana. The idea came to me in a flash one morning as I studied the dust motes swirling inside the mosquito tent. Why not enclose the outdoors, blocking out the lizards and the bugs?

Now, in the United States, I find that someone has beaten me to the punch. But I'm glad to see my idea brought to life, even if it steals my thunder. I'm so glad this house has a totally screened-in patio. I'm glad to be in the United States, where everything is reasonable and new and perfect. I'm so glad to be in Paradise, among friendly strangers.

I've been driven miles and miles to this house to meet the family that wants to take me in. I've been driven here by the husband of a friend of my mother who has somehow arranged for this family to rescue me from the refugee camp at Homestead. He's using up his only day off that week to take care of this.

I've been living in the camp for two weeks now, ever since I was separated from Tony at the airport. As soon as we cleared Immigration, we were loaded into different vans and taken to different camps. Tony went to a camp for teens in Kendall, I went to a camp for preteens in Homestead.

Already, I miss Tony terribly.

Already, I've seen my first Cuba cloud.

I've also learned the word *spic* from the freckle-faced girls from the Air Force base who yell it out every time they approach the chain-link fence surrounding the camp.

I've almost eaten shredded metal along with my ravioli in the camp dining hall. It was just there, this big twisted hunk of metal. I bit into it and almost cracked a tooth. Then the guy next to me also bit into one. And the guy next to him cut his tongue on one. Within one minute the whole dining hall was buzzing with alarm and with children crying out in pain. Somehow shreds of metal from the cans of ravioli had made their way into the ravioli. We were told to throw out the ravioli and line up for peanut butter sandwiches instead.

I've also gotten married to a Coca-Cola bottle by accident.

It caught my eye, that rounded glass lip from the top of a Coke bottle, perfectly and cleanly severed, laying on the ground. It looked like a beautiful jade ring. I slipped it on like a ring, but it was too tight and it cut off the blood flow and my finger began to turn purple and swell. The harder I tried to slip it off, the worse it hurt. I felt so stupid. This wasn't at all like the time I'd gotten my head stuck in a church pew. That had been a mystical experience; this was just plain idiocy. I ended up at the camp kitchen and the cook took one look and started to laugh. "Guess I'll have to saw off your finger now," he said in a totally serious voice. He was Cuban, so I believed him and started to panic, especially when he brought out a huge serrated knife. Then he laughed some more and applied lots of dish soap to my finger and worked the glass ring off. But not without taking off most of my skin along with the ring.

I've also been permanently transformed by a nun, without knowing it.

Nuns ran the camp at Homestead. Don't ask why. It was a camp established by the Central Intelligence Agency and run by Cuban nuns. Anyway, it was Holy Week, and one of the nuns told us, a room full of about eighty boys and girls who had just left all of their family behind in Cuba and were now in a foreign land, that when Jesus willingly embraced the cross on his way to Calvary he saw in it every sin that had ever been committed and would ever be committed in the entire history of the human race, including each and every sin that each one of us in that room would ever commit in our entire lifetime. Somehow she looked us all in the eye at the same time, with a look I'd never seen before, not even in a priest's eye. I knew this nun had been somewhere none of us had never been, and probably would never, ever go, at least before death. Her eyes were living flames, hotter than the Cuban sun, and they sent out rays more concentrated than those that pass through a magnifying glass at high noon at the Tropic of Cancer. She didn't talk to us about our present situation. Though she could have very easily dwelt on very particular, and very immediate problems, like the shrapnel in the ravioli, she talked to us in universal terms about our faults and about redemption from them. She went for the biggest problem of all, and the biggest solution. She told us that Jesus was actually very happy to take up His cross and that He wept with joy upon seeing all of the world's sins embedded in those mean, raw pieces of wood that meant death for Him at the age of thirty-three. She told us Jesus was God made flesh, a God who loved us and had suffered and died so we could choose redemption freely. She spoke of Free Will redeemed by grace and of eternal life.

I walked out of that metal Army surplus prefabricated building in a stupor, wondering what had hit me. What she had said, and the way she had said it pierced me and stuck with me like no other religion lesson I'd had or any Mass I'd ever attended.

So I've been converted without realizing it. And to top it all off, I haven't seen my parents or any other relatives for two long weeks. Meanwhile, my powers of denial are working just fine. This exile thing is a breeze. It's even fun.

In that living room of the small house in Miami, I'm introduced to the family that wants to take me in. They seem like such nice people. They're both younger than my parents, and they also have two little boys they've adopted. One is about a year and a half old, the other is about eight months old. I am delighted to learn that the youngest has the same name as Tony Curtis' character in *The Vikings*. And they also have a huge German shepherd who, for now, barks on the other side of the glass doors, out in the screened-in patio. Such nice people. We talk mostly through my mother's friend, who acts as an interpreter. My English is not quite up to speed, even for the simplest conversations. I can only say rudimentary, yet essential things, such as "I don't eat chicken," and "I don't eat fish. Too much like lizards." All this with a very heavy accent.

These nice people ask me very nice questions about my family, my hobbies, and the camp at Homestead. They listen attentively. They seem to like me. They tell me that the house next door has a very nice pool, and that the neighbors have a boy my age, and that they've already offered to let me swim there any time I want.

Tony is there, too. After we're done at this house, we'll go over to another house, to meet the family that wants to take him in. As luck—or Divine Providence—would have it, the folks that want to take in Tony are good friends with the family that wants to take me in. They live about ten blocks away, near Rockway Junior High School, where Tony would be enrolled. They have a teenage son Tony's age and a teenage daughter slightly younger.

My mother's friend's husband, Juan Becquer, has arranged all this under the oddest circumstances. He had been a lawyer in Cuba, where he represented the interests of the Hilton Hotel. Now he is working as a janitor, mopping floors for an interior decorating firm in Miami, the very same firm that had decorated the Havana Hilton. When he landed in Miami, the first thing Juan did was to seek out every American businessman he'd come to know in Cuba. One of them was the interior decorator, who gave him a job as a janitor in his warehouse. It was the interior decorator who wanted to take in Tony, and their friends who wanted to take me in.

Divine Providence. My mom had alerted her friend Marta about our arrival, and her friend had pestered her husband Juan about our plight. I've often tried to put myself in his place. I'm a lawyer mopping floors, I've got two babies, a wife, and both of my in-laws to feed, and now my wife wants me to do something about these two boys I barely know. If I'd been in his place, I think I might have forgotten to ask the boss about the boys. I might have asked for a raise instead.

Lucky for us, he didn't forget to ask. That's the kind of stuff Cubans did for one another in Miami back then. Everyone went the extra one hundred miles. Juan knew we were coming and had spoken to his new employer about Tony and me. He barely knew us, or we him. I think I'd seen him maybe three or four times in Havana, at the most. His boss had replied that maybe he could take one of us, and that he had some friends who might be able to take the other one.

Talk about miracles. This was close to the parrot fish. Very close.

Both families were Jewish. They wanted to take in two Catholic Cuban boys who barely spoke English. They'd have to feed and clothe us, and force us to do homework, and make sure we took showers and brushed our teeth, and stayed out of trouble, and they'd receive no help from any government agency for doing it. They already had kids of their own, and their houses weren't very large. Yet they wanted to do it. They wanted to do something good, just because it needed to be done.

There were fourteen thousand of us, homeless. Fourteen thousand orphans, waiting for their parents to receive visas and exit permits. All of us had been sent here by parents who thought they'd follow just a few months later, maybe a year at most.

None of us knew we'd be orphans for much longer than that.

And I'm sitting there in that living room, with these nice people, and I look around, and I stare at the Picasso print with the three musicians and at the babies and at the dog out on the patio, and I listen to the English being spoken, and I notice that the sunlight outside is just slightly duller than the light I had grown up with, just a fraction of a fraction less bright.

And I realize that I'm not the same anymore, and that I never ever will be.

I miss my mother. I miss my father, even. I miss everyone so much, except Ernesto.

I miss the sunlight.

I miss my model Viking ship and my comic books.

I'm not the same. I'm not the same. Maybe I'm dead!

All of this sweeps over me like a tidal wave, wordlessly.

What's this? Why am I sobbing? Uh-oh, now I've done it. What's this nice family going to think? Why? Why? Why am I crying like this? I've never cried like this before. Oh God, please, make it stop. *Coño, qué mierda!*

But I can't stop. *No puedo, no puedo parar . . . no, no, no.*

Juan Becquer, the lawyer-turned-janitor takes me outside, as far from the house as possible, beyond the screened-in patio. He talks to me; he asks me questions. I look at the lizards in the yard. They're all over the place. Green ones and brown ones, cursing the screen that stands between them and the patio. I see a frog, too, a big brownish one, just sitting there on the thick grass like a stone. All I can do is sob and tell Juan that I don't know why I'm crying.

But he keeps telling me that I have to know, that everyone knows why they're crying. He reminds me how important this "interview" is and points out in great detail what I stand to lose if I continue crying. He is firm, precise, and as cold as Kant.

To get him off my back, I say to him: "I'm crying because I'm not worthy of living with this nice family. They're too good for me. They're too nice."

"Nonsense," he says. *"No seas tan comemierda."* Don't be such a fool.

My dad had never spoken to me like this.

Slowly, gradually, he wears me down with a lawyer's resolve. It's not anything he says in particular that calms me down, but simply the fact that he's standing out there with me talking to me and trying to crush the poor logic of my made-up reason for crying. I barely know this guy, and he's treating me as if I were his own kid. Maybe the nice people inside the house will be the same way.

Maybe you don't need your own parents.

Maybe it'll be nice to live without Ernesto.

Maybe life after death can be good.

So I stop sobbing and I go back in, and the nice people offer me something to drink and some cookies, and we talk some more, and we forget all about my crying fit.

Louis and Norma Chait take me in. And their friends Sid and Carol Rubin take in Tony. Two days later, the house with the screened-in patio and the Picasso print becomes my home. And these nice people give me a room of my own and a small transistor radio.

Such brave people. Such nice people. Such fine, fine proofs for the existence of God.

(My sixth proof, by the way, snuck in, as an aside.)

My new parents, Lou and Norma, give me an allowance every week. They let me take out the garbage and teach me to cook my own scrambled eggs. They encourage me to ride my bike to school. They seek out friends for me in the neighborhood. They make me call Tony every other day, and urge me to visit him. They make me write to my family twice a week. They insist that I go to church at Saint Brendan's, and give me money so I can put something in the collection basket, even though they are Jewish. I start to think of them as my mother and father, and I begin to love them. My new dad takes me places. He takes me fishing. He takes me to the beach. He takes me out to restaurants. He takes me to the jazz sessions at which he plays the saxophone. My new mom cares for me with all the attention and tenderness of my old mom. And she is so funny. She makes me laugh. And she teaches me not to plagiarize articles from the encyclopedia for school reports.

"You didn't write this!"

"Yes, I did. It's my handwriting there, you see?" (My English pronunciation is getting better, but I still have a long way to go before I can compete with Desi Arnaz, who seems to speak flawlessly.)

"No, I mean, these aren't your words. *Eschew? Altruistic enterprise? Flawed, fragile premises?* I don't think you can write like a college professor—"

"What do you mean?"

"I mean, you took this straight out of the encyclopedia."

"Yes, *The World Book* is a very nice encyclopedia. It has very good articles. My teacher said I should use it, so I went to the library and used it there today."

"But you can't just copy the whole article word for word and turn it in as your report. That's too easy. And it's wrong. It's called plagiarism. You should try to find your own words. Always use your own words. Didn't you have to write reports in Cuba?"

"No. We had essays and exams, but no reports like this one."

"Well, you should always use your own words in a report. You can research the facts in encyclopedias or books, but you should always use your own words when you put it all together. You can always find your own way of saying things."

Too bad they couldn't keep me for longer than nine months. They just couldn't. Marie Antoinette never showed up as she was supposed to. No one was allowed to leave Cuba after the Missile Crisis of October 1962. My mom and the parents of about twelve thousand other children were all trapped on the island, and no one knew when they would be allowed to leave. So the Chaits had to let me go and their friends the Rubins had to let Tony go.

And on the day I left that house I died again. And I buried the pain a little deeper this time around.

They loved me while they could, Norma and Lou, and did more than they should have. I was such a bad liar, and they knew it and put up with it. They gave me many gifts that have lasted a lifetime. And I loved them, and still do, and am ever mindful of the fact I'll always fall short in the good deeds department when compared to them.

They put me on the right path, in my new land. The land of eventuality.

Eventually, I found out I could be my own father and mother, and for a while I convinced myself that I was doing a much better job than Marie Antoinette and King Louis.

Eventually, I found a life that didn't include movie parties in palatial homes with statue-ringed swimming pools, but did have all sorts of other wonders to offer. Like videotapes of *Demetrius and the Gladiators,* and one *Seinfeld* episode that featured the male bra that Victor Mature could have used: the "Bro." (I'm ready to wager that there was at least one Cuban on *Seinfeld*'s writing staff.)

Eventually, I acquired English. It's mine. All mine. I bought it word by word, on credit, the American way. And English owns me, too. I think in English; I even dream in English, except when Louis XVI shows up. Spanish stopped growing and is now a homely, misshapen dwarf. An all-wise and almost mystical dwarf, keeper of the keys to my soul, but a dwarf nonetheless.

Eventually, I lost my accent. Well, almost. I prefer to think that I can pass for Jimmy Stewart, or Captain James Tiberius Kirk, but if you listen carefully, you can tell there's something funny about the cadence of my speech, and the way I pronounce some words, like *eschew.* And don't ever talk to me when I'm angry or tired; you might mistake me for Desi Arnaz.

Eventually, I even earned the right to plagiarize myself, using material from one encyclopedia article in another. I did, I swear. *Lo juro. Mal rayo me parta.* It was marvelous. I did it last week. And I got paid for doing it, too. Don't ask me to be specific, though. One can get in trouble for plagiarizing even oneself, if one gets caught.

Especially if one uses the word *eschew* too often.

37

TREINTA Y SIETE

The tourists' Havana was dotted with nightclubs, bars, casinos, and whorehouses; my Havana was dotted with pools. And I gave all of them names: shark pool, five-statue pool, Popeye's pool, screwdriver pool, never-full pool, tire pool, eye-killer pool, invisible pool, blue lava pool, giant toilet pool, pool of my dreams.

So it's not surprising that when I think of my final days in Cuba the first image that leaps to my mind is that of my uncle's pool.

Some pool it was. Right next to the turquoise sea, and bone dry. No trees within a hundred-yard radius, and in the deepest shade. Nothing but rough, dusty, gray cement. It smelled of concrete, even four years after the cement had been poured. It was an enigma.

My uncle Amado, an architect, had built himself a pool *under* his house. This wasn't an indoor pool I'm talking about. No, it was an outdoor pool, under the house. From the street the house looked like a nice normal building with a three-story façade. But it really had no ground floor beyond a foyer. What would have been the first floor, behind the foyer wall, was the open space for the pool, and the house itself stood above the pool. When you looked at the house from the rear, you saw it all clearly.

Uncle Amado had all sorts of reasons for leaving the job unfinished. Knowing his reasons didn't make it any less enigmatic. It was a cement hole: no tiles, no smooth surfaces, no water, in the deepest, deepest shade.

I had always been drawn to pools. In water you are weightless, and weightlessness frees your mind. But as the Revolution progressed, the number of pools began to shrink. Gone were the private clubs we had frequented. Some were trashed in an orgy of retribution against privilege, others were summarily closed, and those that survived were opened to the public, free of charge. But the funds for maintaining so many clubs soon ran dry and so did the pools. So towards the end I spent a lot more time reminiscing about pools than enjoying them.

I was especially fond of remembering Popeye's pool, probably because it was the one in which I had learned to swim.

Popeye's pool had gotten its name from the man who took care of it, who hated us. It was at Manuel's and Rafael's beach club, and it was tended by a man who was simply known as *El Marinero*—the sailor. Of course, he instantly became Popeye to us. He looked a little like Popeye, too, except he had no pipe. He even wore a cap like Popeye's. He hated us because we often rolled around in the sand with our wet bodies, and then jumped into the pool and watched the sand vanish into the water. It made such a nice cloud when we jumped in. We did this repeatedly, even though he always yelled at us, "Hey, you're going to clog up the filter with all that sand again." He always gave us the evil eye, and with good reason.

We were spoiled brats, *niños bitongos,* who thought we'd never have to worry about cleaning out pool filters. Served us right, it did, to be hurled down to the bottom of the heap when we reached the States. I once spent an entire summer, between high school and college, working sixty hours a week at my mother's factory, inserting thousands of screws in the morning and taking out the very same screws in the afternoon, day after day. They were temporary screws, put in place to speed up the bonding power of a special glue between two parts. The holes into which my screws fit would later be filled by different screws, driven in by somebody else down the assembly line.

I thought I was in hell.

Marie Antoinette was one of the star assemblers at the factory, which made photocopy machines. There wasn't a single job she couldn't do better than anyone else, bum leg and all. Rutger, the ex-Nazi German manager, loved her. She'd sometimes show him how there would be a better way to assemble the pieces, or how to improve their design. Rutger would then call over the engineers and they'd shake their heads, and agree, and walk away looking puzzled.

Cubans weren't supposed to be smart. And most of the workers at that factory were Cubans. Some had been professionals or businessmen before they fled. One of the janitors had been a lawyer in Havana.

I, too, ended up as a janitor, but not in a factory. It was at a housing project in a very poor neighborhood, in a very poor New England town, while I was in graduate school. My worst task at that job was peeling off old wallpaper, under which cockroaches had built their nests. Dodging the rats near the trash dumpsters was not much fun either, but it was still much better than having to read Kant.

But I digress. The point is this: those pools spoke to me of the privileged life that I knew was mine. I knew that I had pools to choose from and that the boys in Regla only had their stinking wharf. I knew it, and I loved knowing it. I loved it up to the last fraction of a second that I stood on Cuban soil, even though by then I'd lost my pools.

God bless the roaches behind the wallpaper, and the screws at the factory, and the broken dishes at the Conrad Hilton Hotel. God bless especially the freckle-faced girls who leaned on the chain-link fence and shouted *"spic!"* my first day at the refugee camp in Homestead. Thanks to them I became a Regla boy, and that pride turned quickly into a burning shame—a shame that still hangs around my neck like a festering dead iguana. So those Regla boys are in there, in my mind, swimming away, diving for coins in their underwear. They swim infinitely, eternally.

My mind is filled with images of pools that never were, too. I loved thinking of new pools I could invent someday, when I became an architect and engineer, just like my uncle Amado. Someday, I thought, I would build bridges and tunnels and houses and churches and schools and pools. Especially pools.

Wonders such as the Jell-O pool.

That was perhaps my most brilliant idea: to build a giant pool, bigger than any in Havana, and fill it with Jell-O rather than plain old water. I don't mean a pool full of chunks of Jell-O, trucked in, but a pool in which the Jell-O had set. The world's largest Jell-O mold. One colossal, shimmering, quivering, shaking pool of Jell-O, its surface smooth as glass, reflecting the blue

blue sky and the clouds. It would have to be outdoors, of course, and ringed with diving platforms of tremendous height. The trick would be how to find a way of getting the Jell-O to set in the tropical heat.

I had big plans. I drew blueprints in my head for the retractable refrigeration dome that would allow the Jell-O to set overnight. I was there, with the retractable roof, before the SkyDome and all those other inferior versions of my invention that dot North America. I'm sure if I'd stayed in Cuba, I could have pulled it off.

I also had great plans for a bicycle slide pool. This would have been a very long and deep pool with a giant slide about the length of a ski jump, ten stories high, down which you could ride your bike and go careening through the air into the pool. I imagined myself sailing through the air for five minutes before hitting the water, and then sinking slowly, slowly, with the bike, all the way to the bottom of the pool.

One morning when the dust motes were whirling especially fast, I had the great idea of combining Jell-O pool and bicycle slide pool. I was very pleased with myself that morning.

Of course, I gave no thought at all to how one might get out from under in a deep Jell-O pool once one had plunged into it. It was the plunging that interested me: the very thought of slamming into Jell-O, especially from a great height. I thought one might bounce a couple of times before sinking in.

If I had been my uncle Amado, that's the kind of pool I would have built next to my house. No shady pools under the house for me. But, of course, who am I to talk, or trade places with my uncle? At least he started building a pool. Mine never even made it to paper.

Amado was a riddle of sorts during my childhood in Cuba. I knew him about as well as I knew his pool. He was our nearly invisible uncle. He was always present by name in our conversations, but seldom there in the flesh. But he was the solid rock of my father's family. Clearheaded, practical to the core, a tower of strength, a problem solver. And always somewhat distant, even seemingly cold. I came to know later that he loved deeply, maybe more deeply than all the others in his family, but had trouble showing it. He had two daughters almost exactly the same ages as Tony and me, and lived just a few blocks from us, but we hardly ever spent time with him. He and King Louis were not at all close to each other.

Divine Providence would see to it, though, that Tony and I would end up living with Amado and his family. We were rescued from the orphanage near the Orange Bowl by the one uncle we hardly knew. And, as it turned out, the two years, two months, and two days I lived in his house were among the happiest of my entire life.

Back in Havana, I can count the times we saw him and his family, it happened so rarely. I remember going to their old house a couple of times. It was somewhere near Tropicream, the ice cream and milk shake place where our dad would often take us. I remember asking my parents why his oldest daughter seemed so weak and unstable as she walked. I remember them telling me that some children are born that way. I remember going to his new house by the sea when they moved there, and marveling at the empty pool in the shade.

I also remember the day they invited us to swim at their house. It was so near to our vanishing. Tony and I were still waiting for our exit permits, but Amado and his family already had theirs. In just a few weeks they would leave their beautiful seaside house and unfinished pool, and fly off to an uncertain future. Amado had no idea he'd end up working as a simple draftsman in Bloomington, Illinois, for ninety dollars a week.

Amado's wife, Alejandra, had asked us to wear sneakers that day, because you couldn't walk or even swim barefoot on the razor-sharp rocks at the shoreline by their house. They were called *dientes de perro,* those rocks. Dog's teeth. So we wore our sneakers to swim in that gorgeous transparent water. Alejandra had told us to bring diving masks, so we wore them too.

What a world inside that water! The fish. The coral. The black, spiny sea urchins. The starfish. The anemones. The colors. And that was just at the coastline. There was a whole sea out there, full of this stuff. The sharks were so lucky.

Tony sensed it and said, "This is great! I'm going out farther."

We were there with Marie Antoinette, who made one of her rare forays into the water. Louis XVI had not joined us, as usual. Uncle Amado was there, and Aunt Alejandra, and their two daughters Marisol and Alejandrita. But neither Amado nor Marie Antoinette tried to stop him. Probably because they had no idea what he meant by "farther."

He swam straight out from the shoreline. He swam and swam and swam, until his head was nothing more than a dot between the sea and the blue sky, a period at the end of a sentence written by God.

He was so fearless, and so full of good ideas.

He was the one who came up with the idea of pulling the blossoms off the hibiscus hedge next door and tying them shut overnight. He was the one who discovered that cold water could make hot lightbulbs explode. He was the one who invented a new alphabet. We started writing notes to each other in that secret alphabet and within a few weeks we were using it fluently.

He was one of the funniest people I've ever known. When videocassette recorders were still rare, he once showed me a videotape of *Mr. Rogers* he had dubbed over with his own voice so that Mr. Rogers, the children's show host *par excellence,* spoke like a drunken, raving lunatic. It was a work of genius.

My fearless brother wouldn't adjust to exile easily. I don't think he ever adjusted at all. But I suspect that by the time we left Cuba, he was already seriously damaged. It's not easy to have an adopted brother foisted upon you, especially when he is a pervert.

Tony's life was never stable after we reached the United States. He realized that he could be his own father and mother as soon as he got off the plane, and he ran with that insight, full throttle. And as I have only myself to blame for my many bad choices, so does he. But because he was three years older than me, he was able to make some very bad choices at critical times, and he's paid for this dearly.

But back then, on that day at Uncle Amado's house, he swam out to the very edge of the shallow sea floor that surrounds Cuba. He says he swam past sharks and barracudas and giant stingrays and fish that defied description. And he says he got to the edge of a great abyss, deeper and darker than anything he'd ever seen. It was as if he'd swum out to the very edge of night, he said. He looked down and saw nothing but deep, unfathomable darkness, darker than the night sky, for there were no stars at all. Not one light below. Nothing but black. The blackest black of all.

He said it was beautiful. And I believe him.

I've seen him do other brave, foolish things. I've seen him hold a huge firecracker in his hand until the fuse was no longer visible, and I've noticed how his hand didn't shake at all. I've seen him hold a cigarette in his teeth and dare someone to knock it off with a large rawhide bullwhip. I've seen him totally scraped up from head to foot after being dragged by a car for a block or so in Miami. He'd accepted a dare to hold on to the car's bumper while staying on his bicycle, and he'd be damned if he'd let go, even after he'd fallen down. I was there when he rode his bicycle out to the middle of the frozen lake in Miller Park, in Bloomington, Illinois, when we were living with Uncle Amado. It had just frozen over a couple of days before and the ice wasn't very thick yet. I could hear it cracking and pinging, as if it were about to give way. I've seen him jump off a third-story porch into a snowdrift. I was with him as he drove a Jeep down the runways at O'Hare Airport, right into the path of incoming planes, and he shouted at me, over the roar of the plane's engines: "I love this! I try to do it once a day!" I've seen him come home with a bullet lodged in the palm of his hand, and I've heard him say, "Naah, it's nothing, really." I've seen the machine guns and grenades in his bedroom closet. I've heard him boast about the twenty-five hundred parking tickets he collected and threw away without a second glance.

"Hey, guess what? I'm number two on the list. I'm second! Only one other guy in Chicago owes more in parking tickets than I do! My name was in the paper this morning—front page! I owe the city over seventy thousand bucks! Ha!"

I've had to deal with my mother's panic countless times as he's disappeared off the face of the earth without saying good-bye to anyone, not even his wife. And I've had to deal with the aftermath of his returning home with fantastic tales to tell.

I've seen him eat a huge hot fudge sundae after he became a diabetic, on a day when his sugar level was dangerously high.

He said that abyss was beautiful. And I believe him.

He calls me once a day now—sometimes more often—and he talks about the weather and his dogs and the deal he's got going with the mayor of his town, who lives across the street. And he talks to me about his illnesses, and how he has so little time left to live. He also talks a lot about our childhood.

He likes to tell me about the abyss. It's one of his favorite topics. He loves to tell the story, with exactly the same details, time after time, as if I've never heard it before.

And in the same way he can't get the abyss out of his mind, I can't get that unfinished pool out of mine, the unfinished pool in the unlikely spot, reeking of misbegotten ideas and sour fate. Uncle Amado, the architect at the peak of his career, had built his dream house. But this architect had a daughter who wasn't as agile as other children. That pool spoke of her needs and his pain. It spoke of the Revolution, which had wrecked or interrupted everything. It spoke of twists of fate and of an infinite number of things.

In the dark just before dawn, years and miles away, the biggest pool of all merges with Uncle Amado's in my mind's eye, and the images intertwine. I see the sea that was a stone's throw away, that turquoise pool in which floats the island of Cuba. A pool full of sharks and abysses and wonders and darkness.

I see my brother's head out by the horizon, a speck bobbing in an ocean of turquoise tears, poised over an invisible chasm. Invisible to me, alluring to him. He made me laugh, but now he makes me cry. He was brave; he was reckless. And his recklessness was often paid for by others. He lived for the moment, and loved it. He searched desperately for substances that would reproduce the abyss, and loved the strongest ones way too much. He was drawn to the dark by the dark itself. In the dark you see no images. None at all. In absolute darkness, there is no remorse, nothing to forget. Nothing at all. Nothing, nothing, nothing.

Nada, nada, nada.

Which, by the way, also means "swim, swim, swim" in Spanish.

My seventh proof for the existence of God: a boy swimming out to the abyss from a house with an empty, unfinished pool. Seventh and final proof.

38

TREINTA Y OCHO

It was a hot day. An ordinary day in Havana, on the eve of my departure. The sunlight screamed in utter delight, as always, blasting everything in its path.

Too bad. The loudspeakers ruined it. They were mounted on the utility poles on every street corner, broadcasting from the Plaza of the Revolution. The Maximum Leader was going to give a speech again that day, and the loudspeakers were seeking to do what the sun itself could not: to reach even the darkest, most hidden, innermost rooms in every house in the Ensanche de La Habana, my grandparents' neighborhood.

We were all being bombarded. I shielded my brain from the Maximum Leader's words, and for most of that day I succeeded. The words bounced off my ears and fell to the ground mortally wounded, gasping for meaning. But every now and then I'd let my guard down, and a few words would get through.

Revolution this, Revolution that. *Yanquis* are evil. Fidel is great. Hail to our Maximum Leader. He's given us genuine freedom. All are free now, truly free, under the Maximum Leader's careful guidance. We shall triumph. We shall build an ideal society. We shall all think alike, think freely, as one with our Leader. Revolution this, Revolution that. Death to Imperialism. Death to Capitalism. Long live Communism and Marxism-Leninism. Death to the Worms.

It was a special day for the Maximum Leader and his Revolution. The best nation in the whole world had deemed Cuba worthy of a visit by the first human ever to orbit the earth. Yury Gagarin was in Havana that lovely day, and he was going to put in an appearance at the Plaza of the Revolution.

I had to see him. I didn't care if he was a Communist and an atheist. I didn't care one bit that Yury had told Nikita Khrushchev that he'd seen no signs of God in outer space.

So I'd spent the night at my grandparents' house, which was near the parade route for Yury. That was the very first night I'd ever spent away from my own house, and it had been hard to go to sleep. It had been even tougher to wake up and find that I wasn't anywhere near my parents.

This is what it will be like, I told myself. *This is what awaits me in a month or two.*

Like Yury when he prepared for his launch into outer space, I was preparing myself for my launch into an alien world. I think that's one of the reasons I wanted to see him in person. It wasn't just the fact that he was the first human being to fly so high above our atmosphere: I was impressed with his utter calm in a strange environment.

Yury had balls. *Cojones.* The size of coconuts, and probably just as hard. The kind of balls I'd need in exile. You just can't get into a tiny metal capsule and sit atop the largest *cohete* ever made without balls like coconuts. He was a messenger from the world of the brave, and from the future too. Someday, I'd be going into outer space also. Surely, by the time I'd reach fifty, we'd all be vacationing on the moon. I'd be taking my kids to the moon in July 2000, and I'd be able to tell them on the way there, as the earth got smaller and smaller behind us, that I'd seen the very first cosmonaut in the flesh.

Havana was full of billboards welcoming Yury. BIENVENIDO GAGARIN. The billboards also had the same message in Russian. It looked like such an interesting language. Almost as good an alphabet as Tony had invented, except it had too many letters.

Yury had a very red face. That's what struck me when I laid eyes on him, his face was about the same shade of red as hibiscus blossoms. He rode through Havana in a motorcade on his way to the Plaza of the Revolution, sitting in the backseat of a convertible with the top down. Well, not exactly in the backseat, but rather above it, with his rear end on the body of the car and his legs on the backseat.

He was getting one hell of a sunburn. Cuba was more perilous than outer space for a pale Russian. That sunlight howled with delight as it slammed onto the cosmonaut's red face.

A Russian on parade in Havana. What a sight. I didn't know at the time that the Soviet Union also contained Uzbeks, Ukrainians, Lithuanians, Tatars, Armenians, and dozens of other subject nations. I thought everyone in the Soviet Union was Russian, like Yury. I had no idea it had been an empire for so long, and that Cuba was not its first colony. But I did know one thing: everything they made was a piece of crap. Russian cars were junk. Russian appliances were junk. Russian bicycles were junk. Russian toys were junk. Russian oil and gasoline were worse than junk. The streets of Havana had become rivers of sludge. Louis XVI explained it had something to do with the Russian oil, which was either too thin or too thick for the American cars most Cubans still drove, and which leaked from the cars onto the asphalt. And the sludge was getting thicker and thicker.

Once, trying to cross a wide boulevard in a hurry, I lost my shoe to the sludge, and Louis XVI laughed out loud at the sight of my shoe glued to the median strip.

King Louis and I were doing a lot of walking then, in early 1962. During that one year when I didn't go to school, as I awaited my departure, Louis XVI took me on a few of his errands into the heart of Havana. It was the best time I ever had with him. What I remember best of all is simply walking by his side, hearing him talk. He had a memory for every place we visited, a history. I knew by then that my dad's history was not necessarily an account of the real past. But I loved to hear him bring the past alive, even a false one.

His past was so much more interesting than his present.

I often wonder what it must have been like for him to take me along and talk to me, knowing that he'd lose me soon. What did it feel like for him to know that Tony and I were leaving, with no assurance that he'd ever see us again? What did it feel like to know that he had chosen to stay with his art collection and Ernesto rather than to join us in the States?

He never talked about it. All I know is what he said in a letter shortly before he died, years later. It was an odd letter, full of emotion. Perhaps he knew he was close to death, for he seldom revealed his feelings. He told me that he had known all his life that he would have children and lose them. He said that he knew when Marie Antoinette first proposed sending us to the States by ourselves that this was our fate and his. That it was meant to be. He'd resisted the idea, he said, but not strongly and not for very long, because he knew that God had already planned it this way.

He also told me that when our airplane had taken off he had felt as if his heart were being ripped out of his chest. He said nothing had ever hurt so much in his entire life. He added that it was a pain that had stayed with him constantly, every single day.

I still don't understand him.

And he certainly didn't understand me. Or else he wouldn't have adopted Ernesto. And he certainly wouldn't have made me buy a record I didn't care for at all, which is what he did on one of those days when we walked around Old Havana.

I had about five pesos to spend, and I thought I'd buy myself a record. My first. Louis XVI said he knew of a very good record store that still had lots of records to sell, and we both went there on the bus, somewhere in the oldest part of the city.

It looked ancient and full of ghosts, that part of Havana, even in the daytime. It was gritty and crumbling and beautiful all at once. The record store was one of many in a long arcade, near a place called La Plaza del Vapor. Where the Plaza had once stood there was a giant hole the size of a city block filled with dark green water. It was a Revolutionary urban renewal project gone wrong; too high a water table had surprised the engineers, and they didn't have the means to fix their mistake. So Old Havana had gained a perfectly square lake.

The same shape as the covers of the long-playing albums in the record store. It was a great place. They had every kind of music: classical, Cuban, jazz, rock and roll, you name it. They also had a listening booth in which you could ask for a record to be played. I must have made about ten trips to that booth, and with each trip my dad grew more impatient and irritated.

He didn't like the choices I was making.

"That's jazz, you know. That's trash. You don't want to buy that."

"But I like it."

"It's still trash. You don't really want to buy that."

"But this guy Miles Davis sounds so good. I like this album a lot."

"You still don't know what's really good. It's just trash."

We went on like this for a long time. Finally, he wore me down and convinced me that all my choices had been bad ones. Especially those jazz records. So we ambled over to the classical section, and guided by his expert advice, to which I had now totally surrendered, I ended up buying *Arthur Rubinstein Plays President Eisenhower's Piano Favorites.*

Jesus H. Piano-tuning Christ.

I succumbed so totally to my own maximum leader that when I got home I actually played the record many times. I waited for my taste to improve with each revolution of the disc, but instead the opposite happened. As each note receded into the past and another stood poised to take its place, my taste in music declined exponentially. Two days after I'd bought the record, which had a goofy-looking picture of Dwight D. Eisenhower on the cover, I had come to loathe myself for being such a Philistine. I hated the record. I hated every single note and chord. And I hated myself for hating something good and beautiful.

Something was awfully wrong with me.

But that damn record of mine was so dull and dreadful. It even sounded miserable on the old clavichord Louis XVI had rigged up with a couple of stereo speakers on the inside. If it didn't sound good coming out of the clavichord, then it must have been me who was at fault.

Miles Davis sounded so much better. I had no idea who the guy was, but I could hear the music playing in my brain, and I liked it so much more than the Eisenhower piano pieces.

I stopped listening to the record after a couple of days and left it behind gladly. Louis XVI enjoyed that record a lot. He played it all the time during those last few months I spent in that house with him. Probably played it a lot after I left too, the way I've been playing Nirvana these past few months. Full blast.

Havana was far from Nirvana on that day Gagarin came to visit. Every third word that shot out of those infernal loudspeakers was "Revolution" and every other word seemed to be *Yanquis*. It was pure cosmic dualism, good versus evil, battling it out. Light versus darkness. It was also an apocalypse. The light had not triumphed yet, but was well on its way. The glorious Revolution would wipe the cosmic floor with the heinous *Yanqui* imperialists very soon.

Not even the Christian Brothers who spoke of Satan and hellfire and the final judgment had painted such a grim view of history.

But who could really think of an apocalypse on a day when the sun could crack the stones, as Cubans liked to say? Forget about a sun hot enough to fry eggs. This wasn't enough for Cubans, who probably did that all the time without giving it any thought. No, our sun had to be powerful enough to crack stones.

And Yury was surely getting one hell of a sunburn in the back of that convertible. Come to think of it, his face was the same shade of red as that of good old *El Colorado* of my early childhood dreams. But he was a genuine sport: he waved back at the crowd with a goofy grin on his face. Not quite as goofy as Eisenhower's on the cover of my new record album, but goofy enough, especially for a hero.

I waved at the goofy atheistic Russian space hero and he waved right back.

Contact. I was one with history.

From the parade route, my grandfather Amador and I made our way to the Plaza of the Revolution to get a glimpse of Fidel.

"I need to see that bastard who stole everything from me," said my grandfather.

You have to understand that my grandfather had worked hard as a truck driver for more than three decades. He wasn't a rich man. He was an immigrant who'd had too many bad breaks, someone who would have been much better off if he had remained in Spain but was too ashamed to return as a failure. Now Fidel had taken the little that he had saved up. And at just about the same time that all of his money was stolen from him, he crashed his truck and broke his leg in so many places that it couldn't really be fixed at all. So he walked with a cane now, just like his daughter.

He was the kind of guy that the Revolution was supposed to help.

So we went to see the Maximum Leader. We had to, as long as we were that close.

We walked in the hot sun to the Plaza of the Revolution, along with hundreds of other Cubans. We gathered in the vast space under the monument to the Cuban patriot José Martí, a poet who had died fighting for independence from Spain. The tower at the center of the plaza was about twenty stories high, and directly underneath there was a broad platform with a pulpit from which the Maximum Leader preached to the multitudes. The tower looked like a permanent exclamation point.

It was a sea of people. I'd never seen so many bodies gathered in one spot. Tens of thousands, for sure. Some were curious, like me. Some were there because they were genuine believers in the Revolution. Some were like my father, who was there because it was required of him, in the section assigned to all the judges. There were thousands of Cubans in the same situation, in their own assigned sections. The guardians of the Revolution took attendance. If you didn't attend, there would be unpleasant repercussions: they reminded you constantly that it was their goal to make it tough for anyone who didn't show true Revolutionary spirit.

And Radio Havana proudly broadcast its programs announcing that Cuba was the only free nation in the Western hemisphere.

The crowd frightened me. It spoke in unison and seemed to think in unison, too. It roared and chanted slogans like *Cuba sí, Yanquis no!* at the appropriate moments. Other slogans too. It was a lot like church, I thought. It was a ritual, a liturgy of correct thinking, punctuated by responses from the congregation.

And the high priest was the Maximum Leader.

I saw him. My grandfather saw him, too. He was a pinpoint, off in the distance. A tiny moving speck. Even from far away we could see his tiny little body bouncing up and down as he spoke. He couldn't talk without moving. He jumped and waved his arms as if he were a basketball player or a demoniac. We could hear him very clearly, of course, thanks to all the loudspeakers that dotted the vast space of the Plaza.

You couldn't get away from his voice. Even if you plugged up your ears with your fingers, the sound of his voice was loud enough to find its way to your brain. You could shut out the words, but you couldn't shut out the noise.

He was bombing us.

He was telling us what was good. Telling us how we should think. He was telling us what to choose and how to choose it. He was telling us we had no choice. And he was telling us we were free. Free at last.

That one tiny, insignificant, erasable smudge under the giant stone exclamation point, that speck of nothingness controlled everyone in that Plaza, and everyone on the island. That one little nothing that my cousin

Fernando had planned to erase at that very same spot, two years earlier. Being at that Plaza, that day, was one of the scariest moments of my life. Scarier than any nightmare I'd ever had.

"Let's go, *abuelo,* can we go now, please?"

"Yes, damn it, let's go."

We carefully wended our way out of the crowd that had gathered behind us. It wasn't easy. People were still streaming in as we tried to leave. Some of the latecomers were in groups, and were being herded like sheep.

My grandfather spoke over the din: "Hold my hand. I don't want you to get lost."

I was too old to hold hands, but I did it anyway.

Good thing I did, too, for it would be the last time I'd ever get the chance. I held my grandfather's hand for the last time in my life, there, as Fidel's words fell upon us like hail, or fire and brimstone. We were just two drops in a nearly boundless ocean. But we were two drops who knew what was going on, two drops struggling to free ourselves from the sea around us. An old man torn from his homeland by forbidden love years ago, a boy about to be torn from his by a Revolution.

Two specks moving in the wrong direction.

Two specks about to part from each other forever, thanks to one tiny speck.

One speck bathed in sunlight that day, just like everyone else.

One tiny speck.

Too bad.

39

TREINTA Y NUEVE

"Get Peg-Leg! Get Peg-Leg! Quick, everyone, let's get Peg-Leg!"

Marie Antoinette was being pursued by an angry crowd near the Swiss embassy. She'd been camping out on the sidewalk for a couple of days, waiting her turn to apply for a visa to the United States. Suddenly, a mob had gathered across the street, and they'd started shouting insults at all of those who were lined up outside the embassy. Then they started to hurl bottles.

The bottles whizzed past her and smashed on the pavement. She didn't count them, she just fled in utter terror, as fast as she could. She ran on her one good leg, and her friend Angelita, the mother of my fifth-grade friend Ciro, ran along with her, clutching her arm. But my mother was so used to having conquered her handicap that she had no clue at all that they were after her.

"Who's this *Pata palo* they keep shouting about?" asked Marie Antoinette, as the bottles zipped by and smashed at her feet. Between cries of *Ay, Dios mío,* Angelita let her know: "It's you, *boba,* it's you! . . . and they're coming after us!"

Marie Antoinette stopped dead in her tracks and turned around to face the mob that was pursuing her. They were all on the opposite side of the street and had started to cross it.

"Why are you trying to harm me? What did I ever do to you?"

"You're a worthless worm, that's who you are!" shouted one woman.

"I may be a *gusana,* but I'm a human being, just like you, and a Cuban, too. And I don't know any of you and have never, ever harmed any of you or wished evil on you. So why do you throw bottles at me and call me names?"

"You and all of yours deserve to die, you stinking vermin. We'll kill you all before you have a chance to leave. You don't deserve to live and leave. Death to you and yours!"

"Now you did it," Angelita sighed. "Now they'll kill us for sure!"

Marie Antoinette continued to reason with the mob: "You have no right to shout insults at us or wish us harm. None at all. I'm just trying to leave this country so I can be with my sons. I haven't ever done anything to harm any of you. Get that through your heads!"

"Muerte a los gusanos! Death to the worms! Fatherland or Death! We shall triumph!"

More slogans, chanted in unison, including the Maximum Leader's favorite prayer: *"Cuba sí, Yanquis no! Cuba sí, Yanquis no!"*

When my mother tells me the story, which is at least five or six times a year, it always ends with a bus. Somehow, as the mob continues to harass her and Angelita, a bus magically stops for them. A bus headed for some part of Havana she doesn't even know existed. Marie Antoinette and Angelita jump on the bus and ride it for twenty blocks or so, then get off, panting and wheezing, looking over their shoulders for an approaching mob, and transfer to another bus that will take them back to El Vedado, where Angelita lives.

Marie Antoinette was just doing what the parents of the fourteen thousand airlifted kids were doing all over Cuba: trying to find the quickest way out of the country so they could be reunited with their children. Angelita was doing the same thing. She had three kids in the States: two girls and one boy. The youngest girl had a congenital heart problem and had been through surgery at the age of three.

Angelita and my mom scurried all over Havana, doing what needed to be done, searching for the rarest commodity of all: correct information. Angelita made it to the goal line before my mom, or at least it looked that way. She obtained an exit permit and a visa for herself and her husband. But when they were about to leave for the airport, they received a phone call telling them that their exit permit had been revoked and that they had to reapply. Her husband died of a heart attack right there and then. He was only fifty years old.

Marie Antoinette wouldn't give up, no matter what. She tried and failed so many times. She had no idea it would take her three and a half years to be reunited with us. She didn't know she would get exit permits, only to be turned back at the airport. "Sorry, *señora,* you can't leave today. A diplomat needs your seat." She didn't know that each time she'd be turned back at the airport, it would take more than a year to get another exit permit. She didn't know she'd end up going to Mexico first, just because a friend of hers there met the right Mexican official at a cocktail party. She didn't know she'd have to spend six months in Mexico, mooching off good friends while she waited for a visa to the States. She didn't know she would hemorrhage in Mexico City and undergo emergency surgery. She didn't know that the blood transfusion she would receive would infect her with hepatitis C. She didn't know that one week after surgery there would be an earthquake. She didn't know that two days after landing in Miami, she'd be caught in a hurricane. She didn't know it would take her another three months in Miami to find a way to join us. She didn't know she'd end up in Chicago. She didn't know Tony and I really wouldn't need her anymore for the rest of our lives, at least not in the ways she thought we would. She didn't know I'd be taller than her when she finally saw me again, wearing size ten shoes that would scare her to death.

And she gave up so much, blindly, just to be with us.

I don't know where Tony and I were at exactly the same time that the mob was pursuing her in Havana. We could have been in any number of places, each of them very far from her.

We were in another world. Tony was probably very unhappy that day. He was always unhappy. I might have been happy. It all depends. I loved the adventure of being on my own, even though on some days the hunger was too hard to take, there, at that orphanage near the Orange Bowl.

Maybe I was swimming in the neighbors' pool at my first house in Miami. Maybe I was reading a library book at the orphanage. Maybe I was delivering newspapers on my bike in Bloomington. Maybe it was at exactly the same moment I accidentally slammed a tightly rolled newspaper into the chest of one of my customers and heard him go *"oooooomph!"* Maybe it was when I broke the glass on a storm door with a newspaper, or that one morning when the angry dog who was usually chained up chased me down the street. Maybe it was when I fell in love with Nancy, a girl with blue eyes like Eye Jesus and a haircut exactly like that of my fifth-grade *noviecita*.

All I knew was that since I'd left my home, my nightmares had pretty much vanished and I had learned to bury my love for my parents and family so deeply I barely knew it was there. And one of the ways I did that was to think of how nice it was not to be living with Maria Theresa, Candlestick Lady, Eye Jesus, Window Jesus, and voodoo people anymore.

Of course, every now and then, what I'd buried would bubble up to the surface and scare me half to death. But that didn't happen very often. I was the King of Denial, sitting on the throne at the age of eleven.

I couldn't bury the lizards, though. I'd killed so many I'd never be able to bury them.

All of the stains on my soul are lizard shaped. And some of them are missing their tails. And the severed tails are wriggling madly.

I came after them like a mob, thirsting for blood. I pursued them throughout my entire childhood. I thought they were evil incarnate. But one day topped them all: the day of the Lizard Apocalypse.

"Let's wipe out all of the lizards in the neighborhood," I said to my friend Jorge.

"You can't do that. There are too many of them."

"Then how about our block? Just this one square block. We won't cross any streets. We'll just kill all of the lizards on this one block."

"Okay, that sounds great. Let's go!"

So we each grabbed a broom and went hunting. Brave hunters, seeking to free our neighborhood from fearsome lizards, wielding brooms like baseball bats.

I won't tell you what we did, exactly, because it was so unholy. Suffice it to say that we were immensely successful. So successful, in fact, that I'm still haunted by their tiny ghosts, thirty-eight years later.

The skin, that magic skin still makes me so envious. As wondrous as the changing colors of parrot fish in the turquoise sea. Those tails. Why can't I have one? Every now and then I'd like to leave my tail wriggling in danger's jaws. Those eyes. Eyes that can rotate like the earth itself; eyes that follow you wherever you go, like Eye Jesus.

They were so beautiful. Especially the green chameleons with the *pañuelo* on their throats, that little red kerchief of skin that they furled and unfurled. They were the most beautiful. And they were the ones I hated and feared the most.

Jorge and I killed them all. We started at my house and made a circuit around the entire block. I was most successful at one spot: behind the abandoned building where the pervert had held a knife to my face. There were a lot of lizards back there. I knew this because they had stared at me indifferently on that awful day. In the bright, blinding sunlight and in the darkest shade we killed them. We were as thorough as good historians chasing down every footnote. We climbed trees like mad that day, and jumped fences, and trampled shrubs all around our block.

Of course, almost all of the people who lived in those houses were new to the neighborhood. I didn't know most of them, and I certainly didn't care about jumping their fences or trampling their shrubbery. They were no better than thieves themselves, living in houses others had left behind.

I was on my way out. We'd received our exit permit. I knew the day and time of my departure. April the sixth, at six o'clock in the afternoon.

No more Jorge, no more Louis XVI, no more Marie Antoinette or grandparents or uncles or aunts or cousins. No more toys. No more comic books. No more baseball cards. No more lizards.

But I could take something with me that no inspector at the airport could ever find, no matter what. I could take with me the exact number of lizards I had killed on that one single day.

Forty-one.

I forget how many Jorge killed. All I know is that his number was smaller than mine, and that he will therefore spend less time in purgatory than me for that sin. Maybe forty-one thousand years less.

Forgive me, hateful, dreadful, ugly, joyous, wondrous creatures. I took it all out on you, and for all the wrong reasons.

Forgive me, Jesus. Didn't you once say: blessed are the lizards, for they shall inherit the earth? I'm sure you did. It's just that those lackluster apostles of yours forgot to write that one down in the final version of the Sermon on the Mount. Isn't that it? I'm sure you said a million things that they neglected to write down. I'm sure you saw a lot of lizards there in Palestine. In the temple courtyard, on the grapevines, and the silent stones, and the fig trees, and the nets hung to dry by the Sea of Galilee, sunning themselves. Maybe they even flocked to you.

I'm sure there were even lizards at the foot of the cross, keeping you company, and that artists have left out that detail for nearly two thousand years, too. If I ever take up painting, I'll include them in a crucifixion scene, Jesus. I'll make sure they have drops of Your blood spattered all over their bodies. And if I ever paint an image of Your Sacred Heart, I'll make sure there is a lizard perched on the thorns that encircle it.

You must have said plenty about them. All those people out there, in Your day, believing that this earth and everything upon it were created by an evil deity; all those people out there, in Your day, who saw lizards, snakes, and crocodiles as the ultimate proof of the existence of an evil creator.

People just like me.

You must have set them straight. It was the biggest mistake of all, wasn't it: thinking that some creatures prove that the Father is evil? The most awful mistake of all, mistaking the serpent for the Creator?

Didn't You also have a lot of lizard parables? Like the parable of the silent tail-less lizard? The parable of the lizard who waited patiently for little boys with brooms? The parable of the escaping iguanas? The parable of the lizard that almost flew into orbit? How about the parable of the lizard-shaped clouds? And the parable of the sinner who had an iguana's soul?

I know I said there was no way You could have kissed them. But I've changed my mind. After years of reflection, I'm sure You kissed them. And they kissed You back. Not like Judas, though. They were incapable of betrayal.

No one forced You to kiss the lizard, Jesus. I, however, can't say the same. I've made my peace with lizards, but I still can't bring myself to kiss a real one. I've only kissed metaphorical lizards, and I can't say that I've done that willingly, much less with affection. It always leaves a bitter taste in my mouth.

At least now I admire their beauty. I recognize that they're beautiful in their own lizard way. But I can't say that I find them kissable. Not yet.

The only lizard I can kiss joyfully is a toy lizard. My youngest son has a beautiful iguana puppet that looks better than a real iguana. I've kissed that. I've also kissed rubber and plastic lizards, and beanbag lizards. When I was a child, I didn't have a single toy that even came close to resembling a lizard. But my children have lots of them. And when we go to Florida and see lizards, they are delighted and don't even think of causing them pain.

I still shun real lizards, though. Apparently because I cling to the illusion that what seems ugly or painful or frightening to me is really ugly and painful and frightening. No letting go of lizards for me. No *gelassenheit*, not yet.

But the day of redemption will come, for sure. Maybe I won't have to wait until I'm resurrected. Maybe it will happen in a dream, in this life. Maybe it will be the dream of a lifetime, better than the one in which my father visited me. Maybe he will come to me again and bring a friend this time.

In the dream of a lifetime I know that I'm asleep, and Louis XVI is wearing his baggy boxer shorts and wingtip shoes. I say, "No, don't do it this way again. Come see me while I'm awake."

"Alguien vino a verte," is all he says. Someone is here to see you.

I see a man standing next to my father, whom I instantly recognize. He extends his hand to me, palm upwards. Something wriggles slightly.

"Kiss the lizard, Cuban boy," says Immanuel Kant.

I stare with delight at the green chameleon Kant is holding. Wordlessly, on behalf of all lizards, the creature says, "We forgive you, we really do."

In this, my dream of dreams, I kiss it fondly, and let go forever.

40

CUARENTA

"Don't you wish you were a kid, Dad?" asked my eldest.

"What do you mean?" I answered. "I *am* a kid!"

A wave hit me hard and nearly ripped off my swimsuit, but I didn't mind. We were awaiting the perfect wave with our boogie boards. Some of the older men in the water were body surfing, but just about everyone else had some kind of board. Some had real surfboards, on which they stood, and the waves were big enough to carry them long distances. The really smart surfers wore wet suits.

This wasn't tropical water. My hands and feet had gone totally numb from the cold about an hour before. But I didn't mind.

Not one bit. It was so good to be a kid again. And it was great to see my own three children playing in the surf, going into very deep water, braving ten- and twelve-foot swells.

No Cuba clouds anywhere. Not a one.

I placed my youngest son on his board, carefully, and steadied him as the wave began to crest right behind us. The wave came and hit me hard. Again, I reeled. But my little son, he flew on that wave, rode it all the way to where the water meets the sand. Then my two other kids and I caught the third wave behind that one and almost made it to where my youngest stood, beaming.

This happened at Nauset Light Beach, on Cape Cod, Massachusetts, thirty-eight years, three months, and eleven days after I died for the first time.

I've died several times since then, and it's getting to be routine. In fact, as I'm writing this I see another death hovering on the horizon. A big one. And I'm starting to feel like my father, with one crucial difference.

Though he claimed to have lived countless lives, each in a different body and at a different place and time, I boast of having lived about five or six lives in the same body. Sometimes even in the same place and at roughly the same time.

I just don't seem to get this reincarnation thing right. I've even returned to a place I once lived, seventeen years later, as a very different person, in an older, more vulnerable body. It would have been so much nicer to have returned with a new body, and a tougher heart.

There are many ways to die. Only one kind is final, of course. But before that one pulls you under, many others come along, like waves at the shore.

The first death is not necessarily the sweetest. But I think mine was. It came on time, as planned, as it does to anyone who's going to be executed. I awoke that morning feeling pretty much the same way Louis XVI and Marie Antoinette must have felt on their day back in 1793. Or the way so many of my cousin Fernando's friends must have felt on their appointed days. I stared at the dust motes in the light, as always, and got out of bed, and washed my face, and got dressed.

I had this gnawing feeling that I was about to slip into unconsciousness. Or maybe that I should try to pass out. Maybe if I fainted, they'd put me on the plane, send me to the States, and I'd just awaken there, without having gone through the trauma of parting. Just as in surgery with anesthesia. One moment you're there, and the next thing you know, you're somewhere else, and the ordeal is over.

But I didn't pass out. I tried, but I just couldn't. I'm not the fainting type.

I had recently begun to roller skate a lot. So, as soon as I'd had breakfast, I strapped on my old pre-Revolutionary skates and went for one more tour of the neighborhood. I skated past all the houses where my friends had lived. All the old friends were gone. I had some new friends, all great guys, but I didn't know them very well. I skated past their houses, too. I skated to the old abandoned movie theater, the Rivoli, which was across the street from Aulet's house and zoo. The Rivoli Theater had been closed since before I was born; now it was just a large building with a bar and a small store that sold soda, candy, and cigars and cigarettes. I'd bought many a soda and lots of chewing gum there back in the good old days. Uncle Filo hung out in the bar back in the old days, too. Whenever he needed a break from his research in my father's library, he'd take a walk to the Rivoli and come back a much happier man.

I stared at my feet. I stared at my hands. I wanted to stare at my face but couldn't. I wanted to remember being there, that moment. I wanted to remain the same, forever. Alone, for that moment, but not at all on my own yet, only one block away from my parents, and my house.

My house made me think of Ernesto, and suddenly I wanted to hurry to the airport. It was there, at the abandoned Rivoli Theater, that I had punched Ernesto hard enough to make him stop his obscene behavior towards me. One day, when we were all having fun exploring the dark, empty, musty theater, he'd grabbed me from behind and tried to press me against his body, when all the other guys were out of sight. I'd elbowed him in the gut, and wheeled around and punched him on the arms and chest. I think I might have kicked his shins, too. Right there, just a few feet from where I stood in my skates, I had delivered myself from my tormentor.

Now I was about to be freed from him for good. For an instant, I wished never to return. For another instant, I wished I could go away for a long time and return as an adult, strong as an ox and capable of beating Ernesto senseless. Maybe even strong enough to kill him with my bare hands. I pictured my grown hands around his throat, and his face as he gasped for air, turning blue, as blue as his eyes, and I imagined his iguana soul escaping from his body, bound straight for hell.

It wasn't a pretty picture. And it still haunts me.

I skated past Aulet's zoo and said good-bye to Blackie the chimp and the mynah bird who talked dirty, like Empress Maria Theresa in my dreams.

I came home, took off my skates, and put on my traveling clothes. Tony and I wore our sport coats and shirts with ties because that was the only way we could take them out of the country. My bag was packed by Marie Antoinette, of course. I was incapable of doing that by myself.

And there I was about to go live by myself.

Louis XVI was nowhere to be seen. He'd left the house early in the morning and showed up around lunchtime to say good-bye to us. He didn't explain why, but he wasn't about to go to the airport. That was that.

We said good-bye to him in the living room, right under the gaze of Maria Theresa and Shepherd Boy Jesus. He told me to be brave.

It was my grandfather Amador who drove us to the airport. Everyone was there except for Louis XVI: grandmother, grandfather, Mario, Lily, Marie Antoinette, and even Aunt Lucía, the woman without desires.

The airport was sheer torture. Apparently, the Revolution felt that those of us who were leaving for the States had to be kept at a safe distance from those we were leaving behind, lest they slip stuff to us after we'd been inspected and frisked. So the authorities built a glass enclosure around the departure gate.

They called it *la pecera*. The fishbowl.

We would have to go into the fishbowl early: about three or four hours before departure. They had to search us thoroughly and inspect all of our documents carefully, and that took time.

All of us milled around nervously for a short while outside the fishbowl, along with other anxious families. Some of them were making the trip as one, parents and children together. I envied them. There were other children who were about to travel alone, like us, other Peter Pan Lost Boys. Strange, but I felt no special kinship with them. None at all.

I don't remember anyone crying. Not one person. We were all trying to be so brave.

And for us it was slightly familiar. Tony and I had been through a rehearsal of sorts when we accompanied Manuel and Rafael to the airport a few months earlier. We had joked around until the very last minute. I remember seeing a travel poster advertising Chicago, and saying to Rafa, "Do you think Americans know what *cago* means in Spanish?"

"Yeah, it must be funny to live there."

"Yeah, I wonder what the place is like."

Rafa and I joked about that again twenty-eight years later atop the Space Needle in Seattle, overlooking the dark blue Pacific Ocean, devoid of parrot fish. We spoke in English, of course. Neither of us felt comfortable speaking our mother tongue.

Tony and I had no friends to joke with that day. But we joked with each other as much as we could. That same Chicago poster was there, and we milked that dry.

As we were just about ready to go into the fishbowl, Louis XVI showed up. Sitting at home must have been unbearable for him. He looked frazzled. He was always sort of frazzled, but on that day he looked halfway electrocuted. He never touched a drop of alcohol and he scoffed at sedatives, so the look was all natural. Nothing but raw nerves, as raw as they come.

If I'd been in his shoes I think I'd have been more like Uncle Filo on his way to meet the King of Spain. Dead drunk. Or stuffed full of *calmantes,* as Cubans called tranquilizers.

Of course, no one at that airport had any idea how long exile would last for any of us. It could be a matter of days or months or years. No one knew for sure. But I'm willing to wager that not a single one of the people milling around the fishbowl that day could have conceived of our exile lasting until the twenty-first century.

The uncertainty made the parting easier, I suppose. It was the ultimate and most natural *calmante.* I remember feeling hopeful that this would be a relatively brief adventure. I also remember feeling certain that my mother would join us in a few months, maybe nine months at most.

If we had known that this would be the very last time that some of us would see one another and press our bodies together and touch, then everyone at that airport would have been wailing. Cubans are very emotional, and very physical. Being cold and reserved is considered a character flaw in Cuban culture.

But that day, there, at that airport, all those Cubans could have passed for Swiss Calvinists in a watch factory. Or Kantian philosophers at a conference. Or Zen monks raking gravel.

We never, ever thought it would take this long. Forty is a biblical number, you know. As I write this, in the year 2000, we've surpassed that by one.

And forty-one is the number of the lizard in the Cuban numbers racket. *La lagartija*. The lizard. If you dream of a lizard, you are supposed to bet on number forty-one that day. Forty-one years of Fidel as Maximum Leader of the lizard island. Maybe we should have bet on the lizard with abandon. I, of all people, should have known this.

But I didn't find out about the number assigned to *la lagartija* until last week. The identity of the number forty-one showed up like a Cuba cloud, by surprise, in a photocopied document passed on to me by a friend. It's one of those coincidences that borders on a proof for God's existence.

Tony and I said our physical good-byes to everyone, warmly and calmly. We'd see them for the next few hours, and hear them faintly through the glass, but we wouldn't be able to touch.

That was the worst torture. Being locked up in the fishbowl, with them on one side and us on the other, talking mostly through sign language and carefully mouthed words that could be lip-read on the other side of the thick glass.

Bastards. *Dios los perdone, compañeros*. May God forgive you all, comrades.

We entered the fishbowl, subjected ourselves to strip searches, explained every item in our luggage, showed our passports, and sat down to wait and wait. Tony and I joked around as much as we could. I still felt the sting of my underwear's elastic band snapping against my waist, and of the inspector's laughter.

We were in the aquarium, the real Aquarium of the Revolution. Were we the sharks or the parrot fish?

The time to leave never seemed to come. Imagine being on either side of that fishbowl, saying good-bye to someone you cherish, not knowing that it will be the very last time you will see them on earth. Imagine being there for three hours, maybe four. You don't need Zen training for this meditation.

I have a glass boomerang-shaped coffee table from the 1950s that's about half as thick as the glass curtain at the fishbowl. I love that table, but it always speaks to me of final farewells. Any piece of thick glass will do that to me.

I just brought the table out of hibernation. I'd been keeping it under wraps for more than twelve years. My lovely wife and I bought the table at auction around the same time that we started having children. Kids and glass tables don't mix at all. We knew that all too well and had been keeping the table in a crate in several basements as we moved from place to place.

But now that my oldest son is exactly the same age I was when I flew away, and my daughter is as old as I was when Cousin Fernando was arrested, and my youngest son is as old as I was when the firecracker blew up in my hand, it's high time for the table to come out of hiding.

It graces my Eisenhower living room, which is a time capsule of sorts. A whole room in a New England Colonial house in the woods that mimics the style of Cuba before Fidel. Havana, 1958.

I won't tell you about my Kennedy dining room, which adjoins it. Or the flock of pink flamingos in the woods. Or the iridescent tangerine mailbox on a taxicab yellow post that the neighbors keep destroying and I keep putting back up.

It's that glass table I want you to see in your mind. Kidney shaped, just like the shark pool. Thick, but not thick enough. Only half as thick as the fishbowl.

That table and this book have come out of hiding at the same time. This book was waiting to emerge for years and years, too, but it didn't until now.

You ask: why now? I say: I have as many reasons as the number of Cuba clouds I've seen in the past thirty-eight years, and none of them matter to you, really. If I told you anyway, all you'd see is a deep, dark abyss in which there are no parrot fish.

So let's get to the end.

Tony and I boarded the airplane at sunset, looking over our shoulders. We could see our family off in the distance, through the glass. Not darkly, but clearly, even in twilight. The last thing I saw before I died that day was my mother waving her cane and my father standing next to her, with his hands in his pockets. Those huge pockets in those ridiculously baggy pants, which he always pulled on over his shoes.

I plunged into the airplane and a whole new void. Tony plunged in too, his beautiful abyss in tow. Airport guy couldn't find it during the strip search, just as he couldn't find my forty-one lizards.

Want to know what it's like to die?

The kind of death I'm talking about has no oceans of time in which your memories swim eternally. No. This kind of death comes in a flash, as quick as lightning. And as silently as a lizard when it's squashed by a little boy with a broom. I heard the engines roaring, yes. I did. Who wouldn't, except a deaf person? I heard the engines clearly, so the silence I'm talking about is of a different kind.

It's the silence we find wrapped neatly inside every paradox.

The silence we can't approach without bowing.

The silence that humbles everyone, even the strongest and most fearsome.

Fidel will reach that silence, too, someday. Maybe soon. Maybe not.

It makes no difference when, really. Reach it he will.

It's the silence beyond words.

The silence beyond reason.

The unutterable unknown.

The all-knowing silence that only the third eye can see.

The joyous silence that accepts imperfection as the absolute perfection.

The burning silence, the sweet flame that knocks off your shoes and makes you cry out: "Fire! Fire! Fire! I'm vanishing, wholly consumed!"

Todo me voy consumiendo.

In the wink of an eye—in a fraction of that, really—you pass through the burning silence, and you emerge in exactly the same spot, in the very same body, gloriously transformed, a glowing blank slate.

It might not seem glorious at first, the transfiguration. But glorious it is, and glowing, and as blistering white as the whitest of clouds.

And as painful as all hell.

I had never flown in an airplane before. This was so exciting. The plane sped down the runway at what seemed an unearthly speed, the force pushing me back into my seat. We gained even more speed and suddenly we were aloft.

We were up in the air, no longer on Cuban soil. Aloft, like Peter Pan. Up among the clouds. And I saw the Cuban countryside below me for the first and the last time. Having been stuck inside beautiful, awful Havana all my life, I'd never really seen most of the lizard island. Louis XVI didn't like to travel, and he never took us very far beyond Havana. He had already seen most of the world in all his lifetimes, I guess.

I stared out the window, transfixed, as Cuba became smaller and smaller beneath us.

Look at all that green! Look at that! It's so, so green!

Imagine how many more lizards there must be down there!

Imagine all those voodoo people and demons left behind, there, right there, hidden in the midst of all that greenery!

Look at that! How funny! Look at those royal palms all over the place! They look just like those little cocktail toothpicks with the colored foil tops that held together those triangular ham salad sandwiches! Like the toothpicks in the sandwiches I ate after my First Communion!

Look at those clouds! They're so much puffier than they seem from the ground!

Look at that sea! It's bigger than I thought, so much bigger! And the waves, where are they? I can't see them. I wonder how many parrot fish are down there right now, and sharks. How many?

And will you look at that! That sun, setting over there!

It's tangerine, again, as always, and glowing like an incandescent host, but it's not setting where I've always seen it set. It's all sea, nothing but sea below us. There is no more Havana. No more tangerine Havana.

"It'll be so, so nice to be able to drink Coca-Cola again, won't it," I said to Tony.

"Yeah, sure, and the chewing gum will be nice, too."

"I'm going to ask for a Coke the minute I step off the plane."

"And I'm going to ask for a whole pack of Doublemint gum."

We had passed through the burning silence. Right through it. And here I am now, writing this. It's over, this part of it. But it's only a small part of the story. The silence can be beautiful. Don't let it ever scare you too much. Don't fear the abyss either.

Dying can be beautiful.

And waking up is even more beautiful. Even when the world has changed. Especially when the world has changed.

Tú sabes. You know.

Imagine a tangerine sunrise that never ends, forever hovering over a swirling cloud of parrot fish in the turquoise sea.

Imagine killer waves coming at you, turquoise waves, under white white Cuba clouds that soak up the tangerine and make it even brighter.

Imagine no end of waves.

None.

No end.

Sin fin.

En fin, sin fin.

Tú sabes.

Acknowledgments

This book has been the greatest surprise of my life. I started writing it exactly two years ago, on the last day of Spring term 2000, with no plan or outline, or any idea of how long it would take to finish. Little did I know what lay in store.

Once I began, I couldn't stop. For the next four months I wrote every single night, from about 10 p.m. to 2 or 3 a.m., while teaching, chairing a department, mowing the lawn, swimming with the kids, and doing other research and writing. The only day I didn't work on this book that summer was the day I went in for surgery.

I honestly thought that by working so late at night I was only stealing time from myself. How wrong I was. My wife, Jane, tells me I vanished for four months. And she is right, of course; though I remained here I *was* gone. Off to another dimension, the world of this book. After years of studying the subject of bilocation—the ability to be in two places simultaneously—I had managed to achieve it.

But bilocation exacts a great price. The self who remains at home can't perceive how little of him is actually there, how bilocation dilutes a person, and what an impact that has on his loved ones. Yet, despite my fragmentary existence, Jane encouraged me to keep writing and never look back over the night's work. She also kept telling me to trust in images and to forget everything I had ever written before. I did that too, somehow.

Saying "thank you, Jane" won't ever do. Jane, you were here while I was gone, encouraging me at every turn and pointing me in the right direction. You were here waiting for me, ready to embrace the unknown when I emerged from the silence at the end of the book, a changed man. *Gratitude* is such an insufficient word in this case, even a lame barbaric concept. Some other language would have to be invented to convey my thoughts and feelings adequately, some whole new way of thinking and speaking. I hope I can find it, learn it, and put it to good use, for if anyone ever deserved poems in a new superior tongue, and love undiluted, it would be you, Jane.

And the same goes for our children. Every night for four months they listened to me as I read them the previous night's work, and then they watched me fade away, only to reappear whole the following night with newly written pages in hand. No one could ask for a better audience than the three of you, or a more honest one. You kept me from faltering or choosing the wrong path. You also gave me the passport I needed for bilocation, and the visa too. For this and an infinite number of reasons, all of which I hope you will discover on your own, I dedicate the book to you, John-Carlos, Grace, and Bruno.

Needless to say, I am wholly indebted to those who appear in this book, both living and dead, the good and the bad and the indifferent. They *are* the book. My memories may not match theirs exactly, but I hope that they take no offense at seeing their own past as I have captured it. I would especially like to thank my mother, Maria Azucena, and my brother, Tony. You two made the past come alive for me so often, sometimes simply by choosing one word over another as you shared your memories with me, and your affection. *Gracias por todo*. I would also like to thank my agent, Alice Martell, for all her efforts on my behalf, for her counsel and her friendship. I'm convinced you're not just an angel, Alice, but one of the highest rank, the epitome of wisdom, energy, efficiency, humor, and compassion. Without you I would not have ended up with so many contracts so quickly, or so many translations, nor would I have known what to do when things looked bleak.

Without you I wouldn't have found Rachel Klayman, my editor at The Free Press, who has taught me more about writing than anyone ever has, and whose unerring insight and judgment have made this a much, much better book. Thank you, Rachel, for guiding me so expertly, and for helping me ferret out Kant from his hiding places in my prose. Thanks also for persisting, and for always having my best interests in mind, especially when I was blind to the truth.

I'm also certain that this book wouldn't have been written if it hadn't been for the fact that after decades of isolation from my own people and culture, I was lucky enough to end up working side by side with three extraordinary Cubans. Each awakened me from my slumbers in a different way, but all brought to life within me the same three things: an awareness of the past, an ache for a future forever lost, and a hope for a future yet unrevealed.

Georgina Dopico-Black, what can I say? I owe you far too much. You know what you have contributed and how indebted I am and always will be. Yet I still need to thank you here, no matter what, even if it seems a quixotic gesture, as ridiculous as time itself. *Danke schön.*

I also owe a lot to you, Maria Rosa Menocal. I hope you know how much I treasure our friendship. *Merci,* Maria Rosa, not just for steering me to Alice Martell, but for everything else down to our five-minute chat yesterday.

Roberto González Echevarría, you've helped me more than you could imagine, my friend. *Gracias,* Roberto, for clueing me in to so many things, and for showing me the way to what is genuinely Cuban with every word and gesture.

My dear friends John Corrigan and Sheila Curran, you've also helped in ways unseen, perhaps without knowing it. Now you'll know it for sure, I hope. Thanks, as ever.

Finally, I would like to thank Father Robert Pelton of Madonna House and Father Carleton Jones of the Order of Preachers for helping me face the lizards and the dark night, and for simply being who they are, true ministers of boundless grace and light. *Dominus vobiscum.*

Guilford, Connecticut
May 2002

About the Author

Born in Havana in 1950, Carlos Eire left his homeland in 1962, one of fourteen thousand unaccompanied children airlifted out of Cuba by Operation Pedro Pan. After living in a series of foster homes in Florida and Illinois, he was reunited with his mother in Chicago in 1965. His father, who died in 1976, never left Cuba. After earning his Ph.D. at Yale University in 1979, Carlos Eire taught at St. John's University in Minnesota for two years and at the University of Virginia for fifteen. He is now the T. Lawrason Riggs Professor of History and Religious Studies at Yale University. He lives in Guilford, Connecticut, with his wife, Jane, and their three children. This is his first book without footnotes.

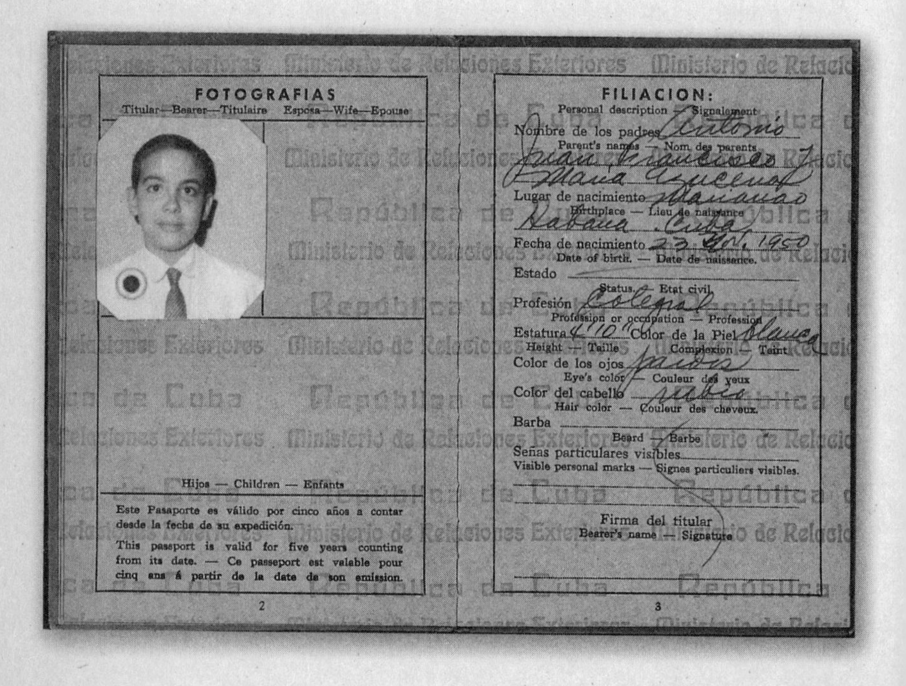
FOTOGRAFIAS
Titular—Bearer—Titulaire Esposa—Wife—Epouse

Hijos — Children — Enfants

Este Pasaporte es válido por cinco años a contar desde la fecha de su expedición.

This passport is valid for five years counting from its date. — Ce passeport est valable pour cinq ans á partir de la date de son emission.

2

FILIACION:
Personal description — Signalement

Nombre de los padres Antonio
Parent's names — Nom des parents

Lugar de nacimiento Marianao
Birthplace — Lieu de naissance
Habana. Cuba

Fecha de nacimiento 23 1950
Date of birth. — Date de naissance.

Estado
Status. — Etat civil.

Profesión Colegial
Profession or occupation — Profession

Estatura 4'10" Color de la Piel Blanca
Height — Taille Complexion — Teint

Color de los ojos
Eye's color — Couleur des yeux

Color del cabello
Hair color — Couleur des cheveux.

Barba
Beard — Barbe

Señas particulares visibles
Visible personal marks — Signes particuliers visibles.

Firma del titular
Bearer's name — Signature

3

A Conversation with Carlos Eire

Waiting for Snow in Havana *is an extraordinary memoir by a man whose boyhood was ravaged by the Cuban revolution. Reading the book is like being transported to Havana, although it's also very much about the universal experiences of loss and separation, and all the joys and cruelties of childhood. Shortly before the book's hardcover publication, Carlos Eire and his Free Press editor sat down to discuss the book and how he came to write it.*

Carlos, you're fifty-one years old, you're a professor of history and religion at Yale, well known in your field, and you have never written anything like this before. Yet, suddenly, you felt compelled to write this book. What triggered this process for you?
The most immediate trigger was the Elián González affair. It reminded me far too much of my own experience as one of 14,000 children who had come to the United States from Cuba alone, and whose parents were intentionally kept in Cuba by the Castro regime. The sheer hypocrisy behind Castro's claim that every child should be with his or her parent was what angered me the most and brought up so many memories. It was like a volcanic eruption. One day I started writing and I couldn't stop. For four months I wrote every night from 10:00 p.m. to 2:00, 3:00, or 4:00 in the morning.
And the results are extraordinary. One thing we especially notice is that your portrait of childhood is so vivid, it's almost tactile. And, as American readers, we notice how dangerous many of the things you did were. Then, layered on top of these more ordinary dangers, you grew up literally in a war zone. So when you look back, do you think of this as a very threatening time in your life?
Yes and no. Mostly I remember it with a certain sense of longing. It was a time for me, as I suppose it is for any child, when I thought, "Death never comes your way, not until you're very old." And there was a certain beauty to the risks that we took. It would be illegal in this country to pile seven children in a car and drive them down a flooded road through ten-to-

twenty-foot waves. But it was wonderful. And throwing rocks at one another was wonderful. That's the way life is: even danger has its beauty.

You write very movingly about being separated from your parents at the age of eleven. When you first came to the U.S. you lived with a foster family and later lived in an orphanage. Your mother was finally able to join you after three years, but your father never made it to the States. Tell me about that.

The original plan was for the children and the parents to be reunited quickly—maybe within three months' time, at most. It seemed unthinkable that Castro could stay in power for very long. It also seemed inconceivable that the parents would not be allowed to follow their children into exile. But we were wrong. Though some families were reunited in the U.S. after just a few months, the vast majority of the parents ended up spending years in Cuba waiting for exit permits. My own mother was turned away at the airport twice over a three-year period, exit permit in hand. Each time it took her a whole year or more to get another permit. There were many children whose parents died while waiting. The father of one of my best friends dropped dead when he was turned back at the airport. Upon hearing the very same words that my mom heard twice—"You're not leaving today; we need your seat for someone more important"—his heart gave out on the spot.

Let's talk not only about leaving but also about going back. I'm struck by the fact that you've never been back to Cuba since 1962, yet you write about the sounds and smells and places of your youth with such nostalgia. Under what circumstances would you consider returning to Cuba, and how does the idea of going back now make you feel?

I will *not* go back while Castro is in power and human rights are routinely trampled. No way. When things change, as they will, I suppose I might go back. But the world that exists in my memory is so vivid perhaps because I have given up on the idea of ever reclaiming it. Unlike most people I know, I can't revisit my childhood haunts physically, so that world survives in my mind and in my soul, intact. I know that going back the squalor and the crushing oppression of present-day Havana would have a devastating effect on me. I got a good sense of that by trying to watch the film *Buena Vista Social Club*. I couldn't watch more than fifteen minutes because the physical destruction of Havana—and of my own people, and my past—is so evident in that film. I started weeping so uncontrollably that I had to return the film to the video store, unwatched. As far as I am concerned, Fidel's Cuba might as well be the deepest circle of hell.